Westward-rolling wagons ford Medicine Bow River, Wyoming, in Samuel Colman's "Emigrant Train." Collection of Hall Park McCullough

America's Historylands

REVOLUTIONARY SOLDIER
CULVER SERVICE

America's

PREPARED BY THE
NATIONAL GEOGRAPHIC BOOK SERVICE
MERLE SEVERY, CHIEF

FOREWORD BY
MELVILLE BELL GROSVENOR
President and Editor, National Geographic Society

INTRODUCTION BY
CONRAD L. WIRTH
Former Director, National Park Service

KEYNOTE CHAPTER BY
CARL SANDBURG
Pulitzer Prize-winning poet and historian,
and world-renowned biographer of Abraham Lincoln

SECTIONS INTRODUCED BY

JOHN BAKELESS
Author of *The Eyes of Discovery; Background to Glory; Daniel Boone; Lewis and Clark, Partners in Discovery*

LOUIS B. WRIGHT
Director, Folger Shakespeare Library; author of *The Atlantic Frontier; The Cultural Life of the American Colonies*

DONALD BARR CHIDSEY
Author of *The Siege of Boston; July 4, 1776; Valley Forge; Victory at Yorktown; The Battle of New Orleans*

JOHN ANTHONY CARUSO
Professor of History, West Virginia University; author of *The Appalachian Frontier; The Great Lakes Frontier*

DAVID LAVENDER
Author of *Land of Giants; Trail to Santa Fe; The Big Divide; Bent's Fort; Westward Vision*

EARL SCHENCK MIERS
Author of *The American Civil War; The Great Rebellion; The Web of Victory; The General Who Marched to Hell*

WILLIAM C. EVERHART
Former Chief Park Historian
Jefferson National Expansion Memorial
St. Louis, Missouri

STEWART H. HOLBROOK
Author of *The Age of the Moguls; Dreamers of the American Dream; Holy Old Mackinaw; The Story of American Railroads*

FRANK FREIDEL
Professor of History, Harvard University; author of *The Splendid Little War; Franklin D. Roosevelt; America in the Twentieth Century*

Historylands

TOURING OUR
LANDMARKS OF LIBERTY

THE COMPANION VOLUME TO
America's Wonderlands

NEW
EDITION

NATIONAL GEOGRAPHIC SOCIETY
WASHINGTON, D. C.

STATUE OF LIBERTY, DEAN CONGER, NATIONAL GEOGRAPHIC PHOTOGRAPHER

A volume in the
World in Color Library

STAFF FOR THIS BOOK

Editor-in-chief
MELVILLE BELL GROSVENOR

Editor
MERLE SEVERY

Associate Editor
EDWARDS PARK

Project Editor, 1967 edition
ROSS BENNETT

Editor-writers
WAYNE BARRETT, THOMAS Y. CANBY
JOHN J. PUTMAN

Editorial assistant
MARY SWAIN HOOVER

Picture Editor
ANNE KOBOR

Design
HOWARD E. PAINE, MERLE SEVERY

Production
JAMES P. KELLY, JOHN M. LAVERY
WERNER L. WEBER

Assistants
BARBARA BOHNENGEL
MARY ANNA BROOKE, JUDITH PETTRY
ROSALYN ROLLO

Engravings and printing
WILLIAM W. SMITH, JOE M. BARLETT

676 illustrations
472 in full color, 38 maps

CONTRIBUTIONS BY
Lonnelle Aikman, Beverly M. Bowie, David S. Boyer, Dorothy M. Corson, Gilbert H. Emerson, Ralph Gray, Anne Revis Grosvenor, Paul R. Hoffmaster, Kathleen Revis Judge, Harnett T. Kane, Thomas Nebbia, Carolyn B. Patterson, Bradford Smith, B. Anthony Stewart, Paul A. Wagner, Volkmar Wentzel, and others

Composed by National Geographic's Phototypographic Division, HERMAN J.A.C. ARENS, *Director*
ROBERT C. ELLIS, JR., *Manager*
Printed and bound at R. R. Donnelley and Sons Company, Chicago
First edition 200,000 copies
Second edition, first printing 150,000 copies

LIBRARY OF CONGRESS CATALOG CARD NUMBER 62-7748

THE LIBERTY BELL IN INDEPENDENCE HALL, PHILADELPHIA
DAVID S. BOYER, NATIONAL GEOGRAPHIC STAFF

Foreword

GETTYSBURG WAS ONLY A NAME to me until my father took me there. As I played sniper in Devil's Den, clambered up Little Round Top, and hiked across the field of Pickett's charge, I felt a mounting sense of excitement. I was walking in the footsteps of men who had fought, suffered, and died there. Then I began to perceive, beyond these fields and the thunder of cannon, the grave and grand significance of what had taken place on this hallowed ground.

When my grandmother and I wandered through Old North Church in Boston, she recited "Paul Revere's Ride" for me. She showed me, too, the witchcraft sites in Salem. Imagine the tingle one small boy felt on learning, in the home of Rebecca Nurse, that this martyr who was hanged on Gallows Hill was an ancestor! So was George Jacobs, executed as a wizard in that dark year of 1692.

The Jamestown colonist, Deerfield settler, the Minuteman, Alamo defender, Oregon pioneer, the sodbuster's wife on the lonely plains, the immigrant family glimpsing the Statue of Liberty—all these are our forefathers, yours and mine. Their story, and the landmarks they left, are the story of this book.

America's Historylands grew out of the Society's immensely popular *America's Wonderlands,* The National Parks. In that book we presented the beautiful face of America. How wonderful it would be, we thought, to create a companion volume that would capture the heart, spirit, and stirring traditions of America in terms of the places where the great events occurred.

This book takes the families of America to those landmarks, to stand on ground trod by their forefathers, and to relive their glorious deeds. Here is exciting history linked with fascinating places you can visit. Here we have people, flesh-and-blood people from many lands, living the dramas that transformed our nation from the wilderness of the wolf howl to the throbbing giant of today.

Much love, much learning have gone into this volume. National Geographic's Book Service staff, sparked and guided by skilled editor Merle Severy, have distilled the essence of diaries, explorers' journals, biographies, histories. They have gleaned authentic scenes and portraits from archives, galleries, private collections the nation over. Staff writers and photographers traveled thousands of miles to make you feel "you are there"; cartographers created easy-to-follow maps.

America's beloved historian, Carl Sandburg, and other famous scholars contributed chapters rich with their knowledge. Researchers, librarians, curators and custodians, owners of historic homes, state and regional historians, Conrad Wirth and the dedicated men in the National Park Service—all helped.

Now, continuing demand for this widely acclaimed volume has necessitated a new edition. We have enriched it with 71 new color illustrations, and project editor Ross Bennett has double-checked with authorities throughout the country to bring up to date this exciting guide to America's Historylands.

Melville Bell Grosvenor

Introduction

A VIGOROUS AND GROWING NATION such as ours must preserve its historic heritage and pass it on to succeeding generations. This heritage tells the story of America's growth, trials, accomplishments, and goals. It provides the key to understanding the present and planning wisely for the future. How well we safeguard and interpret this priceless legacy will determine the kind of nation we shall be tomorrow.

Interest in the American story is surging—we see this in the millions of our citizens who visit historic places all over the land. Beginning with passage of the Antiquities Act in 1906, the federal government has become the custodian of many of these sites. Now the National Park System includes not only Jamestown and Independence Hall but a host of places as varied as the White House in Washington; Hopewell Village, an early ironmaking center in Pennsylvania; and Fort Union, a cavalry post on the Santa Fe Trail.

Today, under my able successor George B. Hartzog, Jr., the National Park Service continues to survey historic areas and buildings to select those that best represent the many-sided story of our nation. These are registered as National Historic Landmarks to encourage their preservation and bring them to the attention of the American people. Many landmarks will remain in private hands—and appropriately so. Individuals and associations were preserving historic sites long before the federal government entered the field. They continue to administer many of the places you will visit in this book.

Mount Vernon, the home of George Washington, was purchased years ago by the Mount Vernon Ladies Association, which still maintains it. The Thomas Jefferson Memorial Foundation is guardian of Monticello. Colonial Williamsburg has been restored in all its glory through an organization founded and financed by John D. Rockefeller, Jr.

Utah, the Southern Pacific Railroad, and the Golden Spike Association held in safekeeping the spot where transcontinental rails met in the desert west of Salt Lake City. The Edison Laboratory in West Orange, New Jersey, was preserved by the Edison family until they transferred it to the National Park Service. Texas joins with the Roman Catholic Church in supporting San José Mission in San Antonio. And the National Trust for Historic Preservation, composed of historical groups throughout the country, uses private funds to secure for the American people many of our treasured sites and keepsakes.

The representative landmarks covered in this book tell the story not just of statesmen and military heroes. Here you will find the blacksmith, farmer, merchant, frontier woman. *America's Historylands* has been organized to show how our people lived and struggled, and to make clear the meaning of what they did.

Independence Hall, home of the Liberty Bell and birthplace of the United States, has witnessed more than 230 Philadelphia winters. The National Park Service, the State of Pennsylvania, Philadelphia, and private organizations joined hands to create Independence National Historical Park and restore its historic buildings.

J. BAYLOR ROBERTS, NATIONAL GEOGRAPHIC STAFF

To follow a strictly chronological approach—lumping together unrelated events just because they happened at the same time—would have broken the thread of our story. Let me illustrate the problem: The Spanish were founding Santa Fe in New Mexico at the same time that Jamestown's settlers were starving in Virginia. And Russians were operating a trading post near San Francisco while Baltimore gunners in Fort McHenry were holding off a British fleet in the War of 1812.

A strictly regional approach would place in the same section events far removed in time. Sir Walter Raleigh's "Lost Colony" on Roanoke and the Wright brothers' flight at Kitty Hawk are six miles—and 316 years—apart.

America's Historylands is organized, instead, around major themes. We follow explorers and colonists as they secure footholds on a virgin continent. We trace the westering surge of our people as they pierce the Appalachian barrier, cross the Mississippi, span the continent from sea to sea, and always we picture the land

America's story begins with lonely ships, freighted with dreams, sailing an empty sea.

MAYFLOWER II BY BILL HADDON, PIX

through their eyes. We pioneer where they pioneered, fight beside them where they fought, triumph where they triumphed. Finally we stand with our own contemporaries and face the limitless challenge of the Space Age.

From Columbus to Cape Kennedy—all this between the covers of one book! To add the zest of discovery to every page of this tremendous adventure, the National Geographic Book Service staff took a novel approach. Hawaii-raised, New York-educated Merle Severy headed for the mountain states. Massachusetts-bred Ted Park explored the South. Alabama-born John Putman went north to maritime New England. Texan Wayne Barrett covered the Great Lakes. Marylander Tom Canby dug his editorial spurs into the Wild West.

They found excitement, inspiration. Now we invite you to share their adventure.

Conrad L Wirth

THE BALD EAGLE HAS LONG REIGNED AS THE NATION'S PROUD AND SOARING EMBLEM. THIS MARITIME EAGLE AND SHIELD, PAINTED C. 1830 BY F. W. VACHE, IS PRESERVED BY THE HOME INSURANCE COMPANY

Contents

FOREWORD 5

INTRODUCTION 7

Freedom's Capital 13

Reminisce with Carl Sandburg at the shrine of Lincoln, reflect on events that shaped the American character. Stroll history's corridors in the Capitol, White House, National Archives. Ascend Washington Monument, glimpse Jefferson Memorial through a haze of cherry blossoms.

The New Land 29

Step ashore with Spaniards at San Juan and St. Augustine; with Englishmen at Roanoke, Jamestown, and Plymouth. Live with the Puritans. Witness Salem's witchcraft and Deerfield's massacre. Join Dutch and Swedes along the Hudson and Delaware. Meet William Penn.

The Colonials 113

Don velvet coat, tricorn, brass-buckled shoes and stride into 18th century Williamsburg. Tour tidewater Virginia and Maryland, moss-draped Carolina plantations, Charleston, Tryon Palace, Old Salem, Savannah. Defend the long frontier against the French and Indians.

CARL SANDBURG

FREEDOM'S CAPITAL

Pilgrims to Washington learn anew the meaning of America

SIXTY-NINE years ago I rode into Washington, D. C., with the Sixth Illinois Volunteers, a militia regiment. We slept on the ground that night in Falls Church, Virginia, and the next day were drilling in military formations. The U. S. battleship *Maine* had blown up in Cuba. The Spanish-American War had begun. We didn't know then we would be the first troops to land on Puerto Rico.

In the same blue uniform that the Union armies wore in the 1860's I went to Washington and saw that city with the zest, the wonder, the reverence of the boy who for years had read about the Capitol, about the White House, about the Washington Monument and the Potomac River.

I had no slightest expectation that a time would come when I, a private citizen, would deliver an address to a joint session of Congress. The occasion was the 150th anniversary of Abraham Lincoln's birth. Two days later I went to the Gettysburg Battlefield, and from a wooden platform located where Lincoln had stood made an address that ended with Lincoln's words: . . . *we can not dedicate, we can not consecrate, we can not hallow this ground. The brave men living and dead who struggled here have consecrated it far above our poor power to add or detract. . . .*

"It was a great day in American history . . . sunset and dawn, moonrise and noon sun, dry leaves in an autumn wind and springtime blossoms, dying time and birthing hour—and birthing hour." With these words Carl Sandburg, the most eloquent spokesman for democracy in America today, commemorated the 100th anniversary of the inauguration of Abraham Lincoln.

The Lincoln Memorial and other landmarks of liberty in Washington, D. C., portrayed on the following pages symbolize the nation's march toward freedom.

JOHN E. FLETCHER, NATIONAL GEOGRAPHIC PHOTOGRAPHER, AND W. D. VAUGHN

Again I never expected until it came to happen that on March 4, 1961, I would speak to a crowd of some 20,000 from the east front of the United States Capitol. Speaking from the wooden platform in replica where Lincoln had stood for his inaugural exactly 100 years before, I looked into the faces of America—men, women, and children—and told them that tomorrow belongs to the children.

There are careless generations who drift, dawdle, decay. Still others leave tall landmarks of liberty, of discovery, invention, and culture. Youth now living and youth as yet unborn hold the seeds and secrets of the folds to be unfolded in the shapes to come. The mystery of justice between man and man, nation and nation, shall take on new phases. Dreamers of deep sacred dreams, finders and welders, sons and daughters of burning quests, shall come. They shall clothe human dignity with wider meanings. Youth when lighted and alive and given a sporting chance is strong for struggle and not afraid of any toils, punishments, dangers, or deaths.

What shall be the course of society and civilization across the next hundred years? For the answers read if you can the strange and baffling eyes of youth.

THE FUTURE is always packed with surprises. It unfolds one scene after another and seems to say, "This one, now you didn't expect this one," and mocking, "or if you did you expected it different, it came from under and from over and it came sidewise in shapes and explosions you didn't expect." We of the American

Beacon of liberty, the United States Capitol dominates the Washington skyline. Freedom sculptured in bronze crowns the great dome, 287 feet above the plaza. Twenty-four Presidents have taken the oath of office before the east front. House wing (left) balances the Senate.

U. S. CAPITOL HISTORICAL SOCIETY

Our nation's laws are hammered out on the anvil of debate in the Capitol. Senators, Representatives, Cabinet members, and press heard Britain's Prime Minister Winston Churchill

Union of States are a swift and furious people—when we get going. We rate easily among the most original, inventive, unpredictable people in the world. Those of the living generation of any given time can be saying to each other, "We shall walk together toward the future."

One of the founders of religious liberty or freedom of conscience in America, Roger Williams, had a vision of a republic of free men doing their best in the practice of a disciplined democracy. This he hoped might come from seeds planted at Providence, Rhode Island. Graphic and unforgettable, almost a little shocking at the first reading of it, is Williams's little sentence: "Forced worship stincks in

JOHN E. FLETCHER, NATIONAL GEOGRAPHIC PHOTOGRAPHER

in 1952. The House Chamber was jammed again when Carl Sandburg addressed a joint session on Lincoln's Birthday, 1959. Passes enable visitors to watch Congress in action.

Gods nostrils." Freedom of the mind, the right to think and to speak your thoughts so long as it does no harm to the rights and privileges of fellow citizens—this freedom, this liberty, is a theme weaving through the chapters of this book. Here are scenes which hold something of the aura of that mystic, hazardous, and almost indefinable thing called the American Dream. The ghosts of Roger Williams and Ben Franklin, of Thomas Jefferson and Abraham Lincoln, of Emerson, Thoreau, Walt Whitman, and Elijah Lovejoy—they are here in many pages.

There has been in the past and there can be seen in our present time a thing not easy to look at, termed "slavery of the mind." Abraham Lincoln referred to it in a

lecture he read at Bloomington and in Springfield, Illinois—its title, "Discoveries and Inventions." He touched on man's first discovery of clothes, of speech, of wind power for sailing, of printing. Rulers and laws in time past had made it a crime to read or to own books. He said then: "It is difficult for us, *now* and *here,* to conceive how strong this slavery of the mind was; and how long it did, of necessity, take to break its shackles, and to get a habit of freedom of thought established." A new country, such as America, "is most favorable—almost necessary—to the emancipation of thought, and the consequent advancement of civilization and the arts."

Dominant in the paper Lincoln read was a love of books, of pure science, of knowledge for its own sake, of a humanity creeping out of dark mist toward clear light. Lincoln was of a pioneer generation. The farthest west he ever traveled was into eastern Kansas. A railway to the Pacific then was often called "a fantasy."

THERE HAD BEEN PROPHECIES, one in 1780 when the colonies were struggling for independence. In that year John Luzac wrote from Leyden, Holland, "If America becomes free, she will someday give the law to Europe." Twenty years earlier a traveler named Burnaby, after a journey over the eastern fringe, wrote: "An idea, strange as it is visionary, has entered into the minds of the generality of mankind, that empire is travelling westward; and every one is looking forward with eager and impatient expectation to that destined moment, when America is to give law to the rest of the world."

The struggle for independence was in the going when William Pitt spoke to the British Parliament from a brief text, "You cannot conquer a map." Beyond the fringes of the 13 colonies stretched a vast continent—mountains, plains, valleys not yet explored. The ragged and often barefoot men who stuck it out with Gen. George Washington for eight long, hard years—they had a name, the *Continental* Army, authorized by the Continental Congress. The pamphlets and the predictions emphasized that what they were fighting for was an independent nation with a continent to grow and expand on.

More than a half century later, Henry Clay of Kentucky, nicknamed "Handsome Harry," trained hard to be President. He hoped for the White House and never reached it, though leaving us his alibi, "I would rather be right than President"—one of his enemies saying definitely that he could never be either. Henry Clay one day rode along the Wilderness Road in Kentucky and had his carriage stopped. Then, stepping out, he crouched, bent on his knees, leaned forward, and put his ear to the ground. Asked why he went through this action that seemed queer or theatrical, he replied, "I am listening to the tread of unnumbered millions to

"We the People of the United States. . . ." Young and old read the charters of their freedom—the Declaration of Independence, the Constitution, and the Bill of Rights (the first ten amendments to the Constitution)—in the National Archives under the watchful eyes of the Founding Fathers. "Eternal vigilance is the price of liberty"—these words are inscribed on the sentinel at the portal.

"I have never stopped thinking about that statement so timeworn," writes Carl Sandburg, "and it no longer sounds stale and sometimes has a fresh taste to the tongue: 'Eternal vigilance is the price of liberty.' And often now I find I couple it with counsel from Georges Clemenceau: 'Rest is not a word of free peoples. Rest is a monarchical word.' "

GEORGE TAMES

come." He was under the intoxication of the American Dream of his day, of tomorrow's children moving out to the Great Plains and beyond into the flaring sunsets farther west.

Nebraskans several generations later, far from the frontier Clay knew, finished a noble architectural poem and fixed on their new State Capitol at Lincoln the inscription: "Honour to pioneers who broke the sods that men to come might live." By their slogans and mottoes the earlier generations made clear their belief that any new world gained and held would come by toil, struggle, hardship, and often flirting with death.

The Latin motto of the State of Kansas has been translated, "To the stars through difficulties," and "To the stars by hard ways." A society of Californians long ago nailed up its slogan: "The cowards never started and the weak died along the way." There were reports, true in some instances, of covered wagons leaving the Midwest with the motto painted on canvas, "Pike's Peak or Bust," later heading back east with a new slogan on the canvas, "Busted, by Gosh."

When Lincoln, on March 4, 1861, delivered his inaugural address at the east front of the Capitol in Washington, it was telegraphed to St. Joseph, Missouri. And while the new President slept his first night in the White House, Pony Express relays were rushing west with the inaugural address. They would be seven days and seventeen hours reaching Sacramento, California.

Of course, what all of us modern smart alecks know is that a jet airliner could make it now from St. Joseph to Sacramento in two and a quarter hours, and that with radio Lincoln could have been heard on the West Coast, and if they had had TV, he would have been seen and heard.

There were in the time of the Pony Express verses sung by people on covered wagons heading west. One by the Quaker poet Whittier, titled "The Kansas Emigrants," went to the tune of "Auld Lang Syne":

We cross the prairie as of old
The pilgrims crossed the sea,
To make the West, as they the East,
The homestead of the free!

History abides with the Presidents at Washington's most famous address, 1600 Pennsylvania Avenue. All lived and worked here except George Washington, who selected the site and approved the design. The White House has grown with the nation. From earliest days citizens, who elect the tenant, have inspected the house they own. More than a million visitors a year tour its stately rooms.

B. ANTHONY STEWART, NATIONAL GEOGRAPHIC PHOTOGRAPHER

VICTOR R. BOSWELL, JR., AND (BELOW)
DEAN CONGER, BOTH NATIONAL GEOGRAPHIC STAFF
LEFT: THOMAS NEBBIA

Springtime in Washington:
A haze of cherry blossoms.
Giggling school children
hushed by the simple dignity
of the Jefferson Memorial.
An elderly couple
strolling marble halls of
the Supreme Court building
where even whispers echo.
The Smithsonian Institution,
beloved by generations,
where boys by the busload
crane at "The Spirit of
St. Louis," and girls cluster
around costumed
First Ladies.
Families posing in front of
the White House; and inside
a long, shuffling file
awed by glittering rooms
of state where Lincoln paced,
perhaps, in carpet slippers.
A retired rancher straightening
as the Marine Band passes
with a tingling Sousa march.
Monuments, museums, vistas
of green, memories of how
the nation began, reminders
of what it means today.
All this is Washington.

MERLE SEVERY AND (ABOVE) B. ANTHONY STEWART,
BOTH NATIONAL GEOGRAPHIC STAFF
CENTER: WILLIAM W. CAMPBELL III

Markers spangle slopes around Arlington National Cemetery's Amphitheater, where fallen heroes are honored. Here, across the Potomac from Washington, a sentry keeps vigil at Tomb of the Unknowns.

Or again, with an authentic coloration that marks a distinctive period piece, we have the hymn verse:

We are living, we are dwelling,
In a grand and awful time,
In an age on ages telling,
To be living is sublime.

Always in the American story has been the movement out of the familiar and known into the Unknown. With each new test and each new time, it cost, and there were those prepared to pay the cost. To the west of the gaunt tragedies of Plymouth and Jamestown there was the Unknown of a vast continent of unmapped wilderness. At Philadelphia in the writing of the Declaration and later in the cold and filth of Valley Forge, there was to the west beyond the Alleghenies the Unknown again, no precedents or forerunners to guide. Later in the trials of crossing the Great Plains

Eternal flame in Arlington burns before the unlowered casket of President John F. Kennedy, assassinated November 22, 1963, in Dallas, Texas. The millions who visit his grave pause to ponder the stirring challenge inscribed on his memorial: "Ask not what your country can do for you—ask what you can do for your country."

JAMES P. BLAIR AND (OPPOSITE) DAVID S. BOYER, BOTH NATIONAL GEOGRAPHIC STAFF. LOWER LEFT: THOMAS NEBBIA

and pioneering the West Coast and in the bloody sectional struggle that hammered national union into a finality, there was ever the Unknown.

In a certain letter of Lincoln may be seen a sentence strange with a bittersweet and curiously sharp with challenge. His beloved friend, Representative Owen Lovejoy, had died in March of 1864 and Lincoln replied to a letter from friends of Lovejoy that pressure of duties prevented his helping them toward a marble monument for Lovejoy. Lincoln's letter ended with this sentence: "Let him have the marble monument, along with the well-assured and more enduring one in the hearts of those who love liberty, unselfishly, for all men."

When I first met this sentence and looked at the word "unselfishly" between two commas, I felt the odd adverb encumbered the free flow of the sentence. Then the more I looked at the word and saw Lincoln's intention, I caught his vital and almost terrible meaning. Across history, unfailingly, there have been those who played selfishly, not unselfishly, with the word and the idea of liberty. Lincoln had met these selfish men in Illinois politics, and, of course, later when he was President. These same selfish players with liberty are to be met in the story of George Washington, whose letters and addresses so often make use of the word "calumny." Over again and again there were those who foully calumniated Washington's superbly stubborn and faithful fighting for independence and liberty.

We are free to weigh and to ponder the wide array of meanings that lurk in

those words: "The hearts of those who love liberty, unselfishly, for all men." These are words with implications, that could well have discussion in all schools and colleges, at any street corner in Washington, D. C., Chicago, Little Rock, or New Orleans, or most any place in the American Union of States where there is debate, rhetoric, or fireworks in the name of "liberty" or its synonym "freedom."

What is a landmark? It is a visible place, object, or document which reports an impression of an event in the past. There are many kinds of landmarks. In most any city you can point to a street corner where John Smith shot to death Bill Jones. Or, again, on the battlefield of Gettysburg, they can show you the troubled acres crossed by Pickett's men in the ill-fated charge that resulted in the first victory of the Army of the Potomac over the Army of Northern Virginia.

Here are streets and roads, buildings and people. The new is here and the old, the past and the present laid before you for your contemplation.

The past is prologue? Yes. Prologue to what? Prologue to the present? Yes!

And we of the present, are we not the prologue of the future?

These may be intelligent questions, proper to ask, when starting on a journey to see our landmarks of liberty.

Brave men in bronze raise the Stars and Stripes on Iwo Jima. The United States Marine Corps War Memorial, overlooking the Potomac and Washington, D. C., immortalizes the historic moment atop Mount Suribachi during World War II. This is one of the few places in the land where the flag flies 24 hours. Beyond the Lincoln Memorial the Washington Monument pierces the sky. Some two million visitors each year ascend it by elevator or 898 steps to see spread out below them Freedom's Capital.

THOMAS NEBBIA

THE DISCOVERY OF NORTH AMERICA
Spain
France
Portugal
England
GRONLANDE
META INCOGNITA
ESTOTILAND
Fretum Davis
Davis 1585 (England)
Frobisher 1576 (England)
Gaspar Corte Real 1500 (Portugal)
Freisland
Sebastian Cabot may have been in Hudson Bay, 1509. (England)
Gaspar Corte Real 1501 (Portugal)
CANADA
St. Laurence Bay
1535
1534
Bell Ile
Cape Bonavista
Cartier 1534 (France)
The Lake of Tadousac the boundes wherof are unknowne
C. Britton
I. St. John
John Cabot 1497 (England)
Cape Santa Maria
Cabot 1498 (England)
VIRGINIA
OCEANUS ATLANTICUS
Hatorass
Croataon
Route of Hernando de Soto 1539-43 (Spain)
Las Bermudas
Cape of Feare
Narváez 1528 (Spain)
Gordillo 1521 (Spain)
Verrazano 1524 (France)
Cabeza de Vaca 1528-36 (Spain)
Pineda 1519 (Spain)
La Florida
Ponce de León 1513
Bahama
Columbus 1492 (Spain)
San Salvador
The Gulfe of Mexico
Mayaguano
TROPICUS CANCRI
Havana
CUBA
HISPANIOLA
Virgines
Cortes 1519 (Spain)
Columbus 1502
Santo Domingo
Antigua
Columbus 1493
Dominica
Teguantepeque
Cape Gracias a Dios
1503
Barbadas
Trenidado
Columbus 1498
Hojeda and Vespucci 1499 (Spain)
Darien
Balboa 1513 (Spain)
Sir Francis Drake to New Albion, 1579 (England)
GUIANA
AEQUATOR
280
290
300
310
320
330
340
70
60
50
40
30
20
10

JOHN BAKELESS

THREE ANCHORS SPLASHED, the cables of three ships tightened. Christopher Columbus had arrived.

His sailors sniffed appreciatively. A land breeze after a long voyage is always welcome; but these winds of the New World bore the fragrance of tropical flowers—much the same fragrance that to this day rolls out to sea in the lee of San Salvador and other West Indies isles.

In the first 300 years after the discovery of America, one traveler after another commented on the fragrance that greeted sailors as they approached the coast. "The land is smelt before it is seen," wrote an early Dutch voyager. In a poem "To the Virginia Voyage," Shakespeare's contemporary Michael Drayton mentions "the luscious smell of that delicious land." Probably Drayton was remembering what Capt. John Smith had said of the sweet odors drifting out to sea at Dominica in the West Indies.

A Quaker sea captain scented pines while still 80 leagues offshore. And on Manhattan Island a Flemish missionary "sometimes encountered such a sweet smell that we stood still, because we did not know what we were meeting."

Columbus always gets (and probably deserves) credit for discovering America.

NATIONAL GEOGRAPHIC MAP REDRAWN FROM THE MOLINEAUX-WRIGHT CHART PUBLISHED IN ENGLAND ABOUT 1600, WITH EXPLORERS' ROUTES ADDED

But of course the Indians or their Mongoloid ancestors arrived thousands of years before him. They crossed Bering Strait, moved down the Alaskan coast, then spread, over the centuries, southward to Patagonia and eastward to the Atlantic. Legends hint at Chinese junks being blown across the Pacific in the third century B.C. and the fifth century A.D. Their sailors may have touched the coast and returned with news of their discovery, but nothing came of it. Norsemen reached the Atlantic coast of America in the 11th century, made a settlement, fought the "skraelings" (probably Indians, but possibly Eskimos), and sailed away.

NONE OF THESE early voyagers ever learned much about the strange new land to which he had come. Columbus himself was convinced he had found a new sea route to Asia, a continent white men had known for centuries. In 1492 Columbus and his sailors had not yet seen either the North or South American mainlands. And in all four of his voyages Columbus glimpsed only a little of continental North America. But the few islands the discoverers did visit on their first voyage were marvelous enough—extraordinary places filled with lush tropical trees and plants, strange animal life, and stranger

ENGRAVING BY THEODORE DE BRY, 1594, LIBRARY OF CONGRESS

Columbus, bearing royal letters to the Grand Khan of Cathay, lands on Hispaniola in 1492.

people of a queer copper color. No European had ever beheld Asiatics quite like these. Yet no one at first thought them anything but "Indians"—one or another of the innumerable races of India or the East Indies.

Columbus's discoveries inspired a generation of explorers who crossed the Atlantic and learned that he was wrong: This was not Asia, but a wild and impenetrable barrier to it. John Cabot, a Venetian backed by English merchants, scouted Nova Scotia and Newfoundland in 1497. A Portuguese, Gaspar Corte Real, followed in his wake in 1501, and Cabot's son Sebastian coasted all the way from Hudson Strait to Delaware. Yet it awaited Amerigo Vespucci, the Florentine who traced South America's shoreline, to theorize that this was a major land mass. A New World he called it, and by a cartographer's error, his name was attached to it—an honor that perhaps he merited, after all.

In 1524 another Florentine, Giovanni da Verrazano, probed most of the east coast of what is now the United States, sailing right into New York Harbor. Yet Verrazano learned little about the shore he cruised past. It would take a hundred years after Columbus before white men gained any clear idea of what North America's east coast was really like.

Many of these explorers, sons of the Renaissance yet haunted by ghosts of the Middle Ages, expected an Eden gleaming with treasure and peopled by plumed knights, beautiful Amazons, mermaids, and half-human beasts like Shakespeare's Caliban. Dragons would surely roam the forests, and sea monsters thrash offshore. It took a while for eyes so dazzled by dreams to see the richness of reality.

As passing centuries proved, the forests, plains, and abundant fertility of the land meant enormous wealth to America. But it was not at all the kind of wealth the first explorers sought. They came for spices and gold. Modern America produces no spices worth mentioning, and though great gold deposits cropped up in the 19th century, they eluded those early seekers. Gold-hungry Spaniards occupied California for generations without realizing that nuggets lay right under their noses in the sands of streams.

GLITTERING HOPES of gold mines and jeweled cities spurred two remarkable Spanish expeditions into the interior (see historical map in back of book). Cortés had found a great city and abundant riches in Mexico, so it seemed obvious to his men that there must be more of the same. Rumor magnified the Southwest's Indian pueblos into the fabled "Seven Cities of Cíbola." In 1540 Coronado and his gaudy party trudged across miles of desert and plain, moving north and east of Sonora in Mexico, exploring as far as central Kansas, but they searched in vain.

Hernando de Soto had served with Pizarro in Peru and seen the wealth of the Incas. He led a strong force, decked in bright armor, north and west from Florida to find gold. His men became mired in swamps, stifled in the heat, but stumbled on into the Carolinas, then across the Appalachians to Tennessee and south again into Alabama and Georgia. They butchered Indians who stood in their way; they starved and sickened; their armor rusted and their clothes turned to rags. They crossed the Mississippi, reaching Arkansas and Texas on their profitless quest.

Once De Soto's men gaped excitedly at some glistening green objects in an Indian's tomb. Emeralds? No, just fragments of glass left by other Spaniards a few years earlier. They collected fresh-water mussel pearls from Indians. Perhaps De Soto was fortunate to die without learning that these, too, were worthless.

Such mistakes continued. Early Virginians sent back to England two shiploads of what seemed gold ore. It turned out to be only "gilded dirt"—probably quartz, mica, or iron pyrites.

The Spaniards had tried their fortunes in this very same region. Jesuits were certainly in Virginia long before Jamestown's settlers. Relics on the Susquehanna near Athens, Pennsylvania—at a point called Spanish Hill—and stonework at Pemaquid, Maine, suggest that Spaniards also pioneered there and vanished.

The French came to Canada for other reasons than acquiring mineral wealth, though one unfortunate mistake about quartz crystals made "un diamant de Canada" proverbial for anything worthless. Fishing vessels had doubtless been making transatlantic voyages as early as Columbus and probably long before. As fishermen do, the crews kept secret their knowledge of good fishing grounds. When Jacques Cartier arrived off Canada in 1534 he met a vessel from La Rochelle that was fishing in waters well known to its crew. And when Cartier nosed up the St. Lawrence, he was following the route of a Norman captain who had sailed 200 miles up the river and brought Indians back to France as early as 1508.

Cartier reached the Indian village that stood on the site of Montreal. There he learned of western waters where one could navigate "for more than three moons." These were the Great Lakes, and Cartier imagined them a mighty waterway leading west to Cathay. Years later the rapids above Montreal were named *La Chine* (China), deriding the old dream.

Samuel de Champlain came to Canada in 1603 convinced that the St. Lawrence offered a route to the "South Sea." He founded Quebec and blazed the way to the Great Lakes. Generations of *coureurs de bois,* slipping through forests in moccasins and riding foaming rivers in canoes, followed his trails.

Champlain befriended the Indians—with one fateful exception. Rashly, he helped a band of Hurons, Algonquins, and Montagnais battle the Iroquois at Lake Champlain. With arquebuses, Champlain and his men routed the Iroquois war party. So doing he set the powerful Five Nations against the French, a hostility that, in large part, was eventually to cost France its hold on North America.

Dreams of gold lured conquistadores through southland swamp and burning desert. Seeking a route to China and souls to save, French explorers and black-robed missionaries (right) ascended rivers of the north, discarding their heavy pinnaces for the canoes of the Indians.

CHAMPLAIN EXPLORES THE ST. LAWRENCE RIVER
AND (OPPOSITE) CORONADO BRAVES THE SOUTHWESTERN DESERTS;
SKETCHES BY PAUL R. HOFFMASTER

Other French explorers followed Champlain. Radisson and Groseilliers probed the Great Lakes, probably entering Minnesota. "The further we sejourned the delightfuller the land was to us," wrote Radisson. "We weare Cesars, being nobody to contradict us."

The Vérendrye family reached Lake Winnipeg and pushed south and west, perhaps as far as Wyoming, searching for a western sea. Like others afoot in the new land, the Vérendryes were convinced that just beyond the next range of hills would lie the great ocean. Englishmen, pushing up the James River to the falls at Richmond, thought that from there it would be about 10 days' march to the "topps" of hills from which "the people saie they see another sea."

French missionaries, plunging into primitive America "to convert some of those foraigners of the remotest country," were first to see many of its wonders—including "a waterfall of dreadful height," Niagara. Jolliet and Fathers Allouez and Marquette explored the Mississippi, following the path of Father Nicolet from Green Bay up the Fox River, down the Wisconsin, and into the Father of Waters itself. Characteristic of French hopes, Nicolet stepped ashore at Green Bay expecting to greet the Emperor of China.

The French were more interested in furs than in settlement, and their few small communities posed no threat to Indian hunting grounds. Besides, French habitants intermarried freely with the Indians. Blessed, then, with the friendship of most tribes, French explorers penetrated the interior of North America before Englishmen did—all but one Englishman. That was David Ingram.

A sailor with Hawkins and Drake, Ingram was beached after a fight with the Spaniards in 1568. With a few companions, he *walked* "about eleaven monethes" across much of North America, from near Tampico on the Gulf of Mexico to a spot on the Atlantic coast thought to be Cape Breton Island where a passing French ship picked him up. At the time no one in England paid any attention to Ingram's story, and his two surviving companions died unknown.

Years later, when Elizabethans were gathering every scrap of information they could about the New World, Ingram was called on for his report. He spun a wondrous tale of buffalo, plains, forests, flamingos, auks, bears, and deer. Richard Hakluyt, chronicler of Elizabethan explorations, published it, then doubting it, omitted it from subsequent editions of *Principall Navigations, Voiages, and Discoveries of the English Nation.* Ingram described "white" bears with "sylver heare" and also "Eliphants." He certainly saw neither polar bears nor elephants—but there could be an explanation.

A MUSKETEER OF EARLY COLONIAL DAYS, FROM JACQUES DE GHEYN, "MANIEMENT D'ARMES," 1608, FOLGER LIBRARY

Lewis and Clark in 1805, like later explorers, described grizzlies as "white." Westerners still call them "silvertips." As for those elephants, the ivory tusks of mammoths, not very long extinct, still lay about at the Big Bone Lick in Kentucky and probably elsewhere. They were still there when Daniel Boone arrived and a long time after. Ingram could have seen those tusks and described them in the speech of his day when "elephant" sometimes meant "ivory."

Ingram's accuracy has also been questioned because he describes buffalo as "Beastes as bigge as twoe Oxen in length almost twentye foote." Buffalo are not 20 feet long. But if those who question Ingram will walk into a modern half-domestic Montana herd, they will see why buffalo *looked* 20 feet long to Ingram, passing through the enormous wild herds on the plains 400 years ago.

At any rate, Ingram's yarn was just what Elizabethans wanted to hear. Interest in America mounted, especially as successful colonization would establish a Protestant bulwark against Catholic Spain. Sir Humphrey Gilbert, who had heard Ingram talk, sailed off to colonize Newfoundland. Sir Humphrey perished at sea in 1583, cheerfully shouting to another ship as his own went down that the way to heaven was "as neere by sea as by land." The royal patent went to his half brother Sir Walter Raleigh, who began the great effort that would give birth to Jamestown. So even Ingram, the poor, illiterate tar with more imagination than memory, had a hand in England's settlement of the New World.

EARLY EXPLORERS FOUND plant life in unimaginable abundance and luxuriant growth. Trees of the eastern forests were enormous. Oaks were "far greater and better" than in England. White cedars, today rather small trees, rose 70 or 80 feet. A thick keel 88 feet long could be hewn from a single maple trunk, so the whole tree was a good deal taller. White pines grew to 150 feet with trunks six feet through. Sycamores in Pennsylvania and the Middle West often had 15-foot trunks. A whole family of settlers could and sometimes did use for a cabin one of the great trunks lying hollow on the ground.

Though magnificent to see, these eastern trees created a dark forest world. Up the trunks scrambled vines, their leaves forming a heavy canopy spread out above the treetops. The abundance of grapes led the Norsemen to name the new coast "Wineland" or "Vinland the Good." But the leaves created a shadow so deep that songbirds and many wild animals could not live in the heart of the forest. One pioneer journeyed a mile without finding a spot "the size of a hand" where sunlight could penetrate. And in thick evergreen woods one could not see 20 feet in any direction.

There was an odd and fortunate circumstance about the darkness. Poison ivy, too, had to seek light above the treetops, where it could do no harm. Except for one mishap of Capt. John Smith's, there is no record of ivy poisoning until well on in the 18th century. When the white man cleared the forests, the gleaming trilobed leaves with their poisonous oil came down to earth where victims could touch them.

There were mosquitoes, of course, the "vexatious, glory-minded, musical winged, bold denizens of the shady forest." Champlain notes "it was wonderful how cruelly they persecuted us."

The perpetual forest gloom depressed white men who passed through it. The darkest parts were sometimes called "the Shades

A CHIEFTAIN OF VIRGINIA, ENGRAVED BY THEODORE DE BRY, 1590, FROM WATERCOLORS BY ROANOKE GOVERNOR JOHN WHITE, LIBRARY OF CONGRESS

of Death." Travelers found themselves unconsciously talking in whispers. This somber forest swept westward, with pines and hemlocks in the northern states, rather more hardwoods in the mid-Atlantic region, and palms and palmettos starting as one went south. In Ohio small openings began to appear, but even in Indiana it was rare to find any place where one could see 200 yards ahead.

Along the Ohio and southward down the Mississippi huge canebrakes grew. The green, jointed, bamboolike stalks towered 30 feet, high enough to conceal a man on horseback from his enemies. Across the Mississippi the Great Plains began, rolling expanses of grass and the parti-colored flowers of spring. There were few trees except cottonwoods and willows along the streams.

In and beyond the Rockies the forest commenced again, with trees that overshadowed any in the East, even in unspoiled virgin forest. Along the Columbia River they rose 200 feet. One astonished Easterner declared Oregon trees were so tall it required "two looks to enable one to see the tops," and the gigantic stumps that still dot the Oregon countryside suggest the man was very nearly right. Redwoods along the Pacific coast reach more than 350 feet.

ANIMAL LIFE TEEMED in Columbus's America. The small Indian population, probably no larger than 900,000 in the whole United States, armed only with bows, arrows, spears, and stone axes, could not possibly deplete the game. Moose and elk ranged northern forests. Elk probably wandered as far south as the Susquehanna Valley. Deer of one species or another roamed the entire continent. Bison spread eastward to the Susquehanna. Pennsylvania had a herd of 400 as late as 1799, and the state's last buffalo is said to have been killed near Lewisburg in 1801. East of the Mississippi, buffalo usually moved in small herds. But on the plains, a man could ride a horse for 25 miles with the great beasts around him all the way.

With its boundless fertility, its woods full of game, its rivers and lakes teeming with fish, America seemed a new-found Eden to many an early traveler.

"The country was so pleasant, so beautifull and fruitfull that it grieved me to see y^{t} ye world could not discover such inticing countrys to live in," one wrote. "Europeans fight for a rock in the sea against one another, or for a sterill land and horrid country [while these] kingdoms are so delicious & under so temperat a climat, plentifull of all things, the earth bringing foarth its fruit twice a yeare, the people live long & lusty & wise in their way."

Into this bounteous continent came the Spanish, the French, men of many lands. The English came to found homes and stay. And it was they, in the end, who took over most of North America--only to lose it at last to other Englishmen like George Washington, Benjamin Franklin, Thomas Jefferson, the Adamses, who were willing to do battle for traditional English rights. By this time "development" had started, and the unspoiled beauty of primitive North America was on the way out. But so vast were North American resources, so huge the land, that it took nearly 400 years after Columbus before Americans knew what they had. By then no region of North America had missed the white man's tread.

And what did he do with his discoveries? That is the theme of this book.

Primeval wilderness greeted the New Land's explorers. Insects buzzed; blood-red cardinal flowers brightened marshes like this along Virginia's Chickahominy River.

THOMAS J. ABERCROMBIE, NATIONAL GEOGRAPHIC STAFF

"For gold,
for praise, for glory"
empires clash over

FOOTHOLDS IN THE NEW WORLD

TUMBLING MOUNTAINS like rumpled green velvet caught the eye of Columbus on his second voyage to the New World. Now "Admiral of the Ocean Sea" with 17 ships and 1,500 soldiers at his command, he anchored in a spacious bay November 20, 1493, and proclaimed the land Spain's. This was the only time Columbus visited territory today under the United States flag.

He christened the island San Juan Bautista. The name might have stuck had not his gold-seeking companion Juan Ponce de León, returning 15 years later, found a rich port—*un puerto rico.* Island and port later exchanged names.

Puerto Rico yielded little gold, but Spain recognized its strategic position astride the gateway to the Spanish Main. San Juan must be fortified. Settlers laid the first stone blocks of El Morro Castle about 1539, but not until late in the century was the fortress formidable enough to daunt a pirate. One of a cordon of citadels stretching through the Caribbean, El Morro was built ever stronger to prevent Queen Elizabeth's corsairs from seizing the rich colonies in tropical America. Legend says that Spain's King Philip II, appalled at the expense, snorted: "Surely so much gold has it cost, one should be able to see it from here!"

In 1595 Sir Francis Drake with a powerful armada saw it from a half mile offshore. El Morro's soldiers were ready. Cannoneers in striped shirts and knee breeches raked Drake's fleet with shot, swabbed out hot guns with vinegar, then fired again. From the ramparts a gunner sighted past the ornamental dolphins on his bronze cannon and arched a ball into the sea dog's cabin, almost hitting him.

PAINTING BY BIRNEY LETTICK

Hurricane-lashed Spanish soldiers from St. Augustine slog across swollen rivers to raid Fort Caroline in 1565. Slaughtering 132 inhabitants of the Huguenot colony, they later put to the sword 200 men trapped at Matanzas Inlet and drove the French from Florida.

In the dark of night the English took to small boats and attacked the Spanish frigates that blocked the harbor. They set one ablaze, but the strategy backfired. "The burnte shippe gave a greate light," noted Drake's chronicler, "the enemie thereby playinge upon us with their ordinance and small shotte as if it had been fayre daye." Drake plucked his beard in anger and sailed away.

Elizabeth commanded the Earl of Cumberland to even the score. With the queen's glove waving like a plume from his helmet, he led an amphibious assault in 1598 that breached the earthworks behind the fort. The Spaniards, weakened by dysentery, surrendered. But Elizabeth's prize slipped from her grasp; the same disease enfeebled the English, and they soon abandoned El Morro.

In the years to follow, Spain strengthened the citadel until it resembled a great battleship, trailing 27 lesser castles and batteries in its wake. Besieged in 1625 by the Dutch, and again by the English in 1797, San Juan's defenders counterattacked

to drive off the enemy each time. Despite damage from cannon, earthquake, and hurricane, El Morro still stands—a symbol of Old Spain's might. Today at San Juan National Historic Site visitors walk El Morro's massive walls, 140 feet above the ocean, and explore musty casemates where soldiers slept beside their guns.

In the United States only Florida's St. Augustine rivals San Juan in age. Here visitors turn off U. S. Route 1 and stroll narrow streets past the Cathedral of St. Augustine, the Spanish governor's house, and Ponce de León's statue.

Searching for gold and a life-giving fountain, Ponce de León landed near here in 1513, claiming the "island" of Florida for Spain. Other conquistadores—Narváez, Cabeza de Vaca, De Soto—followed, but Spain didn't stay until French Huguenots planted a colony, Fort Caroline, on the St. Johns River in 1564.

The Florida peninsula was a dagger aimed at the treasure route between New World and Old. Philip II didn't want it in French hands. Smash their plans, he ordered. So Don Pedro Menéndez de Avilés gathered his men and set sail. He sighted Florida on St. Augustine's Day, 1565, and before overwhelming Fort Caroline, established himself at an Indian village which he renamed St. Augustine—first permanent white settlement on the United States mainland.

St. Augustine, capital of a domain stretching north to Canada and west to the Mississippi, guarded Spain's gold shipments. For more than a century it barely hung on, harassed by Indians and pirates.

In 1586 Sir Francis Drake—who else!—his ships burdened with Spanish booty, chanced upon the "little Towne or village . . . of wooden houses." Its tiny garrison exchanged a few cannon shots, then fled into the woods while the English raiders applied the torch. From smoldering ruins St. Augustine rose anew, a sanctuary for Franciscan friars. But the sanctity of missions didn't deter Robert Searles. In 1668 his pirate band swept through the streets on a midnight massacre. Mounting pressure from the English, now solidly entrenched as far south as Charleston, South Carolina, moved Spain in 1672 to bulwark St. Augustine with something stronger than its "wooden walles." Work began on a great stone fort.

Castillo de San Marcos, a quarter century in building, proved impregnable. James Moore in 1702 and James Oglethorpe in 1740 blunted their swords against its coquina "shell rock" walls, 30 feet high and up to 12 feet thick. It withstood every attack until its drawbridge was lowered to armies of tourists who daily swarm through the national monument. They gaze down at the broad moat and explore guardrooms,

St. Augustine's colonial past lives on along St. George Street just inside the City Gate. Old Spanish Inn dates from early 1700's.

ALBERT MOLDVAY, NATIONAL GEOGRAPHIC STAFF

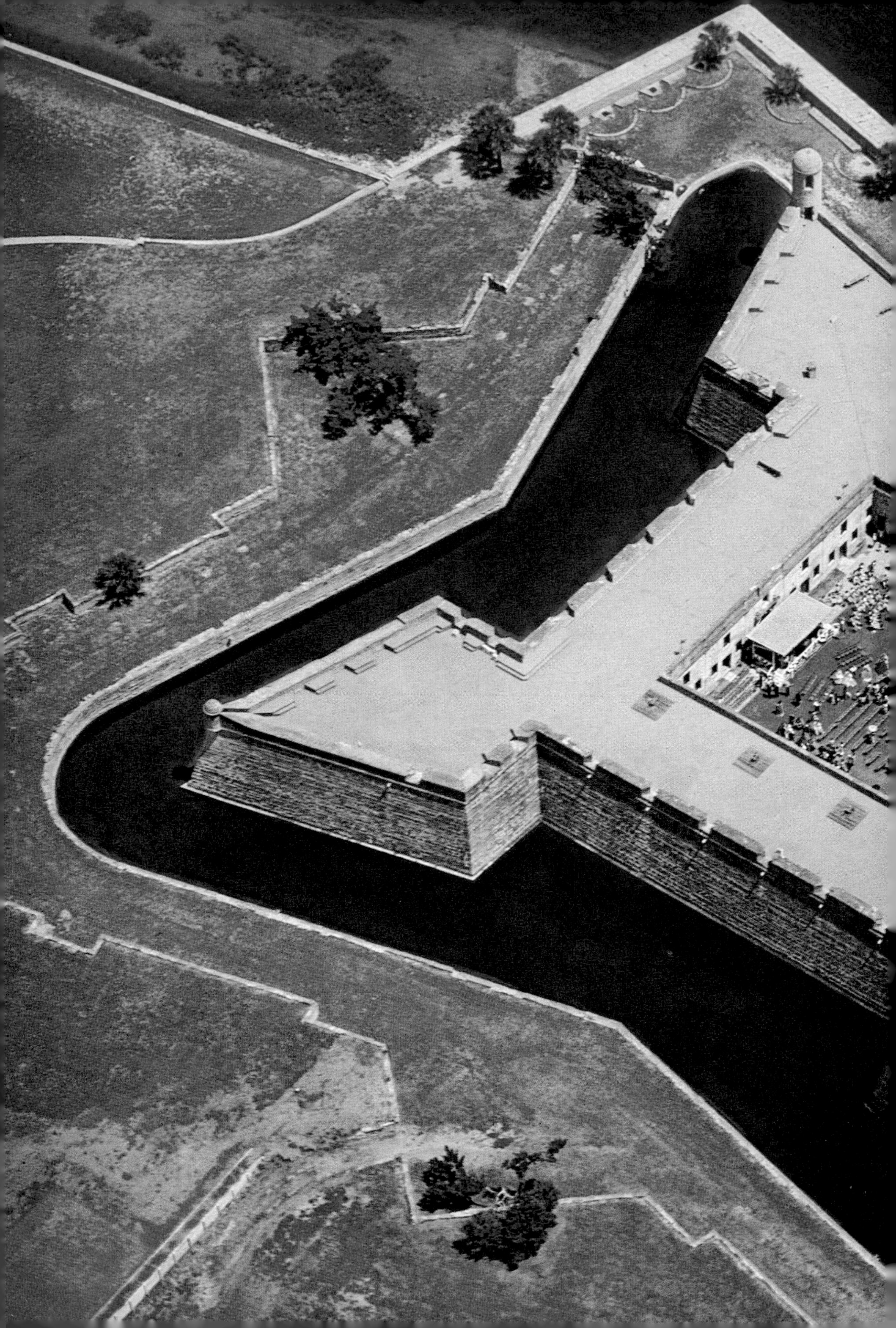

IMPREGNABLE THROUGH THE CENTURIES, *Castillo de San Marcos and its bristling bastions held Florida for Spain. Protected by jagged outer wall and tidal moat, the fortress spreads a four-pronged fighting deck over barracks, chapel, jail, and armory. Visitors crowd the courtyard.*

KODACHROME BY VICTOR R. BOSWELL, JR., NATIONAL GEOGRAPHIC STAFF © N.G.S.

quarters, storerooms, and chapel. A shudder runs along their spines when they stand in a dank dungeon and the guide snaps off the light!

England's first colonists in North America fashioned no sprawling castles. With Elizabethan fervor they came to build an empire: "To seek new worlds, for gold, for praise, for glory," Sir Walter Raleigh said, echoing England's spirit of adventure. Sea-roving Philip Amadas and Arthur Barlowe, scouting for Raleigh, touched coastal North Carolina in 1584 and claimed it for their "rightfull Queene." They returned to England extolling the "pleasant and fertile" island "which the Indians called Roanoke." They brought two tribesmen, Wanchese and Manteo, bearing gifts of tobacco and potatoes. With history looking over his shoulder, Raleigh filled a pipe with the Indian weed and planted the "humble root" in Ireland. But first he drove a wedge into Spain's New World monopoly.

He enlisted 108 colonists, placed his cousin Sir Richard Grenville in command, and next spring bade them Godspeed to "Virginia" (inspired by Virgin Queen Elizabeth). Swashbuckler Grenville swung south to the West Indies, in Puerto Rico seizing two Spanish frigates and a supply of salt; in Haiti dining with an uneasy Spanish governor to the "sound of trumpets and consort of musicke." By late July another fanfare was in order: The colonists had landed on Roanoke.

They built "the new Fort in Virginia," a star-shaped redoubt of earth and brick, and flanked it with thatch-roofed houses. It wasn't Devon, but it would do—at least until Grenville brought more supplies from England. Autumn of 1585 wore into winter. Friction with Indians sparked open war. Food dwindled. Colonists groveled for shellfish and scanned the sea for passing ships. At last, in June, 1586, sails broke the horizon. It was the irrepressible Drake, St. Augustine's smoke still strong in his nostrils. He took the famished settlers aboard and sailed for England.

Their campfires had scarcely cooled when a supply ship sent by Raleigh arrived to find the fort abandoned. Soon after came Grenville. He was "unwilling to loose the possession of the country," so left 15 men with two years' provisions. Back in England, Raleigh rounded up 150 colonists, including women and children. They crowded aboard three ships and in late July landed at Roanoke. The colonists found nothing but the bones of one man. The fort had been razed. John

ENGRAVING BY THEODORE DE BRY FROM A PAINTING BY FORT CAROLINE COLONIST JACQUES LE MOYNE, LIBRARY OF CONGRESS

Piracy by some of the French settlers who raised triangular Fort Caroline spurred the 1565 attack by Spaniards, who renamed the fort San Mateo. Two and a half years later, vengeful Frenchmen returned to the St. Johns River and with the aid of Indians wiped out the Spanish garrison. Spain, however, maintained the fort during the colonial period. A reconstruction of the stockaded earthwork east of Jacksonville memorializes France's brief hold on the peninsula.

White, veteran of the first voyage, now governor of the colony, put the settlers to work building "newe cottages." One sheltered White's daughter Eleanor, wife of Ananias Dare. On August 18 she gave birth to the first English child born in the New World—Virginia Dare. Governor White saw little of his granddaughter, for before she was a month old he had sailed to England for supplies.

War with Spain scuttled White's schedule; not until 1590, two years after the defeat of the Spanish Armada, could he return to Roanoke. What he saw then struck him numb. Deserted, overgrown, palisaded with tree trunks, the settlement gave no clue to the fate of the colonists, though White saw "a certaine token" in the enigmatic word CROATOAN carved on a tree.

Roanoke's mystery fascinates motorists who cross Croatan and Roanoke sounds to Fort Raleigh National Historic Site. In 1950 the Park Service resurrected the bastion, rebuilding its parapet. Imaginations need barely a nudge to see high-booted colonists striding up the ramps to man gleaming brass cannon. The visitor center has coins, clay pots, and reproductions of John White's drawings.

History dubbed Sir Walter Raleigh her leading man in the Roanoke tragedy, but he never appeared in North America. Turned out at court, fortune gone, this brightest star of the Elizabethans fell after James I rose to power. He was beheaded in 1618 in the Tower of London.

But Jamestown had taken firm root by then. Raleigh was right in his prophecy for Virginia: "I shall yet live to see it an Inglishe nation." WAYNE BARRETT

CULVER SERVICE AND (LEFT) AYCOCK BROWN

Sir Walter Raleigh beguiles Queen Elizabeth with poetry on Roanoke Island near the theater where they perform in *The Lost Colony*. Paul Green's pageant re-creates for summer vacationists the ill-fated settlement, which left only the word CROATOAN to puzzle searchers—and generations to come. Some Carolina Indians claim the Roanoke settlers for ancestors.

JAMESTOWN

England's gentlemen-adventurers sink roots in the fertile soil of Virginia

AT THE LOOKOUT'S SHOUT, sea-weary men tumbled from their narrow bunks and raced to the rail, searching for the Virginia shore. The *Susan Constant,* with the *Godspeed* and the *Discovery* trailing her like ducklings, slipped into the mouth of Chesapeake Bay. Eagerly, a party put ashore.

"Wee could find nothing worth the speaking of," reported George Percy, "but faire meddowes and goodly tall Trees; with such Freshwaters running through the woods, as I was almost ravished at the first sight thereof."

Nothing worth speaking of! In other words, no gold. For years the English had eyed Spanish treasure from America—and raided Spanish galleons. But to control this wealth, they wanted to carve a slice of America for themselves. Sir Walter Raleigh, who had failed, languished in the Tower. Now the Virginia Company of London had sent forth these ships under Capt. Christopher Newport to plant a colony 100 miles upriver, safe from attack. It must be on unoccupied land where a 50-ton ship could set provisions ashore. It must be healthful.

If there was such a place the explorers failed to find it. Instead they chose for their "Jamestowne" a swampy fist of land jutting into the James River, where ships could snuggle up to the bank in six fathoms of water. On May 13, 1607, the fleet made fast to trees. Next day men and supplies went ashore—and the first permanent English settlement in what is now the United States was born.

"Now falleth every man to worke," wrote a member of the party, "the Councell contrive the Fort, the rest cut downe trees to make place to pitch their Tents; some provide clapbord to relade the ships; some make gardens, some nets &c."

The colonists' council had elected as president Edward Maria Wingfield, well-born, but pompous and unimaginative. Though Indians were all about, Wingfield failed to drill his men or to build any defense but a barrier of loose boughs. On May 18 the chief of the Paspaheghs strolled up to the flimsy fort. A hundred armed braves "garded him in a very warlike manner with Bowes and Arrowes."

The chief signaled the English to lay aside their arms. They refused. He boldly entered the fort with his men. One Indian stole a hatchet. An Englishman snatched it back, striking him on the arm. "Another Savage, seeing that, came fiercely at our man, with a wooden sword, thinking to beat out his braines." The English raised their muskets. Silence. Each side waited for the other to move. The chief gave an angry command, and the braves trooped out of the fort.

The Indians soon struck in earnest. Captain Newport, returning from a voyage upriver to where Richmond now stands, learned that Jamestown had been attacked: two dead, 14 wounded. A cannon shot saved the colony by knocking a tree bough upon the redskins and scaring them off. An arrow had pierced Wing-

James Fort rose from wilderness to guard the first permanent English settlement in America. Colonists lived behind a palisade in thatched half-timbered houses. The reconstructed fort stands in Jamestown Festival Park.

B. ANTHONY STEWART, NATIONAL GEOGRAPHIC PHOTOGRAPHER

field's beard. Observed a diarist: "Hereupon the President was contented that the Fort should be pallisadoed, the ordinance mounted, his men armed and exercised."

But rations were running short. In June, Newport sailed away to England, leaving 104 men with scanty provisions to maintain their toe hold in Virginia.

Soon the daily menu was half a pint of wheat and half a pint of wormy barley, boiled in water. Sickness struck. "Scarse ten amongst us coulde either goe, or well stand; such extreame weaknes and sicknes oppressed us," the record reads. By September 10, half the settlers had died. Wingfield had blundered enough. The other council members told him he was through. "You have eased me of a great

Tiny ships like these park replicas brought settlers: *Susan Constant* (left), *Godspeed, Discovery.*

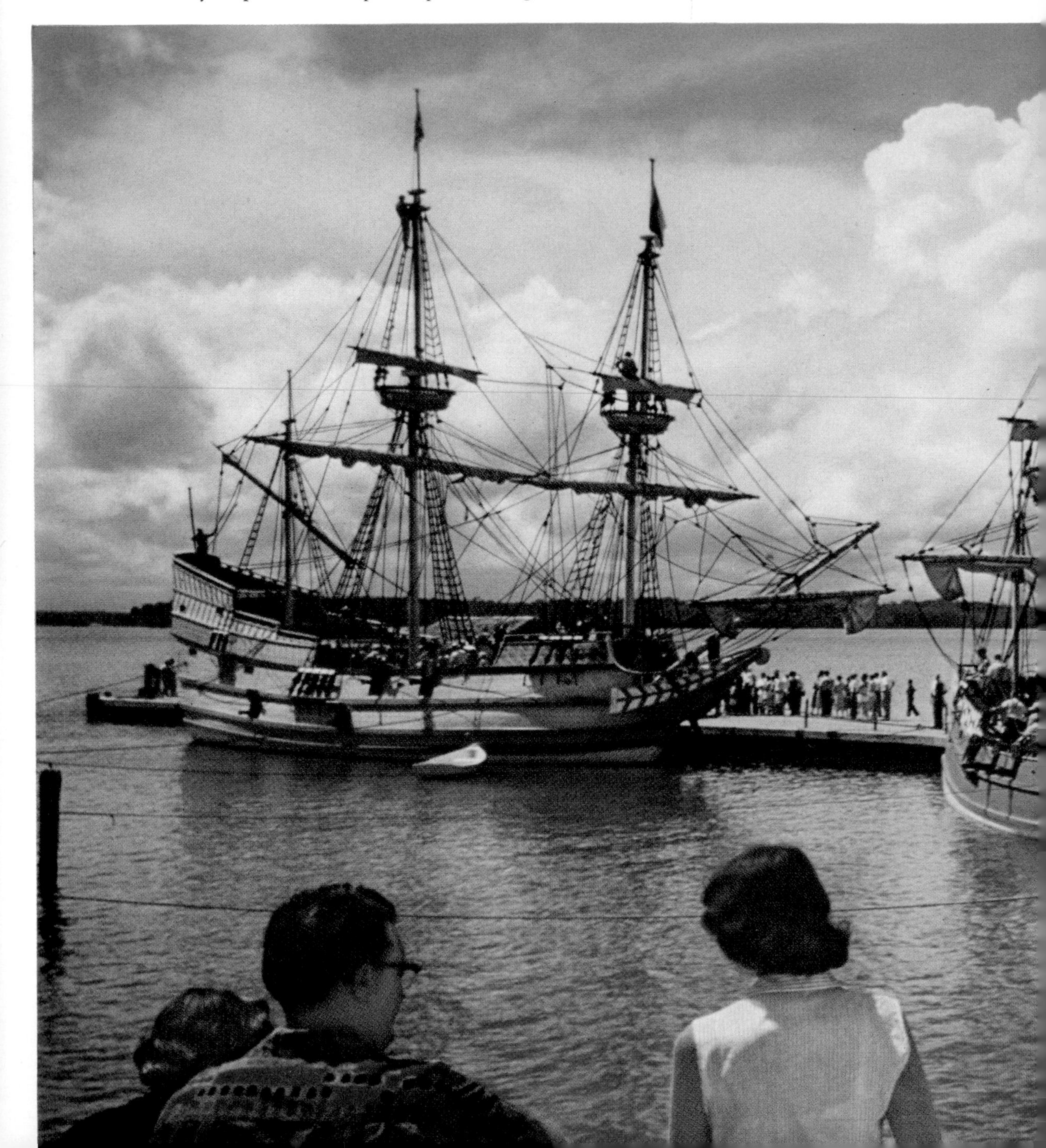

deal of care and trouble," he replied. The weakened colony now leaned upon John Smith, sturdy, bristle-bearded, and contentious, who had the irritating habit of telling people how to do things, and usually proving himself right.

When Smith took over, no houses had been built, the tents were rotting, scarcely five men were well enough to mount guard.

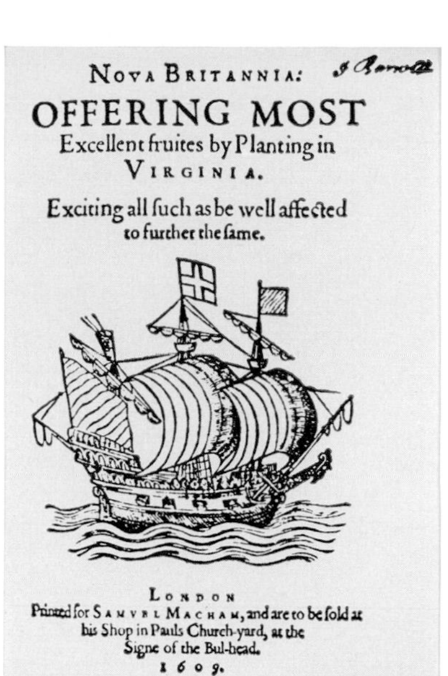
NOVA BRITANNIA:

OFFERING MOST
Excellent fruites by Planting in
VIRGINIA.

Exciting all ſuch as be well affected
to further the ſame.

LONDON
Printed for SAMVEL MACHAM, and are to be ſold at
his Shop in Pauls Church-yard, at the
Signe of the Bul-head.
1609.

Pamphlet (right) extolled Virginia while the colony starved.

THOMAS J. ABERCROMBIE, NATIONAL GEOGRAPHIC STAFF. INSET: NEW YORK PUBLIC LIBRARY

Even those who recovered, snorted vigorous John Smith, "would rather starve and rot with idlenes, then be perswaded to do any thing for their owne reliefe." He set them to mowing, binding thatch into bundles, building and thatching houses. The result was a tiny village of huts crammed within a stockade.

Smith headed up the Chickahominy River to get badly needed food by trading with Powhatan, Indian ruler of the lower Chesapeake area. He finally waded ashore in a marsh and headed into the woods with an Indian guide. In a few minutes he heard Indians yelling behind him.

Grabbing his guide, Smith bound him "to his arme with his garters, and used him as a buckler." An arrow whistled out of nowhere and struck Smith in the thigh. Spinning about, he saw two Indians drawing their bows. More sprang up. Firing his pistol and holding his Indian in front of him, he kept the attackers away. Then he backed into a quagmire. At last, "being neere dead with cold, he threw away his armes."

The Indians dragged him off to their village, and after dancing around him with "hellish notes and screeches," they thrust him into a long house and served him enough food for 20 men—"which made him thinke they would fat him to eat him," Smith wryly remarked.

Finally the Indians led him to Powhatan. The old chieftain was "proudly lying uppon a Bedstead a foote high, upon tenne or twelve Mattes, richly hung with manie Chaynes of great Pearles about his necke, and covered with a great Covering of *Rahaughcums*" (raccoon skins). After a long powwow a crowd of braves, hideously painted, rushed at Smith and threw him to the earth, pressing his head against two huge stones. Others raised their clubs to beat out his brains.

At the last moment, as Smith tells it, "Pocahontas the Kings dearest daughter, when no intreaty could prevaile, got his head in her armes, and laid her owne upon his to save him from death." Pocahontas was a charming girl of 13 or 14—just the age to be fascinated by this handsome white stranger. In an impulsive act of pity, she wrote her name imperishably into American history.

SMITH was saved, but starvation and disease stalked Jamestown. Only 38 hungry, desperate survivors greeted Newport's ship when it sailed up the James loaded with good English food and drink. And hardly had the colonists become accustomed to the taste when disaster struck again. This time fire swept through the flimsy settlement, destroying buildings, tools, supplies, and the minister's books. After rebuilding, the colonists chose John Smith as president. Bursting with energy as usual, he extended the fort from three to five sides (our first Pentagon), drilled the men, repaired the boats, and sent out trading parties.

Newport arrived again with orders to find gold, a passage to the Pacific, and survivors of Raleigh's lost colony. With him came nearly a hundred new colonists—and not an ounce of food for winter! To top all, he was ordered to crown Powhatan and give him royal presents—a waste of time, Smith barked, when they should be trading with the Indians for their newly harvested corn.

Powhatan's presents had to be carried almost a hundred miles by water. When it came time to crown the Indian chieftain, "a foule trouble there was to make him

STATUE BY WILLIAM COUPER; THOMAS J. ABERCROMBIE, NATIONAL GEOGRAPHIC STAFF

Capt. John Smith kept Jamestown going despite hunger, hardship, and strife. He still guards it—in bronze. A soldier of fortune at 16, Smith claimed he beheaded three Turks in single combat! Information from Smith guided his friend Henry Hudson toward the river that bears Hudson's name. Smith's New England explorations helped the Pilgrims.

NATIONAL GEOGRAPHIC MAP REDRAWN FROM TENTH EDITION OF JOHN SMITH'S MAP OF VIRGINIA

Corn meant life to Jamestown, yet the gentlemen-adventurers disdained to plant and harvest it. Then John Rolfe raised "sweet-scented" tobacco (far right) that fetched good prices; soon colonists cultivated the very streets.

In 1616 they shipped 20,000 pounds, though James I dubbed smoking "harmful to the brain, dangerous to the lungs."

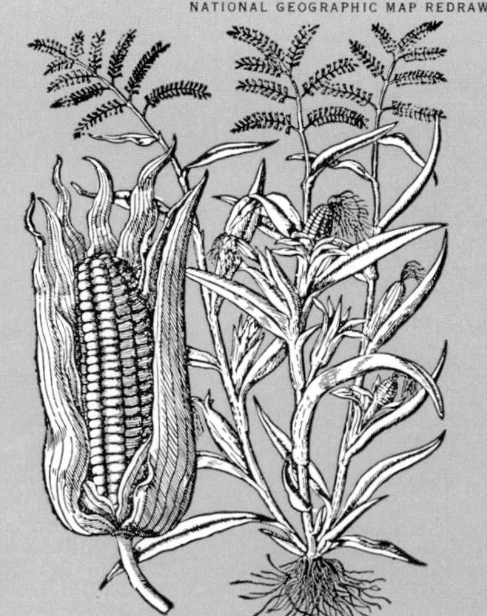

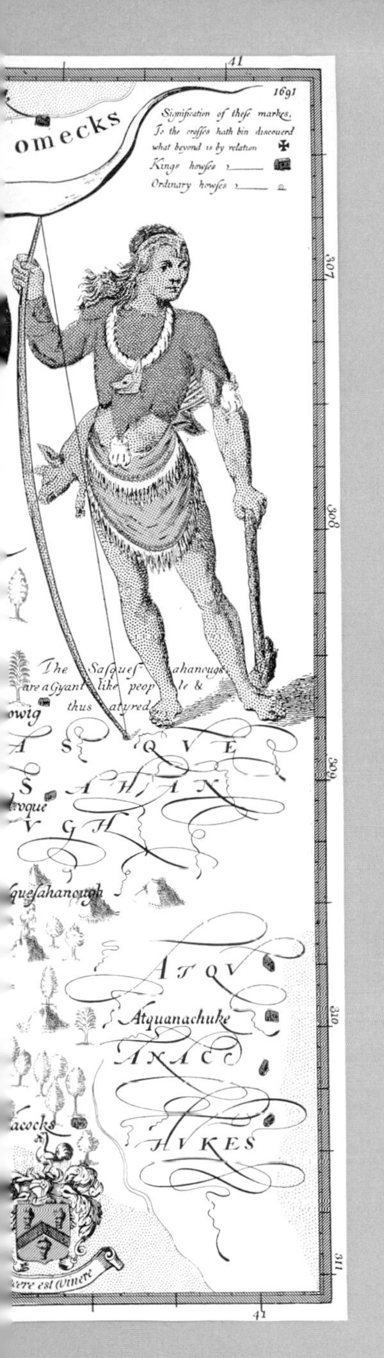

John Smith's map portrays the domain of a savage king and a lovely princess

Time and again the restless captain probed the broad rivers of the "Chesapeack" region, bartering with the Indians for corn, searching for a passage to the Pacific, charting the "mother map" of Virginia. His best known trip, up the Chickahominy River, ended with his rescue by Pocahontas from her father Powhatan.

After that the princess often came to James Fort, bringing food, sometimes turning cart wheels for the delighted colonists. In 1613 she was held hostage to prevent impending Indian raids. Clad in an English gown and baptized Rebecca, she won the heart of young John Rolfe.

BY AN UNKNOWN ARTIST IN ENGLAND, MELLON COLLECTION, NATIONAL GALLERY OF ART

Persuaded after much soul searching that he was moved, not by "the unbridled desire of carnall affection" but "for the good of the plantation, for the honour of our countrie, for the glory of God, for my owne salvation, and for the converting to the true knowledge of God and Jesus Christ, an unbeleeving creature, namely Pokahuntas," Rolfe popped the question and was accepted.

Two years after their marriage the Rolfes visited England. Calling on them, John Smith found not the laughter-loving child of the forest, but modest Lady Rebecca stiffly dressed in brocades (above). Pocahontas never saw America again. She died at Gravesend as she was about to sail for home. But her little boy Thomas became the forefather of many of Virginia's first families.

FROM LEFT: PIETRO ANDREA MATTIOLI, "DISCORSI," 1585, LIBRARY OF CONGRESS; ANTHONY CHUTE, "TABACO," 1595, HUNTINGTON LIBRARY AND ART GALLERY; NICOLAS MONARDES, "JOYFULL NEWES OUT OF THE NEWE FOUNDE WORLDE," 1577, FOLGER LIBRARY

The glasshouse, rebuilt above, raised hopes for a colonial industry, but Polish artisans produced little before the "starving time" closed shop. Clay oven (right), heated with hot stones, baked bread.

Archeologists have dug up artifacts like "scratch" ware (left) and bottles for wine and Dutch gin.

THOMAS J. ABERCROMBIE, NATIONAL GEOGRAPHIC STAFF (ALSO TOP RIGHT)

B. ANTHONY STEWART, NATIONAL GEOGRAPHIC PHOTOGRAPHER, AND (ABOVE) THOMAS L. WILLIAMS

kneele to receive his Crowne." At last the English, leaning hard on his shoulders, forced him to stoop a little, then popped the crown on his head. At a signal the boats in the river let go with a volley. Powhatan, thinking the whole ceremony a trap, started up "in a horrible feare." But at last they convinced him all was well. Powhatan gave his old shoes and his mantle to Newport. That mantle can still be seen in the Ashmolean Museum at Oxford, England.

Newport sailed for home; winter brought more threats from Indians, more deaths. Finding himself the only surviving council member, Smith told the settlers: "He that will not work shall not eat, except by sickness he be disabled." And he set them to making tar and soap ashes, digging a well, building houses, and erecting a fort across the river on a bluff—known today as Smith's Fort Plantation. Before it was finished, President Smith found that the casked corn, which was to have seen the colony through till next harvest, was half rotten, and hordes of rats were rapidly eating the rest.

On July 10, 1609, a ship sailed in from England bringing great news: The Virginia Company had been reorganized, and heavy reinforcements of men and supplies were soon to come out. No one knew that the ship had been wrecked, that months would pass before survivors reached Virginia. Meanwhile, plagued with food shortages and insubordination, the colony barely held together.

In the fall of 1609 John Smith returned to England. He had been badly burned in an accident and was still plagued by enemies within the settlement. Yet Smith had fallen in love with America, not for the dream of gold or of a passage to the South Sea but for its own sake. He returned to explore the New England coast, but he never saw Jamestown again.

With his departure, Jamestown fell apart. Weapons were traded to the Indians, who slaughtered the settlers; some survivors sailed for England without permission; all hogs, chickens, and other livestock were eaten. That terrible winter of 1609-10 came to be known as the "starving time." Men wolfed the meat of dogs and rats and searched the woods, eager to "feede upon Serpents and snakes and to digge the earthe for wylde and unknowne Rootes." They dug up the dead for food. Of nearly 500 people, only 60 miserable creatures were alive when the shipwrecked leaders, Sir Thomas Gates and Sir George Somers, turned up in May.

Shocked, Gates wrote that Jamestown appeared "raither as the ruins of some auntient fortification, then that any people living might now inhabit it: the pallisadoes tourne downe, the portes open, the gates from the hinges, the church ruined and unfrequented . . . the Indian as fast killing without as the famine and pestilence within."

It seemed the only thing to do with Jamestown was abandon it. On June 7, survivors set sail for England. Hope of a British America was dead. But next day as they dropped down river, they met a longboat bringing dramatic news: Lord De La Warr was in the bay with new supplies. The colony was saved.

But Jamestown still had no firm economic base. Everything – gold, glass, tar,

soap ash—had failed. Sassafras and clapboard could not pay big profits to the Virginia Company. Then in 1612 John Rolfe discovered how to cure sweet tobacco, and with this new export the colony began to get on its feet.

In July, 1619, Governor Sir George Yeardley called together America's first legislative assembly. Burgesses elected from 11 settled areas gathered in the church choir where the governor sat with his council. Before they adjourned they fixed the price of tobacco, recommended "that no injury or oppression be wrought by the English against the Indian," and decreased punishments for idleness, gambling, and drunkenness.

A few days after adjournment a Dutch ship sailed up the river and sold some 20 Negroes for badly needed provisions. Thus began the "peculiar institution" of slavery which was to affect the whole history of America.

In London, meanwhile, the Virginia Company sought 100 "woemen, Maides young and uncorrupt to make wifes to the Inhabitantes and by that meanes to make the men there more setled & lesse moveable." The girls arrived next summer, gladdening an equal number of eager males. Unfortunately, the newlyweds had only two years of bliss before disaster struck. In 1622 some Englishmen

ENGRAVING BY THEODORE DE BRY, 1628, LIBRARY OF CONGRESS, AND (LEFT) THOMAS L. WILLIAMS

Plastering clay over a network of twigs, settlers slapped together their wattle-and-daub homes. But they failed to cement a lasting friendship with the Indians. In 1622 Opechancanough, Powhatan's successor, turned his braves loose on outlying plantations. They slaughtered 347 unwary colonists.

murdered a respected Indian. On Good Friday the Indians fell without warning on settlements up and down both sides of the James. Jamestown itself was saved by a friendly Indian.

Then came plague. Of the thousands who had come to Virginia, only 300 were left in 1623. More planters arrived after James I made Virginia a royal colony, and by 1625 there were a score of settled areas. Brick dwellings rose in Jamestown, including the home of Gov. John Harvey, which became the first statehouse. A brick church was begun about 1639. Part of its tower still stands.

Though endlessly beset by Indians, disease, and fires, the Virginia Colony grew to a prosperous community of 80,000. Then in 1700 the capital moved to Williamsburg. Jamestown declined into an "Abundance of Brick Rubbish."

Thanks to the National Park Service, the Association for the Preservation of Virginia Antiquities, and Virginia authorities, that rubbish has been turned into a meaningful site where all Americans can pay homage to the brave settlers whose trials were a source of our strength.

The tower, rising above this rebuilt church, is the only standing ruin of 17th century Jamestown. Loopholes pierce its three-foot walls. Gravestones carry such honored names as Berkeley, Byrd, Lee, Blair, and Harrison. In 1619 the first representative legislative assembly in the Americas convened on this site. Here, too, came worshipers in Sunday best.

B. ANTHONY STEWART,
NATIONAL GEOGRAPHIC PHOTOGRAPHER

B. ANTHONY STEWART, NATIONAL GEOGRAPHIC PHOTOGRAPHER

Thomas Rolfe inherited 150 acres from his mother Pocahontas. His friend Thomas Warren built this house on the property in 1652. Traces of Smith's Fort remain behind dwelling.

St. Luke's, "a time-hallowed relic of the past" in Dwight D. Eisenhower's words, is a link with medieval Gothic churches. Though greatly restored, its walls have weathered 300 years. Right: "Old Brick's" 17th century alms box.

Famous landmarks of early Virginia

Though early records speak of "James Citty," Jamestown was never bigger than a village. But it became the nucleus of a widespread community of planters who cleared the land and built homes and churches (see map, page 138).

WILLARD R. CULVER AND (RIGHT) HISTORICAL PICTURE SERVICE

Adam Thoroughgood House on Lynnhaven Bay may be the nation's oldest brick home. "Good Adam" died rich in 1640. He rose from servitude in true American style.

DAVID S. BOYER, NATIONAL GEOGRAPHIC STAFF (ALSO LEFT)

Bacon's Castle, built by Arthur Allen about 1655, recalls an English country mansion, with Flemish gables, triple chimney, Tudor dungeon, and a ghost that haunts the garden. Bacon's men held it during the uprising.

Bacon's Rebellion

NATHANIEL BACON had an ear for the woes of his fellow planters. In the 1670's they faced ruin, for tobacco glutted England. Governor Berkeley packed the assembly with cronies, barred elections, and levied crippling taxes. When Indians attacked in 1676, Berkeley made no move to check them.

Without the governor's authority, Bacon and 300 men went to fight redskins. Berkeley declared him a rebel and set out after him, but Bacon whipped the Indians and became Virginia's hero. He marched triumphantly into Jamestown, where the raging governor tore open his fine clothes and shouted, "Here! Shoot me! 'Fore God a fair mark, shoot!"

Bacon replied that he only wanted "a commission to save our lives from the Indians . . . and now we will have it before we go." And his men echoed, "We will have it!" shaking their guns.

They got it. But Bacon couldn't decide whether to fight Indians or Berkeley, who alternately pursued and fled him. Finally the rebels laid siege to Jamestown and burned it (above). Bacon planned reforms, but dysentery killed him. Berkeley returned and hanged 37 of Bacon's followers.

"That old fool," said Charles II, "has hanged more men in that naked country than I have done for the murder of my father."

Thus ended Bacon's rebellion against many of the same injustices that brought on the American Revolution a century later.

WAYNE BARRETT

NEW ENGLAND

Pilgrims plant freedom on Plymouth's shore

JAMES THE FIRST arched a pious brow at the Pilgrims' petition. "What profits may arise in the parts to which they intend to go?"

"Fishing," he was told.

"So God have my soul, 'tis an honest trade! 'Twas the Apostles' own calling." And he let them go in peace. Yet the Pilgrim Fathers sailed from England, September 6, 1620, with very little fishing tackle. They sought less tangible profits

DEPARTURE OF THE "SPEEDWELL" FROM HOLLAND, 1620, BY ROBERT W. WEIR, IN U.S. CAPITOL ROTUNDA

than cod and mackerel when they established the first permanent European settlement in New England.

Norsemen probably explored parts of the region in the 11th century. In 1497 John Cabot sailed among codfish so plentiful they could be scooped up in baskets. The fishing lured vessels from Portugal, Brittany, the Basque country, Holland, and Devon. By 1600 scores of ships flying many flags sailed off the coast.

After the fishermen came fur traders, finally would-be settlers. Both France and England stubbed colonial toes on New England's "stern and rock-bound coast" before the Pilgrims gained a foothold. In 1604 France, spurred by her enthusiastic explorer Samuel de Champlain, planted a short-lived colony at the mouth of the St. Croix River, now the boundary between Maine and Canada. In 1607, the year Jamestown was founded, English settlers headed by George Popham built Fort St. George on the Kennebec River, but soon abandoned it after fighting Indians, winter, and the "malice of the Divell."

About this time in England, Separatists were battling the devil in the pulpit. They considered the Anglican Church "a pudle of corruption" and met in secret to restore "primative order, libertie, & bewtie." They had better conform, King James bellowed, "or I will harry them out the land." Royal wrath sent a small band scurrying to Leyden, Holland, in 1608.

Fearing absorption by the Dutch—some preferred "ye prisons in England rather than this libertie in Holland"—the Pilgrims looked to the New World. London merchants, sensing quick returns, financed them and swelled their ranks with 61 "strangers." These were humble folk who sought only to better their lot. For God and profit 102 colonists, a melting pot from the beginning, boarded the *Mayflower*.

The Leyden Pilgrims were no plaster saints. Passionate, curious, daring, they typify the Elizabethan Age. They spoke sharply, liked plain food and "strong waters," married early, and demanded "freedome of Religion." They broke cleanly

Ye Lord's free people, "well weaned from ye delicate milke of our mother countrie" by their exile in Holland, now set faces and hearts toward "those vast & unpeopled countries of America."

with the Church of England instead of trying to purify it, as did the Puritans. One tie bound them all: They came "from the cottages and not the castles of England."

Frugality cost them the services of Capt. John Smith, who had charted the New England coast in 1614. "My books and maps," he acidly noted, "were much better cheape to teach them, than my selfe."

Nine weeks after putting to sea the Pilgrims dropped anchor in Cape Cod Bay. Safe in harbor they "fell upon their knees & blessed ye God of heaven, who had brought them over ye vast & furious ocean, and delivered them from all ye periles & miseries thereof, againe to set their feete on ye firme and stable earth." And there, off Provincetown, they drew up the Mayflower Compact to "combine our-selves togeather into a civill body politick" and frame "just & equall lawes."

DECEMBER blew in cold and wet. Weary colonists huddled aboard ship while some in an open shallop explored the coast. Icy spray bit their faces and froze their clothes into "coates of iron." At last they found "a place fitt for situation." The *Mayflower* ferried the colonists to Plymouth Harbor, and on December 20th they stepped ashore, tradition says, near a great boulder on the beach. With "victuals being much spente, especially our Beere," they voted to "plant" on the high ground above the rock.

The first months were cruel as only a New England winter can be. Fever and scurvy decimated the colony: "This month [March] thirteen of our number die. And in three months past dies halfe our company . . . scarce fifty remain, the living scarce able to bury the dead."

As spring finally came, fortune smiled. Out of the woods strode a naked Indian. "Welcome!" spoke Samoset, who had learned English from fishermen in Maine. He bridged the gulf between white man and red. Samoset introduced the Pilgrims to Massasoit, sachem of nearby tribes, and to Squanto, who "had been in England & could speake better English than himselfe." Pilgrims learned how to build fish traps, raise corn, and stalk game. October's harvest, though lean, was reason enough to "rejoyce together." They celebrated their first Thanksgiving playing

"After they had injoyed faire winds and weather they met with many feirce stormes"

Taking aboard Pilgrims from the unseaworthy *Speedwell,* the crowded *Mayflower* sailed from Plymouth with 102 "saints and strangers." On its 67-day voyage of some 3,500 miles, two children, Oceanus Hopkins and Peregrine White, were born. Two persons died. "After longe beating at sea, they fell with that land which is called Cape Cod . . . they were not a litle joyfull."

Loath to leave the Pilgrims alone on such a "wild & savage" coast, Capt. Christopher Jones stood by all that first terrible winter. When the *Mayflower* weighed anchor, severing the Pilgrims' last link with England, not one homesick, haggard settler chose to desert his wilderness home.

ROBERT F. SISSON, NATIONAL GEOGRAPHIC PHOTOGRAPHER

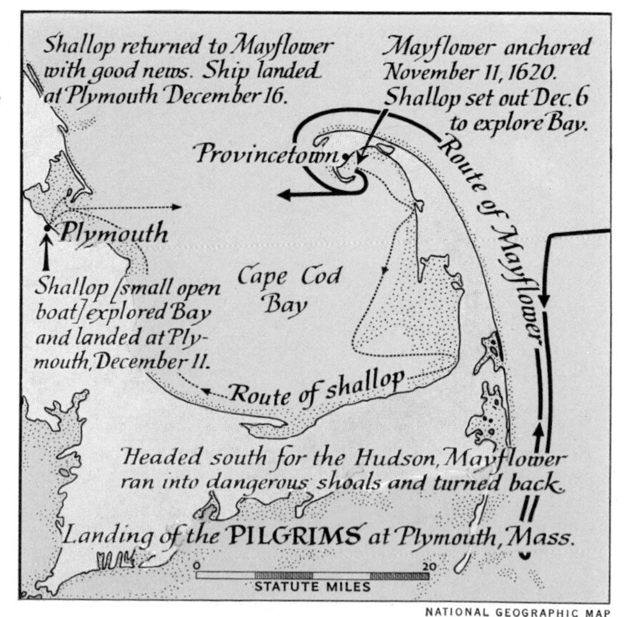
Shallop returned to Mayflower with good news. Ship landed at Plymouth December 16.
Mayflower anchored November 11, 1620. Shallop set out Dec. 6 to explore Bay.
Provincetown
Route of Mayflower
Plymouth
Shallop [small open boat] explored Bay and landed at Plymouth, December 11.
Cape Cod Bay
Route of shallop
Headed south for the Hudson, Mayflower ran into dangerous shoals and turned back.
Landing of the PILGRIMS at Plymouth, Mass.
0
20
STATUTE MILES

NATIONAL GEOGRAPHIC MAP

Thousands throng beach where Pilgrims landed in solitude

"They had no friends to wellcome them, nor inns to entertaine or refresh their weatherbeaten bodys," wrote William Bradford. But it was standing room only when *Mayflower II* arrived in 1957. A shallop rows out to pick up Capt. Alan Villiers and crew for reception beside the colonnade over Plymouth Rock.

The guide at "this steppingstone of a nation" is costumed in Pilgrim's weekday Lincoln green and russet brown.

The *Mayflower* replica is permanently moored at Plymouth.

LUIS MARDEN AND (LEFT) BATES LITTLEHALES, BOTH NATIONAL GEOGRAPHIC STAFF

games and feasting on venison, roast duck, shellfish, berries, and grapes. A hungry winter followed, more Pilgrims arrived from England, and the colony staggered under the load. But the tattered saints never lost faith.

Imagination must wipe away today's bustling community to see the Plymouth of 340 years ago: A scant collection of hewn-plank and thatch-roofed houses flank Leyden and Main Streets, and a stout palisade girds the town from Town Brook to Plymouth Harbor. On Burial Hill rises "a fort of good timbers, both strong and comely," and brazen cannon look down to overawe the "salvages." Assembling in Leyden Street at beat of drum, Pilgrims march up the hill together in family groups. They congregate in the fort's lower room where Elder William Brewster leads them in worship.

Expanding slowly, New Plimoth became Old Plymouth Colony, stretching from Cape Cod's tip to Narragansett Bay, from Scituate to Nantucket Sound. Pilgrim traders founded outposts from Maine to the Connecticut Valley, matched wits and wampum with French, Dutch, and Indians.

Mecca for modern Pilgrims is famous Plymouth Rock. To most it somehow seems too small: "They expect a cliff, I guess," remarked a guide. Broken off the original boulder, reduced more by souvenir chippers, it now lies safely beneath a classic colonnade at tide's edge. The old town is rich with relics and memories of democracy's growth. Here lie time-yellowed records of Governors Bradford and Winslow; there hangs a portrait of Winslow, the only known likeness of a *Mayflower* passenger. In Plymouth was born the New England town meeting. And from its gray clapboarded Town House, patriots defied King George's Stamp Act: "We will never be slaves to any power on earth."

The Jabez Howland House (1667) echoed to Pilgrim boots. The restored Sparrow House (1640) has a round-cornered fireplace, carved paneling, and a door buttressed "to withstand tomahawk blows." The Harlow House was built in 1677 "from the timbers of the old fort." Children, like the Pilgrims, plant corn and flax in the yard when "oak leaves are the size of a mouse's ear." Plimoth Plantation recreates forefathers' days with old-style dwellings and a replica of the *Mayflower*.

Neighboring Kingston was home to William Bradford. A "father to them all," he governed the colonists 31 years. Duxbury ranks second to Plymouth in early

Before the kitchen fireplace, like this in the Duxbury home of John Alden, Pilgrim families supped on bowls of hasty pudding. Then both men and women lit pipes

Pilgrim associations. Here lived Philippe de La Noye, an ancestor of Franklin Delano Roosevelt. Here also stands the John Alden House, built by son Jonathan in 1653. Now a museum, it has been in the Alden family for three centuries. It saw the death of "Speak for yourself" John and probably Priscilla. They rest in the pine-shaded Old Burying Ground not far from the grave of Capt. Myles Standish, the odd man of that legendary triangle.

Longfellow memorialized the captain in verse; Duxbury honors him in sculpture. His statue atop a 130-foot granite monument is "the highest in the world," wisecrack old-timers. "It's Myles above the sea!" Standish never joined the Pilgrim church, never bowed to its self-righteous code. He kept a tolerant outlook when Pilgrims and, later, Puritans were losing theirs.

Pilgrim Village, rebuilt at Plymouth, mirrors days when forefathers shocked corn for the harsh winter ahead. Exhibits include a saw pit where house planks are hand-sawn from logs, and crafts of the Pilgrims' Indian allies.

PLIMOTH PLANTATION AND (ABOVE) KATHLEEN REVIS JUDGE

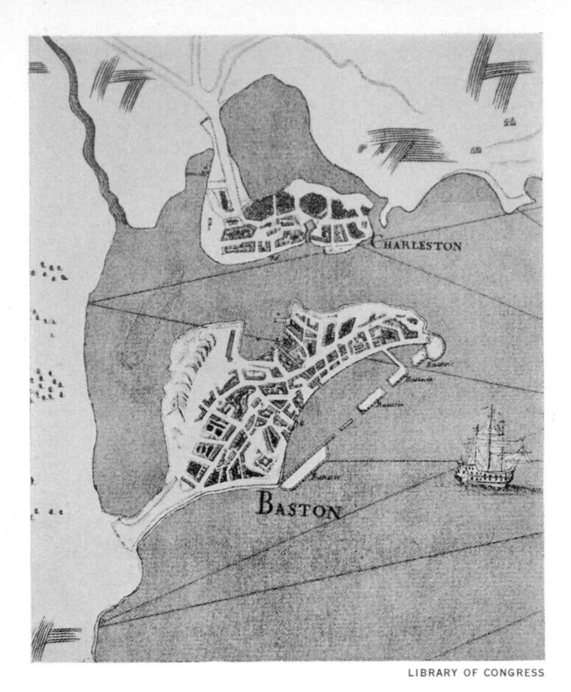

LIBRARY OF CONGRESS

"Baston," as a French mapmaker labeled it in 1693, grew blueberries when Ann Pollard skipped ashore in 1630. Aged 100 (right), she recalled it.

Puritans settle Massachusetts Bay

MEN OF PLYMOUTH scouted north to the Shawmut peninsula in 1621, dropping names—Brewster Islands, Point Allerton, Squantum—that Boston still reveres. They esteemed the Boston Bay country superior to Plymouth and regretted they had not settled here. But as Governor Bradford in true Calvinistic tradition pointed out, "it seems ye Lord who assignes to all men ye bounds of their habitations, had appoynted it for another use."

Thus predestined, Squire John Winthrop, charter in hand, landed at Salem, June 12, 1630. After exploring down the coast, he chose the mouth of the Charles River for his colony and led the Puritans to Charlestown. Scarcity of fresh water soon prompt-

Governor Winthrop's arrival began the great migration

CHARLES HOFFBAUER, NEW ENGLAND MUTUAL LIFE INSURANCE COMPANY
ABOVE: MASSACHUSETTS HISTORICAL SOCIETY

LAURENCE LOWRY

The Common, Boston's oldest landmark, harks back to 1634 when it was bought for $150 to serve as "a trayning field . . . and for feeding cattell." Cow paths winding to the 48-acre pasture became downtown streets. Adjacent Public Garden with its pond dates from 1850's.

ed the governor to shift his flock again. They crossed to the neighboring peninsula of Shawmut, where they could share the spring-water supply of William Blaxton, a hermit who lived on Beacon Hill. On September 7 they named their settlement Boston, after the Lincolnshire town so familiar to the Puritan leaders.

First ashore was "romping" ten-year-old Ann Pollard, who remembered the land being "very uneven, abounding in small hollows and swamps." Soon the peninsula boasted a cluster of sod-roofed and bark-covered cottages, and a fort "which can command any ship as shee sayles into any Harbour within the still Bay."

The first Bostonians, mainly city dwellers, arrived too late to plant a crop had they known how. Scrimping on clams and mussels, ground nuts and acorns, ravaged by disease, some 200 of them—perhaps one in five—died before winter.

Survival lay in the sea: fishing, shipbuilding, trading. In 1631 Puritans launched the first ship built in Massachusetts and soon laid keels for more, some as big as 200 tons. New hope surged in Boston. And before the end of the decade new life throbbed as 20,000 Englishmen, many of them scholars, fled the despotic England of Charles I. With renewed vigor Bostonians cut firewood, pastured cattle on the harbor islands, developed "Farms in the Countrey," and proclaimed their city "the chiefe place for shipping and Merchandize." Like Old Testament patriarchs, their ministers laid down the law from the pulpit on matters affecting the community—excommunicating a heretic, perhaps, or ordering the town butcher to "remove the Stinking garbage out of his yard, nere the street."

In the mid-1600's theocracy grudgingly gave ground to civil rule by laymen gathered in the town meeting. "Puritanism," remarked James Russell Lowell, "believing itself quick with the seed of religious liberty, laid, without knowing it, the egg of democracy."

Boston hatched it, but Salem did the initial incubating. Four years before Winthrop landed, Roger Conant rallied a few defectors from the Plymouth Colony and established them at the Indian fishing village of Naumkeag. They fished and planted, "feeding their fancies with new discoveries at the Spring's approach . . . turning down many a drop of the bottell." Two years later stern John Endecott arrived in Salem and took command. Endecott had cut short the far from puritanical goings on at Wollaston, where rebels from Plymouth's strait-laced society had raised a Maypole to frisk around. He had no trouble setting Salem to rights.

Salem's Pioneer Village makes today's visitors aware of the hardships New England settlers took for granted. As shelter from raw winds and drifting snow, they dug their first homes from the rocky soil or raised wigwams. Green sapling poles, bent to join at the roof, were thatched and shingled with pine bark.

Nearby stands the Lady Arbella House. A well-born Puritan, she came with Winthrop on the ship named for her, but died within a month. Her husband also succumbed, and Cotton Mather noted: "She first deceased, he for a little while tried to live without her, liked it not, and died."

Rev. Francis Higginson, who drew up a confession of faith and a covenant, and Pastor Samuel Skelton established the first Puritan church in America at Salem. When Skelton died, Roger Williams became its pastor. But in 1635 he was hounded out of Massachusetts for advocating a clean break with the Church of England and went south to found Providence. This presaged the day half a century hence when Salem, maddened by "witchcraft," would again loose the dogs of intolerance.

IN THE LANGUAGE of the Old Testament, Salem means "City of Peace." But to any American schoolboy Salem remains best known for the hysteria that gripped the town during a few months in 1692.

By this time New England was as enlightened as any land in the world. Harvard was already a good deal older than many of today's colleges. New Englanders had been elected to the Royal Society of London. Massachusetts scholars had a grasp of physics and astronomy that was second only to the newest learning of Europe. Yet the Puritan church, based largely on the fear of hell-fire, clung firmly to belief in witchcraft—the possession of human souls by the devil. The religious climate remained hospitable to any suggestion that witches might be doing

BATES LITTLEHALES, NATIONAL GEOGRAPHIC PHOTOGRAPHER

No witches' brew for modern Puritans at Salem's Pioneer Village. They're making soap from tallow and wood ash. Complete to brick kilns, saltworks, and pillory, the rebuilt settlement of Naumkeag looks as it did before Winthrop landed here on his way to Boston.

. . . and hangs witches

Satan's work right under the noses of fire-breathing Puritan clergymen.

In the home of Rev. Samuel Parris in Salem, a group of girls aged nine to 19 would gather to hear the tales of magic and sorcery told by his West Indian servant girl Tituba. So graphic were her descriptions of the working of evil spirits that the girls' imaginations ran wild.

Early in 1692 Elizabeth Parris and a few of her teen-age friends began having fits of madness. They took themselves more and more seriously until they believed that Tituba and other Salem women had bewitched them. With the clergy's encouragement, they made accusations.

And so began the mass hysteria. By the time the madness could be stopped at year's end, 19 men and women had been hanged as witches, one had been pressed to death, and scores more suffered in prison.

Recantation and regret followed. All 12 jurors published a "declaration of sorrow" asking forgiveness of God and man. Damages were finally paid to the victims' heirs, and the act of public penance by Salem and the Bay Colony was complete.

Salem's 17th century homes include many with witchcraft associations. The so-called Witch House belonged to one of the judges. Rebecca Nurse, whose home stands in Danvers, was hanged as a witch. The House of Seven Gables and its neighbors, the Hathaway House and Retire Becket House, stood during the hysteria, as did the Pickering House. Gallows Hill, scene of executions, still broods over the old town.

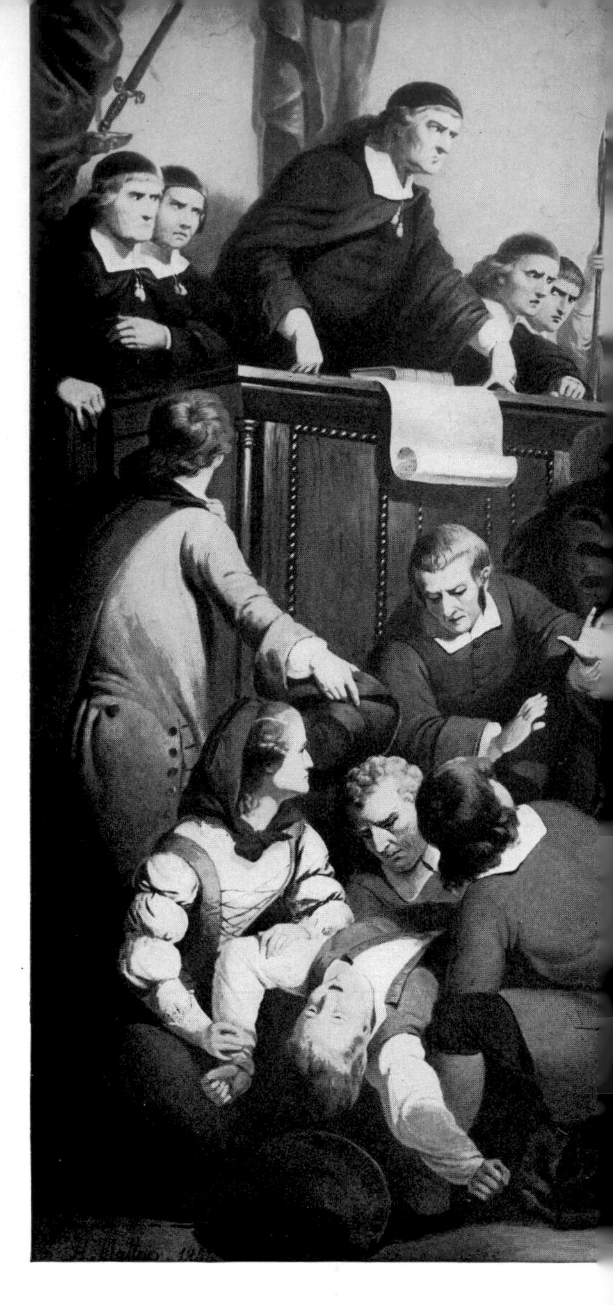

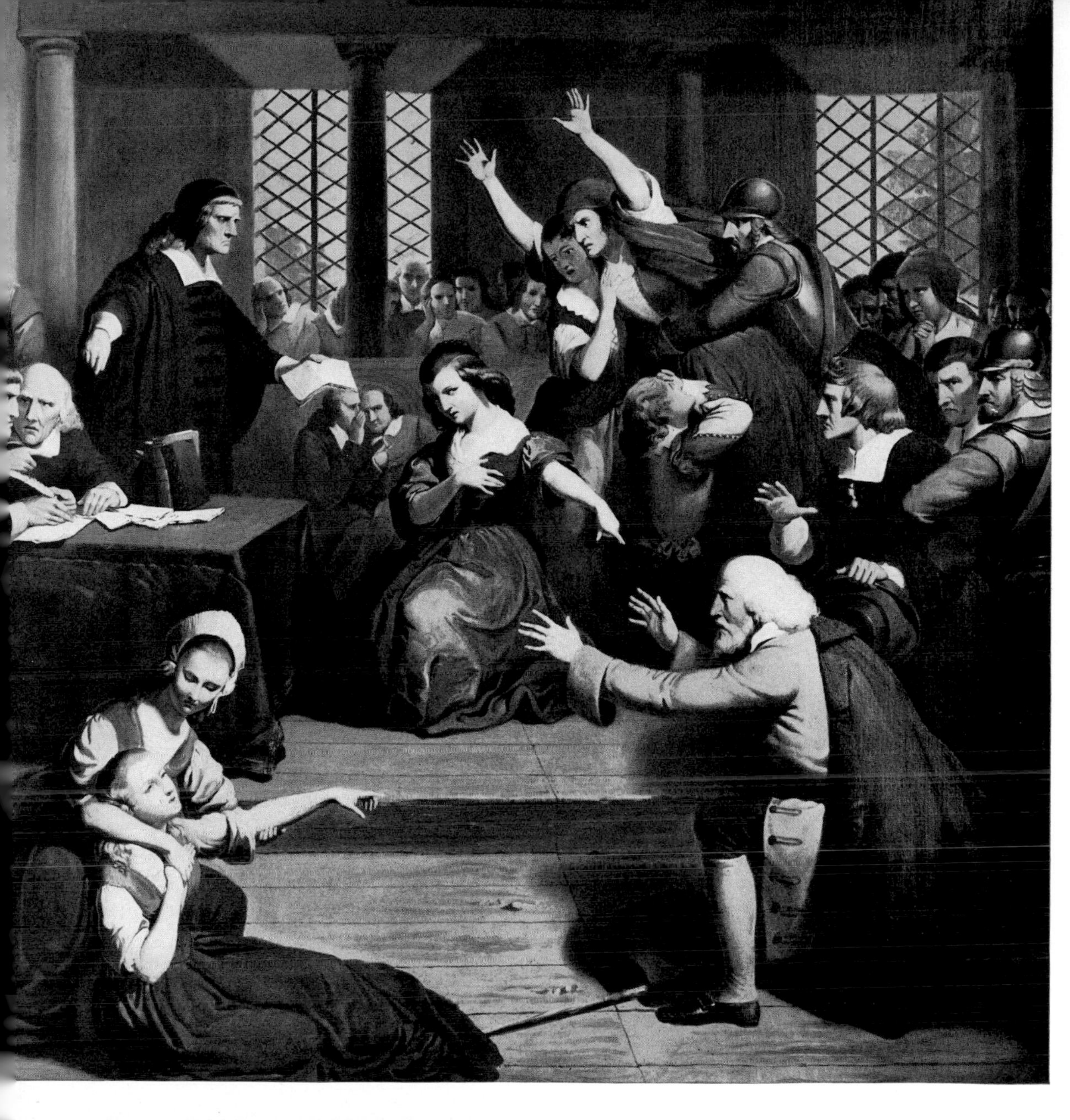

Witchcraft hysteria seizes convulsing girls who point to "sorcerer" George Jacobs. "You tax me for a wizard," he shouts. "You may as well tax me for a buzzard. I have done no harm!" Yet the court sentenced him to die on Gallows Hill.

Jonathan Corwin, a judge at the trials, lived in the Witch House (far left). House of Seven Gables, with its secret staircase, belonged to a cousin of novelist Nathaniel Hawthorne. An ancestor, John Hathorne, was also a judge at the witchcraft trials.

B. ANTHONY STEWART AND JOHN E. FLETCHER, BOTH NATIONAL GEOGRAPHIC STAFF
ABOVE: T. H. MATTISON, ESSEX INSTITUTE, SALEM

WOODCUT C. 1670 BY JOHN FOSTER, MASSACHUSETTS HISTORICAL SOCIETY, AND (RIGHT) HUNTINGTON LIBRARY AND ART GALLERY

MAMUSSE
WUNNEETUPANATAMWE
UP-BIBLUM GOD
NANEESWE
NUKKONE TESTAMENT
KAH WONK
WUSKU TESTAMENT.

Ne quoshkinnumuk nashpe Wuttinneumoh CHRIST noh asoowesit
JOHN ELIOT.

CAMBRIDGE:
Printeuoop nashpe Samuel Green kah Marmaduke Johnson.
1663.

Bible and preacher wielded power in Puritan towns. Missionary John Eliot sought to extend their sway over the Indians, translating the Scriptures into Algonquian (above). Master printer Marmaduke Johnson came from England to print the book "at the presse in Harvard Colledge."

Richard Mather, shown at left in the first American woodcut, was the grandfather of Cotton Mather.

Puritan life centers in the church . . .

PIETY AND HARD WORK were the driving forces of the Puritans. Every member of the large families did his chores faithfully. But by dusk on Saturday work had to cease, for the Sabbath had begun. Beans bubbled in a pot on the great hearth. Pies cooled on a window sill. They could be served without effort for supper and Sunday breakfast.

On Sunday everyone filed into the meetinghouse for a session that might last for hours. Families took square pews, assigned according to rank and dignity. Attention focused on the high pulpit. If thoughts wandered, the watchful tithingman stood near with his long pole. One end was knobbed to rouse those made drowsy by their live-coal footwarmers; the other bore a patch of fur to tickle any maiden caught yawning, tittering, or flirting. The congregation stood while prayers rumbled on past the turning of the minister's hourglass.

Nucleus of the village, the meetinghouse stood at the head of the green, surveying the dwellings that lined the street. In early days it served as a fort, and worshipers leaned their guns in pew corners. Thursday was Lecture Day, and villagers gathered to hear long harangues, to scoff at the town drunkard trussed in the stocks, and to test their aim with matchlocks on the green. Then it was home for supper in low-ceilinged kitchens with huge fireplaces where family life centered.

. . . and in the home

Old Ship Church has echoed Hingham's prayers since ships' carpenters raised its massive timbers in 1681. Puritans shunned altars; pews in the square meetinghouse focus on pulpit. In last hymn, congregations often turned to face choir.

KATHLEEN REVIS JUDGE

The Whipple House at Ipswich grew with the years from austere 1640 to the day of the piano.

Wooden utensils (from top): a wrench to tighten rope bedsprings, bowl, funnel, mortar and pestle, piggin, butter paddle, trencher. Forks were rare.

Spinning and weaving kept families clothed. Children helped at small looms. Simplicity, sturdiness mark early homes like the Whipple House (right) and Topsfield's Parson Capen House.

WHIPPLE HOUSE BY KATHLEEN REVIS JUDGE, WEAVING AT PLYMOUTH'S HARLOW HOUSE BY BATES LITTLEHALES, NATIONAL GEOGRAPHIC PHOTOGRAPHER. TOP: OLD STURBRIDGE VILLAGE. LEFT: FOLGER LIBRARY

FROM HERMAN MOLL'S MAP OF NORTH AMERICA, C. 1710, LIBRARY OF CONGRESS

Cod hooked in Newfoundland's chill waters were split, salted, spread out to dry. Oil was pressed from liver. The fish abounded year round. Cured cod kept indefinitely.

RAY BROWN FOR "STORY OF OUR MERCHANT MARINE"

In ships they built with adz and ax, New Englanders carried their corn and salt fish to West Indies marts.

WITHOUT the bounty of the sea, Pilgrims and Puritans could scarcely have scratched a living from New England's rocky soil. Indians taught them to plant dead fish along with their corn. Herring or alewives served the purpose, and towns boasted of their coastal brooks where alewives ran in spring.

The corn crop, ground into meal, furnished a family with pudding, porridge, and tough crusty journey cake. Even now New Englanders eat "johnnycake," Indian pudding, and corn meal mush sweetened with maple syrup.

Sacred cod hangs in the Massachusetts State House, honored as lifesaving food for settlers, first export, and the humble origin of mercantile wealth.

PAUL R. HOFFMASTER

One for the cutworm, one for the crow,
One for the woodchuck, and two to grow.
So says the Yankee farmer, planting five kernels of corn and a fish or two in each hill.

MASSACHUSETTS DEPARTMENT OF COMMERCE

To grind corn settlers first hollowed a log for a mortar. Streams later powered mills. Where winds blew fresh, as on Cape Cod and Nantucket (above), windmills turned.

New Englanders discover corn, codfish, and coastal trade

But cod was the fish that fed early New England. Big and meaty, they nosed close to shore in spring and fall. Settlers were quick to realize the profit from fishing. Their fishing vessels were nodding to each other on the cod-rich Grand Banks in 1645. Gloucester earned its fame from the codfish—and New England learned how to sail.

The day in 1631 when Gov. John Winthrop launched his 30-ton *Blessing of the Bay* to carry cargoes between settlements, the future of the region became certain: trade.

Gloucester's Madonna, cradling a schooner, welcomes fishermen home. This old port's fleet is manned today mostly by Portuguese whose ancestors fished the Grand Banks a century and more before the Pilgrims came.

LUIS MARDEN, NATIONAL GEOGRAPHIC STAFF
LEFT: KATHLEEN REVIS JUDGE

KATHLEEN REVIS JUDGE AND (RIGHT) SAUGUS IRONWORKS RESTORATION

Ironworks of the Puritans surge to life again

Churning power for the rolling mill delights young visitors as they explore the birthplace of America's steel industry on the banks of the Saugus near Boston. Blast furnace, forge, warehouse, wharf, and ironmaster's house also have been restored to their 17th century prime.

At Saugus, water wheels spin tales of New England's first industry

As 17th century New Englanders turned from soil to sea for their livelihood, they created a demand for ships and the iron that went into them: nails and bolts, chains and anchors.

At first the iron came from England, slowly and expensively. Settlers moving inland would burn their houses to recover the nails. But after 1640 the Bay Colony was pouring "pigs" and forging wrought iron at a plant "as good as any worke England doth afoarde"—the mighty ironworks on the Saugus River.

Hammersmith, the investors called it; and in its day the blast furnace, forge, and giant water wheels were a wonder. Yet by 1678 the ironworks lay silent. Perhaps it was too big, too grand for the modest community it served.

Almost three centuries of neglect saw the site overgrown with brambles and its story obscured by legends. Only the ironmaster's house remained, thanks to zealous guardians. The American Iron and Steel Institute finally poured more than $1,500,000 into six years of painstaking restoration. Archeologists uncovered some six tons of relics, including a mighty water wheel far beneath the town's busy Central Street.

A rusty scum on Massachusetts bogs indicated iron ore in the muck beneath—and inspired the original project. Timber for charcoal abounded. Rock from the nearby coast added a fluxing material to remove impurities. English and colonial investors, the "Company of Undertakers," raised capital.

John Winthrop, son of the Bay Colony's governor and organizer of these backers, set up an unsuccessful blast furnace in Braintree, south of Boston. Richard

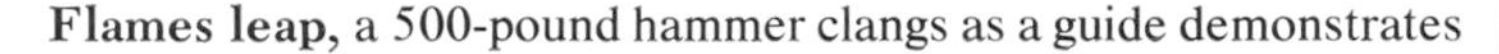

Flames leap, a 500-pound hammer clangs as a guide demonstrates

In the 17th century great labor produced small quantities of a much-needed metal: wrought iron

STEP BACK IN TIME at Saugus and in your mind's eye you'll see sweating colonials in leather aprons charge the blast furnace with layers of charcoal, "bogge" ore, and rock. A water wheel pumps the flapping leather bellows; smoke billows from the furnace top. To the bottom seeps iron "made so very fluid by the Violence of the Heat," to be forged into the tools of a wilderness civilization.

The tap plug is broken and liquid fire flows out. Some is molded into brittle castware. The rest runs into furrows in the floor. The main channel hardens into a "sow" bar while side rivulets become "pigs"—like a sow feeding her young.

Amid a spray of sparks and the ring of metal against metal, craftsmen in the forge heat and reheat the pigs, and hammer carbon from the cast iron to produce wrought "merchant bars." Some are sold at the site, some shipped to Boston and to other colonies. Others go next door to be rolled into strips or to be slit into "small barres or roddes to serve for the makyng of nayles and other thyngs."

Leader, a man of "skill in mynes, and tryall of mettals," replaced Winthrop, moving the operation to Saugus, north of Boston, where a river navigable below the works could be dammed. In 1648 Governor Winthrop noted, "the Furnace runnes 8 tun per weeke, and their barre Iron is as good as Spanish."

Saugus employed some 185 ironworkers, miners, woodcutters, and boatmen, and housed them in a "company town." Included were Scots, captured in battle by Cromwell, indentured to the ironworks, and bedded down, some say, in the "Scotch"-Boardman House. No fortunes grew from America's first "big business," but Saugus trained the men who built much of the colonial iron industry.

for Saugus visitors how wrought iron was forged. In rolling and slitting mill the guide rolls a bar flat.

SAUGUS IRONWORKS RESTORATION. LEFT: KATHLEEN REVIS JUDGE. BELOW: PAUL R. HOFFMASTER

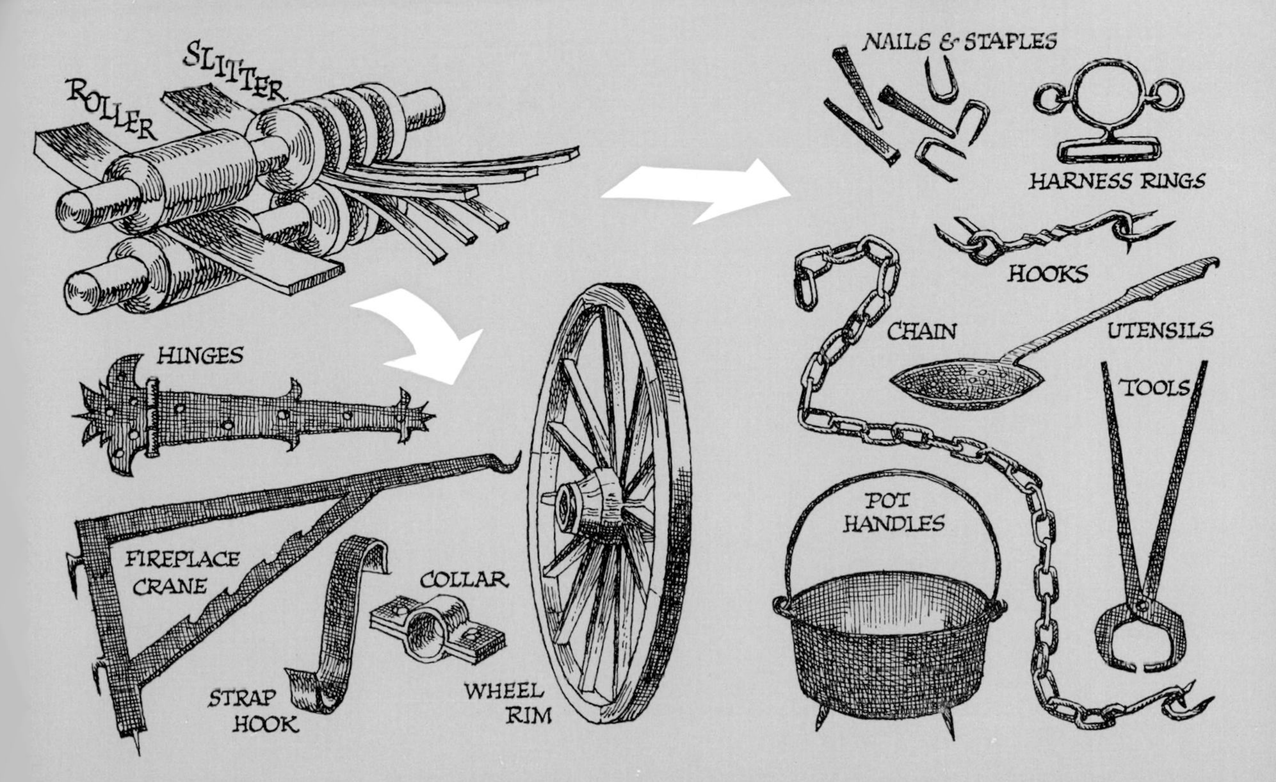

Roger Williams, champion of the rights of red man and white, flees in exile to found a refuge.

Rebellious Puritans spread out

PURITAN ELDERS sought iron, but when they found it in Roger Williams's unbending opinions they liked it not. Williams, pastor of Salem Church, denied the Bay Colony's right to take Indian lands and preached that the state could not control man's conscience. "Forced worship stincks in Gods nostrils," he later wrote.

Ordered to deny these views, Williams, whose hot Welsh temper made him "passionate and resentful under provocation," refused. Banishment was the only answer to this rebel. To escape deportation to England, Williams plodded south through snowy wilds to Manton's Neck on the Seekonk River. There, with 12 companions, he founded a settlement named "in commemoration of God's Providence," and drew up America's first document separating church and state. This covenant provided a local government "only in civill things." No cleric would deal out civil punishments in Rhode Island. In 1638 Williams helped found America's first Baptist church.

The Boston elders labcled Rhode Island a "sewer" to catch the "Lord's debris." But the colony thrived on its tolerance.

Anne Hutchinson, an ambitious Bostonian of "nimble wit, active spirit and voluble tongue," became a sort of evangelist, stridently naming those citizens who deserved to be saved and those who did not. When she included some of the most prominent clergy in the latter category, her fate was sealed. Out she went, and Roger Williams purchased from the Indians some land for her followers at what is now Portsmouth, Rhode Island.

Rev. Thomas Hooker of Cambridge Church thought freemen, not just church members, deserved the vote; that a congregation's authority should reside in itself, not stem from the elders. When his flock tired of fighting the sandy soil and cramped quarters around burgeoning Boston, he got permission from the General Court, the Bay Colony's ruling body, to remove to the fertile region along the Connecticut River, discovered and claimed for Holland in 1614 by Adriaen Block.

In the summer of 1636 Hooker led 100 men, women, and children and 160 head of cattle westward along an Indian trail into the wilderness. Living on milk from their cows, they fought through swamp and thicket. At what is now Hartford they found wide meadows around a Dutch trading fort.

Three years earlier a small expedition from Plymouth Colony had sailed up the

LIBRARY OF CONGRESS AND (LEFT) BETTMANN ARCHIVE

Villages dotting this late 17th century map contrast with New England's howling wilderness two generations earlier. Puritans, overcrowded around Boston, moved as entire congregations, seeking elbowroom to build towns.

river, defied the fort's two cannons, and staked out Windsor to the north. Immigrants from Watertown had planted Wethersfield while William Pynchon, destined to prosper in fur trading, settled a dozen families at Springfield.

These scattered villages with their thatch-roofed, salt-box houses braving the edge of the unknown sought unity in the Fundamental Orders, America's first written constitution. Hooker spread the seeds of democracy from his Hartford pulpit: "The choice of public magistrates belongs to the people.... The foundation of authority is laid, first, in the free consent of the people." This principle, in Connecticut's royal charter of 1662, affected New Haven (founded by London merchants in 1638) and 11 Long Island communities, Gravesend to Southampton.

But Puritanism still ruled daily life. Worshipers at Hooker's church might see one Walter Gray publicly corrected for "labouring to invegle the affections of Mr. Hoocker's Mayde." For the average God-fearing Puritan such "sinful dalliance" went down as hard as Venice treacle, a popular cure-all of boiled snakes, white wine, herbs, and opium. Public whippings for inveterate idleness and pil-

Lady Pepperrell House graces Kittery Point, Maine. Victor over the French at Louisbourg (1745), her husband was first Yankee baronet.

Roger Williams preached at Smith's Castle, near Wickford, Rhode Island, rebuilt in 1677 after burning by Indians. Colonists killed in the Great Swamp Fight are buried nearby.

Clemence House, Providence "stone-ender," is tied to a huge fireplace. Most New England homes had a central chimney.

FROM LEFT: MAINE DEPARTMENT OF ECONOMIC DEVELOPMENT, WILLARD R. CULVER, L.F.KINNEY, E.J.CYR. BELOW: ROBERT F. SISSON, NATIONAL GEOGRAPHIC PHOTOGRAPHER

Sheldon's Tavern, one of the fine white buildings in historic Litchfield, Connecticut, was raised in colonial simplicity in 1760, then embellished with a mansard roof and Palladian portico.

Washington, in 1781, had upstairs room on the right.

Thomas Lee House stands in stark dignity beside a quiet road in East Lyme, Connecticut. It began in 1664 as a single room with a chamber above but grew with the family. The owner had 15 children.

SEDGE LEBLANG AND (ABOVE) EDWARDS PARK, NATIONAL GEOGRAPHIC STAFF

Rev. Henry Whitfield built Connecticut's oldest stone house at Guilford in 1639-40.

Settling on Long Island, New Englanders built saltbox homes like the Thompson House at Setauket.

Newport stood as a beacon of religious freedom. Jews founded a congregation in 1658 and dedicated Touro Synagogue (above), America's oldest, in 1763. Nearby, Quakers built Friends Meeting House in 1699. At Old Colony House (right), where Rhode Island's General Assembly met, Catholic Mass was celebrated in 1780.

lorying for unreligious talk kept minds fastened on the virtues of work and of reverence for God, not the king. Consumed with his fight for survival on the frontier, the Connecticut settler forgot England, forging a fierce independence that became his legacy to America.

But religious freedom still centered in "Rogue's Island." William Coddington, a friend of Anne Hutchinson, quit Portsmouth in 1639, moved down Aquidneck Island, and settled Newport. It became a religious asylum. Spanish-Portuguese Jews soon took root there and gave the country its oldest synagogue. Quakers, who in Massachusetts risked having ears lopped off, tongues bored with hot pokers, or necks stretched, congregated at Newport and built a meetinghouse. Presbyterians, Moravians, quietists, even freethinkers abounded.

Newport soon outstripped Providence in commerce. By the early 1700's it

ARTHUR P. MILLER, JR., AND (LEFT) ROBERT F. SISSON, BOTH NATIONAL GEOGRAPHIC STAFF

throbbed with shipbuilding and West Indies trade. Along the waterfront silk-stockinged gentlemen in scarlet coats and swords, silver-buckled shoes, and lace ruffles mingled with Friends in straight-skirted coats, broad-brimmed hats, sober gowns, and drab poke bonnets. Fat-hulled merchantmen loaded and discharged cargoes of rum and molasses at the wharves.

Occupied with trade, unfettered by a church-controlled state, such free spirits acquired a strong distaste for central authority. No fixed government ruled them until the patent of 1644, and even then they fought over land titles, taxes, and government. More than a century before the Bill of Rights, Roger Williams wrote freedom of worship into a royal charter. Little Rhode Island kept that charter as its constitution until 1842. It's no accident that a statue of the Independent Man graces the State House at Providence.

Deerfield— a massacre in the wilderness

An ox sledge creaked under the last load of wood, women served supper from glowing hearths, and by nine o'clock Deerfield's 290 settlers were abed on the bitter cold night of February 28, 1704. Toward dawn the sentinel dozed at his post.

Stealthily, a horde of Abenakis, Caughnawagas, and French Canadians crept over drifted snow and dropped inside the palisade. Shrieking hideously, they fell upon the settlers in their beds.

Hacking their way into Parson Williams's home, the savages bound him fast and murdered two of his eight children. John Sheldon's nail-studded door stayed them, but they broke in at the rear and dashed out the brains of his two-year-old daughter. Torches fired 17 houses. Leaping flames sent a vivid message, and mounted men from other Connecticut Valley settlements finally routed the attackers.

They say the moon was red over Deerfield the night of the slaughter. The Massachusetts village was left a smoking ruin with half its inhabitants killed or dragged off to the north.

To the French, the massacre was coldly political. "We must keep things astir in the direction of Boston," wrote Canada's Governor Vaudreuil, "or else the Abenakis will declare for the English."

Deerfield's wretched sur-

KATHLEEN REVIS JUDGE
RIGHT: HISTORICAL PICTURE SERVICE

Howling savages, clambering over the snow-drifted palisade, split John Sheldon's massive oak door but could not hack it down. Thrusting in a gun, they shot his wife. The original door with tomahawk imbedded stands in Memorial Hall.

vivors refused to abandon their wilderness outpost, and a farm village rose again, prospering from the rich soil.

Today visitors find "The Street" lined with lovely elm-shaded 18th century homes—also grim reminders. One gravestone recalls the 48 killed in 1704; another that Parson Williams's wife, taken captive, "fell by the rage of Ye Barbarous Enemy."

FRONTIER life was not usually so violent. Massasoit honored a peace treaty 40 years. Fair laws protected and soothed the red men. When Arthur Peach and his gang murdered an Indian trader, Plymouth hanged them. Her settlers paid for Indian land. The Bay Colony's intolerant Puritans, however, saw the devil in the non-Christian savage, and so felt justified in seizing his property. The Indians in turn watched with growing alarm as settlers overflowed into their hunting grounds.

Philip, son of Massasoit, nursed a hatred of whites that in 1675 erupted into King Philip's War. Savages from encircling forests attacked half New England's towns. Lawmakers saw God's judgment on the colony for immodest clothes and hairdos. After a year of terror, militia tracked down Philip's band in Rhode Island, butchered them in the Great Swamp Fight.

Atrocities continued in the north as French and Indians swept down in Queen Anne's War. Jesuit historian Charlevoix noted complacently that in 1703 "they effected some ravages of no great consequence; they killed, however, about three hundred men." The next year they fell on Deerfield. The Peace of Utrecht in 1713 finally pacified New England until the French and Indian War a half century later.

Old Deerfield's quiet charm bespeaks peace; its tombstones tell of sudden death. A survivor's marker notes he "was twice Captivated by the Indian Salvages." Connecticut Valley homes with

MERLE SEVERY, NATIONAL GEOGRAPHIC STAFF. BELOW LEFT: AL DAIGLE

unpainted clapboards, narrow, unshuttered windows, and dignified doorways line the mile-long street, evoking life on the frontier 75 miles west of Boston. A fiery Tory preacher lived in the Ashley House (right). Locked out of church by townsmen, story has it he axed his way in. Sheldon-Hawks House, also open to visitors, stands next door. Only Frary House witnessed the 1704 raid.

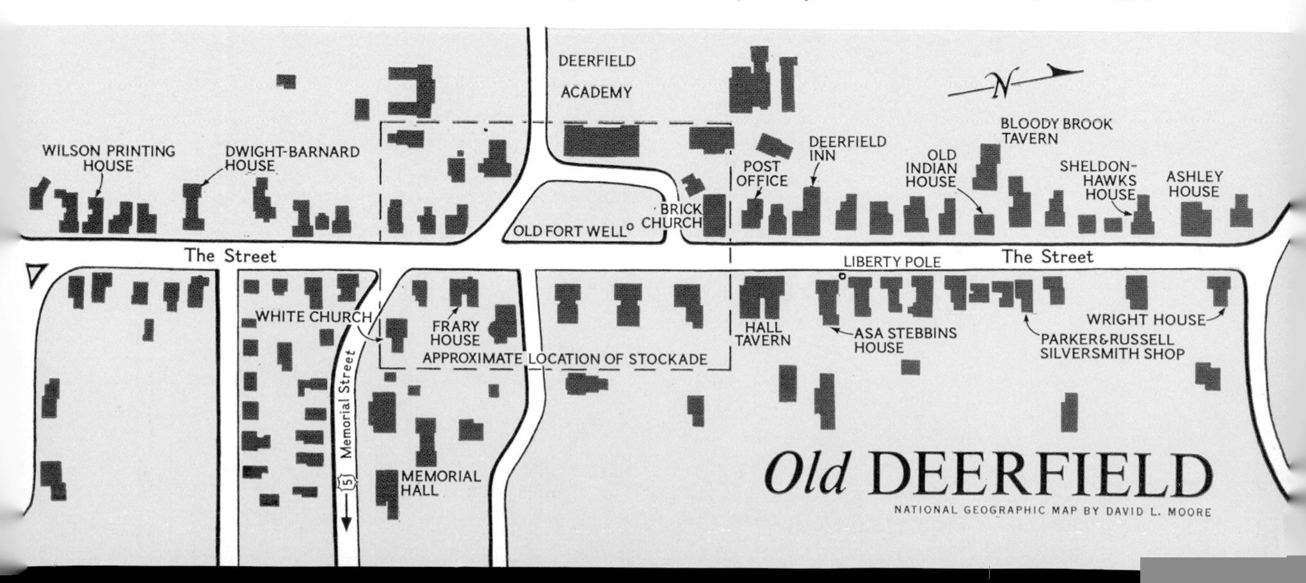

NATIONAL GEOGRAPHIC MAP BY DAVID L. MOORE

Peter Stuyvesant ruled New Amsterdam with a fist of iron, 1647 to 1664. His town stood at the lower end of the island Peter Minuit bought from the Indians for "$24 worth of trinkets." In this first view, drawn about 1626, the fort is exaggerated, the landscape reversed. The Dutch settlers would hardly recognize Manhattan today!

Amsterdam op de Manhatans

STOKES COLLECTION, NEW YORK PUBLIC LIBRARY, AND (LEFT) BROWN BROTHERS

DAVID S. BOYER, NATIONAL GEOGRAPHIC STAFF

THE DUTCH ON THE HUDSON

THE *Half Moon* sailed slowly up the "great streame" that led into the wilderness. Henry Hudson and his men gazed in awe at wooded mountains and watched cautiously as "swarthy natives" paddled out to trade. Hudson, an English captain, had been hired by the Dutch in 1609 to find a new route to China. Instead, when shallowing water turned him back near present-day Albany, he had established a Dutch claim to the river that bears his name.

Fur traders followed. Then in 1624 the Dutch West India Company settled a few Walloon families on the site of Albany. They built Fort Orange and traded trinkets for pelts with the Iroquois who came from the darkly wooded Mohawk Valley to the west. A year later the company established New Amsterdam on Manhattan Island. But growth was slow. Dutchmen were reluctant to leave their prosperous, tolerant homeland. The West India Company was more interested in quick fur profits and raiding the Spanish treasure fleets than in colonizing. Its governors proved inept; strongest of the lot was peg-legged Peter Stuyvesant.

Thumping ashore in 1647, this truculent old soldier declared he would "be as a father over his children." And it was a rowdy family he took on. New Amsterdam was by then a lusty frontier seaport. Thatched wooden homes huddled about the fort, and the blades of the lumberyard windmill moved in drowsy arcs across the blue sky. Blond children darted down rutted dirt streets, dodging creaking carts

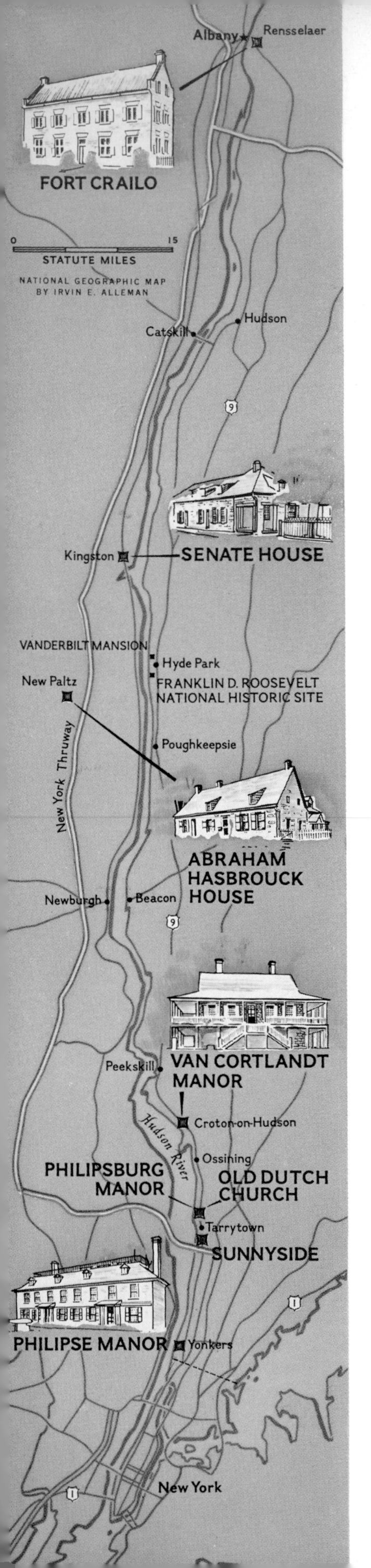

and snorting hogs. Burghers in broad-brimmed hats and baggy trousers strode purposefully in and out of warehouses. From the White Horse and other taverns came oaths and raucous laughter. Backwoods traders and foreign sailors sought to drown months of hardship with mugs of beer and brandy while they spun wild tales to townsmen who listened through the smoke from long-stemmed pipes. Tongues babbled in Swedish, French, Danish, German, and Portuguese, for the colony welcomed all.

Beyond the town sprawled the domains of the *patroons*. The Dutch tried to spur colonization by importing feudalism. Any member of the company who would bring 50 families to settle was offered 16 miles of river frontage. This patroon "would forever possess all the lands . . . fruits . . . and lower jurisdictions" thereof. But vassalage did not fit the frontier; only the 700,000-acre estate of Amsterdam jeweler Kiliaen Van Rensselaer prospered under Dutch

NEW YORK TIMES AND (LEFT) B. ANTHONY STEWART, NATIONAL GEOGRAPHIC PHOTOGRAPHER

Philipsburg Manor and the Old Dutch Church recall Hudson Valley days when haughty aristocrats held sway. Building his stone home in 1683, Frederick Philipse provided a secret passage so he could eavesdrop on his indentured servants. In church, his family sat in pews while the servants stood in a gallery. Ichabod Crane glimpsed this Sleepy Hollow church as he fled from the Headless Horseman. Washington Irving lies in the churchyard.

rule. Tenant farmers who tired of paying rents settled at Esopus, now Kingston, and won their own charter and *schout,* or sheriff. Here and there along the river hearty *boers* carved homesteads in the forests.

These men did not bow easily to Stuyvesant's tyrannical rule. But if the governor spoke often in "foul language better befitting the fish market," he did have cause. Swedish settlers defied Dutch claims on the Delaware. New Englanders pushed down the Connecticut River and spread over Long Island. Indian wars flamed as hotheaded Dutch spread their farms into ancient hunting grounds and the redskins struck back with tomahawk and fire. Raiding the Esopus settlement in 1663, they left the fields strewn with "roasted bodies, like burning sheaves behind the mower."

Stuyvesant faced a showdown when four English ships dropped anchor off Manhattan in 1664. Their commander claimed the colony for the Duke of York, the king's brother. Hopelessly outgunned, the burghers feared destruction of their gabled homes with yellow brick walls and red tiled roofs. They remembered that the governor had hamstrung their efforts for representative government. They refused to fight. Stuyvesant fumed and stomped, then sighed, "Let it be so."

New Amsterdam became New York, in honor of the duke. But the Dutch stayed on, and so did their ways. The great estates, converted to English-style manors, now flourished. Philipsburg Manor, built by one of Stuyvesant's former officials, provides a glimpse into the old life.

A brook bubbles by the reconstructed grist mill that ground the corn the tenants carted from miles around. The church Frederick Philipse built still stands. On Sundays its pealing bell brought in neighboring families, children well scrubbed, women in crisp white caps and billowing dresses. Within the two-foot walls of the great house are tables and chairs the lord of the manor chose for comfort rather than style. Rows of pewter glimmer on dining room shelves. In the kitchen's huge fireplace chickens once turned on the spit, browning over crackling logs. In smoke-darkened pots bubbled fruit preserves, giving off sweet aroma. No wonder Dutchmen loved to eat.

Other Dutch-built houses stand today to delight the visitor. Van Cortlandt Manor and Fort Crailo bear loopholes designed for use in Indian attacks. The hipped roof of Philipse Manor in Yonkers reflects English influence in the colony. Less pretentious are the Ten Broeck House, now called the Senate House, in Kingston, and the Abraham Hasbrouck House, one of several built by French Huguenots who settled New Paltz. Dutch names abound in New York City. The Bowery recalls *bouweries,* or farms, that once dotted Manhattan and spread along the Hudson. Wall Street follows the earthworks that once marked the city limits. And village names *Breuckelen* and *Haarlem* are recognizable in anglicized forms. Nearby Yonkers is named for a *jonker,* or nobleman, who once owned the land.

THE RICH flavor of Dutch life on the Hudson is perhaps best preserved in the writings of Washington Irving, who made his first trip up "this glorious river" in 1800. The sensitive young man wandered among shaded hollows and sleepy villages around Tarrytown, noting "a contagion in the very air . . . it breathed forth an atmosphere of dreams and fancies." His acquaintances served as models for fictional characters. The "ripe and melting" Katrina Van Tassel, courted by Ichabod Crane, is reputed to be a Van Alen girl from Kinderhook—a sweetheart of Irving's. Ichabod himself was modeled on another friend, Jesse Merwin, who generously applied the rod at the village schoolhouse.

Making a name with his lighthearted *Knickerbocker's History of New York,* Irving wrote *Rip Van Winkle* and *The Legend of Sleepy Hollow* in England after he failed there in business. He lived abroad for years, but returned to build Sunnyside and stay in the valley his pen had peopled with goblins and Dutchmen.

Bluish haze still shrouds the Hudson's mountains and coves, and you can sense there a timeless air of mystery and majesty. Legend has it that on dark nights along the Tappan Zee you can hear the splashing oars of Rambout Van Dam, a young Dutchman condemned to ply the river until judgment day. He broke the Sabbath by rowing home from a party. And Irving tells us that thunder from the Catskills signals the return each 20 years of Henry Hudson and his *Half Moon* crew, who play at ninepins and look down on the great river they explored long ago.

JOHN J. PUTMAN

Rip Van Winkle finds his village changed when he returns after a sleep of 20 years. Rip's creator, Washington Irving, lived at Sunnyside (lower), a house "made up of gable-ends, and as full of angles as an old cocked hat."

PAINTING BY JOHN QUIDOR, MELLON COLLECTION, NATIONAL GALLERY OF ART, AND (BELOW) PAUL JENSEN

SWEDES ON THE DELAWARE

CAREFULLY the two ships drew near the rocks where Wilmington, Delaware, now stands. A trumpet blared, hushing the little group of Swedish settlers that clustered before Fort Christina that February day in 1643. On deck, the new arrivals gaped at their wilderness home. Then all eyes turned on Lt. Col. Johan Printz as he came ashore to take charge of the five-year-old colony of New Sweden. Printz invariably commanded attention: "A man of brave size, he weighed more than 400 pounds."

In New Sweden he had little chance to throw his weight around. Failure stalked the Delaware Valley's first permanent settlement. The English had explored the region; the Dutch had built forts there; both claimed it. Swedish investors sought big fur profits, yet offered only niggardly funds. Few colonists came; Swedes saw little point in leaving their own forests for others even wilder.

Undaunted, Governor Printz went to work. Finns, accustomed to clearing land with fire, came to the new colony and set fresh blazes. Swedes raised log cabins with corner fireplaces, as they used to at home. Stout housewives stuffed straw into cloth bags for mattresses. Children played in the shadows of oaks and tulip trees by day and shivered at the cries of wildcats by night. Lenni-Lenape Indians sold land and pelts to "Big Guts," as they called Printz.

Driving his colonists, Printz built forts to tack down his domain stretching from Cape Henlopen to present-day Trenton. But crops failed; the powder magazine at Tinicum Island blew up. When the Dutch built Fort Casimir (New Castle), cutting off Fort Christina from the sea, Big Guts went home. In 1655 the colony surrendered to the Dutch, who in turn yielded to the English. New Sweden vanished, but its Lutherans and log cabins remained to help shape a New World.

LIBRARY OF CONGRESS AND (LEFT) PAUL JENSEN

Dovetailed logs of Morton Homestead at Prospect Park, Pennsylvania, cling tightly after 300 years. Swedes' cabins, hewn from virgin forests, served as models for frontiersmen.

ROBERT F. SISSON, NATIONAL GEOGRAPHIC PHOTOGRAPHER

Philadelphia's *Gloria Dei* Church was built in 1700 by descendants of original Swedish Lutheran colonists. Episcopalians now worship under a model of the first settlers' ship.

PENNSYLVANIA ACADEMY OF THE FINE ARTS AND (RIGHT) MERLE SEVERY, NATIONAL GEOGRAPHIC STAFF

PENN'S WOODS

"A fit place for younger brothers and men of small estates"

THE BROAD Delaware River in its lovelier stretches mirrors the white summer clouds as they pass overhead. In such a manner did the colony of Pennsylvania reflect the mind of its gentle Quaker founder.

William Penn, son of a hard-fighting English admiral, wrote, "If we would amend the World, we should mend Our selves." He sought to mend himself by turning his back on the glittering life of a courtier and embracing the "honestly simple" beliefs of the Society of Friends. For preaching against the ritual and dogma of the Church of England, he was tossed into prison. He decided "there can be no reason to persecute any man in this world about anything that belongs to the next."

William Penn pledges eternal friendship with the Delawares at Shackamaxon (now in Philadelphia), in this idealized painting by Benjamin West. The Quaker leader welcomed Indians and colonists alike to his home, Pennsbury Manor. Reconstructed above, it overlooks the Delaware near Morrisville.

But England did not agree, and Penn turned to America. Perhaps there "an example may be set up to the nations . . . an holy experiment." Pressing a debt owed his father by the Crown, Penn won the grant of a huge colony. He called it Sylvania (woods). Charles II added "Penn" to honor the old admiral.

Penn's first settlers sailed up the Delaware in 1681 and found the cabins of Dutch, Swedes, and English dotting the wilderness. But Penn, landing in 1682 at New Castle, then convening his first General Assembly at Upland (which he renamed Chester), pioneered in men's minds. He decreed not only religious freedom but that "no Law can be made; nor Money raised, but by the Peoples consent."

At Shackamaxon and other meeting places Penn welded a bond of friendship with the Indians. Instead of making them the usual token payments for land, he insisted on a fair price and told his settlers to "sit down lovingly among them." No Indian massacre stained Penn's Woods while he was there.

At the mouth of the Schuylkill Penn gazed with pleasure on the "greene

HOWELL WALKER, NATIONAL GEOGRAPHIC STAFF

Half-timbered walls of Gideon Gilpin's farmhouse at Chadds Ford (map, page 212) evoke early Quaker days. Brick and cobble grace New Castle (below), where Penn landed, adding Delaware to his domain. Old Dutch House and Amstel House are museums.

Country Towne" laid out by his agent and gave the streets names like Walnut, Chestnut, and Pine. Here at Philadelphia, City of Brotherly Love, a stream of colonists landed. By 1685 more than 7,000 had come, stirred by advertisements of "Pennsylvania . . . a fit place for Younger Brothers, and Men of Small Estates . . . The Air is generally clear and sweet . . . Corn produceth four hundred fold."

English Quakers settled early in Philadelphia, Chester, and Bucks counties. Welsh Friends spread along the Schuylkill. Germans, the vanguard of a huge migration, founded Germantown in 1683. Their fellow countrymen spread in a broad arc across the southeast of the colony. Scotch-Irish pushed past them to the western mountains. Some, finding land taken, filtered into the Shenandoah

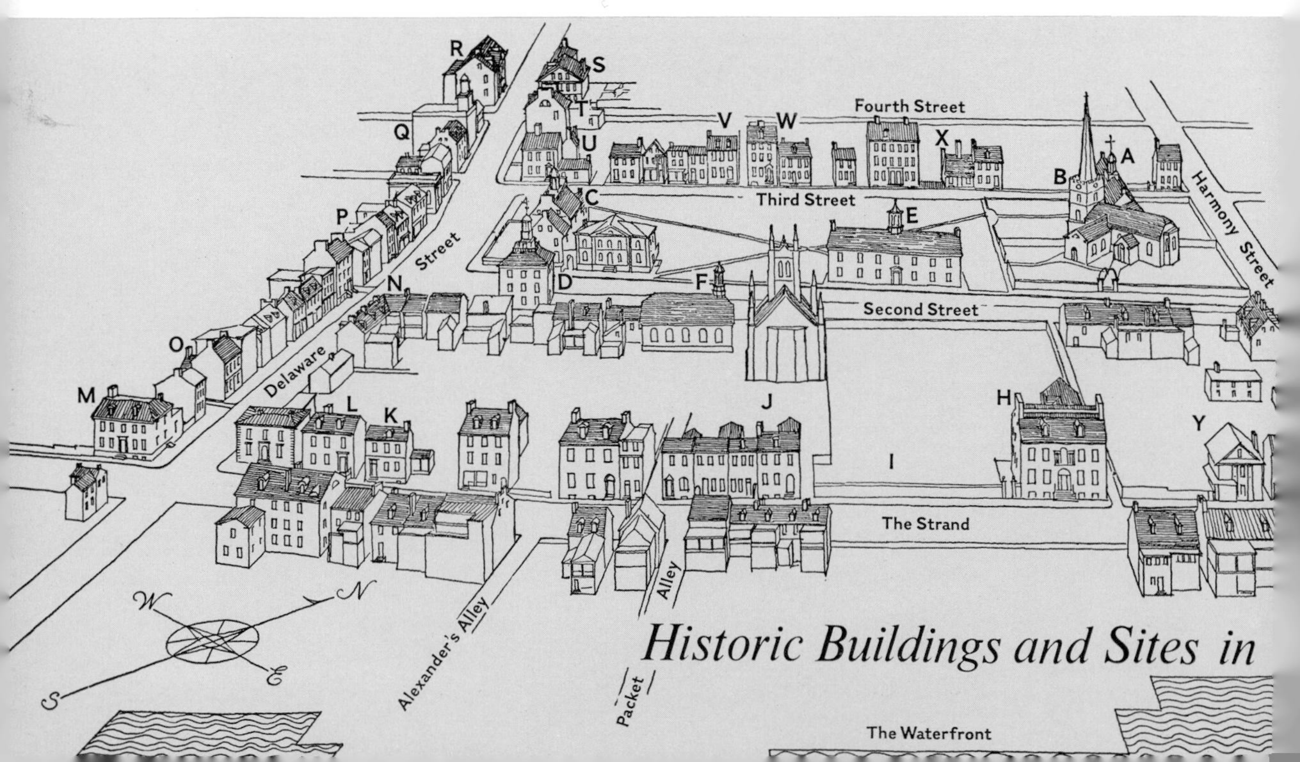

Historic Buildings and Sites in

Valley and the back country of North Carolina.

It was a good life for the Quakers, who could "thee" and "thou" as they wished, and trade diligently in grain, beef, and salt pork from the countryside. Inside neat brick dwellings such as the Letitia House (now in Fairmount Park, Philadelphia) plump housewives loaded tables with "ducks, hams, tarts, custards, porter and punch." Officials built big country homes like Graeme Park and Stenton (see map, page 212).

Modern visitors sense the plain, deeply sincere nature of Quaker worship at the Buckingham Meeting House at Lahaska, near New Hope. Here the Friends gathered on "First Days." There was no clergy. When a man felt the call to pray he prayed. Others stood, broad-brimmed hat in hand, until the prayer ended.

ROBERT F. SISSON, NATIONAL GEOGRAPHIC PHOTOGRAPHER

New Hope, on the Delaware, preserves much of the flavor of Pennsylvania's past. Visitors examine an antique spice cabinet of pewter, brass, and copper.

A THE ACADEMY
B IMMANUEL CHURCH
C COURT HOUSE
D TOWN HALL
E ARSENAL
F PRESBYTERIAN CHURCH
G THOMAS HOUSE
H READ HOUSE
I 1st READ HOUSE SITE
J DUTCH BURIAL GROUND
K McWILLIAMS HOUSE
L GUNNING BEDFORD HOUSE
M VAN LEUVENIGH HOUSE
N CLOUD'S ROW
O ROSEMONT HOUSE
P "PENN" HOUSE
Q K. J. VAN DYKE HOUSE
R NICHOLAS VAN DYKE HOUSE
S AMSTEL HOUSE
T CHANCELLOR JOHNS HOUSE
U KENSEY JOHNS HOUSE
V RODNEY HOUSE
W GEMMILL HOUSE
X OLD DUTCH HOUSE
Y TILE HOUSE SITE

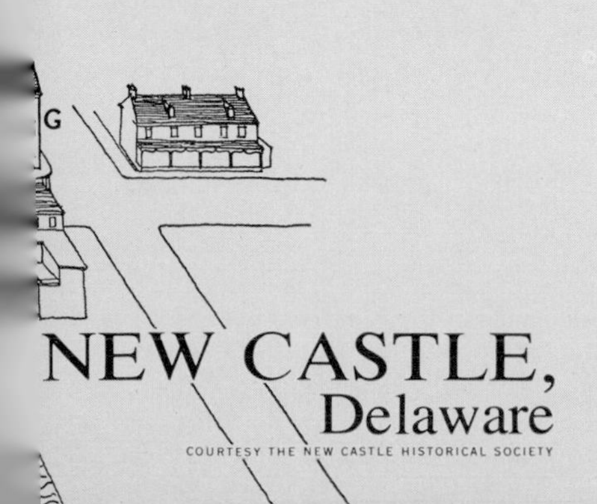

The Plain People of Pennsylvania

TO NO PEOPLE did Penn's promise of a "free colony for all mankind" mean more than to the war-weary, persecuted Germans of the Rhine Valley. Reaching Pennsylvania they told their new neighbors they were *Deutsch*. To English ears this sounded like "Dutch," hence today's "Pennsylvania Dutch."

They planted a variety of religious sects in the new land. German Seventh-Day Baptists built Ephrata Cloister and lived in austere piety like monks and nuns. Moravians practiced their "General Economy" at Bethlehem. The Amish still cling to their folkways. Their neat homes in Lancaster and other farming counties are bare of curtains and lack such worldly luxuries as electricity. Their black coats

J. BAYLOR ROBERTS, NATIONAL GEOGRAPHIC PHOTOGRAPHER, AND (ABOVE) M. DUSSINGER

HOWELL WALKER, NATIONAL GEOGRAPHIC STAFF, AND (BELOW) PAUL R. HOFFMASTER

At Ephrata Cloister (upper left) Conrad Beissel's followers wrote hymns, revived the art of *fraktur* (illuminated writing), and slept on wooden blocks for pillows.

Amish children (above) wear shirts and dresses like their parents', but on grownups bright colors hide beneath dark coats or aprons. A beard means an Amishman is married. They shun cars for buggies like those below bearing Mennonites to church.

MAYNARD OWEN WILLIAMS AND (BELOW) INDEX OF AMERICAN DESIGN

"Oompah" sounds sweeter from a green tuba garnished with hearts and flowers! Pennsylvania Dutch daub tulips and *distelfinks* (allegorical birds) on everything from *taufscheine* (baptismal certificates) to tin coffeepots.

and unadorned dress earn them the name "plain people," which they share with somber-suited Mennonites, Brethren, and others. All farmed wisely. Today the "Dutch" country is renowned for fat cows, green pastures, Broadleaf tobacco, and big red barns with mysterious "hex signs."

Penn provided his colonists with a beneficent frame of government, but his relations with them were not always happy. He learned that democratic precedents lead to fresh demands. In 1701, badgered by quarrels and debts, he returned to England. No more would he live in his beloved Pennsbury Manor on the banks of the Delaware. But he had planted well.

"Had New England, New York, and Virginia been swept out of existence in 1800," wrote Henry Adams, "democracy could have better spared them all than have lost Pennsylvania."

JOHN J. PUTMAN

The Kutztown folk festival inspires bonneted Aunt Sophia Bailer to share her cure for warts. Other "Dutch" women exchange cherished recipes for *schnitz un knepp* (dried apples and dumplings) and *hinkle bott boi* (chicken pot pie).

LOUIS B. WRIGHT

The Colonials

WHY DID THOUSANDS OF IMMIGRANTS to America risk the hazards of the sea, the greed of ship captains, the tomahawks of savages, and the uncertainties of life in an alien land? Why did they endure incredible hardships to establish homes that stretched, by the middle of the 18th century, from Maine to Georgia? The firstcomers hoped for quick wealth; others sought adventure or escape from a tyrannical father, a railing wife, or the imminence of debtors' prison. Some wanted freedom of worship. Some came unwillingly at the behest of sheriff and judge, for the authorities regarded exported criminals as good riddance—and just possibly they might rehabilitate themselves and do some good for the new country.

The strongest single appeal to most immigrants was the opportunity to own land, ever the symbol of status in Europe. Land was so easy to acquire in the colonies that anyone with a little capital could become a landed proprietor. Younger sons with no hope of inheritance in England remedied that defect in America.

Even indentured servants faced a hopeful future in the colonies. Unable to pay their passage, they contracted to serve their masters four to seven years in return for transportation. After they became free citizens again they could buy land on easy terms and establish themselves as small planters. A few, like the three Dulany

"THE COPLEY FAMILY" BY BOSTON'S JOHN SINGLETON COPLEY (C. 1775) CAPTURES THE WARMTH AND ELEGANCE OF GENTEEL COLONIAL LIFE. THE ARTIST PORTRAYS HIS WIFE, CHILDREN, AND FATHER-IN-LAW, RICHARD CLARKE, A PROMINENT MERCHANT. HE HIMSELF LOOKS OUT PENSIVELY FROM BEHIND. NATIONAL GALLERY OF ART

brothers who arrived in Maryland as servants in 1703, later rose to prominence and political importance through shrewd investments in land.

From its earliest days America offered the greatest opportunity in the world for a man to benefit from the work of his two hands. Wages were high and the demand for labor was pressing. Anyone could raise himself to a higher economic position through his own enterprise, and a craftsman might hope to become well to do and gain respect in America's flexible society. The dignity of labor and the virtue of diligence, part of the basic doctrine of England's rising commercial class, took firm root in the New World.

PURITANS WERE CONVINCED that "piety bred industry." Refusal to work was a sin against God, while incessant industry was evidence of godliness and would be rewarded with prosperity. The career of John Hull of Massachusetts Bay provides a classic statement of the success that came through ingenuity, industry, and imagination.

As a child Hull helped his blacksmith father with the farm work, then became a goldsmith's apprentice. Turning to commerce, he traded Virginia tobacco for English textiles and manufactures; dabbled in the wine and sugar trade between Boston, the West Indies, and Spain and Madeira; shipped horses from his farm to Barbados. Indeed there was scarcely any trade that honest John Hull did not engage in. He was, moreover, a skilled craftsman. Through his perseverance and resourcefulness, Hull became one of the first citizens of Boston, owner of a fine house, of many ships, of town lands and farms.

The Brown family of Providence was founded by a pious Baptist who combined business and preaching. His descendant James Brown took the sloop *Truth and Delight* to Martinique with a cargo of corn, cheese, tobacco, tar, lumber, shingles, and 11 horses. He returned with sugar and molasses for his rum distilleries in New England. Pious as Captain Brown was, he had no compunctions about evading the sixpence-per-gallon tax on foreign molasses that was established when Parliament passed the Molasses Act of 1733. He gave his shipmasters careful instructions on ways to elude the customs agents. Obadiah Brown followed his brother's footsteps, adding a "chocklit" mill to his enterprises. He began the manufacture of spermaceti candles, which became an important industry in Rhode Island.

William Phips, an obscure Maine frontiersman and ship's carpenter, married well, became a shipbuilder, took command of one of his vessels, and on a trading voyage to the West Indies heard of the treasure that lay in sunken Spanish galleons. In 1685 Phips and his crew raised a hulk off Haiti and recovered so much gold and silver that he retired a rich man with a knighthood. Lady Phips bought a mansion in Boston's fashionable Green Lane so that Sir William could live in the style to which he was not accustomed.

The vastly rich Derby family of Salem had a progenitor who started as a soap boiler and owner of a small shop that sold Bibles and psalm books. Like the Hancocks of Boston (who looked back to a village cobbler as ancestor), the 18th century Derbys prospered on trade. They often flouted the British Navigation Acts—in other words, smuggled. Many merchant families stationed members at strategic points; perhaps Newport, Charleston, in the West Indies, and in England. Thus they kept in touch with each other and watched over the family businesses.

Quakers, Huguenots, and many Anglican planters shared with New England Puritans the gospel of work, which emphasized diligence, sobriety, and thrift. If the planters sometimes lapsed in sobriety they rarely disavowed diligence. Even elegant William Byrd II, the Samuel Pepys of Virginia, supervised the planting of orchards and crops and commented in his diary on the ruin of his stockings and the need of washing his feet.

Merchant aristocrats of New York like the De Lanceys, Livingstons, and Van Cortlandts were noted for their love of comfort and the increasing luxury of their households. But the Quakers of Pennsylvania, shrewd, careful of credit and reputation, built Philadelphia into the greatest center of wealth in the American colonies. Blessed with prosperity, Quaker merchants often indulged themselves beyond the simplicities that their creed urged. James Logan, Jonathan Dickinson, and others had houses as fine as any Anglican. When Isaac Norris in 1713 ordered a coach "like Jonathan Dickinson's," he drew the line at having a crest painted on it and settled for initials only. He blamed his wife for the ostentation of liveries for his coachman and footmen and compromised by ordering them "Strong and Cheap, Either of a Dark Gray or Sad Coullour."

In the agrarian South, too, the rise to success through trade was respected. No planter was too proud to turn an honest penny in business. Henry Laurens, aristocratic South Carolina merchant and plantation owner and a leader in the Revolution, was the son of a saddler. And the famous Manigault family of Charleston stemmed from a barrelmaker and tavern keeper who made enough money to set up his son as merchant, slave trader, and planter.

Englishmen who obtained huge land grants in America failed in their efforts to establish feudal baronies. Settlers in Maryland were tenants of the House of Calvert, the absolute lords of the domain. But the immigrants had come to better their condition and did not willingly accommodate themselves to an outworn system of land tenure. Only by compromise were the proprietors able to collect their rents and fees. The proprietors of New Jersey, John, Lord Berkeley and Sir George Carteret, tried to make their grant attractive to immigrants by issuing a body

COMMERCE FLOURISHED IN 18TH CENTURY AMERICA, AND RAW MATERIALS FROM THE COLONIES BROUGHT WEALTH TO THE MOTHER COUNTRY. HERE ON A CHESAPEAKE BAY WHARF MEN LOAD HOGSHEADS OF TOBACCO FOR SHIPMENT TO THE LONDON MARKET. CLEMENTS LIBRARY, COURTESY COLONIAL WILLIAMSBURG

of "Concessions" which guaranteed liberty of conscience and a representative assembly and made easy the procurement of land.

Berkeley and Carteret also were among the eight courtiers to whom Charles II had granted the Carolinas in 1663. These lords of the land drew up a remarkable instrument of government called the Fundamental Constitutions. This provided for a ruling aristocracy based on land ownership, with landgraves, caciques, gentlemen-commoners, and yeomen. The grandiose scheme failed because Carolina settlers preferred to exchange their labor for land of their own.

Self-made men—planters, merchants, and craftsmen—turned Charleston into "perhaps the most urbane of American cities," reports historian Ulrich B. Phillips, "with a notable semi-public library, thriving bookstores, excellent newspapers, mantua makers and milliners in touch with Paris fashions, a thronged race course, dancing assemblies, and easy-mannered men's clubs."

BLACKBEARD THE PIRATE RAIDED SHIPPING OFF THE CAROLINA AND VIRGINIA COASTS. NEW YORK PUBLIC LIBRARY

Runaway servants, debtors, ne'er-do-wells, and poor but honest settlers had long trickled into North Carolina, in those days a wilderness. New Englanders who had started an unauthorized settlement at the mouth of the Cape Fear River damned the country as unfit for humans. But pamphleteers corrected that libel and proclaimed it was an ideal marriage ground for "any Maid . . . if they be but Civil, and under 50 years of Age."

Quakers, Huguenots, Swiss, Welsh, Scotch-Irish, and Highlanders moved into what remained for years the most isolated communities in America. Pirates haunted the inlets of Pamlico Sound, and some boasted they were welcome visitors to Carolina homes.

One of the most notorious pirates was Edward Teach ("Blackbeard"), who is said to have gone into battle with his beard plaited and with lighted matches stuffed under his hat to illuminate his fierce countenance. Most of his 14 wives were alive to mourn him when he was killed in 1718 off Ocracoke Island. He fell in hand-to-hand combat with Lt. Robert Maynard of the Royal Navy, having been "closely

& warmly engaged . . . till the Sea was tinctur'd with Blood round the Vessel." Maynard sailed off with Blackbeard's head lashed to the bowsprit.

Maj. Stede Bonnet was another infamous pirate, credited with having actually carried out that fabled method of execution, walking the plank. Bonnet is supposed to have left his home in Barbados to escape a nagging wife. He roamed the Carolina coast and was captured with his crew near the mouth of the Cape Fear River. Admirers placed flowers in his shackled hands as he swung on the gallows.

"How harde wyll it bee for one browghte up amonge boockes and learned men to lyve in a barbarous place where is no learnynge and lesse cyvillytie," wrote one of John Winthrop's friends on the eve of his departure for New England. Winthrop advised him to take along books. Inventories of wilderness libraries in early colonial times reveal a surprising distribution of the writings of Homer, Plutarch, Pliny, Virgil, Seneca, Ovid, Horace, Livy, and other Greeks and Romans. Works of piety exerted great influence, and not only dealt with fine points of theology but provided guideposts to everyday conduct. Books on chirurgery, medicine, law, surveying, and engineering were considered essential.

Concern over their children's future led colonials to establish schools. The people of Massachusetts Bay founded a grammar school, Boston Latin, within five years of their arrival. It is still active today. In 1647 the General Court of Massachusetts passed a law looking toward universal literacy because that "ould deluder, Satan," sought "to keepe men from the knowledge of y[e] Scriptures." Every town of 50 householders had to hire a schoolmaster.

The Dutch in New Netherland recommended in 1649 a public school "with at least two good teachers, so that the youth, in so wild a country, where there are so many dissolute people, may, first of all, be well instructed and indoctrinated." William Penn's first Frame of Government ordered the erection of public schools where "all children within this Province of the age of twelve years, shall be taught some useful trade or skill, to the end none may be idle, but the poor may work to live, and the rich, if they become poor, may not want."

Private schools, particularly in Philadelphia, stressed such utilitarian subjects as mathematics, bookkeeping, navigation, surveying, and the rudiments of natural science. Girls' schools taught needlecraft, plain sewing, and various handicrafts.

Southern colonies with isolated plantations experienced difficulty in setting up schools. Some parents of means were so eager to have their children escape a rustic upbringing that they sent them to England almost as infants. Others hired family tutors, who often took on children of less prosperous neighbors. Skillful dancing masters were always in demand in the South, where manners were emphasized. Not to know how to dance was to display lack of good breeding—and to miss the most popular of colonial amusements.

Higher education in English America began with the founding of Harvard College in 1636. As *New England's First Fruits* (1643) reveals, "it pleased God to stir up the heart of one Mr. *Harvard* . . . to give the one halfe of his Estate (it being in all about £1700) towards the erecting of a Colledge, and all his Library: after him another gave £300 others after them cast in more, and the publique hand of the State added the rest: the Colledge was, by common consent, appointed to be at *Cambridge,* (a place very pleasant and accommodate) and is called (according to the name of the first founder) *Harvard Colledge.*"

Harvard's first president, Henry Dunster, dreamed of making it into a university for all the English-speaking colonies, but religious differences prevented that. By the turn of the century Harvard's growing liberalism alarmed strict conservatives. "Places of Learning should not be Places of Riot and Pride," preached the Reverend Solomon Stoddard of Northampton; " 'tis not worth the while for persons to be sent to the *Colledge* to learn to Complement men and Court Women."

Staunch Puritans created a second New England college in 1701 and named it for Elihu Yale, a rich merchant, in gratitude for his bequest of three bales of East Indian goods, a parcel of books, and a portrait of George I. Throughout the 18th century Yale stood as a fortress against heresy, a bulwark protecting the steady habits of Connecticut.

Zeal for an educated ministry prompted the founding of Princeton in 1746. Its president John Witherspoon typified those Scots who combined piety and classical learning, godliness and patriotic ardor for their adopted country. He and the ministers his university in New Jersey sent out to the frontier were a tough-minded lot ready to fight the Prince of Darkness with pen or musket. The churches and schools built by these Scotch Presbyterians during the colonial period were lighthouses of religion and learning in the wilderness.

King's College, later Columbia, in New York was established in 1754 in a radically different spirit. Its charter stipulated that no rule should be made that would "exclude any person of any Religious Denomination whatever from Equal Liberty and advantage of Education, or from any the Degrees, Liberties, Priviledges, Benefits, or Immunities of the said College, on account of his particular Tenets in matters of Religion."

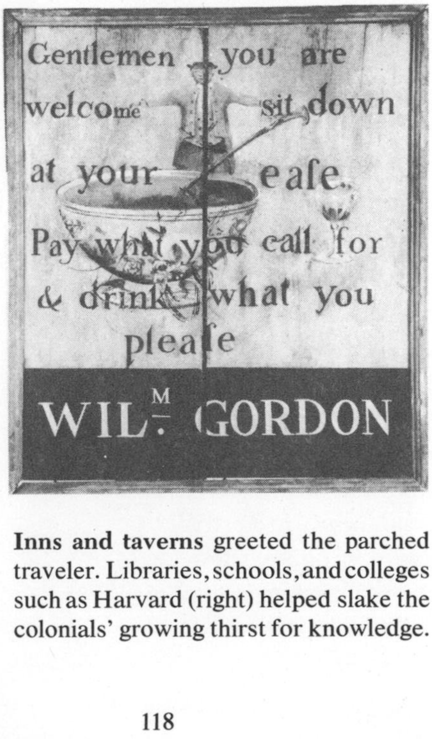

Secular education in Pennsylvania owes a debt to Benjamin Franklin. He proposed the "complete education of youth," and was instrumental in founding the College of Philadelphia, later the University of Pennsylvania. Its curriculum included physics, chemistry, botany, and zoology, and was more modern than any available elsewhere in the colonies.

Thoughtful planters in Virginia had contemplated the need of a college as early as 1619. At last, in 1693, the Reverend James Blair, highest official of the Church of England in Virginia, obtained a charter from their Majesties and named the college William and Mary in their honor. The site chosen was Middle Plantation, soon to be called Williamsburg, and the cornerstone of the first building of this second oldest college in the colonies was laid in 1695.

By 1699 five students at William and Mary had advanced sufficiently to deliver orations in praise of

Inns and taverns greeted the parched traveler. Libraries, schools, and colleges such as Harvard (right) helped slake the colonials' growing thirst for knowledge.

"A PROSPECT OF THE COLLEGES IN CAMBRIDGE IN NEW ENGLAND," ENGRAVED BY WILLIAM BURGESS, 1725-6; STOKES COLLECTION, NEW YORK PUBLIC LIBRARY. OPPOSITE: NEW LONDON INN SIGN; MORGAN B. BRAINARD COLLECTION, CONNECTICUT HISTORICAL SOCIETY

learning before the Governor. "Methinks we see alreddy that happy time," one declaimed, "when we shall surpass the Asiaticans in civility, the Jews in Religion, the Greeks in Philosophy, the Egyptians in Geometry, the Phenicians in Arithmetick, and the Caldeans in Astrology. O happy Virginia!"

IN EARLY COLONIAL DAYS communication between Virginia and London, which usually took six to eight weeks at least, was easier than between Virginia and New York or Boston. The 18th century saw a great improvement, and an increase in intercolonial travel. Peddlers and traders made their way along the trails and tracks of the Atlantic seaboard. Southerners discovered that Newport, Rhode Island, was a desirable refuge from the ague and fever of their own torrid summers. A summer migration regularly set sail from Charleston, and visitors came from other towns and the West Indies. Americans were getting to know each other for the first time.

Communication remained a problem in the far South. Mail sent from New York to Charleston via England often made better time than when sent by postriders through Virginia. When Benjamin Franklin and William Hunter, publisher of the *Virginia Gazette* in Williamsburg, were appointed deputy postmasters general in 1753, mail delivery improved so much in the North that a Philadelphia merchant might mail a letter to New York on one day and receive a reply the next. Travel between Northern colonies was made easy along the network of ferries, bridges, and roads. Though the latter were dusty in summer and in winter deep in mud, they often surpassed the highways of Great Britain.

Carts, wagons, chaises, and coaches traversed them. At first "stage wagons" provided public transportation. Later, stagecoach lines developed, especially in New England, and often made connection with packet-boat lines. Private coaches remained an evidence of conspicuous wealth.

Gregarious Americans exchanged information wherever they met. Pioneers and traders were bringing back tales of good land to be had for the taking beyond the Appalachian barrier. This word needed no newspaper or penny post; it was reported around campfires, at inns, and at church. Taverns were informal men's clubs and meeting places for civic bodies. Coffeehouses flourished in large towns and were resorts of merchants and politicians. And long after the colonial period the country church remained one place where rural people could meet.

THE LAST YEARS of colonial America saw a country very different from the thinly settled strip of British territories that had but a precarious foothold on the continent at the end of the 17th century. From 200,000 in 1689, population increased eightfold to nearly 1,700,000 in 1760. Shipping, lumbering, fishing, and fur trading in Maine and New Hampshire, and farming, trading, and exploiting the pine forests of Georgia gave a livelihood to settlers at the extreme ends of the British domain. The older settlements prospered. In the towns craftsmen plied a multiplicity of trades and put money in their pockets.

Already America was showing hospitality to all people. Although the dominant stock of the colonials remained British, many nationalities were represented in the leading cities. One group in particular influenced the quality of colonial craftsmanship—the Huguenots, driven from France after the revocation of the Edict of Nantes. Some were printers like Louis Timothée, whom Franklin sent to Charleston to print the *South Carolina Gazette*. Some were silversmiths like the immigrant father of Paul Revere. Blacksmiths, gunsmiths, cabinetmakers, joiners, carpenters, sailmakers, weavers—hardly an honest trade was without Huguenot recruits.

Hector St. John de Crèvecoeur, a Frenchman naturalized in New York, commented on the melting pot which produced a new man, an American, different from the Englishman or European who had arrived on these shores. Frenchmen, Germans, Dutch, or Jews modified the prevailing British characteristics, then were assimilated. In New York, for example, Dutch architecture, cooking, and folklore gave a special flavor to British culture. And so it was in all 13 colonies.

A relatively homogeneous people, then, flourished in a vigorous and prospering society. European and American scientists were exchanging information. American towns were becoming cosmopolitan centers of culture even in the agrarian colonies. Maryland began to look to Annapolis. And in Virginia, Williamsburg became a focal point of fashion and formal manners and a sounding board for ideas. America was rapidly coming of age.

BEVERLEY M. BOWIE

WILLIAMSBURG

Virginia's early capital re-creates colonial life

COCKING my tricorn over one eye and giving a tug to my blue velvet coat, I quit my lodgings on Francis Street and strode down the Duke of Gloucester toward Chowning's Tavern. In the yellow glow of the lantern I carried, my brass shoe buckles winked up at me with every step, and from each Yule-decked window I passed, a candle shed its hospitable light.

Chowning's was filled with a goodly company of Williamsburg craftsmen. The master bootmaker waved a tankard of ale in greeting; the apothecary nodded over his long clay pipe. The genial hubbub rose in pitch as platters of steak arrived, and soon the walls resounded to toasts of "The Queen, God bless her," "The Ladies," and "To Ourselves—good men are scarce!"

Warmed and refreshed, we formed behind the bookbinder and his fiddle and marched out of the tavern to the strains of "God Rest You Merry, Gentlemen." The night was crisp, but our caroling spirits were high, and at more than one holly-garlanded door we found welcome and a great bowl of hot spiced punch.

It was outside John Blair House that time caught up with me. We had passed the Magazine where, next morning, militia-

Williamsburg's Capitol, symbol of our colonial heritage, was built by the Crown and helped give birth to the Republic. Here it wears colors of both: Queen Anne's coat of arms and America's first national flag. The city was restored to 18th century grace through the generosity of John D. Rockefeller, Jr.

B. ANTHONY STEWART, NATIONAL GEOGRAPHIC PHOTOGRAPHER

men would fire the Christmas cannon; passed, too, the candlelit Governor's Palace in whose ballroom musicians would be tuning up. The bell of William and Mary, second oldest college in the colonies, had clanged the hour from the Wren Building's slender tower and quivered into silence.

Then, ripping the evening sky with a sound of tearing silk, a jet plane roared by. The 20th century was serving notice: It was not to be so wantonly ignored. I could don knee breeches and buckled shoes, it seemed to say, and traipse about the cobbled streets; but costumes cannot long defy the calendar. The old brick walks I trod concealed telephone cables. My fellow carolers were craftsmen, yes, but on the payroll of Colonial Williamsburg, Inc.

Ale, pecan waffles, and "sallad" are still served at Chowning's Tavern.

Williamsburg, recalled to its 18th century self by John D. Rockefeller, Jr., is not merely old and beautiful: Its every brick is steeped in history. When you stroll its lanes, great men walk beside you—Jefferson, Washington, Patrick Henry, George Mason, nine royal governors, a score of statesmen who helped shape the Republic.

It is hard to link arms with these eminent ghosts in the vacation months when ladies in Bermuda shorts and sunglasses far outnumber those in farthingales. I saw the town first on a morning in late November, still and warm, with the last wizened leaves of autumn drifting silently from the beech trees. From the doorstep of the Bracken-Carter House I could see a boy sweeping out a stable yard, a warder in dun-brown redingote shuffling toward the Guardhouse, and a few pigeons strutting the ridgepole of Captain Orr's dwelling. For the rest, Williamsburg dozed serenely. A lane took me to Duke of Gloucester Street. From in front of Orlando Jones Office I could look for three-quarters of a mile down the broad, uncluttered street past old Bruton Parish Church to the ancient brick buildings of the College of William and Mary. To my right stood the rose-tinted Capitol, as "noble, beautiful, and commodious a Pile as any of its Kind."

Crossing to the Raleigh Tavern, I pushed through a picket gate at one side and entered the brick courtyard next to the bake shop. Windows gave onto it from the tavern's Apollo Room, where young Tom Jefferson once danced with his Belinda. My goal lay in the small outbuilding from which emanated now a rich aroma of cinnamon, apples, molasses, yeast, and the smoke of hickory and oak. Inside I found the baker pressing gingerbread dough into an elaborate wooden mold shaped as a cavalier, while his apprentice raked hot coals from the waist-high oven and shoveled them into a great canister.

"How do you know when the oven is hot enough?" I asked in my ignorance.

"I just put my arm in," the baker grunted. "If it comes out charred, the temperature's about right."

I sat back in an old rush-bottomed chair and watched the morning's baking get under way—cookies, flat round loaves on a broad wooden paddle, a few tarts,

"Sir, I find your arguments as empty as your tankard." Planters in town for the General Assembly and courts swap jibes in Raleigh Tavern, then roll into bed upstairs, half a dozen to a room. Literally "politics makes strange bedfellows."

B. ANTHONY STEWART, NATIONAL GEOGRAPHIC PHOTOGRAPHER

To the Capitol
flock the colonials;
from tidewater plantations,
from scratched-out farms
and piedmont forests.
Rich or poor, they know
the loneliness of a new land;
and here at "Publick Times"
they share a glow of excitement
at seeing friends' faces,
hearing news and the
latest jokes from England,
and happy prophecies of
a good tobacco year.
Flies buzz outside; sheep
graze the green. And inside
the courts convene and
the burgesses set to work.

FROM THE FILM "WILLIAMSBURG—
THE STORY OF A PATRIOT"

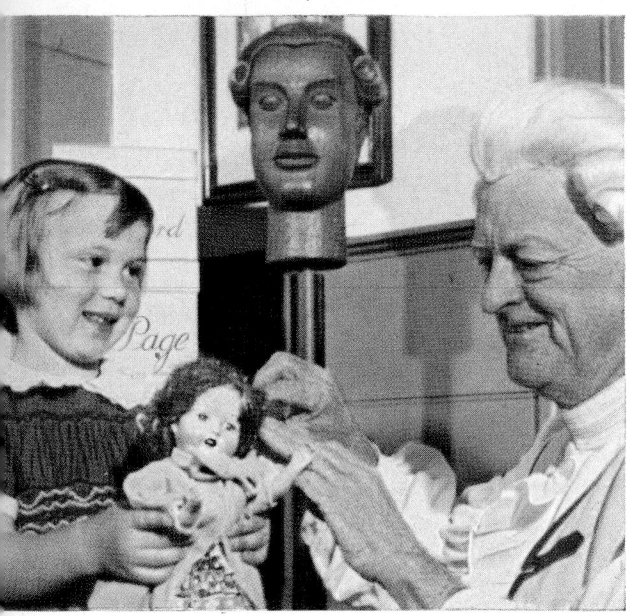

It's business as usual in Williamsburg, where shops representing the colonial crafts of men of "the middling sort" operate year round. On the apothecary's shelves (upper left) are horehound drops, "everywhere commended for those who are bruised, burst, or fallen from high

FROM TOP: BATES LITTLEHALES, B. ANTHONY STEWART, NATIONAL GEOGRAPHIC PHOTOGRAPH AND KATHLEEN REVIS JUDGE. BELOW: JOHN CRANE, COLONIAL WILLIAMSBURG

places." Clockwise from the apothecary's: a fragrant "baker's dozen" fills a wicker basket, flaxen fibers run onto the spinning wheel as thread; cabinetmaker checks his lathe's work; milliner tickles a lady's fancy; the printer inks his type with sheepskin pads; bootmaker pegs shoes that fit either foot; the peruke maker tidies a doll's wig.

B. ANTHONY STEWART, NATIONAL GEOGRAPHIC PHOTOGRAPHER, AND (LEFT) KATHLEEN REVIS JUDGE

Britain's royal lion and unicorn prance again above the governor's doorway, recalling the 169 years that Virginians lived under the Crown. Asked if her family had always lived in Williamsburg, one lady replied quickly: "Oh no! Only since the Revolution."

"Evil be to him who evil thinks," reads the motto.

some mincemeat pies. "Is your bread made just like the colonials'?" I asked.

"Martha Washington herself couldn't tell 'em apart. We get our unbleached flour from an old mill in Louisa County. It's stone-ground. The only difference is we use modern yeast. The 18th century fellows more than likely depended on scrapings from beer vats."

A lady prettily attired in farthingale and lace cap put her head in the bakery door. "I'll take a couple of loaves today, please."

"Ready at noon, ma'am." He shoved the last paddle of bread into the oven and wiped his hands on his apron. "Hostess up at the Capitol," he said with a nod toward the departing gentlewoman. "A lot of the folks in town drop by and leave orders; keeps me busy as a bird dog."

TAKING MY LEAVE, I walked along Duke of Gloucester Street to the Pasteur-Galt Apothecary Shop. The apothecary, well turned out in his sober knee breeches and ruffled stock, took me back into the office used by Dr. John Minson Galt when Williamsburg was young.

"Surgery was a bit rough in Dr. Galt's day," he said. "They had to strap the patient down. No anesthetics, of course. And no idea of antisepsis."

He picked up a sort of brace and bit. "They used this for trepanning—boring holes in the skull. The idea was to let the hot air and vapors out. Prince Philip William of Orange had 17 holes in his head—said to be the most open-minded man in Europe!"

"Did Dr. Galt practice dentistry?"

"Dentistry really hadn't emerged as a branch of medicine. Pulling teeth was about all it amounted to, and anybody would do that; the barber, for instance. False teeth gave a good deal of trouble. Washington's plates, you know, would sometimes lock open in the middle of a speech. Very embarrassing."

I strode down the street to drop in on the wigmaker, the town printer, and the master bookbinder. Before the day was over, I had visited as well the blacksmith, the spinner and weaver, the bootmaker (who kindly sewed tight a loose button on my overcoat), the silversmith, and the candlemakers. My first call on the cabinet-maker, however, yielded me only the sight of a printed notice pinned to his door:

B. ANTHONY STEWART, NATIONAL GEOGRAPHIC PHOTOGRAPHER

The Palace, where Governor Spotswood delighted to wine and dine a good 200 guests, plays host to thousands of visitors each year. They admire the Georgian mansion that cost tightfisted colonials a pretty penny, stroll the gardens, inspect smokehouse and guardrooms.

Serene 18th century music sounding in the candlelit palace ballroom must stir silk-stockinged ghosts to dance a stately minuet

Tinkling harpsichord and mellow strings play at weekly concerts in spring and fall. Here young Tom Jefferson tried his hand at the violin with the amiable Governor Fauquier and "two or three other amateurs." In the adjoining supper room (above) the punch bowl awaited thirsty dancers. On warm evenings His Excellency would linger over coffee, savoring the fragrance of his garden, and fending off pestiferous flies that invaded his unscreened door. Bedtime would send the houschold upstairs to snuff out candles and burrow into beds like the great Tudor oak four-poster with brocatelle curtains (left).

Today, hostesses in farthingales show visitors the Chinese Chippendale chest and gilt bird cage in the governor's office, and bayberry candles being made in the scullery. Antiques gleaned from England and the United States duplicate the original furnishings.

COLONIAL WILLIAMSBURG
ABOVE: B. ANTHONY STEWART AND DONALD MCBAIN, NATIONAL GEOGRAPHIC STAFF, AND (LEFT) KATHLEEN REVIS JUDGE AND DONALD MCBAIN

"I have been obliged through the sheer Weight of Fatigue to quit my Post & repair to my Dwellinghouse until I have recovered my usual Composure."

Aware of a certain Weight of Fatigue myself, I sympathized and made a mental note to return on the morrow, which I did, for it is craftsmen like these who bring the vast museum of Williamsburg to life. Colonial Williamsburg has completely restored or reconstructed more than 500 buildings over 130 acres of the city's original 280-acre tract. Buildings as charming as the Brush-Everard House, as impressive as the Palace engage the eye and imagination. A glowing forge, a printer's shop reeking of ink, a fragrant bakery, a great four-harness loom clicking and clacking—these re-create the past in warmly human terms.

At the information center excellent films on 18th century life, on the process and purpose of the restoration itself, are shown continuously. At the Craft House faithful reproductions of colonial glassware, pewter, silver, brass, linens, wallpaper, paint, and furniture are on display—and on sale.

Smart phaetons with costumed coachmen give visitors an 18th century ride past the Palace (above), old homes, and shops. Facilities include an information center, lodge, inn, day and night tours.

From January to December, hostesses in lace caps and farthingales stand ready to conduct the visitor through the town's great houses and public buildings with such a pleasant informality and ready flow of anecdote that you might imagine they are the proprietors, which in a real sense they are. Thoroughly grounded in the history both of colonial times and of every hand-wrought nail or ancient portrait in the restoration, they take an evident pride and relish in their work.

Everywhere in the restored area, in fact, an effort is made to thaw the polite frost which so easily forms over any museum. In the George Wythe House, evening visitors see the dining room as if the family had just left the table—rumpled napkins, chairs pulled back, wineglasses still rosy damp; upstairs they find night clothes laid out on the beds, slippers ready, a candle guttering beside an open book. At the Magazine, guards startle youngsters by firing old horse pistols with a satisfying roar. At the Publick Gaol, the keeper obligingly leads any parties stricken by guilt to the stocks or pillory. Under a tree near the Courthouse of

B. ANTHONY STEWART, NATIONAL GEOGRAPHIC PHOTOGRAPHER

Bruton Parish Church, completed in 1715, rang out news of independence. Its first organist was also the gaoler—prisoners pumped the organ! George Washington was godfather to 14 slaves baptized here.

Garden of the King's Arms grows jonquils, dwarf boxwood, and flowering shadbush. Town plans urged half-acre lots so each householder might have space to raise herbs and vegetables, flowers and orchard trees.

B. ANTHONY STEWART AND DONALD MCBAIN, NATIONAL GEOGRAPHIC STAFF

1770 a carriage and coachman await those who wish to rattle about behind a spanking pair of high-stepping bays.

Standing in Williamsburg, you command a panorama of American times that stretches back three and a half centuries. From the ill-favored site of Jamestown the seat of government moved to Middle Plantation, surveyed and laid out as the Town of Williamsburg. Politically patrician, Williamsburg was also socially festive and economically stable. Virginia was acclaimed "the happy retreat of true Britons and Churchmen." Its domain extended by charter across the continent to the "South Sea," a vast inland empire many times larger than Great Britain herself. More populous than any other colony, it was also the richest, its income solidly based upon that "Imperial weed," tobacco.

As its capital, tiny Williamsburg threw a long shadow. Laid out as one of Amer-

DONALD MCBAIN, NATIONAL GEOGRAPHIC STAFF, AND KATHLEEN REVIS JUDGE

In the House of Burgesses (left), Patrick Henry thundered defiance to the Stamp Act, rousing legislators to uproarious approval. Here members of America's oldest lawmaking body applauded modest George Washington for his exploits in the French and Indian War. Here, too, George Mason's Declaration of Rights became law.

In these chambers of the Capitol's west wing (above), the General Court of the colony sentenced 13 of Blackbeard's pirates to be hanged by the neck until dead.

ica's most felicitous experiments in town planning, the little city boasted an impressive grouping of public and private buildings, knit by broad avenues and handsomely set off by greens and market square. Fifteen hundred persons normally resided in it. But at "Publick Times," when the courts or General Assembly convened, its population would be doubled or tripled by gentry in from the plantations, merchants, back-country farmers and hunters, sharpers and pickpockets, grooms and craftsmen, solemn Indians, and a sprinkling of slaves.

Over the Raleigh Tavern's chief mantel runs the Latin *Hilaritas Sapientiae et Bonae Vitae Proles*—"Jollity, the Offspring of Wisdom and Good Living."

It might have been the motto of all Williamsburg. Gov. Sir William Gooch noted approvingly in 1727: "The Gentm. and Ladies here are perfectly well bred, not an ill Dancer in my Govmt." Gov. Alexander Spotswood entertained hundreds

BATES LITTLEHALES, NATIONAL GEOGRAPHIC PHOTOGRAPHER

Wren Building of William and Mary is "beautiful and commodious, being first modelled by Sir Christopher Wren," said an early resident. America's second oldest college counts Presidents Jefferson, Monroe, and Tyler as alumni, and Washington as Chancellor. Phi Beta Kappa began here.

Dr. James Blair, college founder, fought hard for its charter and funds. Told it would train ministers to save colonial souls, a royal official snorted: "Souls! Damn your souls! Make tobacco!"

Blair even wrung loot from pirates awaiting trial, promising a word on their behalf.

Smoke from a booming salute veils the Magazine. Gunpowder stored there worried Governor Dunmore in 1775; he spirited it away from rebels. Angry colonists marched on the capital; Dunmore fled.

Today's visitors inspect 18th century pistols.

of guests at the Palace, and the drain on his wine cellars and smokehouses was fabulous. Yet underneath this festivity serious matters were afoot. Bred in a long tradition of self-government, the great landholders would not play second fiddle to the British. Loyalty to the Crown, affinity with the old country—yes. But subservience to authority from abroad—no, gentle sirs.

In the Raleigh Tavern, Jefferson and his friends set up Virginia's Committee of Correspondence. Here, too, burgesses routed from the Capitol by the governor gathered to urge a Continental Congress. Williamsburg's finest hour was upon it. And almost in the next tick of history's clock the town died. In 1780 Governor Jefferson helped move the capital up the James to Richmond, deemed "more safe and central." Williamsburg dwindled into genteel decay.

Then Mr. Rockefeller stepped in with his nonprofit corporation, Colonial Williamsburg, Inc. More than $74,000,000 pumped into the restoration, and sums

COLONIAL WILLIAMSBURG AND (BELOW) B. ANTHONY STEWART, NATIONAL GEOGRAPHIC PHOTOGRAPHER

spent by millions of visitors have given the old town a great shot in the arm. And it, in turn, deals out a measure of inspiration to its guests.

I like the story of the GI from Fort Eustis who came up with his unit during World War II and got separated. He was standing before the Peale portrait of Washington in the Capitol. Suddenly he muttered, "You got it for us, General. And, by God, we're going to keep it!" And he saluted.

When Mr. Rockefeller heard that story, tears came to his eyes, and he said quietly, "Then it was all worth while."

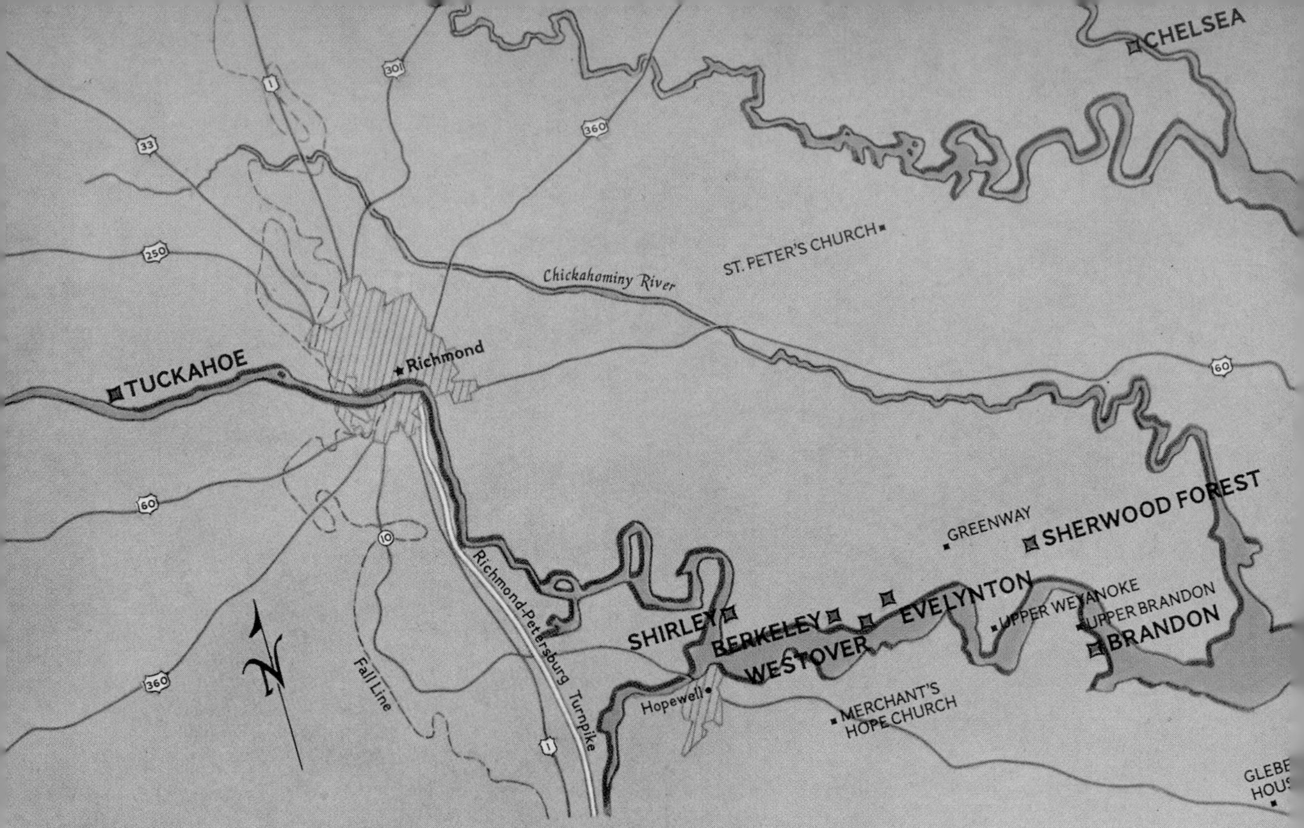

TIDEWATER PLANTATIONS
of the Old Dominion

GAIETY, gossip, and government in Williamsburg were exciting, but the real life of 18th century Virginia centered on the great plantations that lined four navigable rivers—the James, York, Rappahannock, and Potomac. As soon as "Publick Times" ended, planters' carriages lurched along dusty, rutted lanes to isolated Georgian mansions that were the hub of self-contained realms.

Astride a finely bred horse, the planter directed the overseers of slaves in the fields, the blacksmith, the cobbler, the cooper. Tobacco by the hogshead went from his private wharf to England. Back came Chippendale furniture, fashionable gowns, the latest books, and a letter from his London agent suggesting the proper school for his children. Between times he read well. William Byrd II, a learned, lusty, and land-poor aristocrat, notes in his Pepysian diary that "I rose at 6 o'clock and read a chapter in Hebrew and some Greek in Lucian." Emulating the squirearchy of England, Virginia's country gentlemen transplanted London culture to the riverbanks of the New World.

History lives on today in a stately procession of homes, lovingly restored by their owners or by organizations conscious of a priceless heritage. On the James rise Westover, Byrd's magnificent mansion; Evelynton, named for his beautiful daughter; Berkeley, home of the Harrisons who gave the nation two presidents;

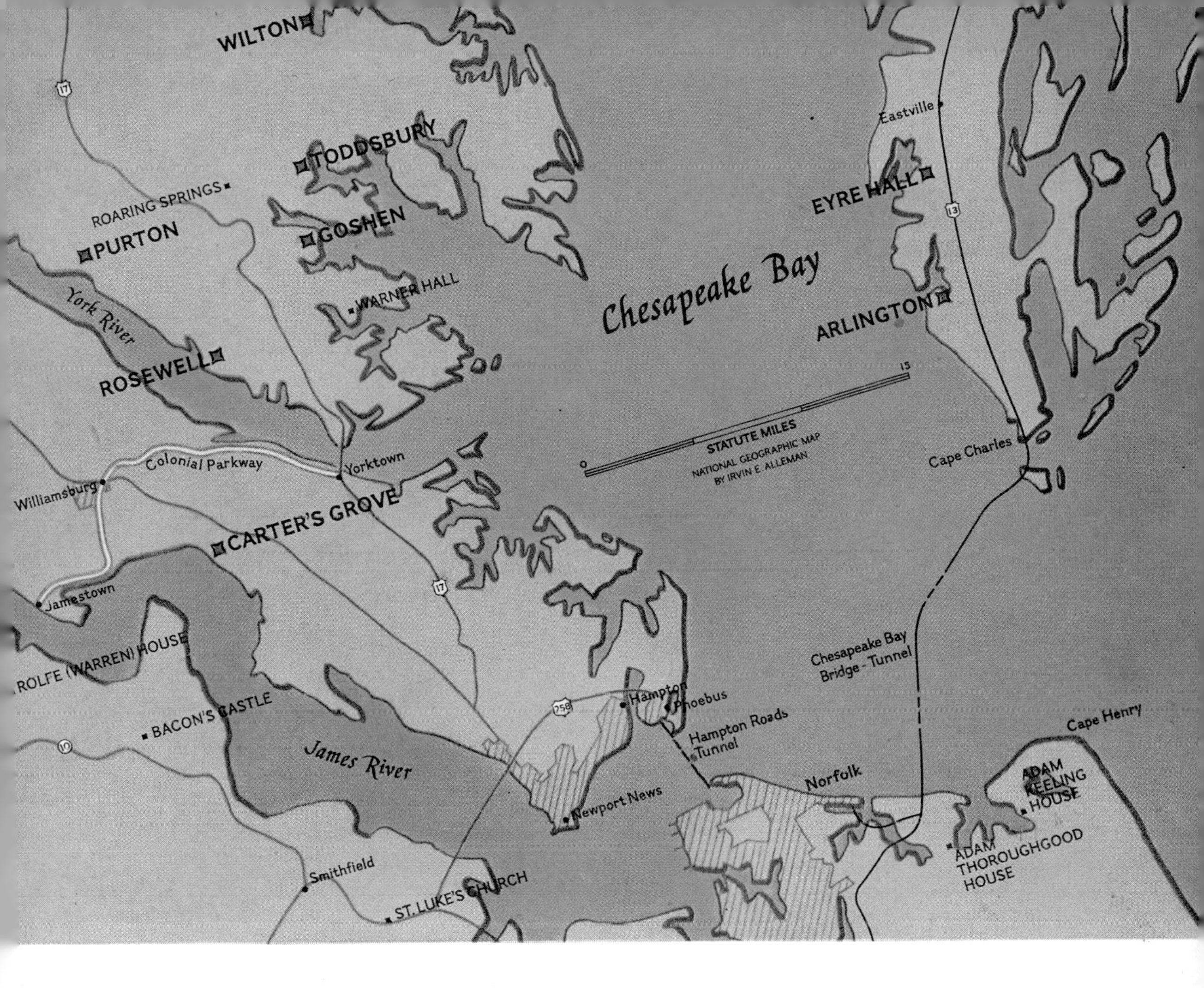

Berkeley, dating from 1726, housed Virginia's illustrious Harrison family. Elegantly restored and furnished, the home (right) is open daily. Terraced gardens march down to the James.

Brandon, still the center of a 5,000-acre farm, is another riverside mansion where history keeps house. Visitors may stroll its gardens.

JOHN E. FLETCHER AND ROBERT F. SISSON AND (LEFT) MERLE SEVERY, ALL NATIONAL GEOGRAPHIC STAFF

Wishing "a very good house," William Byrd II in the 1730's built Westover, Virginia's finest example of Georgian grandeur. Here, shaded by tulip poplars and comforted by an escape tunnel that would take him to the James if Indians struck, he ran his 179,000 acres,

B. ANTHONY STEWART, NATIONAL GEOGRAPHIC PHOTOGRAPHER

read from his large library, entertained lavishly. His descendants include Admiral Richard E. Byrd, the explorer, and U. S. Senator Harry F. Byrd. Like many Virginia homes, Westover receives visitors during Historic Garden Week, late in April. Grounds are open daily.

Shirley, birthplace of Robert E. Lee's mother; 300-foot-long Sherwood Forest where President John Tyler lived; Tuckahoe, Tom Jefferson's boyhood home; and majestic Carter's Grove, built by Carter Burwell, grandson of Robert "King" Carter who owned 300,000 acres and 1,000 slaves. In the brick mansion's "Refusal Room," tradition says Washington and Jefferson both heard "no" from belles they wished to marry.

Along the York and inlets of Chesapeake Bay stand richly paneled Chelsea, the stark ruins of 35-room Rosewell, and well-preserved Purton; Goshen, mossy-roofed Wilton, and Toddsbury, one of the oldest continuously lived-in houses in America. On the Eastern Shore ramble old Eyre Hall, and Arlington of the Custis family. Irascible John Custis, who disliked his wife so much that he proclaimed it in his epitaph, once angrily drove his carriage into the Chesapeake. When his lady asked him where he was going, he bellowed, "To Hell, Madam."

"Drive on," she said coolly. "Any place is better than Arlington."

Visits to other plantations often turned into lengthy stays. Distances were great and southern hospitality was a necessity if the planter was to have the convivial pleasures he loved. Parties were gay; but too much drinking at funerals raised some eyebrows. Intermarriage enhanced the fortunes of Virginia's first families. Washington and Jefferson took well-to-do widows. William Carter, 23, married "sprightly" 85-year-old Sarah Ellyson, "with three thousand pounds fortune." Another road to wealth was government. Tobacco quickly sapped the soil,

The candlelit "Refusal Room" at Carter's Grove, legend has it, saw two famous suitors rejected—George Washington by Mary Cary and Thomas Jefferson by Rebecca Burwell. Carter Burwell built this "most beautiful house in America" around 1750.

Rare silver graces the buffet in Shirley, still operated as a plantation by C. Hill Carter, Jr. "King" Carter gave the tray, 95 percent pure silver, as a present in 1723 when his son John married Elizabeth Hill.

Visitors are welcome at both houses.

Cozy kitchen at Seven Gables on the Eastern Shore dates from 1786. Original hand-cut beam holds pots and pans.

BATES LITTLEHALES, NATIONAL GEOGRAPHIC PHOTOGRAPHER

so planters sought to expand their holdings. Since Williamsburg controlled land grants, getting elected a burgess put one on the inside track. Byrd acquired 105,000 acres for a token £525 by the good graces of the Governor's Council, of which he was a member. Jefferson advised a nephew to hasten to "that public stage whereon you may begin to be useful to yourself," but cautioned, "pursue the interests of your country . . . with the purest integrity."

Unlike Puritan New Englanders, whose churches dominated the towns, Virginia's Anglican gentry ran their parishes. "King" Carter even ordered his parson to pray for rain! Hiring the clergy, levying the parish tax, directing the care of the poor and orphaned were a lesson in government for the tobacco aristocracy.

Trained and bred to govern, the great planters of the Golden Age ruled Virginia capably. Later a new nation would call on four of them—the Virginia Dynasty of Washington, Jefferson, Madison, and Monroe—to guide it during the infant years.

THOMAS Y. CANBY

Sheep and lambs roam Goshen's lawn, children roam old Purton

Gloucester County's Goshen, built in the 1750's, contains a chest of drinking glasses that play *Ach, Du Lieber Augustin* when damp fingers run along their rims. It is a harmonicon, once called a Hydrodaktylopsychicharmonica. Purton, another Gloucester mansion, served as a model for restoration work at Williamsburg. The iron gate comes from Spain. Open doors reveal the York River. Powhatan, father of Pocahontas, reputedly lived on this site.

VOLKMAR WENTZEL AND (ABOVE) HOWELL WALKER, BOTH NATIONAL GEOGRAPHIC STAFF

J. BAYLOR ROBERTS, NATIONAL GEOGRAPHIC STAFF

At Gunston Hall George Mason's pen let freedom ring

In every crisis that rocked America between 1765 and 1790 Mason penned some vital proposal. He devised ways to side-step the Stamp Act and to boycott England after the Townshend Acts. He called for unity in the colonies. Eying the Ohio country, he dug up legal ammunition that buttressed America's claim.

His uncle's large library taught Mason the enlightened thinking of the day: that reason should rule, that just laws make just men. He shared Jefferson's dedication to equal rights, and dubbed the slave trade "disgraceful to mankind."

A widower with nine children, he disliked public office, preferring to manage his 5,000-acre plantation.

Bequeathed to Virginia by Louis Hertle, Gunston Hall on the Potomac boasts carved Palladian and Chinese Chippendale rooms. Boxwood borders the garden aisles.

At right, the Mason seal.

The Virginia Declaration of Rights

GEORGE MASON'S reasoned words expressed the feelings that burned in the breasts of Americans as they moved through discontent, then revolution toward the liberty they felt more precious than life itself. Like other patriots, Mason did not at first seek independence, but the rights of the colonists as Englishmen. In 1770 he wrote, "We owe our Mother Country the duty of subjects; we will not pay her the submission of slaves."

His greatest work, the Virginia Declaration of Rights, adopted June 12, 1776, at Williamsburg, has a familiar ring. For as these excerpts show, Mason struck the chords destined to resound in two world-shaking documents: the Declaration of Independence and the Bill of Rights.

I. That all Men are by Nature equally free and independent, and have certain inherent Rights . . . namely, the Enjoyment of Life and Liberty, with the Means of acquiring and possessing Property, and pursuing and obtaining Happiness and Safety.

II. That all Power is vested in, and consequently derived from, the People; that Magistrates are their Trustees and Servants, and at all Times amenable to them.

III. That Government is, or ought to be, instituted for the common Benefit, Protection, and Security, of the People, Nation, or Community . . . and that, whenever any Government shall be found inadequate or contrary to these Purposes, a Majority of the Community hath an indubitable, unalienable, and indefeasible Right, to reform, alter, or abolish it, in such Manner as shall be judged most conducive to the public Weal.

VIII. That in all capital or criminal Prosecutions a Man hath a Right . . . to a speedy Trial by an impartial Jury of his Vicinage, without whose unanimous Consent he cannot be found guilty, nor can he be compelled to give Evidence against himself; that no Man be deprived of his Liberty except by the Law of the Land, or the Judgment of his Peers.

IX. That excessive Bail ought not to be required, nor excessive Fines imposed; nor cruel and unusual Punishments inflicted.

XI. That in Controversies respecting Property, and in Suits between Man and Man, the ancient Trial by Jury is preferable to any other, and ought to be held sacred.

XII. That the Freedom of the Press is one of the greatest Bulwarks of Liberty, and can never be restrained but by despotic Governments.

XIII. That a well regulated Militia, composed of the Body of the People, trained to Arms, is the proper, natural, and safe Defence of a free State; that standing Armies, in Time of Peace, should be avoided, as dangerous to Liberty; and that, in all Cases, the Military should be under strict Subordination to, and governed by the civil Power.

XVI. That Religion, or the Duty which we owe to our Creator, and the Manner of discharging it, can be directed only by Reason and Conviction, not by Force or Violence; and therefore, all Men are equally entitled to the free Exercise of Religion, according to the Dictates of Conscience; and that it is the mutual Duty of all to practise Christian Forebearance, Love, and Charity, towards each other.

CAVALIER MARYLAND

"Green gold" ushers in a gracious way of life

AN EARLY VISITOR found Maryland and Virginia "two Sister Countries, much of one nature, both for produce and manner of living." The great Chesapeake Bay slashed deep into both colonies, pushing a thousand watery fingers into the land. In such a setting tobacco plantations thrived. Yet Maryland boasted its own character, lighthearted and elegant.

Today's visitor can sense the cavalier spirit in three-centuries-old Annapolis where planters and their families gathered after the crop was in. Walk down to the harbor; the sails of pleasure boats recall days when tall-masted English ships swung on their hawsers there. Nearby stand buildings where colonial merchants offered "European and East India goods . . . on very reasonable terms, for Paper Money, Sterling, Bills of Exchange, Corn, Tobacco, or Short Credit." Stroll into Reynolds Tavern, now a library. Planters met old friends there.

Down Charles Street, the Jonas Green House jabs four chimneys into the sky, a badge of social standing for its owner. When not out back printing his *Maryland Gazette,* Green served as "Punster, Purveyer and Punch-Maker General" of the Tuesday Club. That gay group spiced each meeting with "toasts loyal and amorous," and debated all issues save politics. And while the Virginia planter read his Cicero in solitude, and the New Englander studied his Bible, members of the Tuesday Club argued the merits of popular English novels like *Peregrine Pickle* and *Clarissa.* Their womenfolk, in dresses of India silk, filled paneled salons with the tinkle of laughter as they discussed recent theatricals, *The Beaux' Strategem* and *The Virgin Unmasked.*

From its beginning Maryland was aristocratic. George Calvert, first Lord Baltimore, persuaded King Charles to grant him a slice of Virginia as a fief in 1632. He would hand out baronial manors to lesser lords and pocket their quitrents. He hoped also to provide a refuge for fellow Catholics, persecuted in England.

George died. His son Cecilius dispatched the first colonists in 1634 aboard the *Ark* and *Dove:* 17 gentlemen-adventurers and their ladies, two priests, and about 200 commoners. On Blakiston Island in the Potomac River a lonely cross marks where they landed and "humbly recited on bended knees, the Litanies of the Sacred Cross with great emotion."

On the mainland they founded St. Marys City, now a sleepy, sun-washed community where the first colonial statehouse stands beautifully rebuilt. Calvert urged religious toleration, and an "Act Concerning Religion" was passed in 1649. This guaranteed freedom for all who believed in the divinity of Christ, and fined hotheads who hurled such epithets as "heretik, Scismatic, Idolator," or "popish Priest." But in 1654 Puritans, who were in the majority, seized the government, disenfranchised both Catholics and Anglicans, and ruled with an iron fist until 1658, when the Lord Proprietor regained his authority and restored religious freedom.

Maryland's State House, begun in 1772, rises above Annapolis roofs. Here Washington resigned as commander in chief and the Continental Congress ratified peace with England. Maryland flag is based on Lord Baltimore's coat of arms.

THOMAS J. ABERCROMBIE, NATIONAL GEOGRAPHIC STAFF

FABRICS
Fabric Mart

Hammond-Harwood House beckons visitors through an elegant doorway

When William Buckland came to Annapolis around 1770, he had won fame as architect of Gunston Hall. (George Mason found him quite a bargain as an indentured servant!)

Commissioned by Matthias Hammond, "an able lawyer and political thinker," he wrought this brick masterpiece. Wings with octagonal fronts flank the two-story main building.

Fine carving about the door carries on within the house; acanthus friezes adorn mantels, modillions grace cornices, egg and dart motifs rim fan windows.

They say Hammond's house cost him a bride-to-be; she felt he cared more for it than for her.

Nonprofit Hammond-Harwood House Association opens the property to the public the year round.

W. ROBERT MOORE AND (RIGHT) B. ANTHONY STEWART, BOTH NATIONAL GEOGRAPHIC STAFF

From St. Marys, settlement spread north and across the bay to the Eastern Shore. Old houses still dot the inlets to tell how the cavaliers lived. At massive Readbourne grassy terraces sweep down to the Chester River, a reminder that planters looked on the water as their highway system. Shallops and canoes with blue sterns and red rudders carried them on "Sunday drives." Scows and sloops "trucked" their half-ton hogsheads of tobacco to market. Ketches and barks brought New England skipper-peddlers who sailed from wharf to wharf hawking "Medera-Wines, Sugars, Salt, Wickar-Chairs and Tin Candlesticks."

Marylanders had a way with ships. They borrowed the dugout from the Indians, built up the sides with planks, and added leg-of-mutton sails. Result: the two-masted bugeye that delights Chesapeake Bay visitors today. Shipwrights on the Severn took a hard look at trim Bermuda sloops, then built their own fast vessels for the West Indies trade. Sharp-hulled and sail-crowded, these rakish schooners and brigs evolved into the celebrated Baltimore clipper.

At Wye Plantation giant oysters and diamondback terrapin were prepared in a kitchen painted blue because that "depressed the flies." The "antler" stairway of the Ringgold House once framed red-coated British officers who warmed them-

Little Miss Proctor of Baltimore had not kissed the paint from the doll's cheek when she and her toy sat for artist Charles Willson Peale in 1789. Today her portrait and plaything have ended up in the Hammond-Harwood House. Chippendale and Hepplewhite furnishings stand in the crimson-draped parlor where colonial ladies gossiped. Pewter and brass utensils gleam in the kitchen (below).

MARYLAND
Chesapeake Bay
VIRGINIA
Frederick
Carroll
Baltimore
Howard
Montgomery
Prince Georges
Anne Arundel
Calvert
Charles
St. Marys
Randallstown
Towson
Edgewood
Aberdeen Proving Ground
Mount Airy
Sykesville
Chase
Granite
Fullerton
Drayton Manor
Woodstock
Baltimore
Essex
Damascus
Ellicott City
Fort McHenry
Patapsco River
Clarksburg
RINGGOLD HOUSE
Dickerson
Brookeville
Elkridge
Hinchingham
Glen Burnie
Poolesville
Gaithersburg
Savage
Providence Plantation
Pasadena
Quaker Neck
Corsica Neck
Laurel
Fort George G. Meade
Gibson Island
Rockville
Severna Park
Severn River
Love Point
Kensington
Sandy Point
Wild Acres
Greenbelt
Chesapeake Bay Bridge
Queenstown
Silver Spring
HAMMOND-HARWOOD HOUSE
Whitehall
Dranesville
Bethesda
Stevensville
Chevy Chase
College Park
Annapolis
U.S. Naval Academy
Herndon
McLean
Hyattsville
Kent Island
Washington D.C.
Arlington County
Falls Church
Tulip Hill
Kent Fort Manor
Rich Neck Manor
Galesville
Suitland
Bloody Point
Claiborne
Fairfax
Alexandria
Andrews Air Force Base
Upper Marlboro
St. Michaels
Friendship
Holly Hill
Royal Oak
Occoquan Creek
Fort Belvoir
Mount Vernon
Fort Washington
Brandywine
Patuxent River
Bellevue
Occoquan
Chesapeake Beach
Woodbridge
Indian Head
Waldorf
ROSE HILL
Dumfries
Marbury
Habre de Venture
Hughesville
Gods Grace Point
Prince Frederick
Smallwood's Retreat
Rison
La Plata
U.S. Marine Corps Reservation
Rose Hill
Benedict
Barstow
Madison
Port Tobacco
La Grange
Burnt Store
Cedar Hill
Quantico
Chandler's Hope
Mulberry Grove
Charlotte Hall
Taney House
Cremona
Widewater
Cross Roads
Mechanicsville
PRESTON
St. Thomas Manor
De La Brooke
Three Notch Road
St. Leonard Creek
Stafford
Newburg
Old Spout Farm
Popes Creek
Society Hill
Sotterley
Preston
Riverside
Mt. Republic
Resurrection Manor
Fishing Creek
Dahlgren
Waverly
Wicomico R.
Hollywood
Solomons
Hard Bargain
West Hatton
RESURRECTION MANOR
St. Richard's Manor
Fredericksburg
Leonardtown
Patuxent Naval Air Test Center
Long Lane Farm
HARD BARGAIN
Colonial Beach
Lexington Park
Park Hall
Potomac River
Blakiston Island
Mulberry Fields
Wakefield (George Washington's Birthplace)
West St. Marys Manor
Saint Marys City
St. Inigoes Cr.
Port Conway
Coles Point
Cross Manor
Point No Point
Port Royal
Stratford (Robert E. Lee's Birthplace)
Webster Field
St. Inigoes
St. Ignatius Church
Guinea
Camp A. P. Hill
Rappahannock River
Montross
Bowling Green
CROSS MANOR
Point Lookout
STATEHOUSE 1675?
Callao
Warsaw
Village
Tappahannock
Heathsville
MARYLAND
VIRGINIA
© National Geographic Map
Walter K. Morrison, Cartographer
Design and Art by
William N. Palmstrom and Walter A. Weber
Drawn by Russel G. Fritz and Robert W. Northrop

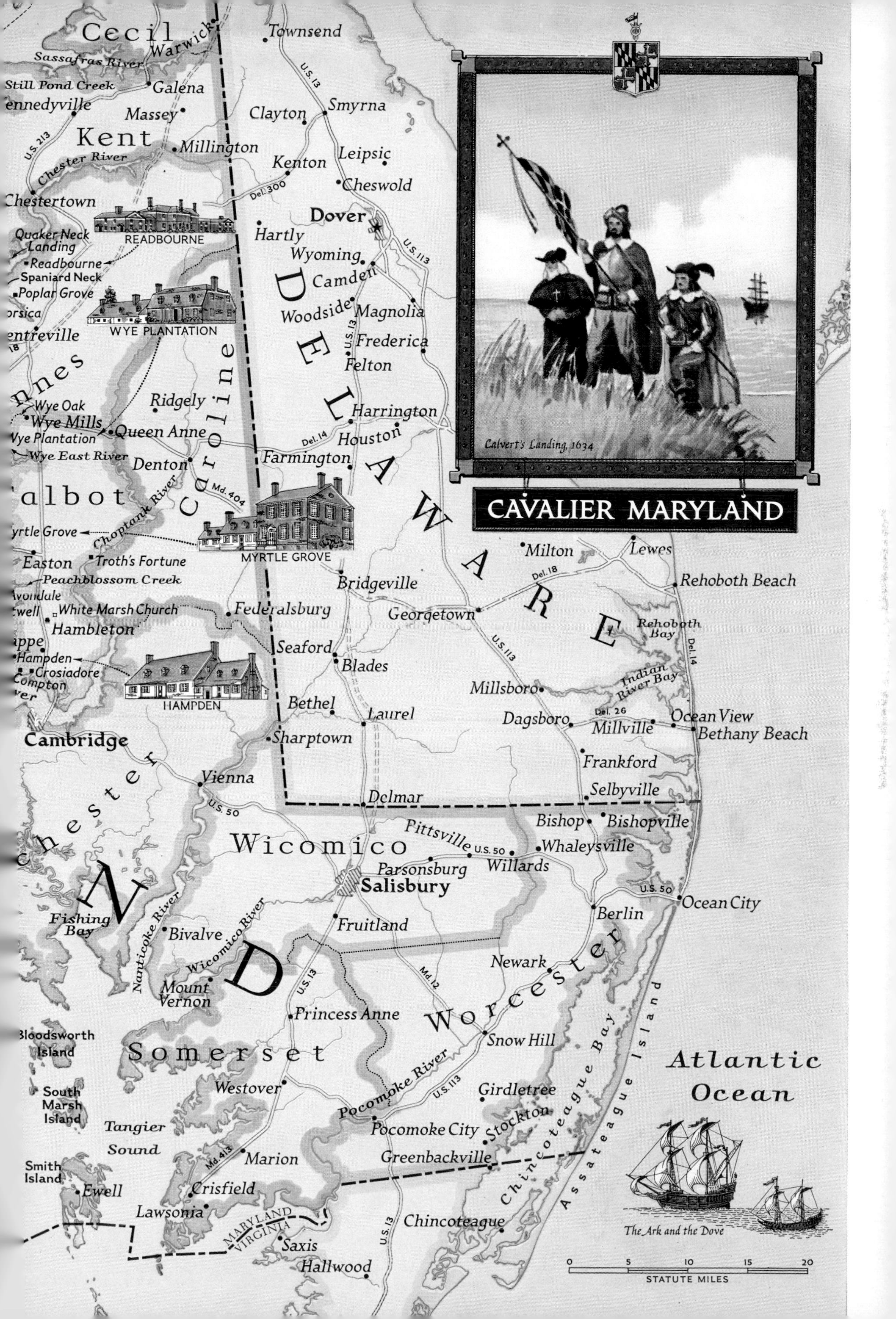
CAVALIER MARYLAND
Calvert's Landing, 1634
The Ark and the Dove
DELAWARE
Atlantic Ocean
Cecil
Kent
Caroline
Talbot
Wicomico
Worcester
Somerset
Dover
Salisbury
Cambridge
Chestertown
READBOURNE
WYE PLANTATION
MYRTLE GROVE
HAMPDEN
Townsend
Warwick
Sassafras River
Still Pond Creek
Galena
Massey
Clayton
Smyrna
Millington
Chester River
Kenton
Leipsic
Cheswold
Hartly
Wyoming
Camden
Woodside
Magnolia
Frederica
Felton
Quaker Neck Landing
Readbourne
Spaniard Neck
Poplar Grove
Ridgely
Wye Oak
Wye Mills
Wye Plantation
Wye East River
Queen Anne
Harrington
Houston
Farmington
Denton
Choptank River
Troth's Fortune
Easton
Peachblossom Creek
White Marsh Church
Hambleton
Hampden
Crosiadore
Compton
Federalsburg
Milton
Lewes
Rehoboth Beach
Rehoboth Bay
Bridgeville
Georgetown
Seaford
Blades
Millsboro
Indian River Bay
Bethel
Laurel
Dagsboro
Millville
Ocean View
Bethany Beach
Sharptown
Frankford
Selbyville
Vienna
Delmar
Bishop
Bishopville
Pittsville
Whaleysville
Parsonsburg
Willards
Ocean City
Berlin
Fishing Bay
Fruitland
Nanticoke River
Bivalve
Wicomico River
Mount Vernon
Newark
Princess Anne
Snow Hill
Bloodsworth Island
South Marsh Island
Tangier Sound
Westover
Pocomoke River
Girdletree
Pocomoke City
Stockton
Chincoteague Bay
Assateague Island
Smith Island
Ewell
Marion
Crisfield
Greenbackville
Lawsonia
MARYLAND
VIRGINIA
Chincoteague
Saxis
Hallwood
U.S. 13
U.S. 213
U.S. 113
U.S. 50
Del. 300
Del. 14
Del. 18
Del. 26
Md. 404
Md. 12
Md. 413
0 5 10 15 20
STATUTE MILES

B. ANTHONY STEWART AND (RIGHT) THOMAS J. ABERCROMBIE, BOTH NATIONAL GEOGRAPHIC STAFF

selves before the fireplace under the first landing. Look on Hard Bargain and you will see why Marylanders call such dwellings "telescope houses." Prospering, planters added wings of varying heights to their homes. From a distance it seems as if a giant could telescope them all into the largest section.

Fine examples of earlier and smaller plantation houses are Preston, seat of the Puritan government in the 1650's; Hampden, raised in 1663; and Cross and Resurrection manors, built on estates of Capt. Thomas Cornwaleys. Rose Hill, sprawling 125 feet along a hillside, was the home of the "chirurgeon" whose patients included a Virginia planter across the Potomac, George Washington. Myrtle Grove, another telescope house, has been in the same family since 1724.

Many of the houses are still lived in, so visitors enter only on special occasions. Others, such as Hammond-Harwood House in Annapolis and beautifully carved Sotterley near Hollywood, open regularly. Apt for tidewater Maryland is the description applied to one of its great sons, Charles Carroll: "Ease may be natural to a man, but elegance—the union of propriety with ease—must be acquired."

JOHN J. PUTMAN

Otwell just rambles along, for its owners kept adding wings. But viewed from the air it forms a neat T. Oldest part dates from about 1670.

Maryland settlers turned wilderness into estates with names like "Penny Come Quick," "My Lord's Gift," "Troth's Fortune," "I have been a great While at," and "Aha, the Cow Pasture."

Green gold to cavaliers, tobacco still hangs high in southern Maryland barns. And there it matures, "by a convenient attendance upon time, to its prefection."

PAUL REVERE PORTRAIT BY JOHN SINGLETON COPLEY, C. 1765, MUSEUM OF FINE ARTS, BOSTON. WALNUT AND BRASS CLOCK, C. 1775, BY NEW YORK'S CHARLES GEDDES, AND THREE PIECES OF COLONIAL PHILADELPHIA SILVER: BOWL BY JOSEPH RICHARDSON, SR., SUGAR BOWL BY WILLIAM HOLLINGSHEAD, COFFEEPOT BY JOSEPH ANTHONY, JR., ALL AT THE HENRY FORD MUSEUM, DEARBORN, MICHIGAN. MAHOGANY HIGHBOY, PHILADELPHIA C. 1775, SMITHSONIAN INSTITUTION, WASHINGTON.

FINE HOUSES like those beside Chesapeake Bay called for fine furnishings. All along the seaboard craftsmen put in their bids for the market England once dominated.

Boston's Paul Revere, silversmith, engraver, and maker of false teeth, fashioned clean-lined teapots and porringers. Philadelphia cabinetmaker Thomas Afflect worked with English model books at his elbow. But from ball-and-claw feet to broken pediment, the highboys he fashioned were no mere copies.

His fellow townsman, David Rittenhouse, made fine clocks, built a telescope (probably America's first), and designed an orrery, a model solar system that showed eclipses "for 5000 years, either forward or backward."

Such skilled work graces many collections, notably the Henry Francis du Pont Winterthur Museum near Wilmington, Delaware.

Colonial craftsmen produce masterpieces of elegance

EDENTON

Albemarle Sound

Cape Hatteras

VIRGINIA
NORTH CAROLINA

Chowan County Courthouse, still in use, is the oldest in the state. It faces the water front of this Albemarle Sound seaport.

BATH

Settled in 1690, it was incorporated in 1705, North Carolina's first town. Charming brick church. The small houses recall those of a New England fishing port.

Raleigh

Alamance Battleground

NEW BERN

Settled by Swiss and Germans in 1710, New Bern contains beautifully restored palace of royal governor William Tryon.

WINSTON-SALEM

Old Salem, now being restored, was founded by Moravians in 1766.

Atlantic Ocean

The Cornwallis House (1771) served as headquarters for the British general during the southern campaign of the Revolution.

WILMINGTON

NORTH CAROLINA
SOUTH CAROLINA

Cape Fear

Orton Plantation evokes the mood of the Old South. Nearby are church ruins and cellar holes of Brunswick, once a thriving colonial port.

Prince George Protestant Episcopal Church (1750) is one of the town's finest buildings.

GEORGETOWN

Columbia

Santee River

McCLELLANVILLE

Hampton Plantation (1735) is a beautiful and well-restored mansion.

Ashley River

Cooper River

White House (1750) is the city's oldest.

AUGUSTA

CHARLESTON

Settled in 1670, this was England's first firm foothold in the southland. Mellow buildings and walled gardens line its twisting lanes. Great plantations stretch away along the Ashley and Cooper rivers.

SOUTH CAROLINA
GEORGIA

Savannah River

BEAUFORT

Charleston on a small scale, with fine old houses and nostalgic ruins.

LOUISVILLE

SAVANNAH

Governor Oglethorpe's planned city. Dignified homes surround its gracious squares.

Old Slave Market, built in 1758, antedates the town.

FORT FREDERICA NATIONAL MONUMENT

Oglethorpe built this fort in 1736 on St. Simons Island to defend Georgia, last of the original 13 colonies, from Spanish Florida. Here stand structures of crumbling tabby, a mixture of oyster shells, lime, and sand. During the War of Jenkins' Ear, the Battle of Bloody Marsh (1742) near the fort halted Spain's raids into Georgia.

GEORGIA
FLORIDA

0 75
STATUTE MILES

NATIONAL GEOGRAPHIC MAP BY IRVIN E. ALLEMAN

ST. AUGUSTINE

EDWARDS PARK

THE COLONIAL SOUTHLAND

A PLANTER from Colonial Maryland could reach South Carolina only after a grueling horseback journey or a perilous sea voyage. No wonder that if he made it safely to Charleston, the biggest city below Philadelphia, he found a setting in many ways foreign.

No longer isolated, Charleston is still a charming world apart. No sooner had I driven on to that narrow neck of land where "the Ashley and Cooper rivers come together to form the Atlantic" than the city's magic engulfed me. For despite French and Spanish raids, an earthquake, hurricanes, great fires, and ordeals of the Revolution and Civil War, the old section looks and feels like the Charleston described in a journal of 1762: "Everything conspires to make this town the politest, as it is one of the richest in America."

Polite it still is, with its accent that caresses vowels, disdains the letter "r," and

Medway, built in 1686 near Charleston, was seat of a landgrave entitled to 48,000 acres under the feudal constitution of Carolina Province. Live oaks shade lawn.

VOLKMAR WENTZEL, NATIONAL GEOGRAPHIC PHOTOGRAPHER (ALSO PAGES 162-3)

throws in the word "sir" like a comma. "Theah has always been grayit affinity between Chawlston and Boston, seh," I was genially informed, after I had admitted to a New England background. "They traded togetheh fo' yeuhs. And you'll recall that it was a Yankee—pawden, a New Englandeh—who brought us the first Madagascar rice in the 1690's."

That sackful of rice put South Carolina on its feet. Planters thrived on the huge baronial domains that the colony's eight lords proprietors had organized. Merchants prospered in town. And beside their mansions rose those of planters who sought sea air as a relief from rice field humidity and mosquitoes. Settlers from Barbados graced their stucco homes with pastel tones. Huguenots brought names that live on—with strange pronunciations: Legare is "Legree," Huger is "Ugee."

To walk Charleston's streets and lanes on a moonlit night is to invite the company of ghosts—the footsteps of young blades come to court their ladies on the balconies or behind some mellow garden wall. I seemed to hear the creak of a wrought-iron gate, a muffled shout of laughter, a whispered curse followed by the clash of swords. Tempers flared when honor was slurred.

Charlestonians are still proud. "No gentleman, seh, is raised away from tidewateh," I was told, and not entirely in jest. And I learned the couplet that blue-blooded youngsters say at night:

I thank my God on bended knee
That I'm half Ravenel, half Huger.

Charleston's Rainbow Row faces port where ships vied for rice, indigo, peltry, and naval stores.

The town and province were "esteemed ye most flourishing of any in His Majestys Dominion of America."

"PROSPECT OF CHARLES TOWN," ENGRAVED 1739, STOKES COLLECTION, NEW YORK PUBLIC LIBRARY, AND (ABOVE) THOMAS NEBBIA

JUSTIN LOCKE

Dark waterways of Cypress Gardens irrigated rice fields near Charleston. Now they thread an enchanted, flower-decked forest.

FRANCES PORCHER (ALSO RIGHT)

Mulberry, beside the Cooper River, served as a fort against Indians in Yamasee War, 1715.

Hampton, ancestral Rutledge plantation along the Santee, greeted George Washington in 1791.

Drayton Hall on the Ashley has **KW** (Cornwallis) carved on it by a Hessian soldier.

EDWARDS PARK, NATIONAL GEOGRAPHIC STAFF

Sheldon Church, where colonial gentry worshiped, slumbers in mossy ruin near Beaufort.

B. ANTHONY STEWART, NATIONAL GEOGRAPHIC PHOTOGRAPHER

"King" Roger Moore built Orton in 1725 as manor house for his 8,000-acre grant on the Cape Fear River. Its rice fields now shelter wild birds.

B. ANTHONY STEWART, NATIONAL GEOGRAPHIC PHOTOGRAPHER

Of the great plantations outside Charleston, enriched by rice and later by indigo, my favorite is Middleton Place. Medway is older; Drayton Hall is grander; Magnolia Gardens may be better known. But at Middleton a smiling Gullah woman accepted my dollar, the usual admission fee, then left me to wander in peace along garden paths, relishing the sweep of lawn, the black pond edged by cypresses, the long view across a marsh to the Ashley winking in the distance. They say Henry Middleton, who built the Tudor mansion, owned 50,000 acres, 800 slaves.

Goose Creek Church nearby recalls proud Barbadian planters who put their scutcheons on its stucco walls. A cavalier once rode up with his lady and demanded an immediate wedding. "Have you proper authority?" asked the rector. The gallant leveled a pistol. "Right here!" said he, and married he was—"the only shotgun wedding wheah the groom held the gun," as my raconteur put it.

Charleston's flavor extends north to Georgetown with its fine Episcopal church, and south to Beaufort (pronounced "Bewfort" in South Carolina), a sleepy little

port with nightmarish memories of Spanish, Indian, and Yankee raids. Near it, in a live-oak forest, stand the brick ruins of Sheldon Church, burned in the Revolution, rebuilt, then burned again in the Civil War. Its gaunt columns seem almost to melt into the moss-draped trees. A haunted place, and one that sums up for me the wistfulness of the South.

NORTH CAROLINA, pirates' paradise, developed slowly along Albemarle Sound and the Cape Fear River. Between the two at New Bern, settled by Swiss, Governor William Tryon built his famed palace, "the most beautiful building in colonial America." Now fully restored to the tune of more than $3,000,000, Tryon Palace is a national show place. I toured the magnificent building, meeting place

Tryon Palace housed North Carolina's royal governors, then served as statehouse until the capital moved from New Bern to Raleigh.

Dining at the "Pallace" in 1791, George Washington noted it was "hastening to Ruins." Seven years later a fire razed part of it.

Miss Gertrude S. Carraway directed the restoration, made possible by the generosity of Mrs. Maude Moore Latham. Realistic detail includes an herb garden for the kitchen (left).

for the Assembly as well as Tryon's residence. Gazing at his six-foot-wide bed and the barber's chair where his valet shaved him, I thought about the royal governor who had planted all this luxury in the wilderness.

"He wasn't exactly popular," said my pretty, soft-voiced guide. "But ah reckon you know all about the Battle of Alamance."

I didn't, but soon learned. Back-country folk howled at the cost of the palace, and some organized as "Regulators" to end this and other grievances. Tryon's militia whipped them at Alamance in 1771.

It was part of the conflict between tidewater aristocracy and backwoodsmen, and they were indeed different breeds. The frontiersmen were Scotch-Irish, Germans, and Highlanders who had fought for Bonny Prince Charlie, been beaten by the English at Culloden, and had hung up their two-handed claymore swords in Carolina cabins.

A band of Moravians from Pennsylvania founded Salem in 1766. Now being carefully restored to its prime, Old Salem stands within the city limits of Winston-Salem, its gentle simplicity a comment on the flamboyance of Tryon Palace.

The long frontier, arching southward from Maine along the Appalachians, demanded courage, resourcefulness, an independent spirit from the lean, tough men who held it against foreign and Indian incursions. Yet Georgia, southern anchor of the frontier and last of the original 13 colonies, began as an experiment in pure regimentation. Gen. James Oglethorpe blueprinted a society that would turn English debtors into productive citizens by regulating every detail of their lives.

Off they sailed, their equipment meticulously itemized: "To every Man, A Watch-Coat, A Musket and Bayonet, An Hatchet, An Hammer, An Hand-saw, A

B. ANTHONY STEWART, NATIONAL GEOGRAPHIC PHOTOGRAPHER

Old Salem preserves an Old World air, with its Home Moravian Church (right) and some of its restored buildings furnished in colonial German style. This North Carolina frontier settlement celebrated its 200th birthday in 1966.

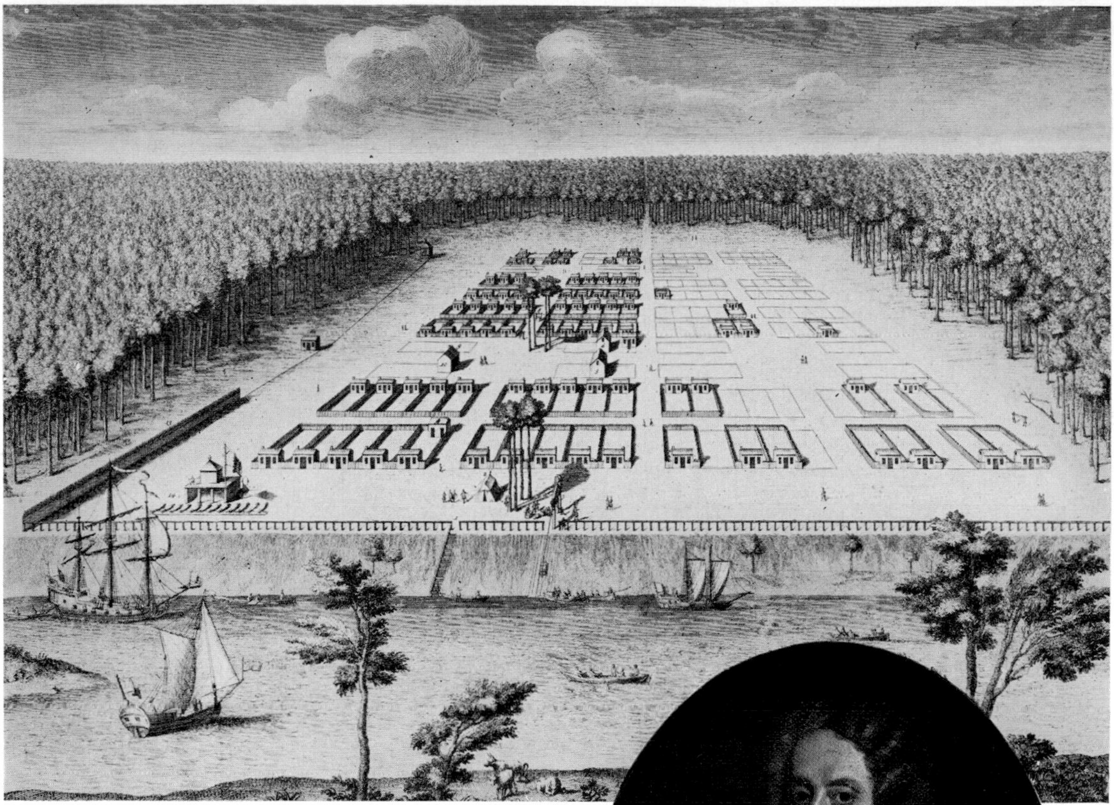

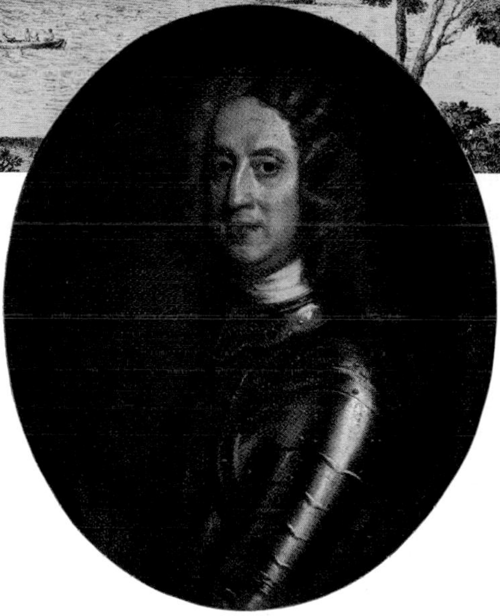

Savannah looked like an army camp in 1734 when Oglethorpe tented beneath the tall pines at center.

shod Shovel or Spade . . . An Iron Pot, and a pair of Pot-hooks, A Frying-pan, And a publick Grindstone to each Ward or Village." etc. Trustees sitting in London limited holdings to 50 acres, forbade selling or willing land, restricted movement, and decreed how many mulberry trees should be planted. Producing silk in the pine barrens was their pet idea.

The regimented colony barely survived. Few of Georgia's many fine homes date from the early years, for wealth could not come until Georgians were free to create it. Noble Jones, one of the first leaseholders, was not granted actual ownership of his Wormsloe estate until 1756.

By the time of the French and Indian War, only some 2,000 whites and 1,000 Negroes dwelt in this tall pine wilderness—little promise of great days ahead when an elegant society would flourish amid the white columns of cotton-rich Georgia. But the colony did serve its strategic purpose by hammering back Spanish ambitions in the War of Jenkins' Ear. And as I drove through Savannah, noting the carefully laid out squares, the gridwork of streets that marched back from the river, I reflected on how much had begun with Oglethorpe and his settlers of 1733.

Wormsloe Plantation, Georgia's oldest, dates from 1733. This house was built later on the original tabby foundations. An old mulberry tree, planted to feed silkworms for the colony's ill-fated industry, yet stands.

HOWELL WALKER, NATIONAL GEOGRAPHIC STAFF. TOP: STOKES COLLECTION, NEW YORK PUBLIC LIBRARY. PAINTING OF JAMES E. OGLETHORPE, OGLETHORPE UNIVERSITY

THE FRENCH AND INDIAN WAR

THREE HUNDRED AXMEN hewed a path. Behind toiled a train of pack horses, wagons, cattle, and cannon. On the flanks red-coated regulars and colonials in blue filed past waterfalls and crags. They forded the Monongahela and entered a ravine. This July afternoon in 1755 Gen. Edward Braddock's army was within seven miles of its objective: French Fort Duquesne, where Pittsburgh now stands.

Suddenly muskets roared under the forest's dense arches. Redcoats dropped. Shouting "God save the King!" the rest volleyed at an unseen enemy. Back came

Strongholds guarding passes and valleys were focal points of conflict along the frontier. Those marked by symbol remain. But sudden battles raged through the wilderness like summer storms. Masters of hit-and-run tactics, Rogers' Rangers, in buckskin and Lincoln green, here skirmish on snowshoes near Lake George.

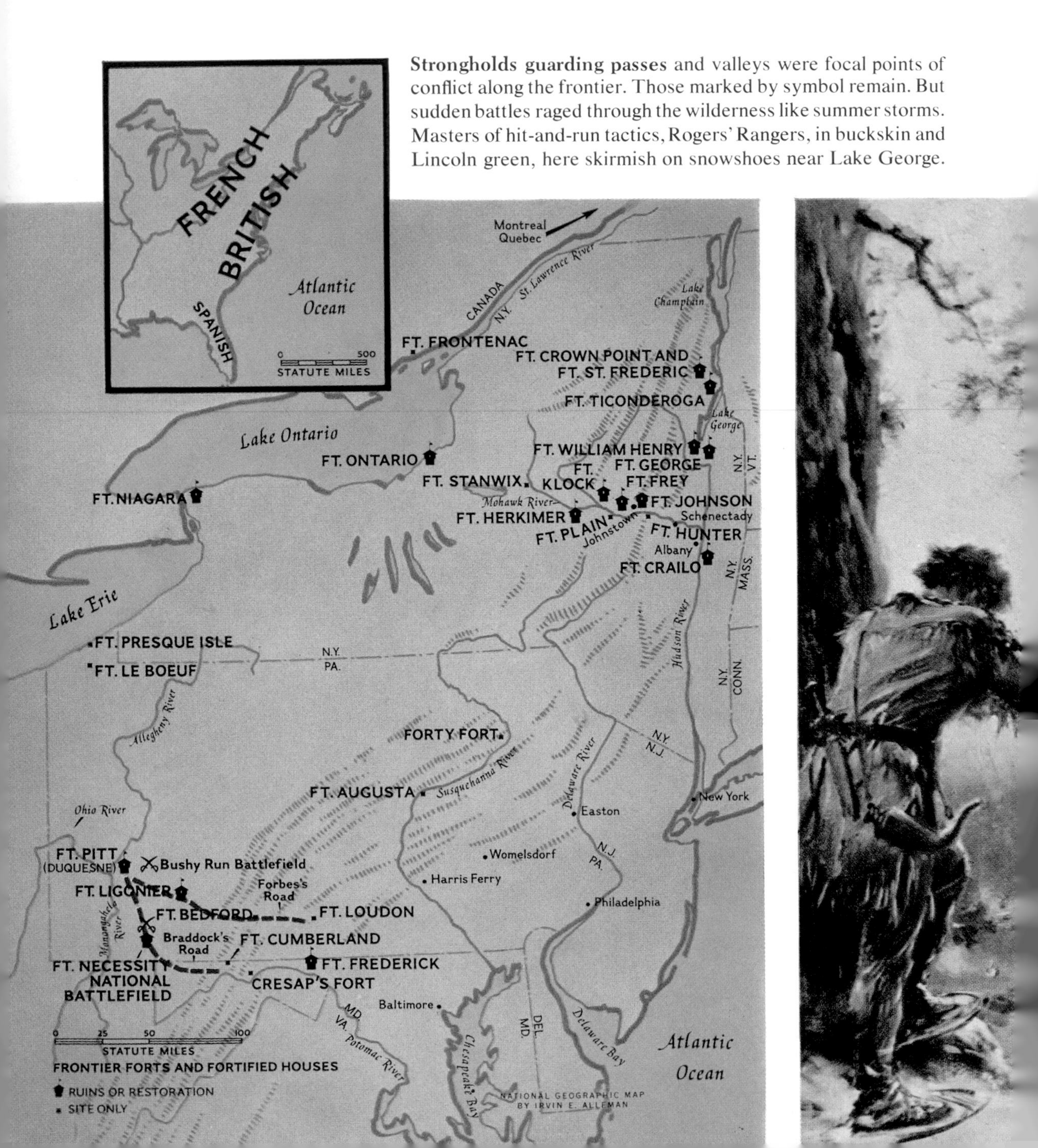

a withering fire. The British broke ranks, huddled, blindly shot into the woods, the air, even into each other. Four horses crumpled under Braddock; finally a ball smashed him down. An aide, young George Washington, lost two horses; bullets shredded his clothes. After three hours of slaughter, with 900 dead or wounded, the British fled, carting off their dying general. Britain's first campaign in the French and Indian War ended in disaster.

For half a century hostilities had smoldered on British America's 1,000-mile frontier. During Queen Anne's War French and Indians sacked Deerfield, and the British captured Acadia (Nova Scotia). In 1745 merchant William Pepperrell led 4,000 untrained New England farmers and shopkeepers against Louisbourg, mighty French naval base guarding the Gulf of St. Lawrence. Firing 9,000 cannon balls during their unorthodox siege, "Pepperrell's Yokels" amazed the world by bringing the proud defenders "to Termcs for us to enter ye Sitty."

France turned to the Ohio Valley, basing its claims on the explorations of La Salle. England countered with Cabot's discoveries and the Virginia Company's jurisdiction "west and northwest to the South Sea." By the mid-1700's Pennsyl-

"THE BATTLE OF ROGERS' ROCK" BY J. L. G. FERRIS, REPRODUCED BY SPECIAL PERMISSION OF THE GLENS FALLS INSURANCE COMPANY

vanians were spilling over the Alleghenies, and Virginians were staking out vast holdings. France wooed the Indians and built stockades.

George Washington, a 21-year-old militia officer, was sent in 1753 to talk the French at Fort Le Boeuf into "peaceable departure." He failed. The next May his small force of Virginians surprised 33 Frenchmen encamped in a glen in western Pennsylvania. The attack plunged Britain and France into a struggle that spread round the world and decided the fate of North America.

Lake George, Lake Champlain, and the Ohio River were gateways to French Canada and the Old Northwest. In 1755 the British tried to force these corridors. The assault on Fort Duquesne died with Braddock. But in New York, trader William Johnson led 3,900 militiamen and Indians to defeat the French at Lake George.

Meanwhile, France's Indian allies raided all along the frontier, scalping within 50 miles of Philadelphia. Panic seized the colonies.

Fearful of an uprising of the French-

From lonely outposts cannon belched death in the

Baptism of fire on the frontier readied Washington for his later role

"I have heard the bullets whistle," wrote 22-year-old Colonel Washington; "there is something charming in the sound." He heard that whistle at Jumonville Glen, at Fort Necessity, and with Braddock; again when defending Virginia's long frontier, 1755-7, and as vanguard commander in Forbes's march on Fort Duquesne.

A powerful six-footer, Washington excelled at wrestling and horsebreaking, and quoted Shakespeare and Addison. By 1772, when Peale painted him in the uniform of a Virginia colonel (far right), he was chafing at "our lordly masters" in England.

A fateful volley in this Pennsylvania glen ignited a global war. Washington's surprise attack killed Coulon de Jumonville and nine French soldiers.

DAVID S. BOYER AND (BELOW FROM LEFT) MERLE SEVERY AND RALPH GRAY, ALL NATIONAL GEOGRAPHIC STAFF

seesaw struggle for a continent. This stockade near Fort Ticonderoga overlooks Lake Champlain.

Expecting reprisal, Washington erected a "small, palisado'd fort" in Great Meadows. Here he surrendered—the only time. Route 40 travelers visit reconstructed Fort Necessity.

CHARLES WILLSON PEALE, WASHINGTON AND LEE UNIVERSITY

Joseph Brant fought the French. Still loyal to England in the Revolution, the Mohawk chief ravaged his home valley. His sister Molly was the wife of Sir William Johnson, Britain's Superintendent of Indian Affairs.

Catholic Acadians, the British herded more than 6,000 onto transports and dispersed them among the colonies and in Europe. Some struggled on foot to Louisiana, where today their name is shortened to "Cajun." Longfellow's *Evangeline* portrays the sufferings of these peaceful farm folk.

In 1756 General Montcalm took Fort Ontario for France, and a year later destroyed Fort William Henry on Lake George. An aroused England made fiery William Pitt minister of war, and in 1758 he sent General Abercromby with 15,000 men against Montcalm at Ticonderoga. For four hours Abercromby hurled his men against the outnumbered French. The defenders cut the redcoats down, regiment after regiment. Nearly 2,000 fell and the English retreated. Abercromby survived the lesson that Braddock died learning: Parade ground tactics of Blenheim and Ramillies invited disaster in the North American wilderness.

Sir William lived in baronial style at Johnson Hall, now a museum in Johnstown, New York. In councils like

But Britain's might pressed upon New France. Jeffrey Amherst and James Wolfe crumbled the walls of Louisbourg, which England had restored to France. A force, largely colonials, took Fort Frontenac on Lake Ontario, severing French lines to the Ohio Valley. John Forbes hacked through the wilderness, and the French evacuated Fort Duquesne before him. He renamed it Pitts-Bourgh after Pitt. The French lost Niagara, and blew up forts at Ticonderoga and Crown Point.

For weeks Wolfe had besieged Quebec. Nature defended it with cliffs, France with the matchless Montcalm. As winter neared, threatening to seal the St. Lawrence, Wolfe resolved on a desperate gamble. Moving stealthily in boats past the French batteries under cover of night, his 5,000 men scaled a precipice to the heights outside the city. When dawn of September 13, 1759, revealed the English drawn up on the Plains of Abraham, Montcalm came out to fight. The battle claimed both generals, but Britain routed France and won the continent.

With French power crushed, the colonies felt less need for the motherland. But England now enforced neglected trade laws. Chief Pontiac bathed the frontier in blood and England drew a Proclamation Line closing trans-Allegheny lands to settlement. Colonials ignored it—except as a grievance. To pay for redcoats billeted in America, Parliament voted taxes. Colonials evaded them when possible. But the British yoke felt heavier and heavier. THOMAS Y. CANBY

this he kept the restive Iroquois nations allied with Britain. The blockhouse at right stands today.

PAINTINGS BY E. L. HENRY, KNOX GELATINE COMPANY, AND (TOP LEFT) WILLIAM VON MOLL BERCZY, THE NATIONAL GALLERY OF CANADA, OTTAWA

A.M.Willard
1876

DONALD BARR CHIDSEY

The Revolution

GEORGE THOMPSON always had taken the militia for granted. Everybody around Pomfret did. "The discipline" was simply one of the chores, without much urgency to it. Indians? Not in northeastern Connecticut in 1775. The French war was over and the frontier far away. Pirates? There hadn't been a pirate in this part of the world since they hanged Tom Tew down in Providence almost a hundred years ago. Anyway, Pomfret was a good fifty miles from the sea. Public order? Well, these were peaceable farm folks. A rough-and-tumble grudge fight behind somebody's barn now and then was about as far as they ever went. They had no habitual criminals and no vagrants.

Yet four times a year George Thompson took his musket down, checked his lead and powder, knapped his flint, and walked two miles to the village to join his company. He'd been doing it since he joined at 16, and it brought none of the thrill of soldiering. After all, this wasn't an honor, only an obligation. It was part of life, like huskings and raisings, like praying, bundling, and soapmaking.

The groups on the village green, wheeling and stamping as men shouted commands, attracted scant attention. The men wore no uniforms, no insignia of rank, and carried the same muskets, of every conceivable size, weight, and caliber, that

"SPIRIT OF '76," THE FAMOUS PAINTING BY ARCHIBALD M. WILLARD, HANGS IN ABBOT HALL IN MARBLEHEAD, MASSACHUSETTS

they used for rabbit hunting. The officers wore no swords for they might easily be voted back into the ranks. They were not superior beings but men you saw every time you went to town and often enough betweentimes. They called the roll, then inspected the guns – empty, of course, since nobody but a beefwit would appear at drill with a loaded gun that might go off when you slammed the butt to earth.

Lining up, the men heard the same old speech from the officer in charge. Then they marched for a few hours, depending on the weather. The local minister preached to them. Finally came the salute, the best part of the day.

They loaded their muskets, each as he wished, measuring out powder and ramming home wadding instead of balls. They put in real flints, taking out the chunks of wood called "nutmegs" that they used in practice. The discipline called for them to snap their strikers at an imaginary foe, pulling the "trickers" more or less in unison. It was the ambition of their officers to have them one day fire a perfect *feu de joie,* very hard to do, even for regular troops.

It meant facing one another in double rank, discharging their guns one at a time into the air, from right to left along the front line, then from left to right along the second line. They never did succeed in this fancy French salute. Whether from nervousness, misunderstanding, or just plain high spirits, somebody would shoot out of turn; and then all those who remained loaded would blast away at the sky with a terrific racket, give a cheer, and make for the tavern. The discipline always ended that way, with them sitting over applejack or blackstrap while they cleaned their guns, joshing, and discussing the latest news. They might stay as late as nine o'clock at night. No, it was hard to take the militia seriously. At least it had been hard until a little while ago. Now everything was changed. . . .

STAMP ACT PROTEST IN THE PENNSYLVANIA "JOURNAL," 1765. EMMET COLLECTION, NEW YORK PUBLIC LIBRARY

George tugged the ox to a halt and stretched, mopping his face. This was only April, but the winter had been the mildest in memory and it had been followed by an early and very warm spring. To George Thompson, toiling behind a plow, it felt like the middle of July.

A couple of hundred yards away, on the other side of a stone fence, George's neighbor had also paused in his plowing, though not for the same reason. Old Put must have been nigh on to 60, but he seldom took any kind of rest; he stopped now only because a horseman on the road was signaling to him. Old Put dropped the reins and strode briskly over that way. George watched him admiringly. Now there was a man who *did* take the militia seriously; wore a sword too. Israel Putnam was a colonel, and more than that a hero of the French and Indian War. He was a myth, a man everyone told stories about.

George knew him as a kind and generous neighbor, yet sometimes avoided him. For Old Put, almost triple George's age, made George feel tired with all that furious activity. He was certainly a hard man to keep up with, was Old Put.

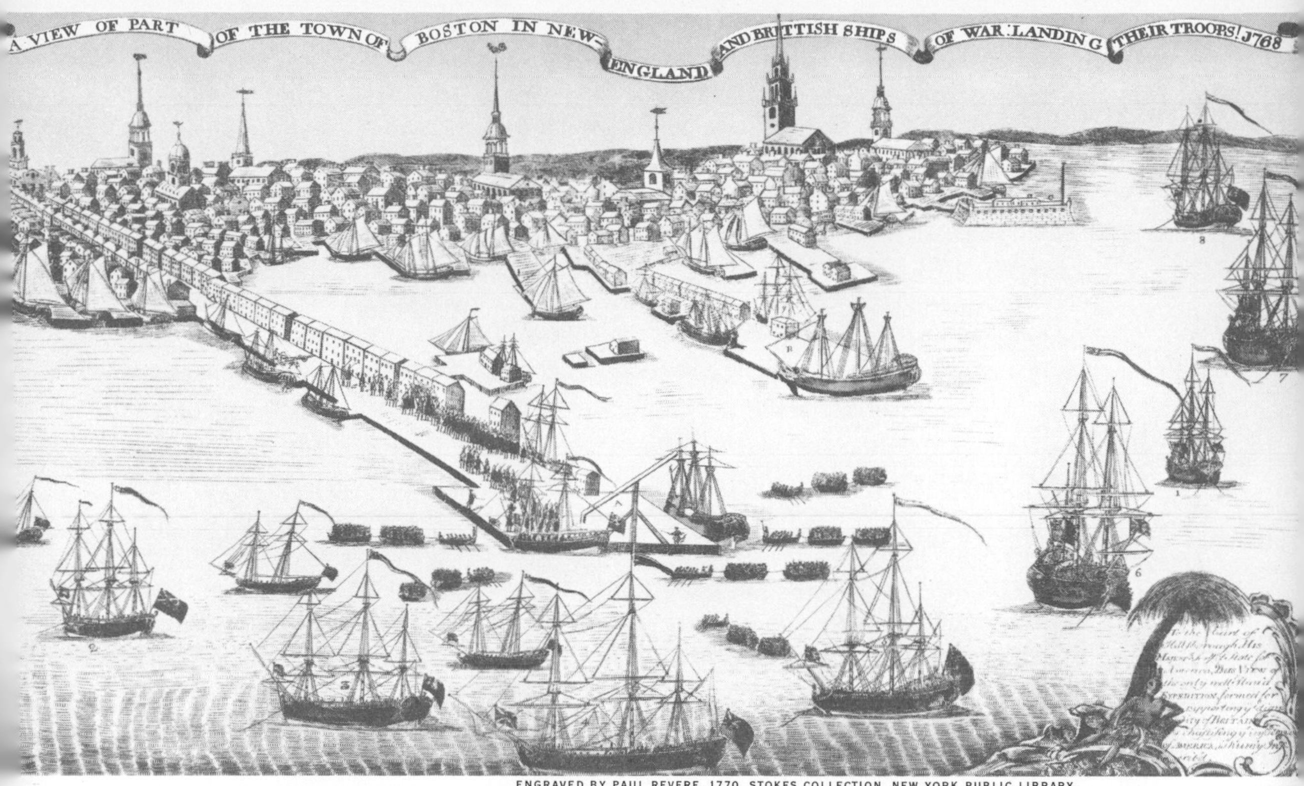

ENGRAVED BY PAUL REVERE, 1770. STOKES COLLECTION, NEW YORK PUBLIC LIBRARY

Unwelcome soldiers march up Long Wharf "with insolent Parade" toward the Old State House. Third cupola from left is Faneuil Hall. Central spire belongs to Old North Church.

The horseman continued south, and George wondered whether he had brought any news from Boston. George hoped so. All up and down the land men were waiting breathlessly for news from Boston.

Death and taxes, they say, we always have with us, and most people tend to think death the more interesting. Not so George Thompson. He knew all about death, or thought he did, for his minister made it clear that he was predestined for heaven or hell. He had nothing to say about it. With taxes it was different. Taxes were a touchy subject, and George liked to think he had a little control over them.

VERY LITTLE in the house that George Thompson had inherited from his father and grandfather was "boughten." The family had made most of the furniture. The womenfolk had hooked rugs and sewn quilts. Even the cedar shakes had been hand-hewn, as had the timbers, mostly oak and ash. Only the glass in the windows and here and there a few strategically placed nails had been paid for with cash. Virtually every piece of clothing that George and his mother and brother wore was homespun or home-knitted.

George seldom handled money; and the same was true of thousands of his countrymen. But the times when they did were almighty meaningful to them. George had been saving for years to buy a brass knocker to spruce up the front door. He didn't want to go to Hartford with the coins only to learn that the price had gone up because of some newfangled tax imposed from 3,000 miles away. Not that the British were taxing door knockers, yet. But there was no telling where they would stop.

George was 20, and he could remember the squawk that had gone up—quite properly, he believed—about the Stamp Tax. Well, the British had backed down and repealed the Stamp Tax. They had taken off other more recent taxes too, the ones they called the Townshend duties after the cabinet minister Charles Townshend. These had been removed from paint, glass, wine—everything but tea.

But why had the British kept a tax on tea? Wasn't that just a foot in the door?

George himself couldn't afford tea. Spring water, milk from his own cows, now and then a cup of beverage brewed from raspberry leaves, or coffee made out of parched rye ground up with acorns—these he drank instead. But the principle of the thing disturbed him. A tax on tea today meant taxes tomorrow on goods that George did have to buy, things like salt and potash. Also, assuming that he could ever put enough aside to marry Deliverance Harris, she'd probably like tea.

ENGLAND INSISTED that the colonies needed soldiers for their protection, and that they ought to pay for those soldiers. To George Thompson this just didn't make sense. Every man in America had a gun—and knew how to use it. Sure, the militia weren't as smart as the redcoats; but maybe over here they might be more effective. Now that the French had been whipped, there were only the Indians to think of, far to the west along the frontier. What good would those glittering redcoats be against Indians, who could heave their tomahawks to cleave heads while never making a sound or showing an inch of skin? A Mohawk could not tell a redan from a redoubt—George wasn't sure *he* could either—but the Mohawk had the trick of keeping under cover, and he would be fighting on his own ground.

The redcoats weren't needed. And they were not ingratiating. Underpaid, brutally treated, they took their fun where they found it, and they were likely to find it in the wrong place. They were hardly the cream of the nation they had been sent to represent. Many had been dragged from jails and given a choice of joining the army or having their necks stretched. You could feel sorry for the poor devils but you didn't want them living next door. And you certainly did not want to depend on them to protect your home. You could take care of that yourself.

The lobsterbacks, as almost everybody called them, had an unpleasant habit of assembling outside churches and meetinghouses on the Sabbath while service was going on, and roaring bawdy songs. They were particularly fond of a tune called "Yankee Doodle." Nobody knew where it came from—probably Ireland—and nobody was quite certain why any American should be called a Yankee. But "doodle," of course, was a common name for a clown, a stupid lout from the country, a clod—just such a person, George reflected wryly, as himself.

It worked both ways, this rasping of nerves. The lobsterbacks didn't cotton to the Yankees either. Especially they disliked the people of Boston, who jeered and sneered at them and hit them with sticks and snowballs, so that one evening a few years back a British detachment, taunted too hard, got out of hand and opened fire.

This was what everybody called the Massacre, a mighty big name, it seemed to George, to pin on such a brawl; but there was no doubt that it had brought about a heap of hard feeling, even way out here as far as Pomfret, Connecticut.

And then there came the Tea Party. When three ships loaded with tea, the *Dartmouth, Eleanor,* and *Beaver,* wouldn't turn back, Committee of Safety members and other patriots dressed like Indians went aboard and dumped the whole cargo – more than 300 chests – into Boston Bay. This had seemed mighty funny to the

PAUL REVERE'S DEPICTION OF THE BOSTON MASSACRE FANNED THE FLAMES OF REVOLUTION. AMERICAN ANTIQUARIAN SOCIETY

Yankees, just at first. The tea was worth about £1,000, and that ought to teach the British a lesson. It didn't. Instead of backing down again, the British got tougher. Instead of recalling the redcoats, they sent more. They passed a series of pesky restrictions on colonial trade known as the Intolerable Acts, and they denied all port privileges to Boston until the tea was paid for, thus as good as besieging the city. Many of Boston's 16,000 citizens might have starved had it not been for the generosity of neighbors—and the activity of smugglers.

PATRIOT TEMPERS BOIL IN THE BOSTON TEA PARTY ON THE NIGHT OF DECEMBER 16, 1773.
CULVER SERVICE

That was why everyone waited so eagerly for news from Boston. All that was needed now was a spark. It wouldn't even have to be a very big spark to set all New England afire.

George Thompson sighed. He flexed his shoulders and returned to his plow. The horseman, he noted, had galloped away, dust standing thick behind him on the New London road. Old Put was returning to his furrow at a trot.

That might have warned George that something was wrong. No man, not even Israel Putnam, goes back to work with the exuberance of a schoolboy getting out of school. But George was so used to seeing Old Put giving forth energy in all directions that he scarcely noticed now and didn't even wave a hand.

One good sign, George reflected as he started the ox forward again and bent over the handles, was that the other colonies were getting interested in this trouble in New England. According to what he had heard, Massachusetts had made old Artemas Ward commander in chief of her militia "for the defense of this and other American colonies." It wasn't just Massachusetts. They were all writing back and forth to one another—men like John Adams in Boston, and John Dickinson the Quaker and Dr. Franklin the philosopher in Philadelphia. And in Maryland Charles Carroll, a Catholic, the richest man in America, was keeping in touch, making plans.

Meanwhile the Second Continental Congress in Philadelphia stayed in session, ready for any emergency.

It was good to know that you weren't alone, George pondered. Why, even standoffish Virginia, where they had no use for the "wise men of the East" and didn't mind saying so—even Virginia was involved in this business. Hadn't the House of Burgesses only the other day passed a resolution declaring that "an attack made on one of our sister colonies to compel submission to arbitrary taxes is an attack made on all British America"? George Thompson was no lawyer, but you didn't have to be a lawyer to understand that. All you had to know was English.

Virginia, a colony that until just lately had seemed farther away than England itself, was the home of Patrick Henry, who was doing plenty of strong talking down there. Even George, tucked away in Pomfret, had heard from dispatch riders about Henry, the man who said, "I am not a Virginian, but an American," and "The battle, sir, is not to the strong alone; it is to the vigilant, the active, the brave." Patrick Henry had also spoken some words at St. John's Church in Richmond that would live for a long time: "I know not what course others may take, but as for me *give me liberty or give me death!*"

Patrick Henry must be mighty wonderful, George reckoned. But even so he could hardly be as eloquent as Sam Adams of Boston. Him George had heard.

ALONG WITH HIS WEALTHY FRIEND John Hancock and handsome Dr. Joseph Warren, Samuel Adams put into words all the grinding, blistering complaints that the colonists had bottled up against the king's ministers and Parliament.

Blasting the Intolerable Acts, Adams wrote: "For flagrant injustice and barbarity, one might search in vain among the archives of Constantinople to find a match for it. But what else could have been expected from a Parliament too long under the dictates and controul of an Administration which seems to be totally lost to all sense of feeling of morality, and governed by passion, cruelty, and revenge?"

Using funds raised by friends—for he had little of his own—Adams had gone all around New England making speeches before Sons of Liberty groups, even ones as small as that in Pomfret, where the Sons of Liberty and the militia were practically the same thing. The first sight of Sam Adams caused a man to feel his heart settle lumpishly into disappointment: twitchy mouth, fidgety hands, untidy clothes, eyes that watered all the while. But as soon as he started to speak you forgot that. It was like a view from a high hill. It was like listening to music.

No wonder people got stirred up and sometimes seemed to be spoiling for a fight, especially the Sons of Liberty. Over in Farmington a year before they had posted handbills informing the town that they would burn "at six o'clock this evening, in honour to the immortal goddess of Liberty, the late infamous Act of the British Parliament for farther distressing the American Colonies; the place of execution will be the public parade, where all Sons of Liberty are desired to attend."

Nowadays the hard feelings sometimes went beyond just touching off a bonfire, raising a liberty pole, and declaiming "That we scorn the chains of slavery; we despise every attempt to rivet them upon us; we are the sons of freedom and re-

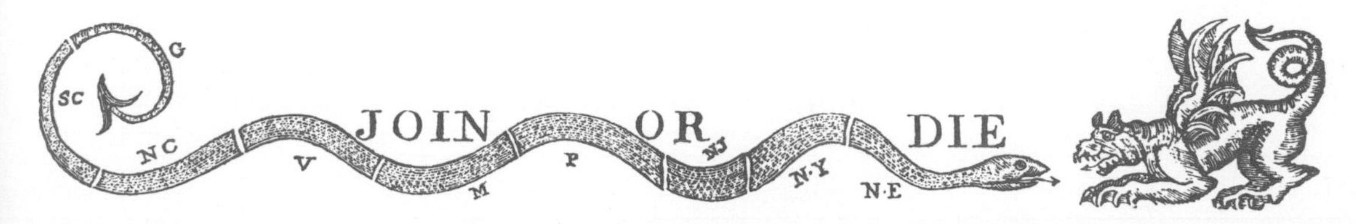

BORROWING THE SEGMENTED SNAKE IDEA FROM BENJAMIN FRANKLIN, PAUL REVERE ENGRAVED THIS SYMBOL OF THE COLONIES CONFRONTING THE BRITISH GRIFFIN FOR THE "MASSACHUSETTS SPY" IN 1774. AMERICAN ANTIQUARIAN SOCIETY

solved that, till time shall be no more, godlike virtue shall blazon our hemisphere." George had heard of Tories being treated to tar and feathers.

He had also heard about the time last fall when the Boston redcoats marched to Charlestown to seize some gunpowder. Within a couple of days thousands of minutemen had come swarming in on Boston from all the towns around, then had drifted off. Tension was so high in Boston that every drunken brawl, indeed every jeering word shouted at a soldier by a street gamin, might bring on bloodshed.

PHEW! PLOWING LAND LIKE THIS was hard work, and soon George was sweating again. He stopped to wipe his neck. Whatever made him glance in the direction of the Putnam farm he was never to know. But when he did he saw only the plow standing alone in its half-completed furrow. Old Put was gone and so was his horse.

While George stared, wondering if there was anything he should do, skinny, stern Hannah, Old Put's cousin, came out of the house and scaled the fence as lightly as any lad. In a moment she was shouting to him. "Israel says that the man came from Boston and there's trouble."

George Thompson looked at her, waiting. The sun felt very hot.

"Big trouble. Killing men right and left. Out in the country too. Place they call Lexington."

George lifted the reins off his neck.

"Israel took the horse so's to get there first," Hannah went on. "He'll have everything laid out."

"I bet he will," said George Thompson.

He left both his plow and his ox standing in the unfinished row. Hezekiah could finish the plowing. He was big enough now.

George met Hez on the road as he neared the house.

"Where're *you* going?" a suddenly frightened younger brother asked.

"To war."

He did not hurry, neither did he hesitate. It had not occurred to him that he might hesitate. He told his mother. She put up something to eat on the way.

"Deliverance will have to wait a mite, I guess," George said.

"She can," his mother replied. "She's used to it by this time."

George took his musket down from over the fireplace, checked the priming, the contents of the horn, and the knapping box where he kept his flints. He pulled his hunting shirt over his head and slipped a copy of the Book into a pocket. He kissed his mother and patted Hezekiah on the head. Then he was gone, heading north toward Boston.

He was not alone. All over New England other George Thompsons were doing the same thing, thousands of them; and within a few days thousands more up and down the Atlantic seaboard would be setting forth on a long road.

Looking at them, a proper general might have said that they weren't ready for war. But generals don't know everything. The waiting was over at last and the decision had been made. In their own hearts the young men thought they were ready. Maybe that is what counted.

Paul Revere's BOSTON

MINUTEMEN looked to Boston for news of a fight, and well they might. There, in British eyes, even the "pulpits were converted into Gutters of Sedition." Today visitors can tread in the footsteps of men who made a revolution.

On State Street, once "besmeared with guiltless Gore," a circle of cobblestones marks where the redcoats shot down rowdies and patriots who taunted: "Bloody backs . . . lo-obsters . . . lo-obsters, who'll buy?"

Walk down Washington Street to Old South Meeting House. Inside, candlelight once flickered on a tense, waiting crowd. Would the British send the tea back? No. And so they marched to Griffin's wharf. Some, "cloathed in blankets," armed with hatchets, and with faces painted copper, broke open the chests of tea and tossed them from the ships.

Faneuil Hall still has market stalls, as it did on the day rumpled Sam Adams rose in the meeting room upstairs to read England's

Paul Revere gallops on in bronze, just as he does in Longfellow's beloved lines, "Listen my children, and you shall hear. . . ." In the belfry of Old North Church, behind, lanterns signaled the British route: "One, if by land, and two, if by sea." That night "the fate of a nation" rode with Revere, "and the spark struck out by that steed, in his flight, kindled the land into flame with its heat."

KATHLEEN REVIS JUDGE

answer to the tea party: "Be it enacted, that no vessel . . . no goods, wares . . . be transported, carried, or discharged or brought from any other country."

From the modest wooden house that stands on North Square, a silversmith often strode at night to meet friends at the Green Dragon Tavern. "I was one of upwards of thirty, chiefly mechanics, who formed ourselves into a committee," wrote Paul Revere. "We took turns, two and two, to watch the soldiers by patrolling the streets." Revere often galloped into the countryside, bearing patriot messages. On the night of April 18, 1775, "booted and spurred," he prepared to ride into history.

Lion and unicorn atop the Old State House recall royal rule. Here in 1761 James Otis argued against the Writs of Assistance—special search warrants. From its balcony the Declaration of Independence was announced. Restored building is now a museum.

Faneuil Hall, called the "Cradle of American Liberty" by Daniel Webster, provided a forum for Samuel Adams, John Hancock, and other patriots protesting British taxes. A combination public market and meeting place, the hall was the gift in 1742 of Peter Faneuil, "topmost merchant in all the town."

Paul Revere House (right), Boston's oldest, had stood for a century when Revere moved in about 1770.

KATHLEEN REVIS JUDGE AND (ABOVE) THOMAS NEBBIA
LEFT: B. ANTHONY STEWART, NATIONAL GEOGRAPHIC PHOTOGRAPHER

PAINTING BY CHARLES HOFFBAUER; NEW ENGLAND MUTUAL LIFE INSURANCE COMPANY

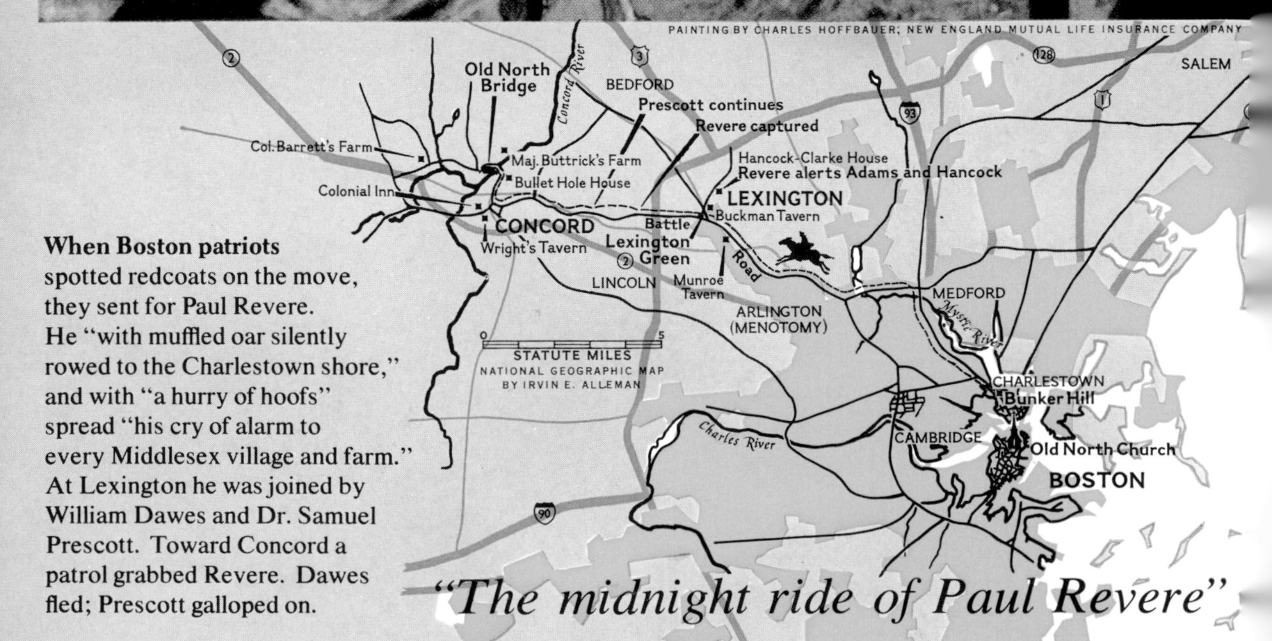

When Boston patriots spotted redcoats on the move, they sent for Paul Revere. He "with muffled oar silently rowed to the Charlestown shore," and with "a hurry of hoofs" spread "his cry of alarm to every Middlesex village and farm." At Lexington he was joined by William Dawes and Dr. Samuel Prescott. Toward Concord a patrol grabbed Revere. Dawes fled; Prescott galloped on.

"The midnight ride of Paul Revere"

The Boston, the shorelines, and roads of Revere's time are superimposed in black line on today's map. Present urban areas, shaded in yellow, contrast strikingly with the little city, confined to its peninsula, that he knew.

LEXINGTON AND CONCORD

"Let it begin here"

LIEUTENANT JOHN BARKER of the King's Own regiment pulled on his scarlet coat, brushed a fleck of soot from its gold braid, then buckled on the broad white strap that held his sword. Stepping out onto the dark Boston street the night of April 18, 1775, he strode toward the common. There 700 picked troops were assembling. Tall, big-chested grenadiers had been plucked from each of Gen. Thomas Gage's regiments. Now they leaned on their muskets, whispering. Beside them stood the wiry, swift-footed men of the light infantry companies. This time, Barker thought, they'd put up with no impudence from the Yankee doodles.

As the column moved silently toward the bay where longboats waited, Barker remembered the abuses these men had taken from the Bostonians. He recalled how Salem citizens had raised their drawbridge and defied Colonel Leslie when he marched to collect their arms. Then there was the day thousands of Yankees had gathered outside Boston, armed and angry, because redcoats had seized some powder and rumors spread of bloodshed. Well, let them stand up this time. General Gage had ordered this strong force to grab the arms stored at Concord, and perhaps to snatch Sam Adams and John Hancock from their refuge at Lexington.

Sailors pulling on muffled oars carried the troops across to Cambridge marsh. They stepped out into knee-deep water, sloshed to solid ground, then stood in the chill wind two hours waiting for rations. Crossing a stream, the column gained the road and swung past Menotomy toward Lexington. Fields and woodland seemed to glow dimly in the moonlight. Now and then Barker heard the clang of a distant bell, the signaling shot of a far-off musket. The Yankees are on to the game, he thought. A horse patrol clattered up to report that minutemen were gathering at Lexington. Barker wondered if they aimed to fight. Probably not. Everyone knew they were "the most absolute cowards on the face of the earth."

ONE OF THE MINUTEMEN at Lexington, Sylvanus Wood, had heard the town bell ring and "immediately arose, took my gun, and . . . went in haste." Capt. John Parker had called out his militia company at midnight after Paul Revere galloped in to warn Adams and Hancock. Since then, some of the men had drifted home. Others had adjourned to Buckman Tavern, to wait before the fire sipping rum. As dawn brightened the edge of the sky, Wood, standing near Captain Parker, saw a scout ride up with a message. The drummer beat a call to arms, and everyone came running. They formed two lines on the green, about 70 men.

Through rising morning mist, Wood saw a bright red column come up the road, then huzzah and form a line of battle on the green. An officer spurred to the front and shouted, "Ye villains, ye Rebels, disperse!" Parker sought to steady his men; a witness said he shouted, "Stand your ground. Don't fire unless fired upon. *But if they mean to have a war, let it begin here.*" There was a shot, then a redcoat volley whizzed over the line of minutemen. Who fired the first shot, no one really knows. But Wood heard Parker order his men to disperse, "every man to take

KATHLEEN REVIS JUDGE AND (RIGHT) DAVID S. BOYER, NATIONAL GEOGRAPHIC STAFF

On Lexington Green this boulder marks where minutemen faced the British regulars. Buckman Tavern nearby still bears the scars of musket balls.

care of himself." As the minutemen fled over a stone wall, the British volleyed again. A few Yankees fired back; Jonas Parker, knocked to his knees by a ball, was trying to reload as a redcoat pierced him with bayonet. Jonathan Harrington, blood streaming from his side, crawled toward his house across the road. He died as his wife ran to him.

Maj. John Pitcairn, commanding the light infantry companies, tried to check his men, but they "were so wild they could hear no orders." Seventeen minutemen were cut down before the redcoats returned to ranks and, with one man wounded, marched off toward Concord.

Men at Concord had been busy for hours; muskets, balls, and powder had been hauled from storerooms and hidden in the woods. At Col. James Barrett's farm, a plow had cut deep furrows, and cannon were laid in them and covered.

When news of Lexington reached the men milling around Wright's Tavern, they trudged out to meet the British on the road. Then, as a minuteman recalled, "we was orded to the about face and march^{d} before them with our Droms and fifes agoing and also the B[ritish] we had grand musick."

The minutemen marched back through town, swung right, crossed the North Bridge, and climbed a ridge. There they stopped.

The redcoats tramped into the village. Grenadiers tossed flour and musket balls into the millpond, then set fire to entrenching tools they found in the town house. British light infantry made for the North Bridge; four companies crossed it and marched toward Barrett's farm, three stood guard. The Concord men, joined by companies from Bedford, Acton, and Lincoln, saw the smoke rise. One asked Colonel Barrett, "Will you let them burn the town?"

Barrett said no. The minutemen marched down toward the bridge. Redcoats faced them across the river; a few began pulling up the bridge planks.

A minuteman corporal remembered the next moments. "Mager Buttrick said if we wair all of his mind he would Drive them away from the Bridge. they should not tair that up. we all said we wood go. We . . . had stricked order not to fire till they fir[d] firs . . . Capt Davis had got I Be leave, within 15 Rods of the B[ritish] when they fir[d] . . . . their balls whisled well."

Minutemen shot back. When the smoke cleared two Americans and two redcoats were dead. A third redcoat lay dying. The British retreated to town and started back toward Boston.

By then minutemen were striding toward Concord from Chelmsford, Framingham, Sudbury, Stow, and other towns. They gathered at the Meriam house and watched the British march by. One redcoat platoon wheeled and fired. The minutemen replied, then raced for a woods a mile down the road. As the British crowded past, the woods exploded with flashes and smoke: "a grait many Lay dead, and the Road was bloddy."

It was like that all the way to Lexington. Lieutenant Barker of

Irises bloom along the Concord River where blood once flowed. At North Bridge (rebuilt in background) Maj. John Buttrick shouted, "Fire, fellow soldiers, for God's sake, fire!" His men drove back the redcoats.

the King's Own would never forget. "The Rebels . . . hardly ever fired but under cover of a Stone wall, from behind a tree, or out of a house; and the moment they had fired they lay down out of sight until they had loaded again."

At Lexington the battered column stumbled into an 800-man relief brigade under Lord Percy. But the rebels were reinforced too. From Watertown, Roxbury, Needham, Danvers, and Dedham came farmers and blacksmiths, storekeepers and artisans, all angered by the British raid. They shot, faded away, then returned to fire into the red mass again. Barker watched his men become "so enraged at suffering from an unseen enemy that they forced open many of the houses from which the fire proceeded and put to death all those found in them."

An incredible day! In 20 hours Barker and his men had marched 35 miles, and fought fully half the distance. Seventy-three red-coated bodies marked the road from Concord; 26 men were missing, 174 wounded. A thought nagged the lieutenant; Lord Percy would put it into words. "I never believed, I confess, that they wd have attacked the King's troops, or have had the perseverance I found in them."

Beside one of the hundreds of winking campfires that faced Boston, a man scribbled a note to his wife: "'Tis uncertain when we shall return . . . let us be patient & remember that it is ye hand of God."

Weeks dragged on and the fires still glowed. "We are besieged this moment with 10 or 15000 men," wrote a humiliated Tory that spring of 1775. But Gage and two new generals, William Howe and Henry Clinton, eyed Dorchester and Charlestown Heights, flanking the rebel line. Seize those hills and the farmers would flee, their rebellion crushed. Plans were laid: On June 18, redcoats would march again. JOHN J. PUTMAN

"The rude bridge that arched the flood"

At Concord, visitors tread the span that echoed "the shot heard round the world." The Minuteman, immortalized in bronze by Daniel Chester French where patriots opened fire, inspired Ralph Waldo Emerson's Concord Hymn:

Their flag to April's breeze unfurled,
Here once the embattled farmers stood. . . .

Bullet Hole House, Colonial Inn, Wright's Tavern survive from that fateful day.

The colonials harried the British all the way back to Boston from behind stone walls that still line Battle Road, now being restored by the National Park Service. Each April 19 groups such as the Sudbury Ancient Fyfe and Drum Company retrace the footsteps of their forebears, sometimes through a late spring snow.

B. ANTHONY STEWART, NATIONAL GEOGRAPHIC PHOTOGRAPHER
RIGHT: IVAN MASSAR, BLACK STAR

BUNKER HILL

The war begins in earnest

THE CRASH of cannon jarred Boston out of bed early on the morning of June 17, 1775. In the harbor H.M.S. *Lively* rocked at anchor as its broadsides pounded a crude redoubt built overnight on Breed's pasture, a lower hump of Bunker's Hill. A day before Britain's planned attack, the rebels had fortified Charlestown Heights.

Gage, Howe, and Clinton hastily conferred over the best way to reduce the works. Clinton suggested throttling the narrow neck that linked Charlestown to the mainland. Howe disliked the look of mud flats at the neck. Also, wouldn't a frontal attack restore the morale of troops still shaken by their debacle on the Concord road? Gage agreed. Regiments marched to the wharves and embarked while the fleet thundered its salvos.

On the sun-baked hillside farmers in round hats and shirt sleeves toiled to finish their earth-

A 220-foot obelisk marks the battlefield. Charlestown hid snipers, so the British burned it. General Warren,

B. ANTHONY STEWART, NATIONAL GEOGRAPHIC PHOTOGRAPHER. "BURNING OF CHARLES TOWN," GARBISCH COLLECTION, NATIONAL GALLERY OF ART

work. "Americans are much afraid of their legs," said Israel Putnam. "If you cover these, they will fight forever." But as the scarlet regiments lined up below, glittering with bayonets, one Yankee fell to his knees and prayed. Others licked parched lips, wiped sweat from their palms, counted their bullets.

Briskly, Howe outlined his two-pronged attack—grenadiers and marines to march straight up at the redoubt, light infantry to trot along a beach, then come in from behind. To meet this, John Stark set his 800 New Hampshire frontiersmen along a fence running to the beach, and piled rocks across the sand. Stark, veteran of Rogers' Rangers, drove a stake 40 yards out: When those white gaiters pass it, open up, aiming low. In the redoubt William Prescott repeated: Aim low; pick off the officers; *don't fire till you see the whites of their eyes.*

In awesome splendor the King's Regulars strode forward, a steel-tipped tide. Closer and closer they came until you could see the hot, glistening faces and hear the panting breath, the swish of boots in tall grass. Then redoubt and fence erupted in flame and smoke and a great scythe slashed through the trim ranks and mowed them into writhing, screaming windrows of torn flesh. On the beach whole companies of light infantry crumpled as the New Hampshiremen got in an incredible three volleys while the British pressed for that last 40 yards. On the hill bewildered grenadiers found themselves standing alone, slipping on bloody grass.

The redcoats recoiled, re-formed, advanced, and were slaughtered. Survivors shed heavy packs, some their wool tunics, and grimly charged a third time. Two volleys smashed them; then the patriots' powder was gone. The British swept into the redoubt, won the field. Their losses: more than 1,000 men—and the assurance of elite troops. No grenadier who fought at Bunker Hill ever felt invincible again.

patriot hero, fell with the redoubt. Two weeks later Washington took command at Cambridge.

"BATTLE OF BUNKER'S HILL" BY JOHN TRUMBULL, 1786, YALE UNIVERSITY ART GALLERY

TICONDEROGA

Green Mountain Boys catch the garrison napping and seize its prized cannon

THE EXORBITANT COST of Bunker Hill shelved British plans for breaking out of Boston. Now a comic-opera adventure that took place a month before loomed in importance. Because of it, the British would be forced to sail from Boston.

On a drizzling May night some 200 ragged backwoodsmen, mostly from the New Hampshire Grants (now Vermont), huddled on Lake Champlain's east shore awaiting boats to ferry them to Fort Ticonderoga. The old French and Indian War outpost seemed a ripe plum to snatch from the British, and two cocky, impetuous leaders planned to do just that. Ethan Allen and Benedict Arnold, squabbling over the command, managed to get 83 men up to the fort's south gate before dawn.

Fort Ti's guns were floated and dragged down to Albany, then sledged across the snowy Berkshires by the muscle of 80 yoke of oxen and the will power of Washington's artillery chief, Boston bookseller Henry Knox.

In March, 1776, the Americans seized Dorchester Heights and Boston's besieged British came under the muzzles of Ticonderoga's guns. The game was up; the redcoats left.

The restored fort (right) is now a museum.

With a whoop they plunged inside. A sentry leveled his musket. It misfired and he fled. Another lunged with his bayonet. Allen, "gigantic" in great green coat, yellow breeches, and cocked hat, cracked him with the flat of his sword and demanded the commandant. The sentry pointed to a stairway.

"Come out of there, you damned old rat!" Allen bellowed.

An officer appeared, clutching his breeches. By what authority did Allen demand surrender, he asked, puzzled.

"In the name of the great Jehovah and the Continental Congress!" Allen shouted, according to his own testimony. Others report that his answer was saltier, that he had about as much respect for the great Jehovah as the British did for the Continental Congress. Anyway, the garrison capitulated without a shot, and the Green Mountain Boys happily broke into the liquor supply.

The fort's capture, May 10, 1775, hardly ranks as a battle. But it opened the way to Canada. That fall Gen. Richard Montgomery took Montreal and Arnold besieged Quebec. And in March, 1776, Ticonderoga's cannon drove the British from Boston. The war shifted to New York, and Washington hurried to meet it.

B. ANTHONY STEWART, NATIONAL GEOGRAPHIC PHOTOGRAPHER. OPPOSITE: PAINTING BY TOM LOVELL, COURTESY OF DIXON "TICONDEROGA" PENCIL COLLECTION

"FORCING THE HUDSON RIVER PASSAGE" BY DOMINIQUE SERRES (1722-93), UNITED STATES NAVAL ACADEMY MUSEUM

Fire from Fort Washington (right) and Fort Lee failed to stop British warships in 1776.

HEARTBREAK AT NEW YORK

Washington proves a master—at retreat

A MONTH AFTER the British sailed from Boston, George Washington reached New York, playing his hunch that Sir William Howe would try to seize the Hudson and split New England from the other colonies. Gradually, Washington marshaled 19,000 raw troops. They came from other colonies besides New England. When they formed on July 9, 1776, to hear the Declaration of Independence, they represented a national army. They cheered the great words mightily, then tore down the gilded statue of George III that stood on Bowling Green.

Over on Staten Island Sir William built up his army to 32,000 and prepared to restore all that the statue stood for. With his redcoats he now had blue-clad mercenaries from Germany to help fight this unpopular war. When Howe landed his professionals on Long Island, Washington gingerly drew up his army in a defensive line and ruefully watched it come apart on August 27 before Howe's perfect tactics and the superb timing of his flank attack. To the wail of bagpipes and the thump and moan of drums and hautboys, Highlanders and Hessians advanced on the American front. Running from those terrible bayonets, patriots blundered into the hard-marching flanking column and were simply swallowed.

The 1776 battle for New York raged over the sites of today's skyscrapers, parks, and avenues

Assembling on Staten Island (1), Howe's army struck across the Narrows, landing unopposed at what is now Dyker Beach Park. Washington sped forces from Manhattan to Long Island, manned crude redoubts at Brooklyn Heights, and formed a battle line (2) through Prospect Park.

Howe engaged the Americans with two columns and led a third that circled to cut them off from behind. Survivors of the trap retreated to the redoubts on Brooklyn Heights (3). Howe, remembering Bunker Hill, mulled over what a frontal assault might cost.

While Howe delayed, a northeaster blew in and kept British warships from patrolling the East River. Washington called for John Glover's Marblehead regiment. These leathery Massachusetts fishermen tirelessly rowed 9,500 Americans back to Manhattan (4). As the wind died, early morning fog screened Washington in the last boat.

The British followed two weeks later. They stormed ashore at Kip's Bay (5) and sent militia scampering from shallow trenches. Hearing the bombardment, Washington galloped along the route of Lexington Avenue to try to rally his fleeing men at a cornfield near Grand Central Station. The Americans finally dug in at Harlem Heights (6), lashed back, and chased the redcoats through the present site of Columbia University.

Howe, deciding against a frontal attack, three weeks later moved up Long Island Sound (7) and landed at Pelham Bay Park for another flank attack. Washington evacuated his headquarters at Jumel Mansion and fell back (8) to White Plains with 13,000 men, leaving 2,000 to garrison Fort Washington and 3,500 to hold Fort Lee.

Washington made a strong stand at White Plains, then melted north. Howe wheeled to engulf the twin forts (9, 10). Collecting remnants of his desertion-ridden army, Washington fled southwest across New Jersey.

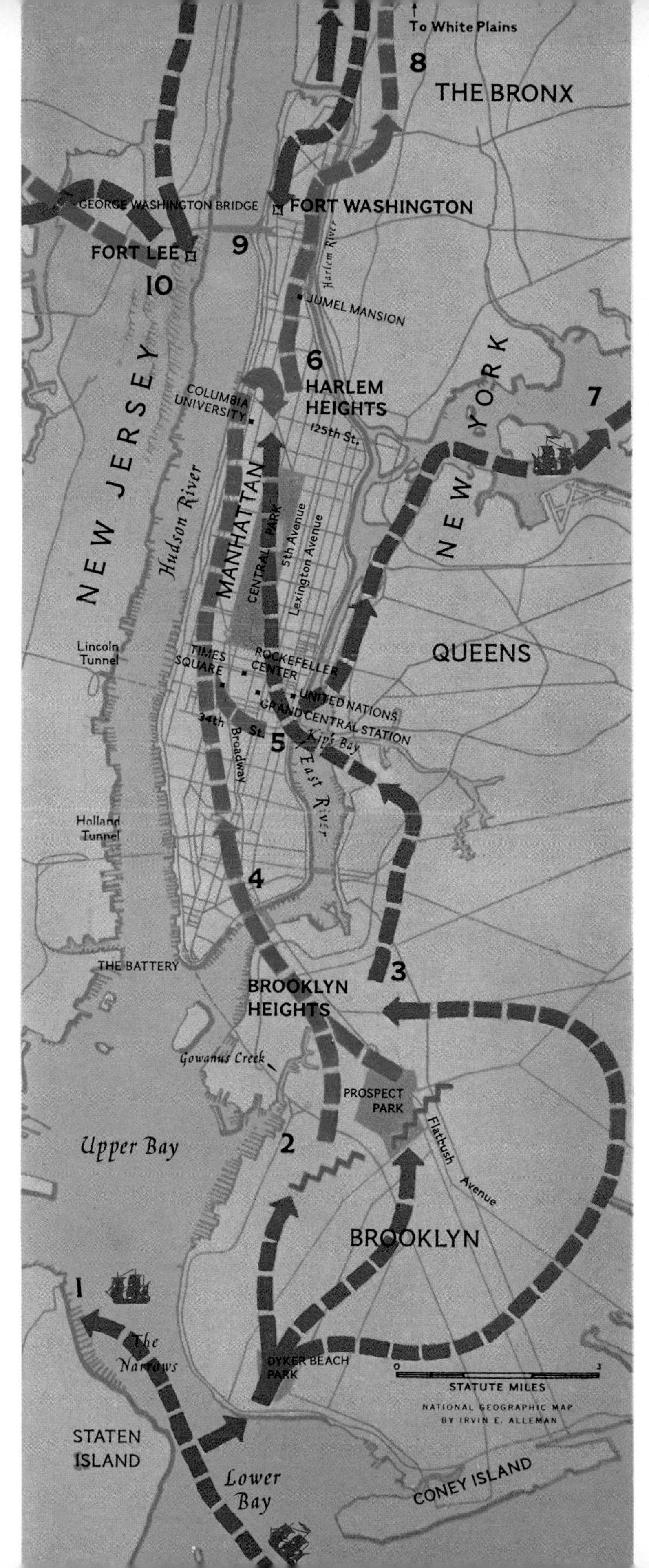

B. ANTHONY STEWART, NATIONAL GEOGRAPHIC PHOTOGRAPHER. BELOW: CULVER SERVICE (LEFT) AND LOUIS FROHMAN

West Point became watchdog of the Hudson later in the Revolution. Here Americans stretched a mighty chain, each link 100 to 300 pounds, to bar the river to British ships.

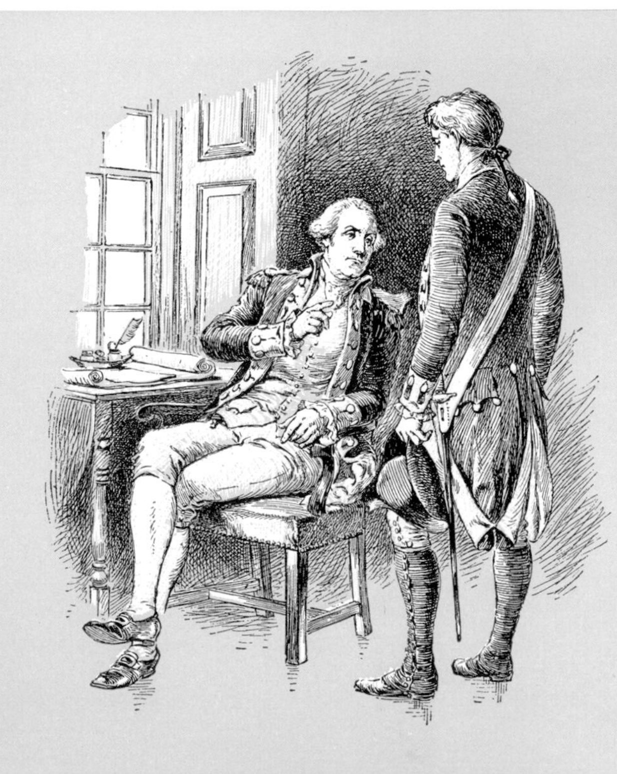

"I only regret that I have but

WHEN Knowlton's Rangers fought the redcoats on Harlem Heights, one of their comrades was missing. Capt. Nathan Hale, entrusted with an espionage mission, was behind the enemy lines.

Disguised as a schoolmaster in frock and broad-brimmed hat and carrying his Yale diploma, the handsome, athletic former teacher crossed to Long Island from Connecticut and worked his way westward among British encampments. They say he got to within a mile of the American lines on Manhattan.

Here his luck ran out. A great fire in New York provoked mass arrests by the British.

"Rejoice, my friend, that we have given the Rebels a d_____d crush," wrote an exultant British officer.

Not all Americans ran. Cut off and surrounded, Lord Stirling with 250 crack Marylanders "fought like a wolf." Florid and fifty, Stirling was born William Alexander of New Jersey, but claimed a Scottish earldom. He drank and fought with equal vigor. On this day he led six smashing charges on the troops that engulfed him before he surrendered. "What brave fellows I must this day lose," grieved Washington.

He changed his tune at the Kip's Bay rout when the militia panicked before Howe's landing party. They discarded muskets, knapsacks, even clothes. He flung his hat on the ground. "Good God!" he roared, "have I got such troops as those?"

Below Harlem Heights the British sounded a taunting fox-hunt call as they drove back Knowlton's Connecticut Rangers. Stung, the Yankees spun round and sent the famed Black Watch regiment flying. Washington nodded approvingly and called his men off before they engaged the whole British army.

But spirits were to tumble. Howe forced the Americans north and wrenched away Forts Washington and Lee and control of the Hudson. Harried through New Jersey in winter, Washington wrote, "I think the game is pretty well up." Still, he had a trick up his sleeve.

one life to lose for my country"

Hale was picked up for questioning. When a search of his person revealed sketches and notes of installations, Hale confessed his mission. At 11 o'clock the following morning the young captain was unceremoniously hanged in an artillery park on Manhattan's East Side. Howe's aide, Capt. John Montresor, transmitted to Americans the familiar last words.

Statues of Hale stand in City Hall Park in New York and at Yale University in New Haven. Nathan Hale Homestead, near South Coventry, Connecticut, has been restored and furnished with his family's possessions.

Jumel Mansion, built by loyalist Roger Morris in 1765, was Washington's headquarters in 1776. Now it is a museum.

TRENTON AND PRINCETON

Washington slashes back in stunning victory

FOR A MOMENT sleet-laced wind blinded the shivering Hessian sentry, half a mile north of Trenton. Then he peered again up the road and swore in disbelief. Dimly seen in the waking day, a horde of fast-moving scarecrows approached! The German, cued hair sticking out as if from fright, fled back toward his garrison with a shout: *"Der Feind! Heraus!"*

"Der Feind"—the enemy—was supposed to be cringing on the Pennsylvania side of the Delaware River, cowed by Howe's advance units at Trenton and Bordentown. Yet here they came, a spectral army in a ghostly December storm.

To Washington, earlier that month, time had seemed a worse enemy than Howe. Enlistments of all but 1,400 of his troops expired December 31, 1776. The patriot cause appeared doomed. Gambling all on one more battle from his army, Washington decided to strike at Trenton Christmas night, when the Hessian garrison would be celebrating in hearty German fashion. (Puritan scruples kept many Americans from making a festival out of Christmas.) Poring over maps at the Thompson-Neely House, which still stands in Pennsylvania's Washington Crossing State Park, the generals plotted a three-crossing attack. One force would hit to the south as a diversion; a second would cut off Trenton from Bordentown; Washington with the main force would sweep down on Trenton from the north.

ROBERT F. SISSON AND JOHN E. FLETCHER, NATIONAL GEOGRAPHIC PHOTOGRAPHERS

Washington's Durham boats would dwarf this rowboat at the crossing; 40-60 feet long, 8 feet in beam, they were built to transport grain, iron, and whisky. That Christmas night their cargo was men, horses, and cannon.

The ice-choked Delaware stalled the first two crossings. But crushing floes and cutting sleet merely delayed iron-willed Washington. Wrestling the current, John Glover's seagoing soldiers rowed 2,500 men to the Jersey shore. At four A.M. the march began. The shoeless trailed blood on the icy road.

At the edge of town a detachment swung left to block the road to Princeton. Henry Knox's artillery rolled to the head of King and Queen Streets and opened fire. Sleep-drugged after their bouts with Christmas wine, the Hessians stumbled out in confusion. Flitting from house to house like shadows, the Americans picked them off.

Col. Johann Gottlieb Rall, commander of the 1,400-man garrison, had spent the night at cards. He tucked a warning of the attack in his pocket, apparently unread; to him the patriots were "nothing but a lot of farmers."

Now he rode into a hail of lead to group his regiment and send it up King Street against those "farmers." Cannon fire drove it back.

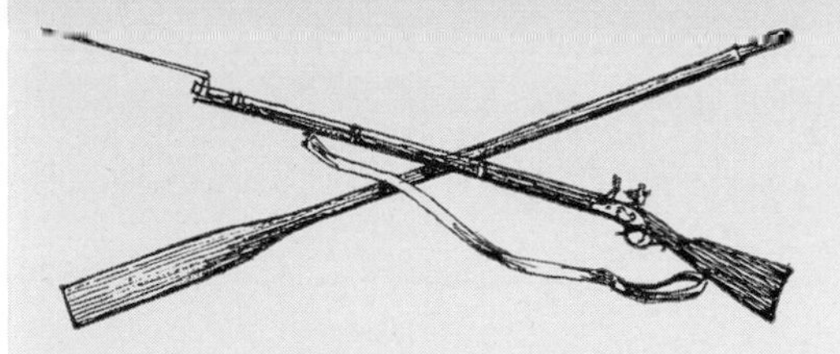

Glover's Marbleheaders

A HANDFUL of crack regiments formed the hard core of the infant army, staying while militia came and went. One was the 14th Continental, mostly Massachusetts mariners who moved fast when a skipper spoke. Under Col. John Glover, merchant and shipowner, they hit the deck whenever Washington needed amphibious troops, or scrappers who wouldn't turn tail.

They rescued the army after the Long Island defeat, helped stem the Kip's Bay rout. When Howe landed at Pelham to flank Washington, they lined stone fences and slowed the redcoats. After ferrying the army across the Delaware, they sealed off the last Hessian escape route.

Glover's schooner *Hannah* was, in his words, "the first Armed Vessell, fitted out in the Service of the United States."

THE 1851 PAINTING, ON LOAN FROM THE METROPOLITAN MUSEUM OF ART, HANGS IN THE MEMORIAL BUILDING AT WASHINGTON CROSSING STATE PARK, PENNSYLVANIA

Washington Crossing the Delaware by Emanuel Leutze idealizes the spirit of '76. Delayed in crossing, the chilled, ragged men massed on the New Jersey shore near McKonkey Ferry House, now a state museum.

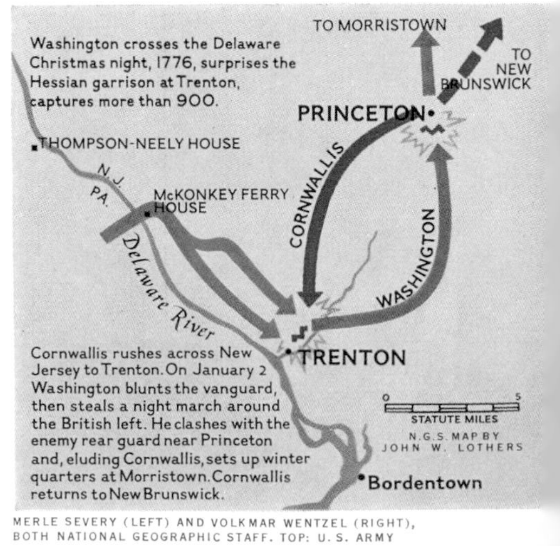
Washington crosses the Delaware Christmas night, 1776, surprises the Hessian garrison at Trenton, captures more than 900.
TO MORRISTOWN
TO NEW BRUNSWICK
PRINCETON
THOMPSON-NEELY HOUSE
N. J.
PA.
McKONKEY FERRY HOUSE
CORNWALLIS
WASHINGTON
Delaware River
TRENTON
Cornwallis rushes across New Jersey to Trenton. On January 2 Washington blunts the vanguard, then steals a night march around the British left. He clashes with the enemy rear guard near Princeton and, eluding Cornwallis, sets up winter quarters at Morristown. Cornwallis returns to New Brunswick.
0
5
STATUTE MILES
N.G.S. MAP BY JOHN W. LOTHERS
Bordentown

MERLE SEVERY (LEFT) AND VOLKMAR WENTZEL (RIGHT), BOTH NATIONAL GEOGRAPHIC STAFF. TOP: U. S. ARMY

Side streets swarmed with Americans. In the melee Rall fell, mortally wounded. With escape cut off to Bordentown, the Hessians surrendered.

The victory turned American despair into confidence. But time was running out for Washington's troops. An eloquent appeal backed by a $10 bonus kept them intact to face Lord Cornwallis, rushing across New Jersey to "bag the fox." Washington engaged the vanguard at Trenton January 2, then side-stepped and drove for British supplies at New Brunswick.

At dawn, near Princeton, the Americans collided with British regiments bound for Trenton. The redcoats charged. The Americans ran, rallied, fell back. Up galloped Washington, waving his hat. "Parade with us, my brave fellows. . . . We will have them!" Stiffened, his men drove the British from the field and mopped up the Princeton garrison.

Cornwallis spun round like a baited lion to smash this elusive Virginian. Washington, seeing his troops' exhaustion, abandoned the New Brunswick sally and headed for winter quarters at Morristown. He had saved his reputation—and the Revolution. But he could not save Philadelphia, where six months earlier independence had been declared. ROSS BENNETT

Young Capt. Alexander Hamilton's guns win a duel at the top of old King Street in Trenton

A New York artillery company under the future statesman opened the attack near the present Battle Monument, cut down opposing troops, silenced the guns they brought up. Hessians spilled from the Old Barracks (far left). This 1758 building and the Trent House (1719), Trenton's oldest, contain fine period furnishings. A week later Hamilton fired on Princeton's Nassau Hall (left); 194 redcoats gave up. The Continental Congress met here in 1783.

PHILADELPHIA

Ben Franklin's fair city proclaims liberty

BENJAMIN FRANKLIN
BY CHARLES WILLSON PEALE
HISTORICAL SOCIETY OF PENNSYLVANIA

JULY 1, 1776, Philadelphians awoke to find the air hot and close. Ben Franklin, trudging down Chestnut Street toward the State House, felt the heat rise from the cobblestones. A summer storm to clear the air would be no surprise. Franklin walked slowly; gout and the exertions of 70 years had sapped his strength. But his eyes sparkled behind his spectacles as he drank in the sights of the city he knew so well.

The white steeple of Christ Church towered into the blue sky above all else. In neat brick buildings shopkeepers arranged their wares in windows made of many small panes. By the public water pumps pretty housemaids gossiped in the sun. Merchants in carriages clattered toward dockside warehouses.

It was fitting that the Continental Congress should meet here. Philadelphians, energetic at their trades and in exporting produce from Pennsylvania farms, had made their city the most populous (some 38,000) and richest in America: the "object of every one's wonder and admiration." And here the Congress must decide if the 13 colonies should stand on their own, independent of their motherland.

Franklin may have thought of the day he came to the city. He was 17 then, and Boston born. On Second Street he had bought "three great puffy rolls," tucked one under each arm, and munched on the third. He had made quite a sight, his coat pockets "stuffed out with shirts and stockings," rubbernecking up and down Chestnut and Walnut Streets. But in seven years he owned his own newspaper; and a few years later his *Poor Richard's Almanack* brought him fame and the beginnings of a "sufficient tho' modest fortune." Practical-minded Pennsylvanians relished Poor Richard's proverbs: "Fish and visitors smell in three days"; "Early to bed and early to rise makes a man healthy, wealthy, and wise." Franklin himself was never early to bed. At the *Junto,* a club he organized, he debated "the nature of vapors" and composed jolly drinking songs.

The city itself reflected his civic leadership. Streets were paved; at night constables and lamps made them safe. He helped found a circulating library (America's first), a "noble hospital" (now the Pennsylvania Hospital), an academy (which grew into the University of Pennsylvania), and the American Philosophical Society (which still meets in the brick building he raised funds for). Even the lightning rods sprouting from the roofs were his invention, and all Europe knew of his kite

Declaration of Independence signers dipped their quills in this inkstand made by Franklin's friend, silversmith Philip Syng, and wrote their names in history.

THE INKSTAND IS PRESERVED IN INDEPENDENCE HALL; FACSIMILE DOCUMENT
 DAVID S. BOYER, NATIONAL GEOGRAPHIC STAFF

America's greatest men gather in Britain's grandest colonial city to forge freedom's most formidable document

experiment. Town and farm folk found that the stove he invented gave more heat with less fuel.

Without a doubt, the old gentleman who stepped into the Assembly Room of the State House that July day was the most famous man in America. Half a hundred other delegates, tricorns tucked under their arms, bustled in and took seats. At noon, as they wiped perspiration from their brows and slapped at buzzing horseflies, John Hancock announced they would consider "the resolution concerning independence."

There was a murmur. The proposal offered three weeks earlier by Richard Henry Lee of Virginia was bold: *That these United Colonies are, and of right ought to be, free and independent States, that they are absolved from all allegiance to the British Crown....*

John Dickinson of Pennsylvania rose, a lean figure in plum-colored coat and breeches. His voice was

THE GEORGE HEAP VIEW OF PHILADELPHIA, C. 1754, LIBRARY OF CONGRESS

"Holes digged in the Ground, Covered with Earth" sheltered the first Philadelphians. By the 1700's, the bustling port was "Noble and Beautiful" with houses "after the Mode in London." Tallest steeple tops Christ Church, standing today. Spire to the left identifies the State House where John Adams, Roger Sherman, Robert Livingston, Thomas Jefferson, and Benjamin Franklin presented the Declaration of Independence to John Hancock, who presides below.

"THE DECLARATION OF INDEPENDENCE" BY JOHN TRUMBULL, U. S. CAPITOL ROTUNDA

charged with emotion: "To escape from the protection of Britain all unprepared as we are, would be like destroying our house in winter . . . before we have got another shelter." Even a year after Bunker Hill the colonies had as yet formed no union or confederation. True, the British had been driven from Boston. But wouldn't it be wiser to wait to see how things went?

Rain began to beat upon the big windows. Dickinson sat down, a handkerchief to his forehead.

Plump John Adams bounced up, said he wished he had the powers of ancient Greek and Roman orators, then pointed out how useless it was trying to bargain with a British government that simply wouldn't bargain.

As he spoke a door flew open. In it stood three men, booted, spurred, and dripping wet. They brought news: New Jersey had swung to independence. A letter from Annapolis lay on Hancock's desk; it lined up Maryland.

ALBERT MOLDVAY AND JOHN E. FLETCHER, AND (RIGHT) DAVID S. BOYER, NATIONAL GEOGRAPHIC STAFF

Shrines that witnessed the birth of the United States renew the faith of Americans

Congress Hall, scene of George Washington's second presidential inauguration, rang with debates from 1790 to 1800 when Philadelphia was the national capital. Here in the restored Senate Chamber, members of the bar association re-enact early lawmaking.

In Independence Hall (below), the Founding Fathers adopted the Declaration of Independence and wrote the Constitution. Visitors inspect the Liberty Bell (page 4), spirited into hiding from the British the winter of 1777-78. Next door at old City Hall, the first U. S. Supreme Court met. Nearby Carpenters' Hall dates from 1770; the First Bank of the United States, from 1795.

Other Philadelphia sites include Elfreth's Alley, little changed since Ben Franklin's day, and the home of Betsy Ross, who tradition says made the first Stars and Stripes.

Candles flickered in the storm-darkened chamber as the chairman polled the delegations. *Massachusetts . . . Rhode Island . . . Pennsylvania.* Franklin rose with John Morton. He felt a pang as three fellow delegates remained seated. His own colony rejected the motion.

The next day Mr. Dickinson stayed away and Franklin led Pennsylvania in voting for the measure. Caesar Rodney of Delaware had ridden 80 miles in darkness and rain to break the tie in his delegation. Edward Rutledge bulled South Carolina into

History Haunts Old Homes of PHILADELPHIA AND VICINITY

Souderton

Montgomery County

Lansdale

MILL GROVE

DAWESFIE

Perkiomen Creek

Norristown

THE HIGHLANDS

MILL GROVE: Home of John James Audubon. Here the French artist began to paint the birds of America in the early 1800's.

Whitemars

Valley Forge

PA. 43

Conshohocken

Schuylkill River

Chester County

Battle of Paoli, Sept. 20, 1777

Paoli

U.S. 30

Wayne

WAYNESBOROUGH: Birthplace of Gen. Anthony Wayne. His father built the main house in 1740. William Wayne, the general's great-great-great-grandson, occupies it today.

Bryn Mawr

Ardmore

PONT READING

Merion

WAYNESBOROUGH

PA. 3

Delaware County

West Chester

JOHN BARTRAM HOUSE: Site of the first outstanding botanica garden in the United States

Media

U.S. 1

Battle of the Brandywine, Sept. 11, 1777

GILPIN HOUSE: General Lafayette's headquarters before the Battle of the Brandywine, September 11, 1777.

GILPIN HOUSE

PA. 291

Chadds Ford

Delaware River

Chester

Brandywine Cr.

U.S. 202

PENNSYLVANIA

DELAWARE

0 10

STATUTE MILES

Map by National Geographic Cartographers W. N. Palmstrom and I. E. Alleman

Wilmington

MT. PLEASANT

POWEL HO

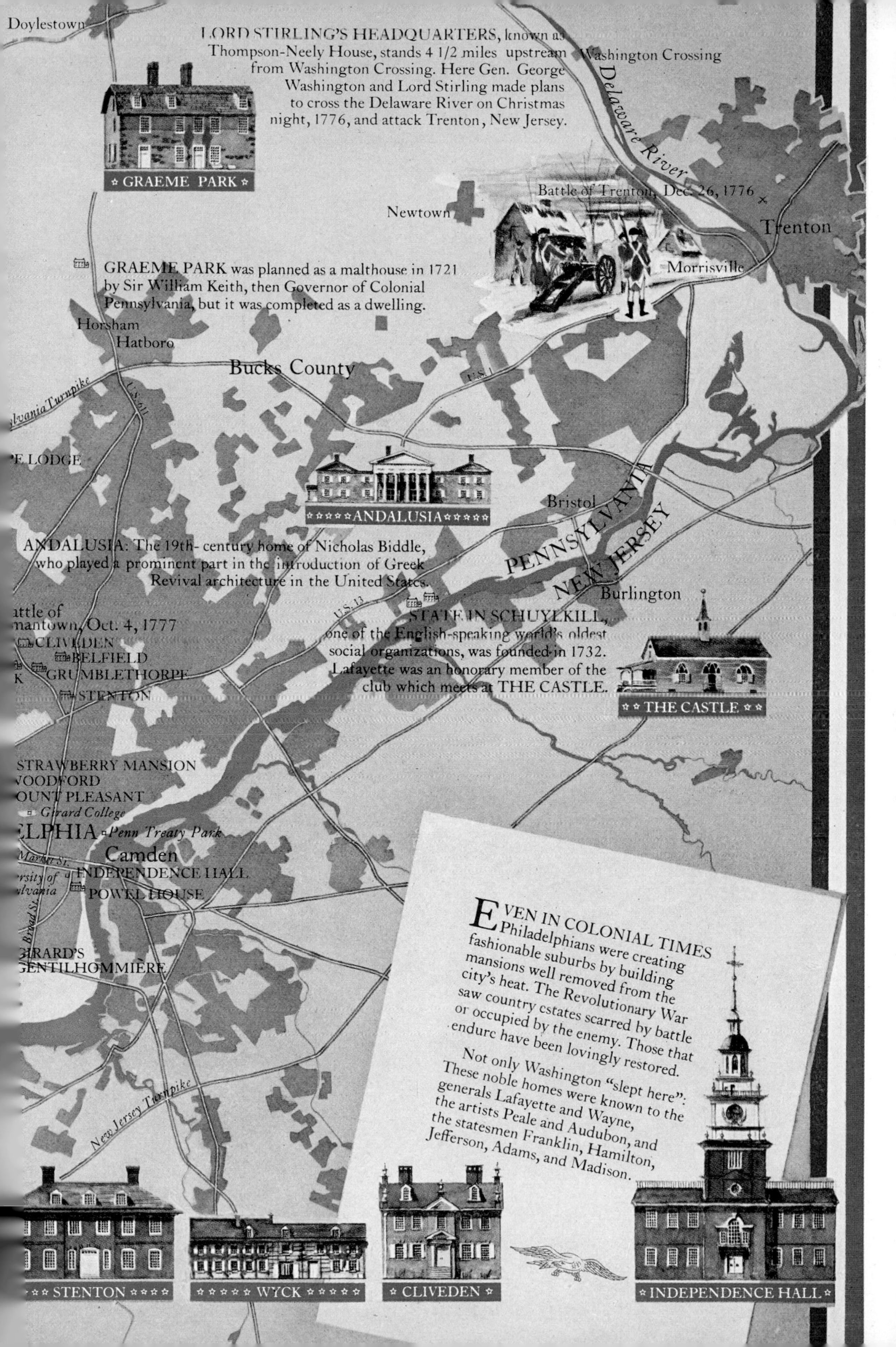
Doylestown
LORD STIRLING'S HEADQUARTERS, known as Thompson-Neely House, stands 4 1/2 miles upstream from Washington Crossing. Here Gen. George Washington and Lord Stirling made plans to cross the Delaware River on Christmas night, 1776, and attack Trenton, New Jersey.
Washington Crossing
Delaware River
GRAEME PARK
Battle of Trenton, Dec. 26, 1776
Newtown
Trenton
Morrisville
GRAEME PARK was planned as a malthouse in 1721 by Sir William Keith, then Governor of Colonial Pennsylvania, but it was completed as a dwelling.
Horsham
Hatboro
Bucks County
U.S. 1
U.S. 611
ANDALUSIA
Bristol
PENNSYLVANIA
NEW JERSEY
ANDALUSIA: The 19th- century home of Nicholas Biddle, who played a prominent part in the introduction of Greek Revival architecture in the United States.
Burlington
U.S. 13
STATE IN SCHUYLKILL, one of the English-speaking world's oldest social organizations, was founded in 1732. Lafayette was an honorary member of the club which meets at THE CASTLE.
Oct. 4, 1777
CLIVEDEN
BELFIELD
GRUMBLETHORPE
STENTON
THE CASTLE
STRAWBERRY MANSION
Girard College
Penn Treaty Park
Camden
INDEPENDENCE HALL
POWEL HOUSE
New Jersey Turnpike
EVEN IN COLONIAL TIMES Philadelphians were creating fashionable suburbs by building mansions well removed from the city's heat. The Revolutionary War saw country estates scarred by battle or occupied by the enemy. Those that endure have been lovingly restored.
Not only Washington "slept here": These noble homes were known to the generals Lafayette and Wayne, the artists Peale and Audubon, and the statesmen Franklin, Hamilton, Jefferson, Adams, and Madison.
STENTON
WYCK
CLIVEDEN
INDEPENDENCE HALL

Hospitality glows in the Powel House, welcoming all to elegant rooms where Washington and other notables wined, dined, and danced.

line. The New Yorkers, informed the day before that a British fleet approached Long Island, still balked. But they promised their vote.

The will of the Congress had spoken. In formal session "the thing was done."

Three weeks earlier a young red-haired Virginian had begun composing a declaration, should it be needed. On July 4 Thomas Jefferson winced as the Congress changed a word here, a phrase there. A paragraph he cherished—condemning slavery—was stricken in deference to plantation owners. At day's end the body adopted the magnificent paper which began:

When in the Course of human events, it becomes necessary for one people to dissolve the political bands which have connected them with another....

FROM Savannah to Boston patriots cheered and cannon boomed at the news. Now, as John Adams wrote, "Nothing will remain but war."

Redcoats seized New York, were hit hard at Trenton and Princeton. In August, 1777, General Howe sailed with a powerful army up Chesapeake Bay. Washington met him at Chadds Ford on the Brandywine, was outflanked by Cornwallis, and withdrew. Congress fled to Lancaster, then to York.

On September 26, British dragoons and Hessians paraded into Philadelphia amid band music and "the acclamation of some thousands of the inhabitants, mostly women and children."

Desperately, Washington struck the main British camp at Germantown. For

Benedict Arnold bought Mount Pleasant for his bride, but betrayed his country before they could move in. The Philadelphia Museum of Art has refurnished the 1761 home with Chippendale by cabinetmakers of the city.

DAVID S. BOYER, NATIONAL GEOGRAPHIC STAFF, AND (LEFT) THOMAS NEBBIA

THOMAS NEBBIA

Waynesborough was ransacked by British. They even bayoneted the boxwood, the story goes. But the owner, Gen. Anthony Wayne, was away at Paoli, where redcoats routed his troops. A descendant of "Mad Anthony" owns the 1724 house.

Hope Lodge sheltered soldiers wounded at Germantown. Visitors now find war echoes faint amid the graceful furnishings, carved moldings, and Delft tile fireplace fronts in this stately Georgian home. Buying it in 1746, Samuel Morris reportedly quipped to friends, "I've got the pen; all I want now is the sow!" His betrothed swiftly broke off their engagement.

hours the battle hung in the balance; then the Americans were forced into retreat. Howe's officers settled snugly for the winter in Philadelphia's fine houses.

Many of those old homes still stand, where visitors recapture the luxury and drama of days when our nation was born. Enter the Powel House and ascend to the great drawing room upstairs with its gilded mirrors, Chippendale furnishings, and carved mantel. Here Mayor Samuel Powel entertained the city's elite. Guest John Adams relished a "most sinful feast . . . curds and creams, jellies, sweetmeats of various sorts, twenty sorts of tarts, fools, trifles, floating islands, whipped sillibubs &c. &c." When the British took over, patriot Powel and his family had to move into the back portion, but their charm parried other reprisals.

In some houses the British were welcomed. At Woodford candlelight shone on officers in scarlet sipping tea with Tory ladies. Rebecca Woodford was a belle of the *Mischianza* honoring General Howe.

For that spring pageant, staged by Capt. John André on the banks of the Delaware, "fourteen young ladies were dressed alike: white Poland dresses of Mantua with long sleeves, a gauze turban spangled, and sashes around the waists." Officers in knightly attire jousted for their favor. Wrote one happy girl to a friend in the country, "You'd have an opportunity of raking as much as you choose. . . . I've been but three evenings alone since we moved to town."

Mount Pleasant opened British eyes with its pedimented door beneath a Palladian window, its hand-tooled cornices, pilasters, and recessed china cupboards. No wonder ambitious Benedict Arnold plunged himself even deeper in debt to buy the house in 1779 for his bride Peggy Shippen. It stands in Fairmount Park

Cliveden, serene and gracious today, was scourged by "a tempest of round-shot, grape and musketry" during the Battle of Germantown. Retreating British barricaded doors, held off Americans who feared "to leave a castle in our rear." The delay helped rob Washington of victory. Built in 1761 by Judge Benjamin Chew, the house is still lived in by Chews.

E. L. HENRY'S PAINTING HANGS IN CLIVEDEN; COURTESY OF SAMUEL CHEW

and along with Woodford, early 19th century Strawberry Mansion, and other historic dwellings regularly welcomes visitors.

Two old houses recall Philadelphia's close tie with the sea. Pont Reading, begun in 1682, became the home of shipbuilder Joshua Humphreys; he designed naval vessels in both the Revolution and the War of 1812. Girard's Gentilhommière has the French flavor of the sea captain who came ashore in 1776, started a store, and grew so prosperous that he founded a bank and left money for a college.

Philadelphia boasted two world-famous naturalists. By the Schuylkill stands the gray stone house John Bartram built with his own hands. Franklin found him a walking encyclopedia "on the subjects of botany, fossils, husbandry, and the first creation." In Bartram's garden youngsters smile at tree names like jujube, ginkgo, and papaw. At Mill Grove on Perkiomen Creek they watch birds in the sanctuary and visit the home where John James Audubon came to live in 1804.

Houses at Germantown witnessed the battle. Redcoats turned Cliveden into a fort; it still bears the scars. The brick-paved hall in Stenton felt the tread of Howe as he directed his army. Stone walls of Wyck and Grumblethorpe echoed to cannon. And in rambling Dawesfield Washington made a fateful decision. His men would winter at a place called Valley Forge. JOHN J. PUTMAN

THOMAS NEBBIA

VALLEY FORGE

Winter seasons the raw Continental Army

THEY ARRIVED on a bitter December evening in 1777 – 11,000 men "without a House or Hutt to cover them." Valley Forge was defensible and near enough to Philadelphia to enable Washington to keep a close watch on Howe. From here he could bar British raids into the Chester Valley "breadbasket" and challenge any large-scale movement out of the city. But it was a desolate post.

How different all had seemed earlier that year! Encamped at Morristown after his victories at Trenton and Princeton, Washington had pinned down British garrisons and all but swept New Jersey free of redcoats. He thwarted their foraging. Even Howe's headquarters in New York, 30 miles away, had felt the pinch. With spring, Continental levies and supplies began to stream in.

When Howe took to ships and threatened Philadelphia by sea, Washington had sped to meet the threat. His Continentals were in good spirits that morning of August 24, 1777, when they paraded in the city where independence had been proclaimed. Each man wore a sprig of green in his hat. John Adams, a witness, was charmed by the thump and squeal of drums and fifes, the sight of these marching men. But he noted: "They don't step exactly in time. They don't hold up their heads quite erect, nor turn out their toes so exactly as they ought."

Now in December – less than four months later – Adams would scarcely have recognized these soldiers, except that they still slouched along out of step. Gone were the green twigs, the hopefulness. Gone, too, was Philadelphia, now a cozy billet for the British. Whipped at Brandywine and Germantown, the Americans marched this time across the Schuylkill to bleak winter quarters. "It snows," wrote a young Connecticut surgeon. "I'm sick – eat nothing – No Whiskey – No Forage – Lord – Lord – Lord."

At first General Washington occupied a tent, refusing the comfort of a local farmhouse until his men had built some huts for themselves. Small wonder that he earned their respect and loyalty. But as winter tightened its grip, many soldiers came close to mutiny. Groups of men huddled around campfires, ragged,

Washington lived in this flimsy marquee until his men had huts. The tent and other mementos of the six-month ordeal are preserved at Valley Forge, Pennsylvania, where bloodstained snow marked the path of freedom.

DAVID S. BOYER, NATIONAL GEOGRAPHIC STAFF, AND (TOP) METROPOLITAN MUSEUM OF ART

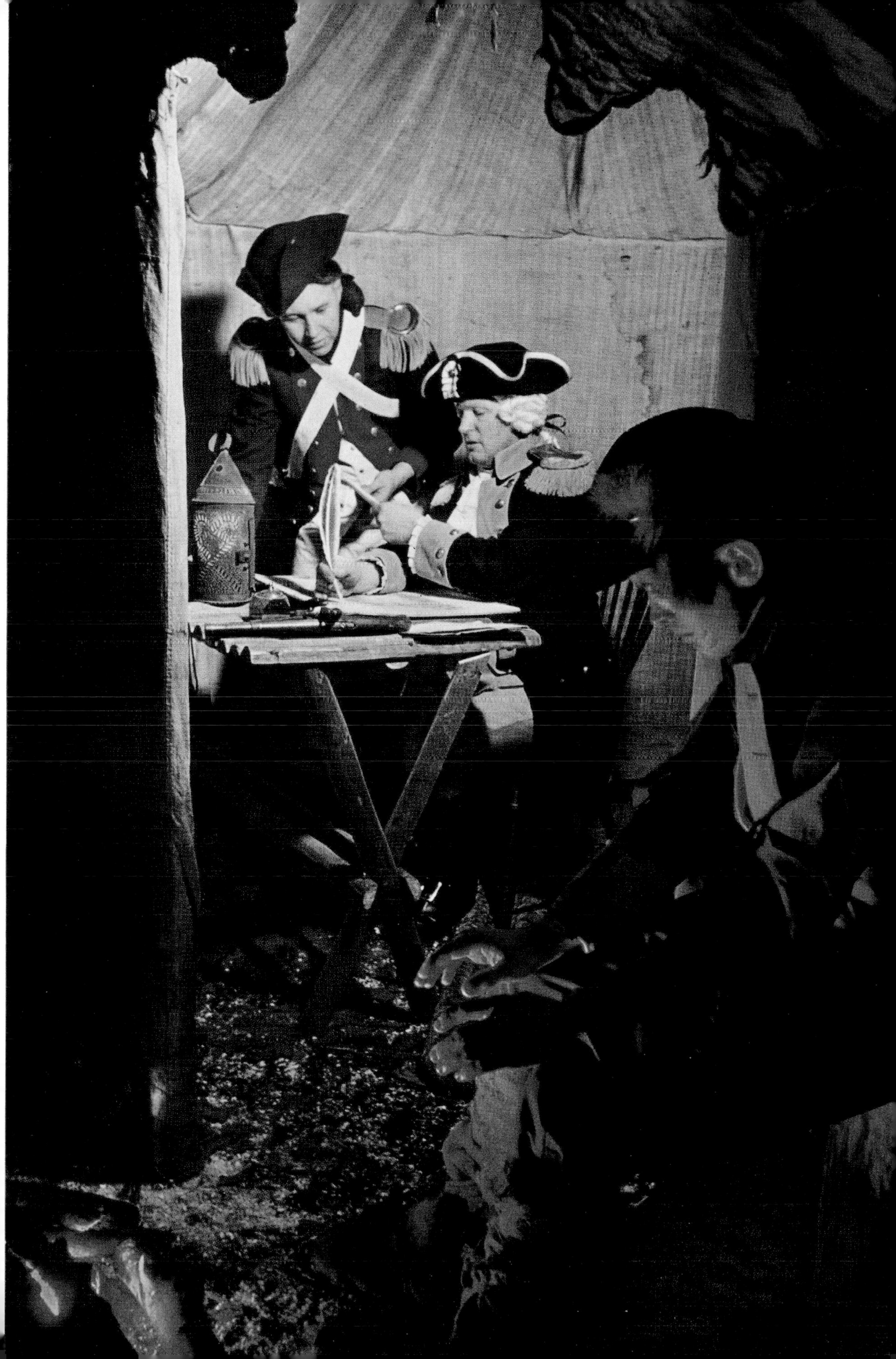

Baron von Steuben conducted drill through an interpreter. He forgot his rank, swung muskets to demonstrate the manual of arms, swore mightily in three languages when he realized orders must be *explained* in this democratic army. The men learned, morale rose.

Patriots fought winter in crude, earth-floored huts like these. Squads of 12 raced each other building them. Tom Paine wrote Franklin: "They appeared to me like a family of beavers: every one busy; some carrying logs, others mud . . . the rest fastening them together."

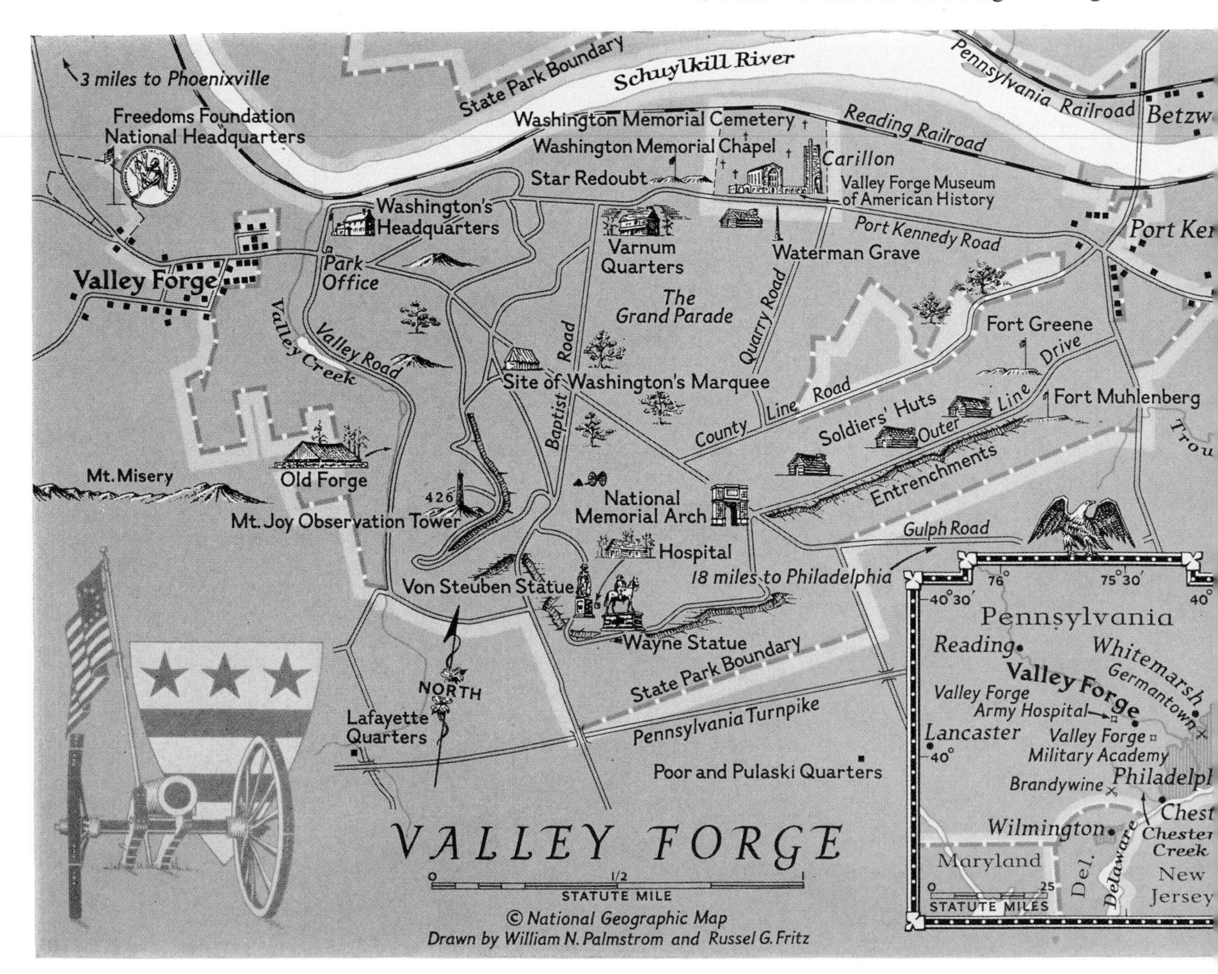

DAVID S. BOYER, NATIONAL GEOGRAPHIC STAFF, AND (TOP LEFT) PAINTING BY EDWIN A. ABBEY, LIBRARY OF CONGRESS

half-starved. Sentries, lashed by icy winds, tramped blood from their raw feet on the frozen ground, or stood in their hats to ease chilled toes.

"I have upwards of seventy men unfit for duty only for the want . . . of clothing, twenty of which have no breeches at all, so that they are obliged to take their blankets to cover their nakedness," reported a New York colonel. "And as many without a single shirt, stocking, or shoe, about thirty fit for duty, the rest sick or lame, and, God knows, it won't be long before they will all be laid up, as the poor fellows are obliged to fetch wood and water on their backs half a mile with bare legs in snow or mud."

Washington tells of seeing a man wrapped in only a thin blanket run from one hut to another. Soldiers who left their quarters to go on duty borrowed clothes from those who remained inside. One soldier was court-martialed for threatening to desert just as soon as he got some shoes. Many murmured about a lost cause and cursed Congress for failing to supply enough food and clothing.

Epidemics of "camp fever" (probably typhus) and smallpox raged, and in February, 1778, Washington wrote: "For some days past there has been little less than a famine in camp."

But hardships or no, General Washington cracked down on his men. He held them to strict military discipline and rigid routine; he executed deserters. Under the stern Prussian drillmaster, Inspector General von Steuben, farmer-recruits took shape as professional soldiers.

Today Pennsylvania's Valley Forge Park Commission is restoring the 2,300-

B. ANTHONY STEWART, NATIONAL GEOGRAPHIC PHOTOGRAPHER

Washington's headquarters brightened under Martha's touch. She dined with officers, made soup and jelly for the sick, and greeted fife-and-drum serenaders on the General's birthday.

Monmouth and Morristown

CULVER SERVICE AND (RIGHT) NEAL P. DAVIS

THE trained veterans of Valley Forge got their chance to fight in June, 1778, when Sir Henry Clinton, who had replaced Howe, led the British out of Philadelphia. Gen. Charles Lee, a reluctant patriot, feebly hit troops convoying Clinton's 12-mile baggage train, then retreated.

Washington blasted Lee as "a damned poltroon," rallied the men, and rolled back the grenadiers in a battle near Monmouth, New Jersey.

A woman carried a water pitcher among the sweltering soldiers and took her fallen husband's place at his cannon. Thus "Molly Pitcher" became a legend as the last major action in the North ground to a halt and Clinton slipped away.

More hardship was in store. In 1779 the Continentals tramped back to Morristown for the century's severest winter—28 snowstorms and bitter cold. For some, "naked as Lazarus," it was Valley Forge all over again. Quartered at Ford Mansion (right), Washington held his ragged army together.

acre reserve to its original condition as a military camp. Log cabins copy those built by Continental troops. Each follows Washington's specifications for 900 12-man "hutts." The reconstructed hospital is a small one-room log structure with a rustic operating table at its center. Surgeons had to amputate frozen, gangrenous limbs without benefit of anesthesia.

Park guides say that the question most commonly asked is, "Where was the Battle of Valley Forge fought?" There was none, of course. But sickness, privation, exposure killed more than 3,000 men. Many were buried where they died.

With one unmarked grave goes a sad little story about a soldier who persistently stole chickens from a neighboring farm. The owner appealed to Gen. Anthony Wayne, who seemed too preoccupied to give attention.

"What am I to do?" the farmer asked impatiently.

"Shoot him," snapped Wayne.

The farmer did.

Tracing old fortifications around the cantonment, visitors come upon memorials to regiments recruited in the 13 colonies, and to Europeans who helped America win independence: Steuben, Pulaski, and De Kalb. Others from overseas served at Valley Forge. And a party of Oneida Indians contributed their scouting talent.

Washington's headquarters, a two-story stone farmhouse, looks today as it did when he lived there. Martha Washington joined him for his 46th birthday, watched his health, and won hearts by referring to him as "the old man."

With spring came the miracle of dogwood blossoms—they still come out on some 50,000 trees. A run of shad right up to Pawling's Ford filled empty bellies with fish. Troops played rounders, forerunner of baseball. Best of all was Washington's momentous announcement: France had joined the war on America's side, thanks to the great victory at Saratoga.

HOWELL WALKER

SARATOGA – THE TURNING POINT

Gentleman Johnny comes a cropper

WASHINGTON, soon to move toward Valley Forge in late 1777, heard news from the north that gave him hope in the face of hardship. A drama had been enacted on the bright autumnal stage of the Hudson Valley. A likely British triumph had been rewritten to give America a smash hit.

The plot was familiar: The British were to push down from Canada and cut off New England. It had been tried before and had failed when Benedict Arnold patched together a fleet of small vessels on Lake Champlain and hurled them against the British at Valcour Bay. This time British hopes rode with Gen. John Burgoyne, an elegant, amusing amateur dramatist beloved by his men, who called him "Gentleman Johnny." He started south with a light heart and 8,000 troops, hoping to join at Albany with Howe coming up the Hudson from New York, and Col. Barry St. Leger sweeping through the Mohawk Valley from the west.

Burgoyne's flotilla slipped down Lake Champlain, a glittering pageant – British in scarlet, Hessians in blue, rangers in green, and redskins leading the way in canoes. Fort Ticonderoga's homespun garrison took off before them. But instead of dispersing, the rebels tore up bridges, burned crops, and felled trees across the

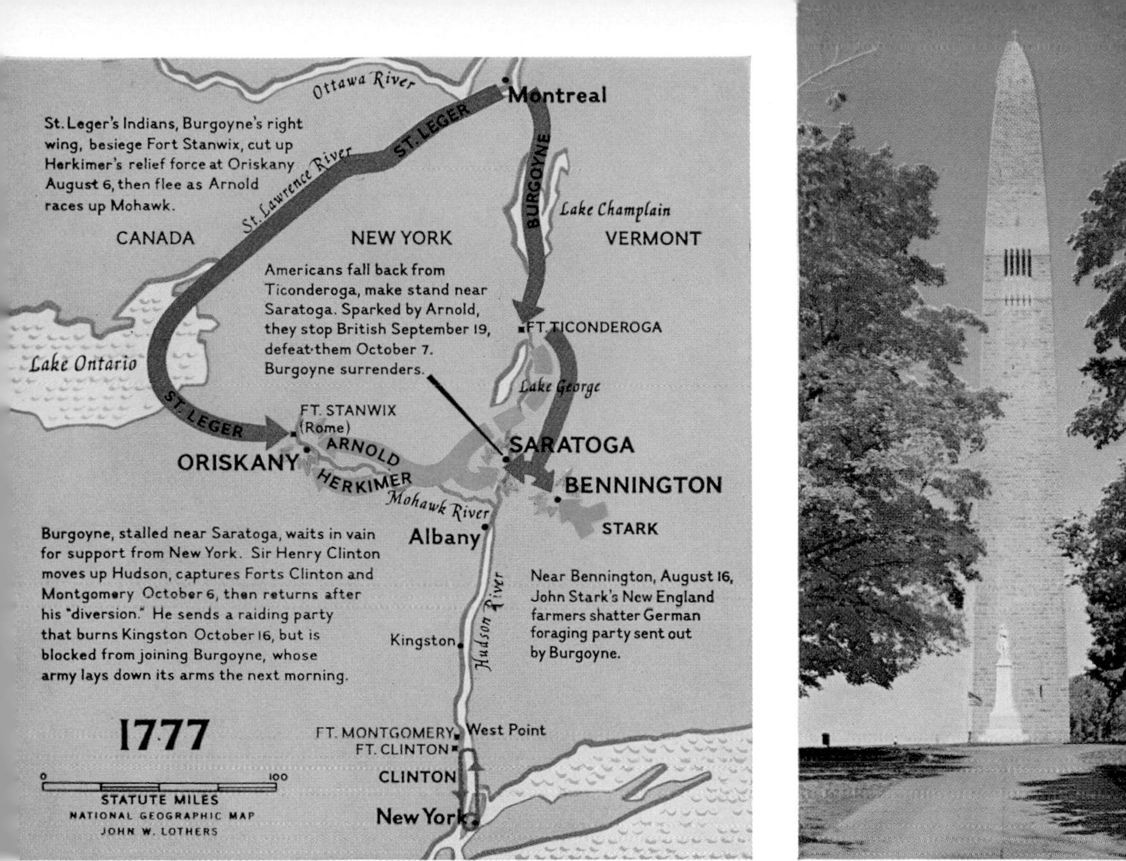
Ottawa River
Montreal
St. Leger's Indians, Burgoyne's right wing, besiege Fort Stanwix, cut up Herkimer's relief force at Oriskany August 6, then flee as Arnold races up Mohawk.
ST. LEGER
St. Lawrence River
BURGOYNE
Lake Champlain
CANADA
NEW YORK
VERMONT
Americans fall back from Ticonderoga, make stand near Saratoga. Sparked by Arnold, they stop British September 19, defeat them October 7. Burgoyne surrenders.
FT. TICONDEROGA
Lake Ontario
Lake George
ST. LEGER
FT. STANWIX (Rome)
ARNOLD
SARATOGA
ORISKANY
HERKIMER
BENNINGTON
Mohawk River
STARK
Albany
Burgoyne, stalled near Saratoga, waits in vain for support from New York. Sir Henry Clinton moves up Hudson, captures Forts Clinton and Montgomery October 6, then returns after his "diversion." He sends a raiding party that burns Kingston October 16, but is blocked from joining Burgoyne, whose army lays down its arms the next morning.
Hudson River
Near Bennington, August 16, John Stark's New England farmers shatter German foraging party sent out by Burgoyne.
Kingston
1777
FT. MONTGOMERY
West Point
FT. CLINTON
0
100
STATUTE MILES
CLINTON
NATIONAL GEOGRAPHIC MAP
JOHN W. LOTHERS
New York

BENNINGTON BATTLEFIELD MONUMENT; FRANK L. FORWARD

trails. Axmen chopped a road for the General's baggage wagons. Unmounted Hessian dragoons limped in their high, tight boots. The supply line stretched thin. Worst of all, Howe sent word that he would head for Philadelphia, not Albany.

There was still St. Leger. He came down the Mohawk as scheduled and paraded his redskins before Fort Stanwix. The rebels refused to panic. Nicholas Herkimer's militia marched to the rescue. In a ravine near Oriskany, St. Leger's Indians led by Joseph Brant ambushed the force and shot Herkimer from his horse. The tough old Indian fighter propped himself against a tree and coolly directed his men as they fought out of the trap.

General Arnold scented battle and stormed off to relieve Fort Stanwix. He sent a false rumor ahead that overwhelming American forces were on the way. The Indians swallowed the tale and vanished like wraiths into the forest. St. Leger could only give up his plans and retreat. He too would miss the reunion at Albany.

Gentleman Johnny was having troubles on his eastern flank. He had sent a detachment, mostly Hessians, to scour the country for horses and food. As they moved toward Bennington (now in Vermont), John Stark, hero of Bunker Hill, met them with 2,000 shirt-sleeved Yankees. "We'll beat them before night," cried he,

"Post two men behind each tree!" Herkimer orders at Oriskany. Seeing that the Indians would rush a man before he could reload, the wounded general told his troops to fight in pairs.

FREDERICK C. YOHN'S FAMOUS PAINTING HANGS IN THE UTICA PUBLIC LIBRARY

IDEALIZED PAINTING BY JOHN TRUMBULL, U.S. CAPITOL ROTUNDA

"The fortune of war, General Gates, has made me your prisoner," said General Burgoyne, tendering his sword in the final act of the Saratoga drama. Colonel Morgan stands at right.

"or Molly Stark will be a widow!" And his farmers rose and mowed down the Germans like ripe wheat.

Far from lighthearted now, Burgoyne urged his weakened army southward, crossing the Hudson near Saratoga (now Schuylerville). Ahead stood Bemis Heights, lined with increasing numbers of well-fed, well-armed country boys spoiling for a fight. They blocked the way.

September 19 dawned clear and crisp. Drums rolled in the British camp. Men lined up and swung off toward Bemis Heights. They didn't know that high in distant trees, hidden by yellowing leaves, American scouts watched every move. The main column of redcoats reached a clearing, Freeman's Farm. Pickets moved into the open, feeling their way across. Suddenly the silence was ripped by the ugly, flat cracking of Pennsylvania rifles. Men dropped in soggy bundles, the rest high-tailed it back to the main force. After them came a buckskin horde led by a towering Virginia teamster, Dan Morgan.

Frantically, the British regulars aligned and sent a crashing volley. The riflemen reeled back, but rallied at the gobble of a wild turkey—Morgan's call. Lead whistled across Freeman's Farm as the battle swayed. Then fire-eating Arnold flung New Hampshire Continentals at a gap in the ragged red line. The king's men wavered, came close to cracking, but Arnold's momentum was spent. He got no help from the cautious American commander, Horatio Gates. As darkness closed in, artillery gave the Yankees "a whiff of grapeshot" at close range. They melted into the forest. Burgoyne held the field—but he had been stopped cold.

Help must come from New York if he was to continue the campaign. But Howe had gone south to Philadelphia. Clinton, his replacement, offered merely to "try something . . . of use."

Burgoyne's last act began October 7 on a tragic note. All that his hungry men had left was courage. He called on it, sending them once more against Bemis Heights. And again Arnold battered them back. Although Arnold had been relieved of command after a quarrel with Gates, he led the Continentals to victory, riding at one point right across the field of fire, a reckless blur in a hail of bullets. He dropped, wounded, as the British and Hessians caved in.

Clinton, at last on the move, seized two forts up the Hudson and wrote Burgoyne: "I sincerely hope this little success of ours may facilitate your operations."

But the curtain was falling for playwright Burgoyne. On October 17 he surrendered at Saratoga.

France had been waiting for just such a victory. She declared herself an ally. ROSS BENNETT

A stone boot honors Benedict Arnold the Saratoga hero, not the West Point traitor. It bears epaulets but no name. A bullet smashed his leg as he led Americans to victory on this field, now a national historical park (below).

ROBERT F. SISSON AND (ABOVE) B. ANTHONY STEWART, BOTH NATIONAL GEOGRAPHIC PHOTOGRAPHERS

Philadelphia
PENNSYLVANIA
MARYLAND
NEW JERSEY
Baltimore
Delaware Bay
DELAWARE
Chesapeake Bay
BRITISH FLEET
Nathanael Greene
Commanding General
Southern Department
Continental Army
CHARLES WILLSON PEALE
INDEPENDENCE HALL COLLECTION
PHILADELPHIA
Charles, Lord Cornwallis
Commanding General
British Southern
Campaign
THOMAS GAINSBOROUGH
NATIONAL PORTRAIT GALLERY
LONDON
Appalachian Mountains
York River
Williamsburg
YORKTOWN
October 19, 1781
James River
Norfolk
FRENCH FLEET
Count de Grasse's fleet from the West Indies beats off a British fleet from New York, September 5, 1781. The French seal Chesapeake Bay—and Cornwallis's fate.
VIRGINIA
NORTH CAROLINA
Dan River
Roanoke River
GUILFORD COURTHOUSE
March 15, 1781
Winston-Salem
Greensboro
Raleigh
Cape Fear River
0 100
STATUTE MILES
NATIONAL GEOGRAPHIC MAP
BY JOHN W. LOTHERS
AMERICAN VICTORY
BRITISH VICTORY
Cape Hatteras
Pee Dee River
COWPENS
January 17, 1781
KINGS MOUNTAIN
October 7, 1780
Wateree River
NORTH CAROLINA
SOUTH CAROLINA
CAMDEN
August 16, 1780
HOBKIRK'S HILL
April 25, 1781
MOORES CREEK
February 27, 1776
Wilmington
Atlantic Ocean
Congaree River
Columbia
EUTAW SPRINGS
September 8, 1781
SOUTH CAROLINA
GEORGIA
Cooper River
CHARLESTON
June 28, 1776
May 12, 1780
Savannah River
SAVANNAH
December 29, 1778

WAR IN THE SOUTH

"We fight, get beat, rise and fight again"

REDCOATS MARCH almost at will through the pine forests. But guerrillas boil up behind them like a ship's wake and the land is never really conquered.... Patriots battle loyalist forces which haven't a British soldier in them. A young militia officer binds his father so the old Tory can't help the enemy.... Hunger, disease stalk the ravaged countryside....

This is the war in the South: sometimes army against army, sometimes patriot against loyalist neighbor in savage civil war. It matched British Col. Banastre Tarleton, who butchered militia even after they raised the white flag, against Francis Marion, the "Swamp Fox," who struck like lightning, then vanished.

Counting on strong loyalist support, General Clinton had tried to invade the South in 1776. But Carolina patriots whipped his Tory allies at Moores Creek and drove his fleet from Charleston. Stalemate in the North brought the British back. They took Savannah late in 1778 and overran Georgia. In 1780 Clinton captured Charleston in America's worst defeat of the war, and left Cornwallis to hold "this miserable country."

Moving north, Cornwallis clashed with the Americans at Camden. Continentals fought stubbornly, but militia ran "like a Torrent." The way clear for his invasion of North Carolina, Cornwallis sent Patrick Ferguson and a flanking force northward in the shadow of the Appalachians. Major Ferguson had invented a breech-loading "rifle gun" that fired five times as fast as a muzzle-loading rifle. Had it been adopted, it might have put a quick end to the war. Certainly it would have helped Ferguson now, trapped on Kings Mountain. Ferguson was everywhere, his silver whistle piercing the din as he rallied his troops for bayonet charges. Then death stilled the whistle. Frontiersmen with long rifles overwhelmed his entire force, then drifted back across the misty mountains.

Washington sent Nathanael Greene, a superb strategist, to take command in the South. With fewer than 1,500 men "wretched beyond description," the mild-mannered Rhode Island ironmaster sparred with the disciplined legions of Lord Cornwallis. He placed part of his force under Daniel Morgan, who made a stand at Cowpens against Tarleton's dragoons. The "Old Wagoner" moved among his nervous militia, joking with them, telling them he'd crack his whip over Ban Tarleton. When the dragoons charged, the militia shattered them.

Stung, Cornwallis pushed forward. But Greene escaped across the swollen Dan River into Virginia. He gathered reinforcements, then struck south to harass the British, now far from supplies in country aswarm with guerrillas. At Guilford Courthouse, Hobkirk's Hill, and Eutaw Springs Greene lost the field but tore redcoat ranks to ribbons. "We fight, get beat, rise and fight again," he reported.

Thus the tireless general, the Continentals, the guerrillas, and drifting militia pushed the British back on Charleston and Savannah. Meanwhile Cornwallis, who had withdrawn to Wilmington, marched north to meet destiny at Yorktown.

These blue stars and stripes saw battle at Guilford Courthouse. A national military park marks the site of Cornwallis's costly victory.

FLAG IN NORTH CAROLINA HALL OF HISTORY, RALEIGH; THOMAS NEBBIA

CLIMAX AT YORKTOWN

BY INTELLIGENCE which I have this day received," wrote Gen. Henry Clinton on September 2, 1781, "it would seem that Mr. Washington is moving an army to the southward [and] expects the co-operation of a considerable French armament." Bland words to introduce the thundering last act of the Revolution!

In "impenetrable secrecy" Washington and Count de Rochambeau marched to Chesapeake Bay, which De Grasse's French fleet controlled. In Virginia, Americans under Lafayette thinly straddled the peninsula between the James and York rivers. Inside this still fragile net Cornwallis with 7,500 men dug in at Yorktown and waited to be reinforced by sea.

THIS CARTRIDGE BOX PLATE FROM HESSIAN REGIMENT VON BOSE WAS FOUND AT REDOUBT NO. 9 ON YORKTOWN BATTLEFIELD

Continentals and militia streamed into Williamsburg. On September 28 the allied army, now 16,000, pressed down the peninsula. Assured by Clinton that "the joint exertions of the navy and army" would soon relieve him, Cornwallis abandoned his outer redoubts to tighten defenses about the port.

Washington's troops shoveled furiously on their first siege line. October 9, French and American batteries opened fire. Day and night they pounded the British. A defender's diary tells of "the

DAVID S. BOYER, NATIONAL GEOGRAPHIC STAFF

"STORMING THE REDOUBT" BY LOUIS EUGENE LAMI, THE CAPITOL, RICHMOND, VIRGINIA

This "Lafayette Cannon" roared defiance at Yorktown's besiegers. The Marquis, triumphantly touring America in 1824-5, recalled its capture by men he commanded as a 24-year-old major general. George II's coat of arms decorates the breech. In bitter fighting (above), Lafayette's infantry, led by Alexander Hamilton, took strategic Redoubt No. 10.

horribly many cannon balls ... men were badly injured and mortally wounded by the fragments of bombs ... arms and legs severed or themselves struck dead."

In the American camp, surgeon James Thacher found the bombardment "sublime and stupendous." The bombs "are clearly visible in the form of a black ball in the day, but in the night they appear like fiery meteors with blazing tails, most beautifully brilliant," he exulted. "When a shell falls, it whirls round, burrows ... and bursting, makes dreadful havoc around."

Sickness decimated the beleaguered troops. In desperation Cornwallis wrote: "we cannot hope to make a very long resistance."

On the night of October 11-12 Washington closed in to start a second siege line. Three nights later French chasseurs and grenadiers stormed one redoubt, another fell to American bayonets. Cornwallis tried to escape across the York, but a squall scattered his boats. On the morning of the 17th he sent a drummer atop a parapet to beat a parley—"the most delightful music" to American ears.

A hush fell over the battlefield.

For two days the combatants hammered out terms. Then the British regulars, some weeping, some sullen, marched out with impassive German mercenaries and nervous Tories, bands playing an old march, "The World Turned Upside Down." The Treaty of Paris was two years off, but America's flag now waved free.

Guns and fraises bristle today from earthworks on Yorktown Battlefield. Starting from the visitor center, sightseers can trace history's path through the fortifications, the cemeteries, the Moore House where the capitulation terms were

Washington and his officers (right) and French commanders (left) watch deputies enact the ceremony of surrender, October 19, 1781. "The play, sir, is over," wrote Lafayette.

drafted, along Surrender Road, and on to the 95-foot victory monument authorized by a jubilant but penniless Congress in 1781 and not begun until a century later.

Yorktown, with its stately Nelson House, preserves some of the "great Air of Opulence" it had when the wharves bustled with tidewater tobacco trade. The Customhouse and the Somerwell House rose in the early 1700's. Grace Church and the Sessions House, oldest in town, have stood since the 1690's.

Now in Colonial National Historical Park, Yorktown is a terminus of Colonial Parkway. This highroad of history sweeps 23 miles from the victory ground of independence, back through elegant Williamsburg to swampy Jamestown, where Englishmen planted the seeds of Yorktown 174 years before. THOMAS Y. CANBY

Nelson House was "wounded" during the siege; cannon balls still lie imbedded in its walls

Built before 1740, this Georgian mansion belonged to Gen. Thomas Nelson, signer of the Declaration of Independence and governor of Virginia.

Cornwallis is believed to have moved here when his earlier headquarters (in another Nelson home at the east end of town) were demolished by artillery. Here, tradition says, he wrote Washington, "I propose a cessation of hostilities. . . ."

Lafayette was gaily entertained here in 1824. Nelsons owned the house, which served as a Union hospital during the Civil War, until the early 1900's.

BATES LITTLEHALES AND (LEFT) VOLKMAR WENTZEL, NATIONAL GEOGRAPHIC PHOTOGRAPHERS
TOP: "SURRENDER OF CORNWALLIS" BY JOHN TRUMBULL, YALE UNIVERSITY ART GALLERY

The world of GEORGE WASHINGTON

INDEPENDENCE had been assured at Yorktown, and Washington was the most honored person in America. A grateful republic would make him its first president, raise statues to him, create godlike legends about him. As the years rolled by biographers would write millions of words about Washington—hero, man, and myth. In reaction to his early portrayal as the paragon of the cherry tree legend and the all-wise "man in the white marble toga," debunkers sometimes went to opposite extremes.

Yet the role Washington preferred was that of squire of Mount Vernon.

As a product of English colonial life, George Washington came naturally by this love for the soil. The son of Augustine and Mary Ball Washington, he descended from a long line of landowners. He was born in 1732 on a 2,500-acre plantation, now Wakefield, in Westmoreland County, Virginia. While George was still a toddler, the family moved up the Potomac to Little Hunting Creek tract, site of Mount Vernon. After a few years the Washingtons established a third home at Ferry Farm, near Fredericksburg. There, when George was 11, his father died.

The boy turned for guidance to his half brother Lawrence, back from war service in the Caribbean. When Lawrence settled down at his inherited estate—renamed in honor of his former commander, Admiral Edward Vernon—George was always welcome. Thus began a historic love affair with a way of life that George once described as "of all others . . . the most delectable." On long visits to the rolling, wooded estate along the Potomac, he swam, rode, fished, and hunted. By the time he was a husky 16 year old he was learning—earnestly if a bit awkwardly—to dance and play billiards and cards, all social arts of Virginia's 18th century gentry. He recalled that time as "the happiest years of my life."

MORE IMPORTANT to Washington's future was a family connection with Thomas, Lord Fairfax. He took a fancy to young George, and knowing that the lad had studied surveying sent him off with an expedition to mark out a vast property in the Shenandoah Valley for farming grants. It was Washington's first taste of frontier life, of camping in the wilderness and sharing the meager accommodations of scattered settlers. To his "Surprize," he confided to his diary, his bed in one pioneer hut was "nothing but a Little Straw—Matted together without Sheets or any thing else but only one thread Bear blanket with double its Weight of Vermin such as Lice Fleas & c." At supper, on another occasion, he found "neither a Cloth upon ye Table nor a knife to eat with."

The trip taught him to meet new situations and develop self-reliance. On his impressionable mind the sweet abundance beyond the Blue Ridge left a lasting appreciation of America's natural wealth—and the right of free people to enjoy it.

NATIONAL GALLERY OF ART

GEORGE WASHINGTON

by Rembrandt Peale

This "Porthole Washington," one of 79 versions, was painted in 1823 because the first President's family wished to show "his mild, thoughtful, and dignified, yet firm and energetic countenance." Sitting in 1795 for four artists of the Peale family, Washington quipped, "I will be well pealed today."

The experience helped fit him for a military career. His subsequent service in the French and Indian War proved his courage and leadership.

Back from war, the dashing colonel married a charming and wealthy widow, Martha Dandridge Custis. After the death of his half brother, George had inherited Mount Vernon. Now, in the honeymoon spring of 1759, he set up housekeeping with his bride and her two children, "Jacky" and "Patcy," already firmly anchored in their stepfather's devotion.

"You must have the House very well cleand," Washington alerted his manager

Washington was born at Wakefield. No plans remain, so the national monument (above) represents a typical Virginia country home of the 1720's. Here George took his early steps, in clothes such as his 11th generation collateral descendant dons at left. At 16 he was surveying the frontier. War brought further travels. In Fraunces Tavern, at Broad and Pearl Streets in New York (below), the commander in chief bade farewell to his officer comrades of the Continental Army. After his inauguration, he toured the nation from Maine to Georgia.

FROM TOP: B. ANTHONY STEWART, JOHN E. FLETCHER, NATIONAL GEOGRAPHIC PHOTOGRAPHERS; LOUIS FROHMAN; LIBRARY OF CONGRESS

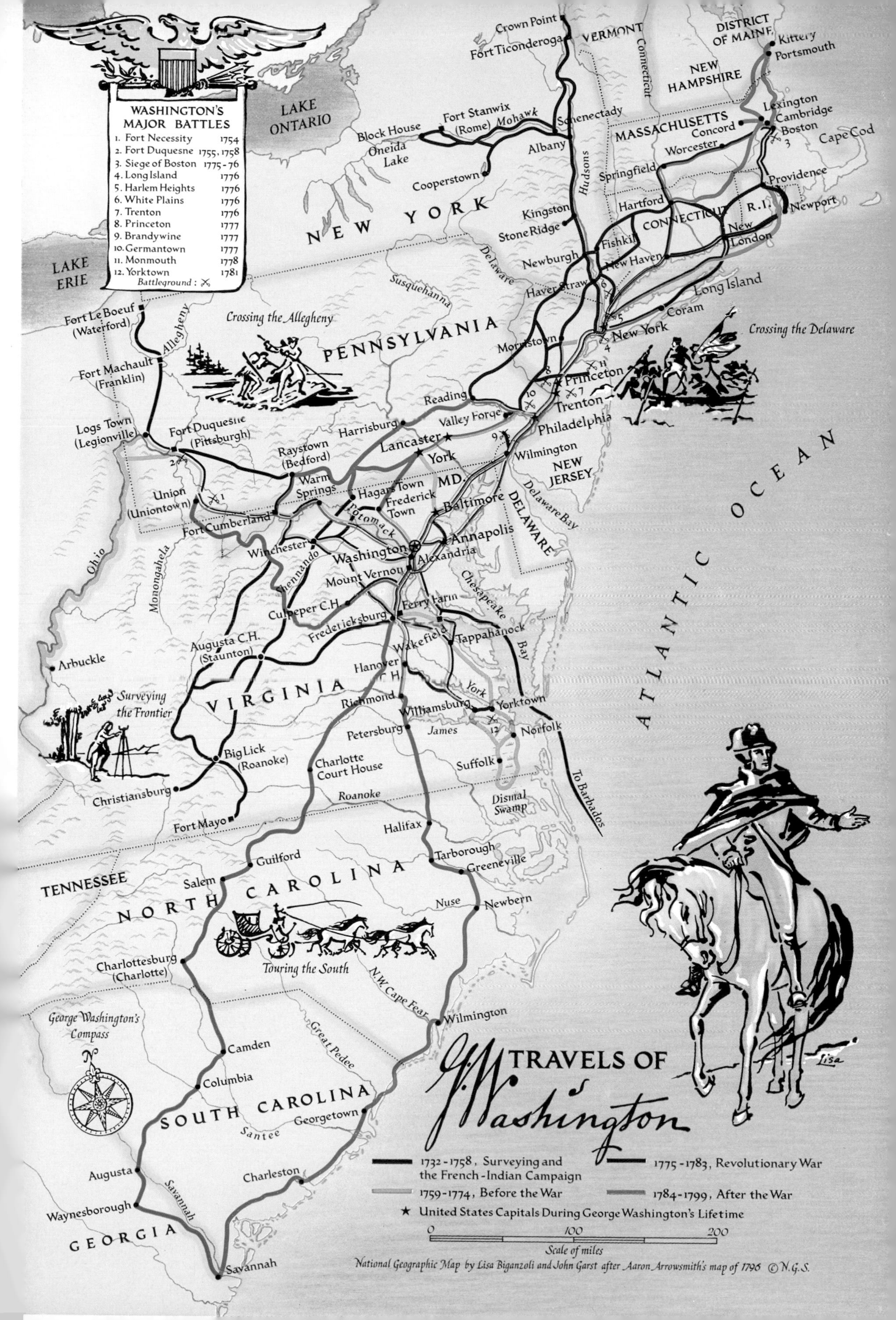
WASHINGTON'S MAJOR BATTLES
1. Fort Necessity 1754
2. Fort Duquesne 1755, 1758
3. Siege of Boston 1775-76
4. Long Island 1776
5. Harlem Heights 1776
6. White Plains 1776
7. Trenton 1776
8. Princeton 1777
9. Brandywine 1777
10. Germantown 1777
11. Monmouth 1778
12. Yorktown 1781
Battleground :
TRAVELS OF G. Washington
1732-1758, Surveying and the French-Indian Campaign
1775-1783, Revolutionary War
1759-1774, Before the War
1784-1799, After the War
★ United States Capitals During George Washington's Lifetime
0
100
200
Scale of miles
National Geographic Map by Lisa Biganzoli and John Garst after Aaron Arrowsmith's map of 1796 © N.G.S.
Lisa
Crossing the Allegheny
Crossing the Delaware
Surveying the Frontier
Touring the South
George Washington's Compass
LAKE ONTARIO
LAKE ERIE
NEW YORK
PENNSYLVANIA
VERMONT
DISTRICT OF MAINE
NEW HAMPSHIRE
MASSACHUSETTS
CONNECTICUT
R.I.
NEW JERSEY
DELAWARE
MD.
VIRGINIA
NORTH CAROLINA
SOUTH CAROLINA
GEORGIA
TENNESSEE
ATLANTIC OCEAN
Crown Point
Fort Ticonderoga
Kittery
Portsmouth
Lexington
Cambridge
Boston
Cape Cod
Concord
Worcester
Springfield
Providence
Newport
Hartford
New London
New Haven
Long Island
Coram
New York
Fishkill
Newburgh
Haverstraw
Kingston
Stone Ridge
Albany
Schenectady
Fort Stanwix (Rome)
Mohawk
Block House
Oneida Lake
Cooperstown
Hudsons
Connecticut
Delaware
Susquehanna
Morristown
Princeton
Trenton
Philadelphia
Valley Forge
Reading
Harrisburg
Lancaster
York
Wilmington
Delaware Bay
Fort Le Boeuf (Waterford)
Allegheny
Fort Machault (Franklin)
Logs Town (Legionville)
Fort Duquesne (Pittsburgh)
Raystown (Bedford)
Warm Springs
Hagars Town
Frederick Town
Baltimore
Annapolis
Union (Uniontown)
Fort Cumberland
Potomack
Winchester
Washington
Alexandria
Mount Vernon
Shennando
Monongahela
Ohio
Culpeper C.H.
Ferry Farm
Fredericksburg
Chesapeake Bay
Wakefield
Tappahanock
Augusta C.H. (Staunton)
Arbuckle
Hanover C.H.
Richmond
Williamsburg
York
Yorktown
James
Norfolk
Petersburg
Suffolk
Big Lick (Roanoke)
Charlotte Court House
Christiansburg
Roanoke
Dismal Swamp
To Barbados
Fort Mayo
Halifax
Tarborough
Greeneville
Guilford
Salem
Nuse
Newbern
Charlottesburg (Charlotte)
N.W. Cape Fear
Wilmington
Great Pedee
Camden
Columbia
Georgetown
Santee
Augusta
Charleston
Savannah
Waynesborough
Savannah

Washington's love affair with Mount Vernon began during his youthful visits

Whether he was fighting Indians, holding his ragged revolutionary army together, or serving as President, his thoughts returned to these beloved acres. "No estate in United America is

JOHN E. FLETCHER, NATIONAL GEOGRAPHIC PHOTOGRAPHER

more pleasantly situated than this," he proudly wrote. Constantly improving it, the General tripled its acreage and efficiently grouped outbuildings and gardens to flank the main house, which he doubled in size. Yet simplicity marked his life here, "free from the bustle of a camp and the intrigues of a court." The road at upper right leads to his grave. Martha lies beside him.

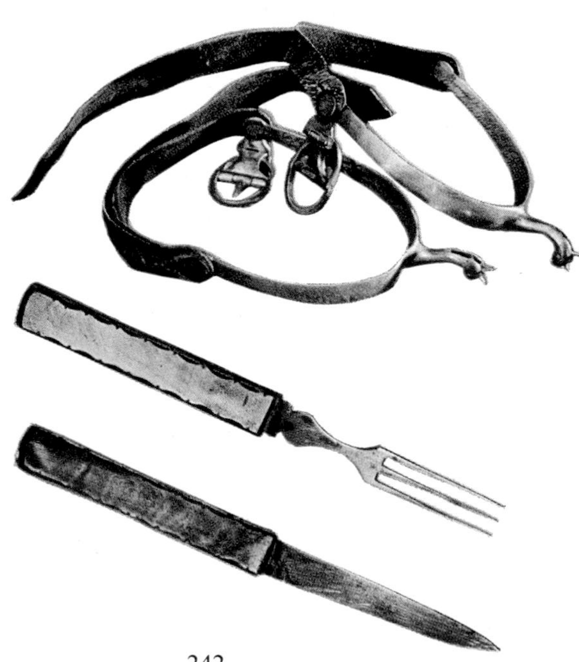

Welcome glow amid winter's snow recalls days when a dozen fireplaces warmed the candlelit mansion. In summer, Potomac breezes cooled the veranda, where Washington relaxed with his family. Here he entertained the horde of callers who turned his home, he wryly remarked, into "a well resorted tavern." A most welcome guest was Lafayette (right) in 1784. Seeing Washington, the Marquis "threw himself into the arms of his adoptive father."

Bone-inlaid knife and fork, whose blade and tines slide protectively into each other's handle, went with the General on his campaigns. Mount Vernon displays them along with silver spurs that Washington gave to a courier at Valley Forge.

before they arrived, "and Were you to make Fires in the Rooms below it w'd Air them."

Besides expanding and beautifying his home, managing family properties, and joining in land-development ventures, Washington took his seat in the House of Burgesses at Williamsburg. A fellow member saw him, "Straight as an Indian, measuring 6 feet 2 inches in his stockings. . . . A pleasing and benevolent tho a commanding countenance, dark brown hair which he wears in a cue."

He was also a contented man. "I am now I believe fixd at this Seat with an agreable Consort for Life," he wrote to a friend, as he contemplated his future as a planter.

But the Burgess of Mount Vernon was hardly "fixd." As resistance to the Crown heightened, Virginia demanded more and more of this quiet, modest, sensible man, "in action cool, like a Bishop at his prayers." He served as a delegate at both First and Second Continental Congresses, led the colonies to victory, presided over the Constitutional Convention, and was unanimously elected first President of the Republic—the highest gift his countrymen could bestow.

Through it all, Mount Vernon remained the

LOUIS MIGNOT AND THOMAS ROSSITER, METROPOLITAN MUSEUM OF ART. LEFT: THE MOUNT VERNON LADIES' ASSOCIATION AND (UPPER) THOMAS NEBBIA

hearthstone of George Washington's world. At the end of the Revolution he bade farewell to his officers, resigned his commission, and wrote his comrade Lafayette, "I am retiring within myself and shall tread the paths of private life with heartfelt satisfaction."

Called away as President, he confessed, "I had rather be at Mount Vernon with a friend or two about me, than to be attended at the Seat of Government by the Officers of State . . . of every Power in Europe."

TODAY, more than a million people a year visit the painstakingly restored showplace that was Washington's pride and joy.

With groups of adults and children—and once with Queen Juliana of the Netherlands paying respect to the American shrine—I walked the shaded lawns and admired relics and reconstructions of those vanished days.

Here is a villagelike 18th century plantation with service buildings clustered about the mansion home. Housekeepers look in vain for a kitchen in the family dwelling. They find it in an annex at the end of an arcade. Its iron skillets, the tubs in the washhouse, looms in the spinning house—even stage-prop hams in the smokehouse—stand ready for ghostly hands to use. Mouths water at Martha's "Grate cake" recipe preserved in the museum. It starts out, "Take 40 eggs . . . work four pounds of butter."

Boxwood-edged flower beds and kitchen gardens bloom, as when Washington gave notice of his coming: "Tell the Gardener I shall expect everything that a Garden ought to produce, in the most ample manner."

Inside the mansion each room and object has its own story. A card table, a set of blue

Tasteful, not sumptuous, rooms typify Mount Vernon. Gift of Lafayette, a key to the Bastille hangs in the central hall (above) between spare bedroom and dining room. In his library Washington balanced accounts, studied crop reports, and wrote letters that shaped history. The globe, telescope, riding crop, and shotgun were his.

B. ANTHONY STEWART AND JOHN E. FLETCHER, NATIONAL GEOGRAPHIC PHOTOGRAPHERS

dishes, white dimity curtains festooned with green all help re-create scenes that Washington knew.

"Too elegant . . . I fear for my . . . republican stile," he wrote of the elaborate marble mantel in the Banquet Hall. It reached Mount Vernon, according to a legend, through the courtesy of a pirate crew. Starting from England respectably enough, this gift was seized by pirates. When the buccaneers noted the famous addressee, they risked hanging by shipping it on to Mount Vernon.

At the handsome secretary-desk in the library, the General and President answered endless letters from friends and favor seekers, and kept meticulous accounts.

From the hall I looked into the music room where the family and neighbors gathered for singing and dancing. Washington loved to dance, but admitted he could "neither sing one of the songs nor raise a single note on any instrument."

The old harpsichord standing open in the room was a gift from Washington to Martha's granddaughter, Nelly Custis. After Nelly married Washington's nephew, Lawrence Lewis, they took it to nearby Woodlawn, built on Mount Vernon land Uncle George bequeathed to them. When the Mount Vernon Ladies' Association was formed in 1853 to save the deteriorating estate and collect its

Washington's day began in this room; from it he and Martha could look down on the Potomac glimmering in the morning sun. And in this four-poster the master of Mount Vernon ended his days. His trunk still rests at its foot.

His rounds included the greenhouse. Rebuilt, it grows oranges as it did then. He prized his grist mill: "I work two pair of Stones, one part of which are French burr." Visitors see wooden gears and a 16-foot water wheel, both restored.

Come Sunday the General would ride to Pohick Church, where it was "not the custom for Gentlemen to go into Church til Service is beginning, when they enter in a Body, in the same manner as they come out." A parish vestryman for 22 years, Washington also served from time to time as "overseer of the poor."

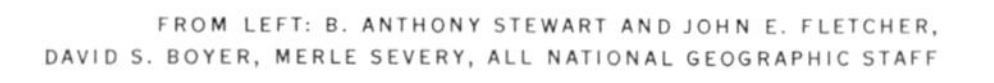

FROM LEFT: B. ANTHONY STEWART AND JOHN E. FLETCHER, DAVID S. BOYER, MERLE SEVERY, ALL NATIONAL GEOGRAPHIC STAFF

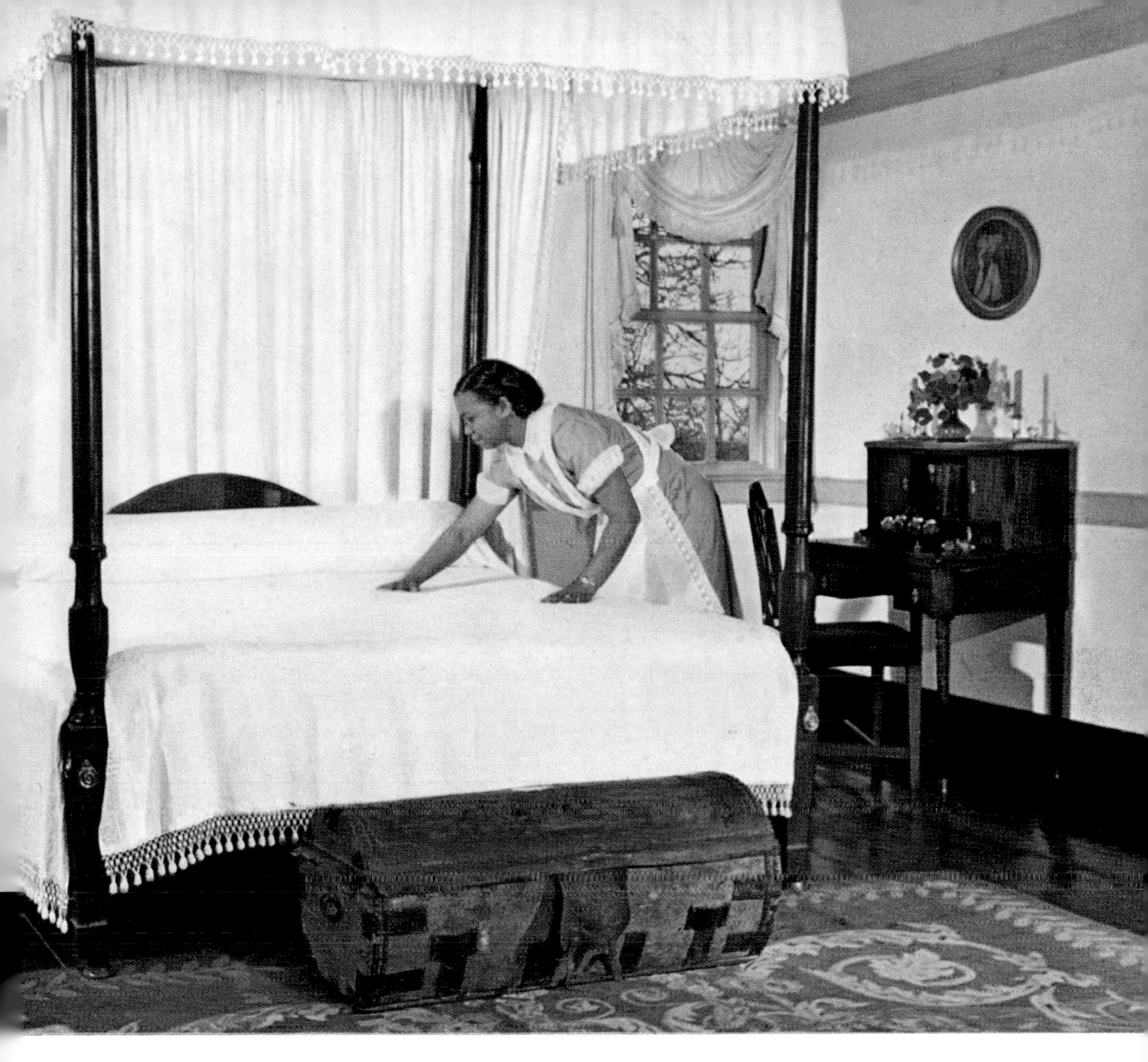

Mary Washington's home in Fredericksburg was a gift from her son. His sister Betty lived in nearby Kenmore.

Woodlawn Plantation, near Mount Vernon, welcomes visitors as it did when Nelly Custis Lewis was hostess here.

Cobbled Prince Street in Alexandria rang to carriage wheels when Washington frequented the thriving port.

FROM TOP: B. ANTHONY STEWART, J. BAYLOR ROBERTS, DAVID S. BOYER, ALL NATIONAL GEOGRAPHIC STAFF

scattered belongings, the harpsichord was the first piece to return.

The most precious possession is the mahogany four-poster in which Washington died, December 14, 1799, after exposure to sleet and snow while making his plantation rounds. His death, between 10 and 11 P.M., was reported by his secretary, Tobias Lear: "He resigned his breath with the greatest composure, having the full possession of his reason to the last moment."

By reconstruction, gift, purchase, and loan, the association has now restored Mount Vernon as it must have looked in its prime. But work is never done. "We are always learning more, and adding details to our scene settings," said Resident Director Charles C. Wall, who has devoted more than 30 years to the restoration.

"In 1956 we acquired our biggest collection of personal and household articles. It came from a descendant and included a charming miniature of Martha Washington believed to have been painted at Mount Vernon in 1772 by Charles Willson Peale."

To protect the mansion and its priceless furnishings, structural reinforcements and fire-fighting equipment have been installed. Guards and watchdogs patrol; searchlights play over the grounds. Engineers, maids, cooks, gardeners, secretaries, stablemen, curators, and librarians maintain this working exhibit that boasts its own cattle, sheep, horses, even beehives.

Ann Cunningham of South Carolina, the association's founder, summed up: "Though we slay our forests . . . pull down our churches, remove from home to home, till the hearthstone seems to have no resting place in America, let them see that we know how to care for the home of our hero."

ROBERT F. SISSON AND DONALD MCBAIN, BOTH NATIONAL GEOGRAPHIC STAFF

Alexandria was George Washington's home town. In parlors like this at Lord Fairfax House, or at Gadsby's Tavern, he would have felt at ease with these clay pipes and cards.

B. ANTHONY STEWART AND JOHN E. FLETCHER, NATIONAL GEOGRAPHIC PHOTOGRAPHERS

Georgetown homes, like these on old Gay Street (left), played host to the General. He may have known the Yellow Tavern, with its stately hall, where merchants and political notables gathered. It is now a 33d Street residence. Today a beautifully restored part of the nation's capital, Georgetown was a proud port before Washington's city was even a plan.

L'Enfant designs a magnificent capital city

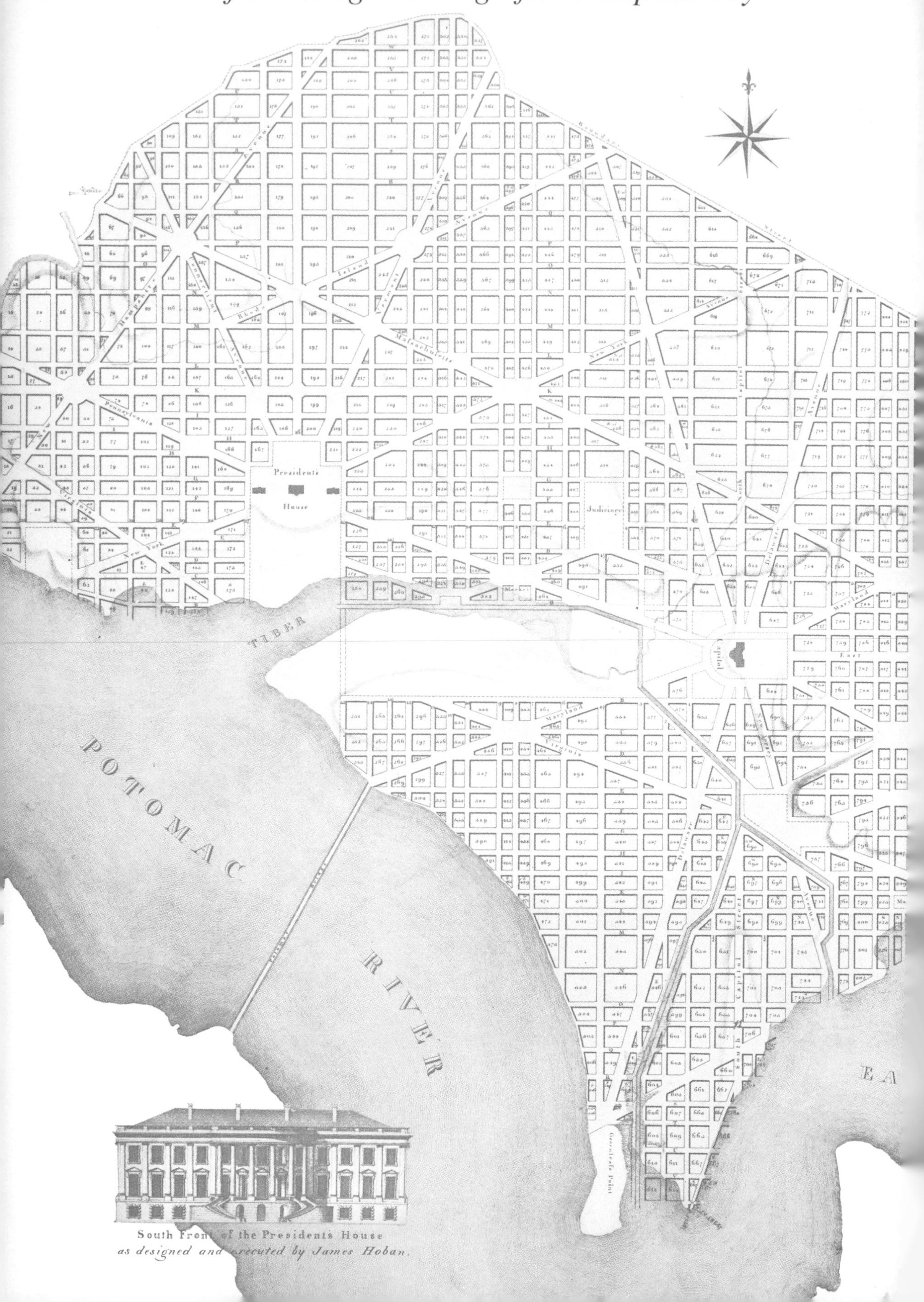

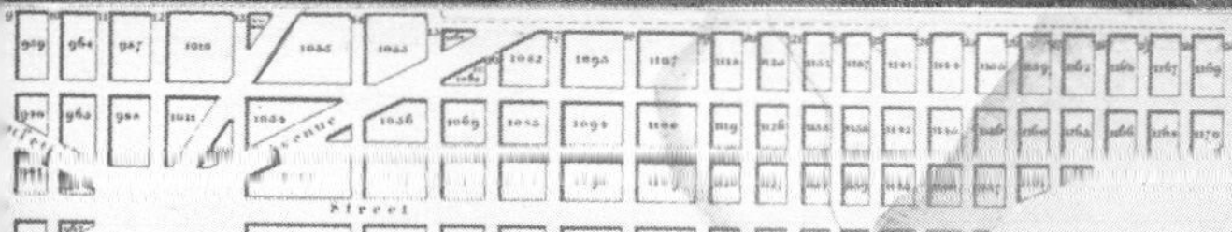

BY EDWARD SAVAGE, C. 1796, MELLON COLLECTION, NATIONAL GALLERY OF ART. L'ENFANT'S PLAN IN AN 1818 VERSION, LIBRARY OF CONGRESS

Washington and his family at Mount Vernon study plans for a federal city on the Potomac

New York was the capital when the General was inaugurated on April 30, 1789. Earlier the seat of government had shuttled among Philadelphia, Baltimore, Lancaster, York, Princeton, Annapolis, and Trenton. In August, 1790, the perambulating legislators returned to Philadelphia to remain ten more years.

Seeking a permanent site between North and South, Washington chose what is now the District of Columbia and appointed Maj. Pierre Charles L'Enfant, French-born Revolutionary War engineer, to draw up plans. L'Enfant centered streets around a mall from Potomac to Capitol (begun in 1793). The President's House (started a year earlier) looks across it. In 1800 the government and all its employees – some 130 – moved in.

The city reflects L'Enfant's design, but grew whimsically at times. When the Treasury burned, President Jackson, out for a stroll, was asked where it should be rebuilt. "Right here!" said he, banging his cane. There it was put, breaking the proposed sweep of Pennsylvania Avenue from Capitol to White House.

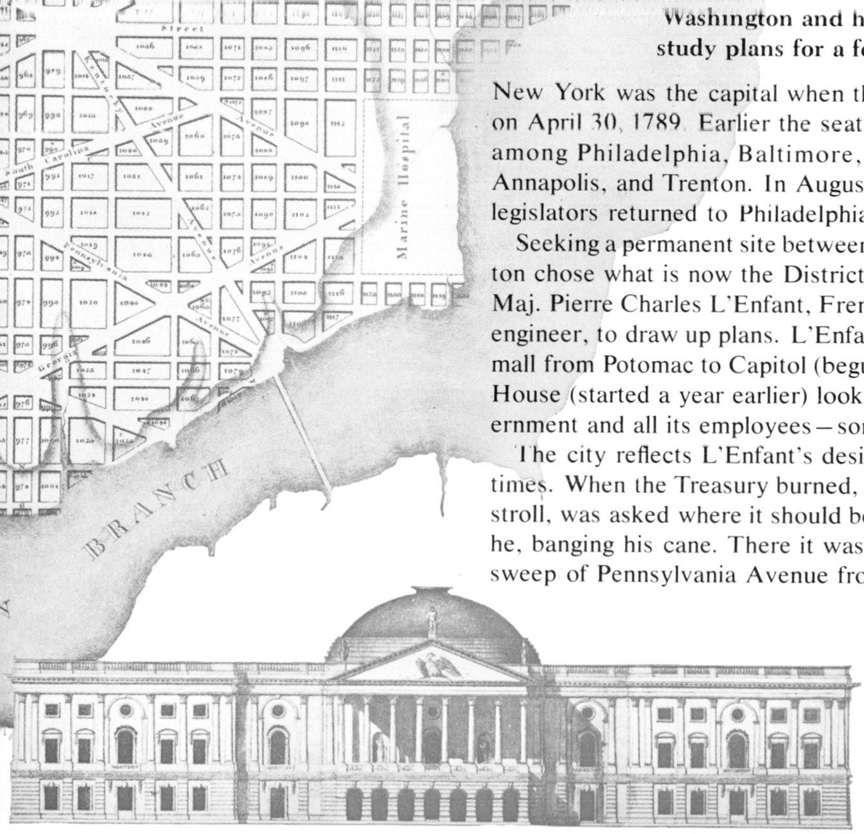

East Front of the Capitol of the United States
as originally designed by William Thornton – and adopted by General Washington – President of the United States.

RICHARD S. DURRANCE

Thomas Jefferson, statesman, sage, architect of American ideals as well as noble buildings, assumed towering stature when his country most needed giants. Yet near Charlottesville he lived, and lingers, as a gentle and kindly neighbor. "All my wishes . . . end at Monticello," wrote Jefferson. He wanted to have inscribed on his grave marker there, not that he had held great offices, but that he was author of the Declaration of Independence and the Virginia statute for religious freedom, and father of the University of Virginia. His own words best capture his character: "I have sworn upon the altar of god eternal hostility against every form of tyranny over the mind of man."

ANNE REVIS GROSVENOR

MR. JEFFERSON *of Monticello*

LAZILY swinging in a hammock, I watched the cloud shadows race across Carter's Mountain, rearing its green head beyond the white fences. What stories it could tell of the days of Thomas Jefferson and his friends who early appreciated its beauty and built homes on its flanks!

I reflected how the spell of "Mr. Jefferson," as local people respectfully refer to him, still lingers about the Charlottesville region of Virginia. At every turn some link suggests this extraordinary man, our country's third President and author of its Declaration of Independence.

Just around the corner of Carter's Mountain perches Monticello, his hilltop home. Through his telescope he could watch the building of his beloved university far below in Charlottesville. Across a vale, spicy boxwood hedges lead to Ash Lawn, the "cabin castle" he built for his friend James Monroe.

Redlands, Carter family stronghold still, scans the countryside from the far end of this ridge granted to John Carter about 1730 by King George II. Beside the James River stands Bremo, another house that reveals Jefferson touches.

With all these reminders about me, I set forth to explore Monticello. Up a wooded road I wound until Jefferson's "sea view" burst upon me, a misty line stretching along the horizon as far as the eye could see. Across hills, valleys, fields, and woods I traced the Rivanna River meandering to Shadwell, Jefferson's birthplace. Left fatherless at 14, Tom inherited "Little Mountain," which he named in Italian "Monticello." Early he began planning the mansion that would one day crown its summit. This was revolutionary in a day when everyone built in the lowlands close to waterways. But first he had to scalp his mountain to level its crest for house and

JEFFERSON SAT FOR SCULPTOR JEAN ANTOINE HOUDON IN 1789 WHILE U.S. MINISTER TO FRANCE; THE MARBLE BUST IS IN THE MUSEUM OF FINE ARTS, BOSTON

Cannon-ball clock in the entrance hall fascinates visitors. Weights drop down the wall at right, marked off with days of the week. Lewis and Clark Expedition brought back the elk and moose antlers.

gardens. Though still in his twenties when he laid foundations, he was in his sixties before the house was finished. During all these years he built, tore down, and built again.

"Architecture is my delight, and putting up and pulling down, one of my favorite amusements," he once said.

The young lawyer's political career interfered too. Starting as the representative of Albemarle County in the House of Burgesses, he rose to be a key delegate to the Second Continental Congress and governor of Virginia. While writing the Declaration of Independence or serving in Washington's cabinet as the first secretary of state, he found time to "dash" home now and then from Philadelphia or New York—an 8- to 13-day trip—to superintend work on Monticello. As minister to France, living abroad for five years, he picked up ideas for his house wherever he traveled—his dome from the new buildings in Paris, and his classical style from the Pantheon in Rome and the 16th century Italian architect, Andrea Palladio.

WALKING OUT on the broad west lawn, I admired the house, as well-groomed as if built only yesterday. Its octagonal dome gleams white and symmetrical against blue sky and copper beeches. Green shutters accent mellow brick. I noted some windows were floor length, the lowest sashes girded by white frets. Mr. Jefferson installed the wooden grills after a visitor, tradition says, leaned too far back in his chair and tumbled four feet to the ground!

I browsed along the flower-lined paths, painstakingly restored by ladies of the Garden Club of Virginia. They were guided by Dr. Edwin M. Betts, botanist at the university, who studied Jefferson's own garden sketches and seed lists. A Negro gardener looked up as I passed. "That takes a lot of snipping," I observed, as he tussled with some tough stems of Spanish iris.

"Time you get around, it's time to start again," he grinned. "Dis hyah purple irish is an o-rig-inal, and I sho' wish Mr. Jefferson never done planted it!"

Then I strolled along a terrace to Jefferson's one-room office. Without realizing it, I was walking over the icehouse, stables, saddle and harness room, and carriage house. Across the lawn a similar platform leading to the Honeymoon Cottage hid smokehouse, kitchen, dairy, and servants' rooms.

To this cottage in 1772 Jefferson brought his bride, Martha Wayles Skelton, already a widow at 23. After their wedding 100 miles away, they traveled in snow until drifts blocked their carriage. Continuing on horseback, they arrived at Monticello in the dead of night to find all the slaves fast asleep and the fires out. But this did not daunt the happy pair in their snug retreat 867 feet above the world.

A stray breeze swayed the weather vane over Monticello's front portico. In the vestibule below I saw its counterpart, a pointer set in a compass rose in the ceiling. By this device the ingenious master could tell accurately the direction of the wind,

"Finest invention of the present age," Jefferson termed the polygraph (right). Twin pens, ingeniously joined, write a letter and make a copy simultaneously.

How far to Philadelphia? The master of Monticello—gleaner of information and lover of gadgets—attached an odometer (below) to the axletree of his carriage and found the distance 269 miles (compared with 240 on today's highways). The device counted wheel revolutions. To measure the countryside around his estate, Jefferson used a theodolite to sight on nearby peaks.

DEAN CONGER AND (BELOW) JOHN E. FLETCHER, NATIONAL GEOGRAPHIC PHOTOGRAPHERS

whether he was indoors or out. He could tell the time too, for the great clock in the front hall is backed by a duplicate outside.

"If you tilt that ladder we use to wind the clock, it will fold up into a mahogany pole," an attendant told me. "Its rungs collapse on pivots." Pointing to French doors, he said, "These work like a streetcar's." He touched one of the glass doors and the other swung open with it. "The works are hidden in the floor below."

I smoothed my hair in a large gilt Louis XVI mirror which Jefferson brought from Paris, and walked across a beautiful floor laid in ten-inch squares of dark cherry with frames of beech. Studying two tiny dumb-waiters built into the side of the dining room mantelpiece, I saw that one descended as the other rose.

"There's a neat trick," exclaimed a bystander. "I'd like to see Jefferson pulling up a bottle from the wine cellar—perhaps to toast his guest James Monroe!"

I wandered through bedrooms used by Monroe and Madison on frequent visits. But there were no beds as we know them today. Instead, three-sided alcoves contained hooks and rope-supported mattresses. On one wall a rough sketch penned by Jefferson himself showed the shirred pattern of the curtains. (Perhaps if Mrs. Jefferson had lived longer than ten years after their marriage, she would have

designed the window hangings.) Jefferson's bed, in contrast to the others, was built in an open alcove between his bedroom and study. On awakening, he could roll out into whichever room he chose.

He could sit or stand to his reading and drawing by adjusting a table's height and angle. And he filed his letters in an octagonal table, some of its drawers shaped like pieces of pie. Gadgeteer Jefferson would be intrigued by the equipment swarms of camera fans bring to Monticello today. He played with an early "Brownie," a camera obscura purchased from David Rittenhouse of Philadelphia in 1794. From shadows his model cast on paper, he traced an exact silhouette.

Jefferson put his ingenuity to good use in farming too. For improving a plow he won the gold medal of the Agriculture Society at Paris. He perfected a threshing machine imported from Scotland. At Edgehill, where his daughter Martha set

Jefferson's personality pervades Monticello. He could step out of bed into bedroom or study. Time exposure blurs his swivel chair, supposedly the first in America. Arms held candles. He designed draperies, windows, tables, even the telescope stand in his study. Remodeling in 1796, he replaced the central staircase with twin doll-sized stairs to save space.

DEAN CONGER, NATIONAL GEOGRAPHIC PHOTOGRAPHER, AND (OPPOSITE) RICHARD S. DURRANCE

Profile of genius: Jefferson's camera obscura captures the image of the patriot, a copy of the bust by Houdon. Viewers see the picture on a mirror inside the casing. Since the image can be seen only within the chamber, a separate exposure was superimposed. In Jefferson's day, the box was used as a sketching aid.

In the restored gardens outside, iris (far left), sweet william (upper), and columbine (lower) recall Jefferson's love of flowers. He experimented with new plants; those found useful or ornamental he passed on to friends and neighbors.

Oak Hill (above) owes its classic beauty to designer Jefferson. Here in 1823 owner James Monroe, the fifth President, drafted his famous doctrine. The home, near Leesburg, is open during Garden Week.

EDWIN STUART GROSVENOR AND (TOP LEFT) DEAN CONGER, NATIONAL GEOGRAPHIC PHOTOGRAPHER

"THE END OF THE HUNT" BY AN UNKNOWN ARTIST, C. 1780; NATIONAL GALLERY OF ART, GIFT OF EDGAR WILLIAM AND BERNICE CHRYSLER GARBISCH. LEFT: WILLARD R. CULVER. BELOW: KATHLEEN REVIS JUDGE

Virginians have chased the fox since the 1600's and take pride in spirited horses, like those below at Montpelier. Orange County home of the Madisons, it grew wings and portico when the fourth President and his wife Dolley, the country's most popular hostess, lived here. Madison was Jefferson's secretary of state.

EDWIN S. ROSEBERRY. OPPOSITE: BETTS COLLECTION AND (TOP) DAVID S. BOYER, NATIONAL GEOGRAPHIC STAFF

up housekeeping as Mrs. Thomas Mann Randolph, Jefferson's slaves dug out a vegetable garden—five tiers in a perfect amphitheater. Aimed to the southeast, the crops got more sun and ripened ten days earlier than neighbors'!

Like other plantation owners, Jefferson had to teach his slaves almost every trade—to make tools, forge nails, mold brick, hew timber, trim woodwork.

As our guide proudly showed us around Monticello, I imagined him as one of Jefferson's own stewards, Martin or Caesar. I could picture him staring at Virginia's Paul Revere, galloping up after an all-night dash. The countryside was alive with British dragoons, Jack Jouett announced. The Governor must leave immediately. Jefferson dispatched his family by carriage to Enniscorthy, then tarried to put away important papers. When a look through his telescope convinced him that soldiers were swarming below, he jumped on his horse and fled. Just in time too, for the troopers soon clattered up and demanded Jefferson.

Martin was handing the last of his master's valuables to Caesar in a hiding place beneath the porch. He dropped the plank and with a noncommittal air conducted the unwelcome visitors through the house. Caesar, trapped below, remained in darkness without food for 18 hours rather than betray the cache.

Eight miles down the road I stopped at Castle Hill, where lived Dr. Thomas Walker, good friend of Jefferson. On that exciting dawn in 1781 Dr. Walker

University of Virginia seniors and faculty crowd the Rotunda just before the graduation procession down the Lawn, shown in the 1824 drawing above. Jefferson fought to locate the university in Charlottesville, listing all persons in the region over 80 to show its healthful climate. He sought every way to cut costs: "If we make the Attic of wood, instead of brick, it deducts 79,920 [bricks] leaving the corrected estimate for the whole Rotunda 1,117,457." He designed the Capitol at Richmond, top, after a Roman temple.

furnished Jack Jouett a fresh mount. Then he detained Tarleton and his troopers with mint juleps for breakfast, so the story goes.

Charlottesville, to scholars everywhere, means the University of Virginia. I marveled how Jefferson chose the beautiful site, worked out the plans, even made the detailed drawings, then kept an eye on stonecutters, bricklayers, plasterers, and carpenters. His masterpiece has been called "the most exquisite group of collegiate buildings in the world." But graceful buildings were not Jefferson's only concern. He outlined the curriculum, selected the first professors, even wrote part of a textbook! His vision and intellectual curiosity are still manifest in the liberal arts course, graduate schools, and many-sided research programs.

With roots in the past, the university faces the future. No one would have approved more than Mr. Jefferson himself.

JOHN ANTHONY CARUSO

THOMAS JEFFERSON in his first inaugural address asserted that the country had "room enough for our descendants to the hundredth and thousandth generation." He had in mind that uncharted vastness sprawling from the Appalachians to the Mississippi. In Jefferson's day population had dammed up on the Piedmont of Virginia and the Carolinas, in the valleys of Pennsylvania and New York, and in the back country of New England. Few settlers had ventured past the Appalachians. But geography has always yielded to the pioneer spirit. Mountains could not hold back freedom-struck Americans.

Beyond the Blue Ridge, beyond the Alleghenies lay mysterious *Ken-ta-ke*—"prairie" or "meadow land." It teemed with deer, buffalo, bear, and wild turkey; was the hunting ground of the Cherokee, Shawnee, Seneca, and Catawba.

One of the first white men to explore this region was Thomas Walker. This Virginia physician and surveyor discovered Cumberland Gap in 1750. The next year Christopher Gist, agent of the Ohio Company, surveyed as far as the Falls of the Ohio (Louisville), returning by Walker's route. Gist's vivid journal inspired adventurers known as Long Hunters (because of their long absence from home) to trek into Kentucky. They hungered, not for new homes, but for the excitement of the chase and the profit in pelts. The greatest Long Hunter was Daniel Boone.

"DANIEL BOONE LEADING A BAND OF PIONEERS INTO THE WESTERN COUNTRY," PAINTED BY GEORGE CALEB BINGHAM IN 1851, HANGS IN WASHINGTON UNIVERSITY, ST. LOUIS

Boone was a restless soul who loved to roam the wilderness. It taught him three things infinitely well: hunting, exploring, and Indian psychology. He had little formal education, wrote with an audacious scrawl, was a hopeless speller. "Let girls do the spelling," said his father, Squire. "Daniel will do the shooting."

DANIEL KEPT HIS FINGER on the trigger of his Kentucky rifle most of his life. When Squire moved the family from their homestead (now restored) near Reading, Pennsylvania, to the Yadkin Valley of North Carolina in 1750, he and Daniel killed so many bears that a stream near the cabin became known as Bear Creek. Proud of his prowess, young Boone recorded it on many a beech tree: "D. Boon Cilled A. Bar." He'd range the forest early in the morning when dew had softened the crackle of autumn leaves, or at moonrise when the deer were feeding. In a fair season he took about 400 deerskins.

During these years Daniel grew to that romantic figure every schoolboy knows. He was broad-shouldered, hard-muscled, with dark hair and a ruddy complexion. His blue eyes reflected courage, his tight lips determination. Such was Boone in 1756 when he married Rebecca Bryan, "whose brow had been fanned by the breezes of seventeen summers." All a man needed to enjoy happiness, he said, was "a good gun, a good horse, and a good wife." Now Boone had all three.

In the next few years he roamed many miles from home. Sometimes he threaded deep into the North Carolina wilderness where the mountains wax misty gray to clear amethyst, depending on mood of day or time of year. In spring the hollows flame with azaleas while mountain laurel and rhododendron, all white and pink, lick at the higher slopes. Boone saw Blowing Rock towering over primeval forest, saw Mount Mitchell's hood of snow. He saw the Grandfather, one of the oldest mountains on earth, and Pilot Mountain, guide to Indians in their ceaseless wanderings. At Linville he watched the shimmering cataract leap into the gorge. The promise of free land lured Boone to Florida. But he found game scarce.

Boone was home in 1768 when John Finley drove a scraggy horse and wagon down Yadkin Valley. The two men had not seen each other since Braddock's campaign more than ten years before. Sitting by the fire in Boone's cabin, Finley unfolded tales of Kentucky—*there* was the paradise for the hunter!

The Kentucky rifle, developed by gunsmiths around Lancaster, Pennsylvania, in the 1740's, owes its name to sharpshooting Kentucky frontiersmen. The spiral (rifled) bore gave it far greater accuracy than a smoothbore musket. From curly maple butt to tip of octagonal barrel, it measured 48 to 62 inches, weighed 8 to 12 pounds. A full powder horn and a pound or two of .30 or .45 caliber bullets would last Daniel Boone a month. He could "bark" a squirrel from the highest tree (shattering the bark under it), and hit a deer at 400 paces. Asked if he had ever been lost while hunting in the wilderness, Boone replied: "No, I can't say as ever I was lost, but I was *bewildered* once for three days."

PAUL R. HOFFMASTER

That very next spring Boone pushed through Cumberland Gap and began his Kentucky adventures. Shawnee warriors robbed him and his brother-in-law John Stuart, and took them prisoner. They fled, were recaptured, escaped again. Then Stuart disappeared while hunting. (Daniel would find his remains five years later.)

The following spring Boone ranged alone to the Ohio River. He came to Big Bone Lick where lay fabulous tusks of mammoths and mastodons, and saw the Blue Licks where thousands of bellowing buffalo rumbled over the salt earth. While Boone stood on a cliff drinking in Kentucky's grandeur, Indians closed in. He got away by leaping over the brink into a maple tree below.

Daniel, now joined by his brother Squire, hunted another year. In the spring of 1771, their pack horses burdened with pelts, they set out for home. Near Cumberland Gap Indians swooped down and stripped them of their possessions.

But Boone had seen Kentucky!

Fired by Boone's glowing descriptions, Judge Richard Henderson and eight associates, envisioning themselves lords proprietors of a frontier colony, formed the Transylvania Company. They sought to purchase from the Cherokee a tract of land comprising most of Kentucky and part of Tennessee. In 1775 Chief Little Carpenter sold out for £10,000 in goods and baubles despite warnings from his son Dragging Canoe that it would turn Kentucky into "the Dark and Bloody Ground."

WHEN THIS TREATY OF SYCAMORE SHOALS was signed, Daniel Boone was not present. Henderson had sent him to blaze the Wilderness Road. Across the Clinch and Powell rivers trudged Boone and 30 men, the Cumberland Mountains rising before them. They pushed through the gap, pursued the Warriors' Path, forded the Cumberland River, then picked up a buffalo trace. Axes and hatchets swung. Through scrub and bramble the men inched to Rockcastle River. For 30 miles more they chopped and slashed through cane and reed. At last the mountains parted.

"Perhaps no Adventureor Since the days of donquicksotte [Don Quixote] or before ever felt So Cheerful & Ilated," wrote young Felix Walker, one of Boone's choppers. "As the Cain ceased, we began to discover the pleasing & Rapturous appearance of the plains of Kentucky, a New Sky & Strange Earth." Walker soon

changed his tune, for he suffered a nasty wound when Indians struck, killing two men. Boone urged defiance. In a valley studded with sycamores he built Boonesboro.

Kentucky frontiersmen, though beyond the clarion call of Philadelphia's patriots, displayed spirit of their own in 1777. In that year of the "bloody sevens," the Shawnee under Chief Blackfish crossed the Ohio, besieged Boonesboro and Harrodsburg, killed settlers, and burned cabins and crops.

At Harrodsburg, first settlement in Kentucky (where pioneer days live on in restored Fort Harrod), George Rogers Clark and his backwoods militia fought stubbornly.

At Boonesboro settlers had barely finished their fort when Blackfish struck. Boone was shot in the ankle and probably would have lost his scalp had not his friend Simon Kenton clubbed an onrushing Indian.

Early 1778 found Boone on his feet leading a party to the Blue Licks for salt. Indians captured him and took him to their camp. Around a huge fire squatted more than 100 Shawnee in war paint, eager to assault Boonesboro. Boone persuaded Blackfish the fort could not be taken, but he had to surrender the men at the salt springs.

At the Shawnee capital, north of the Ohio, he and 16 companions were adopted into the tribe. Boone became Big Turtle, son of Blackfish, and played the role so well he gained the Indians' trust. In June he broke away and, in four days,

George Rogers Clark's "Big Knives" won Vincennes by crossing "Drownded Cuntrey in the Debth of Wintor."

PAUL R. HOFFMASTER

raced some 160 miles through wilderness to Boonesboro. His wife Rebecca, believing him dead, had returned to the Yadkin. Boone roused the townsfolk to strengthen their defenses. When Blackfish came, demanding Boonesboro's surrender, the settlers resolved to fight to the last. "I'll die with the rest," spoke Boone.

The siege lasted two months. Boone's fighters frustrated Blackfish's efforts to trick them into the open, doused his attempts to burn them out, and dug a trench across his path when he tried to tunnel in. When a heavy rain collapsed his mine, Blackfish and his disgusted braves withdrew. The settlers opened the fort and turned their starving cattle out to pasture.

The settlement soon became too tame for Daniel Boone. He wandered on, ever the pathfinder, ever the hunter. At 65, the gleam of adventure still in his eyes, he moved to Missouri, where two young men—Lewis and Clark—were soon to set out to blaze a trail of their own. It is said that Boone hunted in Yellowstone when he was 80 and dreamed of visiting California until death cut him down at 86.

He had carved his own monument, the Wilderness Road. Over it streamed pioneers with pans and plows, dogs and sheep, books and even the printing press.

IMMIGRANTS first settled the over-mountain country: Germans, English, Highlanders, Irish, Welsh, Scotch-Irish. New England stock seasoned the mixture. Dominant were the Scotch-Irish, defiant and aggressive, who seldom neglected an opportunity to better themselves. They had undying confidence in their manhood, were as bold as the Romans, and as Indian fighters won even the Shawnee's admiration. They were Presbyterians, though in the wilderness many turned Baptist or Methodist. They believed in freedom and equality, resented class distinction and the leisurely life. They "preferred the useful to the beautiful and even required the beautiful to be useful." They contributed mightily to the democratization of the United States.

Of Scotch-Irish stock was James Robertson, who founded a settlement (the site of present Elizabethton, Tennessee) on the banks of the Watauga River. For mutual protection against Indians and outlaws, the Wataugans in 1772 formed the first independent government established by white men west of the Appalachians. During the Revolution they placed themselves under the mantle of North Carolina, but had to beat off attack after attack by England's Indian allies.

In 1779 Robertson, acting for the indomitable Judge Henderson, recruited a party and led them down the frozen Cumberland River. On snow-covered bluffs they founded Nashboro (Nashville). Leadership of the Wataugans fell to "Nolichucky Jack" Sevier, handsome Huguenot who lived beside the Nolichucky River. Sevier helped lead the frontiersmen to victory over the British at Kings Mountain.

After the war the Wataugans' Scotch-Irish blood boiled because North Carolina continued to ignore their needs, indeed referred to the settlers as "off-scourings of the earth." In 1784 the Wataugans resolved to break away, "forming ourselves into a separate government." The State of Franklin (see map, page 275), named after Ben Franklin, elected Sevier governor and offered him $1,000 a year—in beaver skins. Financially distressed, Franklin tottered four years, then fell, and North Carolina arrested Sevier for treason. Wataugans seethed with indignation.

They would rescue their leader if they had to burn Morganton, where he was held. The story goes that during the trial one of Sevier's friends asked the judge if he was through with the man. At this point 'Chucky Jack bolted out the door, sprang on a horse, and sped away. In the courthouse an old man crowed, "I'll be damned if you ain't through with him!" and slapped his knee.

North Carolina made no further attempt to prosecute Sevier. In fact, he was pardoned, elected to the state senate, and recommissioned brigadier general.

Sevier's life was tumultuous even by frontier standards. He won 35 battles against Indians, fathered 17 or 18 children, and when Tennessee entered the Union served as her first governor. He was re-elected five times, and ended his days in the United States Congress.

TRIBES OF THE OLD NORTHWEST believed the Great Spirit made the Ohio country for the Indian, not the white man. They were determined the Ohio River should separate them forever. Frontiersmen, on the other hand, regarded the river not as a border, but as a broad avenue to new lands. Defiantly they traveled it to hunt and to settle.

Shots rang out along the Ohio in the spring of 1774. Near present Steubenville, border ruffians murdered eight Indians, including relatives of the Mingo chief, Logan. Long a friend to the white man, Logan now thirsted for blood. He led forays against unsuspecting families. The Shawnee joined him. Terrorized settlers deserted their cabins and fled eastward. In Williamsburg, Lord Dunmore, governor of Virginia, called out militia.

Lord Dunmore's War reached its climax October 10, 1774, at Point Pleasant, West Virginia, where the Great Kanawha empties into the Ohio. In dense forest frontiersmen and Indians—more than 1,000 on each side—flitted among trees, firing, grappling with knives and tomahawks. "Be strong," thundered Cornstalk, fiery chief of the Shawnee. "Lie close; shoot well; drive the white dogs in!"

But inch by inch the Indians were pushed back. As the sun sank, the braves took to their canoes and made for the Ohio shore. Darkness fell with a dreadful silence, and the living buried the dead.

Cornstalk made peace, but one chief refused to bow. "I am a warrior, not a councilor," said Logan. "I have killed many; I have fully glutted my revenge. For my country, I rejoice at the beams of peace. But do not harbor the thought that mine is the joy of fear. Logan never felt fear. He will never turn on his heel to save his life. Who is there to mourn for Logan? Not one."

A young captain of militia, George Rogers Clark, heard these words repeated. One day he would borrow some of Chief Logan's eloquence. Clark had left home in Albemarle County, Virginia, in 1772 to seek his fortune on the frontier. A gangling youth with blue eyes and red hair, he went down the Ohio, surveyed for settlers, and explored in Kentucky for lands of his own.

After Dunmore's War he learned that Judge Henderson's Transylvania Company was fleecing settlers by raising the price of land while keeping the best acres for itself. Clark contested Henderson's claims and, with the help of Thomas Jefferson, won his case. Early in 1777 most of Transylvania became Kentucky

County, Virginia—roughly the same as the present State of Kentucky. But while the Revolution raged, it lay defenseless.

Clark declared that "if a Cuntrey was not worth protecting it was not worth Claiming." Virginia took the hint and gave him 500 pounds of powder to defend Kentucky. After leading the defense of Harrodsburg, Clark hurried to Williamsburg with plans for a bold offensive. In December, 1777, sporting a new coat and linen shirt, he called on Gov. Patrick Henry. His plan: knife deep into the Illinois country, relieving pressure on Kentucky by British-incited Indians. The Governor ordered Clark to "attack the British post at Kaskaskia."

Clark and 180 frontiersmen rowed down the Ohio to the mouth of the Tennessee, then struck off through wilderness. They marched on moccasined feet, their coonskin caps and flintlock rifles bobbing in the shadows. The long butcher knives they carried earned them the Indian nickname "Big Knives."

On the night of July 4, 1778, the Big Knives seized Kaskaskia, on the Mississippi. Here Clark found British dispatches urging the Indians to attack the Americans and offering rewards for scalps. Clark sent word to the French trading posts of Cahokia and Vincennes that France had entered the war on the side of the United States. Within days these settlements declared for Clark.

Winning the red man required sterner tactics. At Cahokia, Indians from all over the region gathered for a powwow with Clark. "I am a man and a warrior," he thundered, "and not a councilor. I carry in my right hand war and peace in my left. . . ." The Indians accepted peace.

But Henry Hamilton, British commander at Detroit whom the Indians dubbed the "Hair Buyer General," launched a drive on Vincennes, and its French garrison surrendered. Clark learned that Hamilton contemplated no offensive until spring. Believing that "a good soldier never ought to be afraid of his life when there was a probability of his doing service by venturing it," Clark resolved to strike first.

In February, 1779, he led his men on the heroic march against Vincennes. Heavy rains had turned much of the 180-mile route into a shallow lake. At night the men dried out by huge campfires and sang of love and war. Reaching the Little Wabash, they found its two branches flooded into a single channel five miles wide. They built a canoe and ferried across. On a spongy hillock they huddled through a drizzly night, now so close to Vincennes that they could hear the morning gun.

Bedraggled and hungry, they waded on, sometimes up to their arm-

CULVER SERVICE

Settlers brought crude tools and New England experience to farm the Ohio country.

pits. At one dangerously deep place Clark blackened his face with gunpowder, gave a war whoop, and lunged ahead. The men followed, and at their leader's command burst into song. The last six miles were hardest—inch-thick ice and chest-high water. The half-frozen men lurched from tree to tree, floated on logs, slogged on to within sight of their prize.

Realizing that he was heavily outnumbered, Clark resorted to stratagem. He marched his men back and forth, drums beating, colors flying, to give the impression of a large force. When darkness fell, his frontiersmen closed in and poured blistering volleys into the fort. Two days later, February 25, Hamilton surrendered.

Clark wanted to march on Detroit, but Virginia couldn't supply him. In 1782 he burned several Indian villages in retaliation for attacks on settlers. Next summer he resigned command, two months prior to the Treaty of Paris in which Great Britain ceded the Old Northwest to the United States. Stripped of his holdings by creditors (for supplies he had bought for his soldiers), Clark retired to a cabin near the Falls of the Ohio. One leg amputated after an accident, his mind crippled by alcohol, "the mighty oak of the forest" fell in 1818.

IN THE WAKE OF BOONE, Sevier, and Clark came "lean, tough Yankee settlers, tough as gutta-percha, with most occult, unsubduable fire in their belly." Typically, the settler lived with his wife and a cabinful of children on a tract of wooded land. He rarely cleared more than 40 acres. He girded trees to kill them and let sunlight reach the soil. He planted his garden among the dead trees. Later he would burn them and dig out the stumps. In early spring he set fire to dry grass so that green shoots could grow for his cattle. He broke the ground with his crude moldboard plow and sowed grain by hand.

The pioneer woman worked as hard as her husband. She cooked, churned, fed and milked the cows, hoed corn, dried beans, chopped wood, carried water, spun clothing, and made clay lamps whose wicks floated in bear grease. Not "a doll to carry silks and jewels," she was dedicated to a life of hardship.

Settlers sought the comforts of religion—often a passionate gospel of hell-fire and salvation. Circuit preachers roamed every corner of the frontier. Their zeal and courage, their defiance of wind and rain inspired the pioneer proverb: "There is nothing out today but crows and Methodist preachers." And Johnny Appleseed.

Born John Chapman in Massachusetts, he was first seen in the Middle West around 1800, drifting down the Ohio on two canoes lashed together and filled with rotting apples. He planted apple trees throughout the wilderness and traveled hundreds of miles to prune his orchards. His price for an apple sapling was a "fippenny bit," but Johnny Appleseed would take a promissory note—and never collect. He quoted Scripture to anyone who would listen. Lying on the floor and rolling forth denunciations in tones of thunder, he was considered a frontier saint. He was known for his quixotic kindness to animals, even insects and snakes.

The Dan'l Boones, the Johnny Appleseeds, the farmers and fighters, surveyors and speculators symbolize America's pioneer spirit. Afoot and on horseback, by Conestoga wagon and flatboat, they rolled back the frontier. They dug canals and built turnpikes. And in a twinkling, it somehow seems, they tamed a wilderness.

SINCLAIR OIL CORPORATION'S PUBLIC SERVICE ADVERTISING

Cumberland Gap National Historical Park: gate west for pioneers following Boone's steps.

ROUTES TO THE OHIO COUNTRY

WITH THE REVOLUTION ENDED, Americans drew breath and took a look at their nation. Like any infant, it wobbled on unsteady legs. But one resource it had in abundance: land. Land enough to glut the hunger of all four million Americans. It lay westward, over the mountains, and now there were ways to reach it. Daniel Boone had blazed a path through Cumberland Gap into bluegrass country, and thousands of settlers streamed over his Wilderness Road. New, all-weather roads were stretching westward. Turnpikes, they called these, for a pike barrier would swing aside when a traveler had paid the toll.

Coaches with silken draperies racketed along the 62-mile Lancaster Pike. This was the finest stretch of the Pennsylvania Road, the major highway west by the turn of the 19th century. Today's U. S. Route 30 roughly follows it. The Catskill Turnpike through New York State funneled New Englanders with "Ohio fever" into the Northwest Territory. In 1808 the National Road, now U. S. 40, started inching across the mountains from Cumberland, Maryland. As wide as 80 feet and largely graveled, it carried a thunderous traffic of Conestoga wagons and stagecoaches and eventually reached Vandalia, Illinois. "Old America seems to be breaking up and moving westward," noted one of its travelers.

The main north-south artery was the Michigan Road, most of it now U. S. Route 31, spilling settlers into southern Indiana from the Great Lakes country. Andrew Jackson's Military Road, between Nashville and New Orleans, lopped about 220 miles off the Natchez Trace, return route of flatboatmen who drifted down the Mississippi. Cars now clip along the old trace on a Park Service road.

Trudging across country, pioneers had to gather wood, herd livestock, watch for Indians. Canals let them sit down. Completed in 1825, De Witt Clinton's "Big Ditch," the Erie Canal, started a frenzied quarter century of canal building. The Pennsylvania Canal, with the aid of a portage railroad, spanned the Alleghenies; Ohio's canals brought downstate points closer to market; and enthusiastic Hoosiers dug the longest ditch of all, the 458-mile Wabash.

With the coming of railroads, many canals went to grass. But the Chesapeake and Ohio Canal, inspired by George Washington, is preserved within the National Park system. It remains a scenic reminder of a restless age.

FAIRVIEW INN ON THE NATIONAL ROAD C. 1825, BY THOMAS C. RUCKLE, JR., MARYLAND HISTORICAL SOCIETY

Stagecoach passengers and wagoners refreshed at wayside inns, the Howard Johnson's of yesteryear

Wheels rumble and hoofs pound a steady counterpoint to jangling harness bells—music of the open road when a Conestoga wagon rolled. Blue-bodied, with red running gear and a canvas top like a billowing sail, it caught a boy's eye as a fire truck does today. At the end of a day's run—about 15 miles—was the welcoming inn. "Whoa, team!" Axles groan. Dogs bark.

Inside, wagoner and stage driver—he does 20 miles a day in his springier Concord coach—swap yarns, smoke Conestoga cigars (stogies), dance to the innkeeper's fiddle. They sleep on the barroom floor, feet to the fire. At dawn whips crack and wagons roll. The Conestoga originated in the Conestoga region of Pennsylvania, the Concord coach in the capital of New Hampshire.

BROWN BROTHERS

"Low bridge!" Erie passengers have to duck 300 times between Albany and Utica alone! At night they squeeze into shelflike berths. Horace Greeley dubbed the 363-mile canal "Old cent-and-a-half a mile, mile-and-a-half an hour." Roistering Irishmen dug it in eight years.

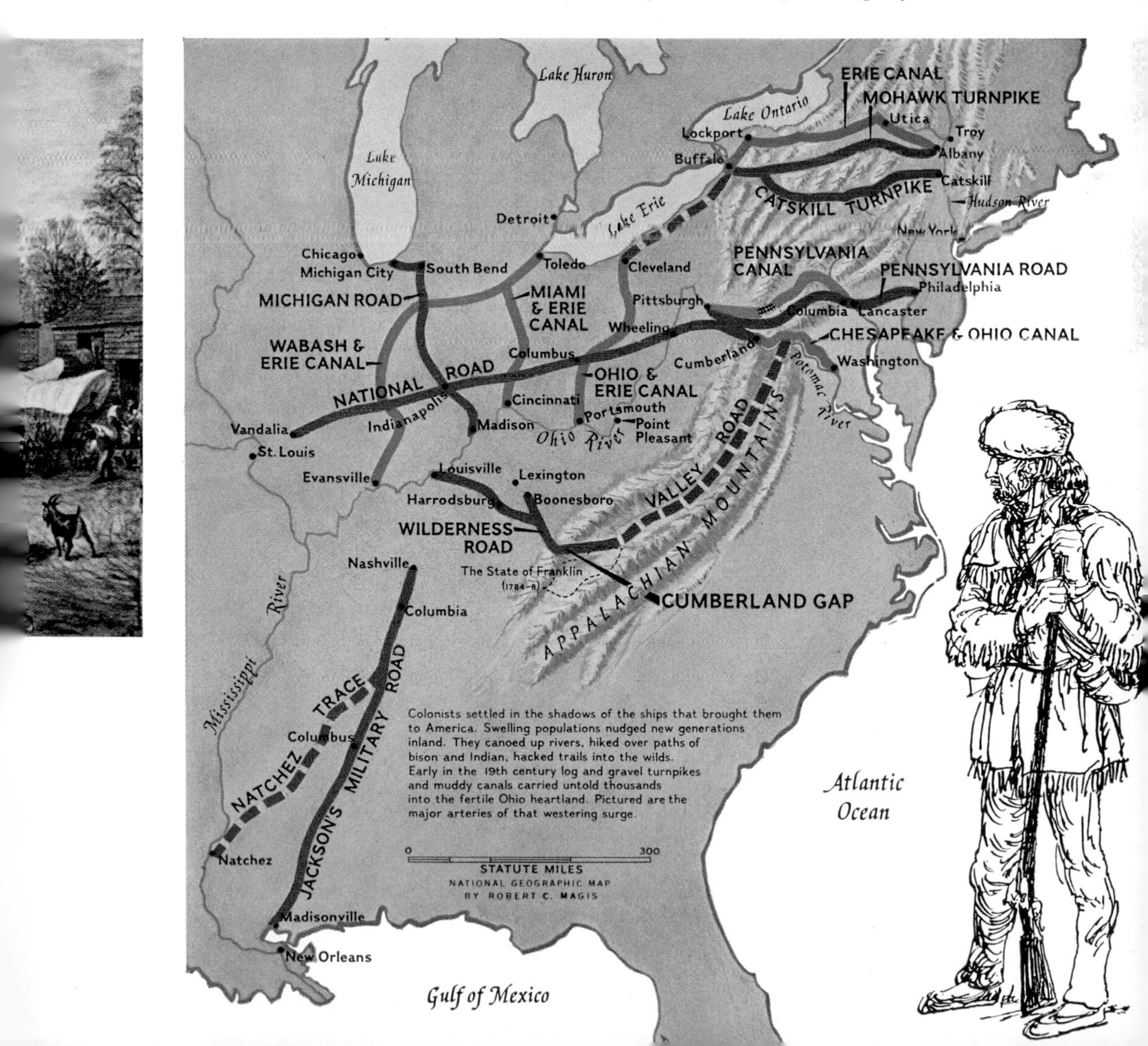

New York Thruway and Erie Canal thread the glacier-gouged Mohawk Valley, historic passage to the Ohio country. Concrete ribbons trace where moccasins trod sun-dappled paths and wagons bumped over corduroy turnpikes. Barge and tug glide west out of Utica

ROBERT F. SISSON, NATIONAL GEOGRAPHIC PHOTOGRAPHER

on the modern Erie. Vestiges of the old canal survive in monumental Schoharie Creek Aqueduct near Fort Hunter, and the locks at Lockport. In lock shanties canalmen gathered on stormy nights for a bit of cheer and harmonizing: *O-o-oh, the Ee-rye-ee was a-rising.*

CANAL CLIPPER

JAY JOHNSTON

A trip on the C & O Canal

A TEAM OF MULES pulled me into a bygone era. With each tug, as the glassy water rippled below, Washington, D. C., slipped farther behind. I was riding the *Canal Clipper,* a flat-bottom craft that carries sightseers up a stretch of the Chesapeake and Ohio Canal along the Potomac River.

Floating between fern-clothed cliffs, in the depths of a dark wood, or past a sun-drenched pasture, you capture the feel of a vanished age. Birds in gaunt pines and towering tulip trees cease their chatter. Then the wind rustles the treetops. A gray squirrel scolds from a sycamore. A turtle plunges off his log solarium. And you think: This is how it was on a spring day a century ago.

My imagination stirs, and around a bend come plodding mules. A barge glides into view. On its bow the skipper cups hands to lips for a singsong cry, the locktender's cue to open the gates.

"Hey-y-y-y-y-y lock!"

The captain and his family lived aft in the cabin. In a stable forward rode the relief mules, heads craning through tiny windows. On sunny days the family wash fluttered from lines strung above-deck. Children, tethered lest they fall overboard, played about the cabin. Dogs and cats dozed on the planking.

Old-timers vividly recall the era. O. P. Matthews, who grew up in western Maryland, could see the canal twisting through the bright-boughed hills.

Towing a sightseeing barge, mules clop across a spillway of the Chesapeake and Ohio Canal at Washington, D. C. The waterway hugged the Potomac for 185 miles.

THOMAS NEBBIA

"I'd lie abed at night," he told me, "and watch the barges inch their way up and down. The light from their bow lamps shone on the water and flashed in the trees. I could hear the music of fiddles, and people singing and laughing in the cabins."

Raleigh S. Bender, retired canalman of Sharpsburg, Maryland, conjured up a tableau of lazy waters and slow-moving boats. "All day long you'd be trying to make time, beat someone else's record for the trip downstream or up. Come dark, you'd put the feed trough out on the banks and let the mules graze or doze. You'd sit around for a spell, smoking and talking, then hit the hay to be up with the dawn for an early start. Sometimes you'd drive the mules through the night." He sat back and the rush of words slowed. "I'll never forget those old canal days."

But for George Washington the C & O might never have been. At Great Falls, ten miles above the capital, the Potomac is a wild creature, crashing through gorges

Locks like these lifted barges from near sea level to 620 feet above it at Cumberland, Maryland. During the canal's post-Civil War boom, 700 boats brought coal, grain, flour, and lumber down here to Georgetown, passing 74 locks.

Now the *Canal Clipper* (below) glides on summer weekends along part of the restored 23-mile Georgetown-Seneca segment.

THOMAS NEBBIA

no boat can navigate. Washington's idea was to bypass such stretches with a new water route. In 1785 he became president of the Potowmack Company. Three years later he wrote Thomas Jefferson that workers had made "very great progress. . . . This will become the great avenue into the Western Country."

The hiker today, tramping the Virginia shore, can see the ruins of locks built in Washington's day.

The Potowmack Company failed, but in 1828 the Chesapeake and Ohio Canal Company revived the idea. Georgetown saw the tidewater terminal take shape. Past Little Falls and Great Falls, Seneca, and

Springtime on the towpath lures hikers and cyclists. Catfish and carp tempt fishermen, and canoeists ripple the placid waters. The National Park Service offers campgrounds, picnic areas.

Great Falls Tavern, the noted Maryland hostelry and lockkeeper's home, has been converted into a museum to tell the canal's story. Here 6 locks (3 are visible) lifted barges 41 feet. Locks are 100 feet long—92-foot barges just fit.

Costing $60,000 a mile, the canal ranged 30 to 80 feet wide, 6 to 8 feet deep, and spanned Potomac tributaries on 12 aqueducts.

President John Quincy Adams dug the first spadeful on July 4, 1828. On the same day, portentously, foundations were started on the Baltimore and Ohio Railroad, which eventually would doom the canal. It ceased operations in 1924.

THOMAS J. ABERCROMBIE, NATIONAL GEOGRAPHIC STAFF, AND (OPPOSITE) THOMAS NEBBIA

Whites Ferry crept the ditch as brawling workmen dug and blasted. Point of Rocks, Harpers Ferry, Snyders Landing, and Williamsport prospered as the canal brought trade. Above Hancock, engineers tunneled a mountain to save seven miles. Finally in 1850 the waterway reached Cumberland. Artillery boomed and brass bands blared as five coal-laden barges headed downstream.

In its heyday the canal floated millions of tons of coal, grain, lumber, and flour from the Alleghenies to tidewater. But rail competition doomed it. Now, for most of its 185 meandering miles, it is dry, weed choked, and tree grown. Yet new life looms for the canal, parts of which are being restored by the Park Service.

"It is a refuge, a place of retreat," said Justice William O. Douglas, who fought to preserve it. The pleasures that he found in walks along its banks—solitude, serenity, and sylvan beauty—await others in abundance.

GERALD R. BRIMACOMBE. RIGHT: "TRAPPEUR," LITHOGRAPH BY LEMERCIER, THE OLD PRINT SHOP. OPPOSITE: CHIEF TRADER ARCHIBALD McDONALD, HOLDING BEAVER TOP HAT, BRAVES RAPIDS ON 1828 EXPEDITION; PAINTING BY A. SHERIFF SCOTT, COURTESY HUDSON'S BAY COMPANY

Grand Portage, Minnesota, saw voyageurs lug 180-pound packs of goods and furs nine miles around falls on the Pigeon River. Hundreds came by canoe each summer to trade at the British North West Company stockade, now part of a national monument. In 1821 North West and Hudson's Bay companies merged. Mackinac Island, famed Michigan resort, and Prairie du Chien, Wisconsin, preserve landmarks of the American Fur Company. Tank Cottage, Wisconsin's earliest, grew from a fur trader's cabin.

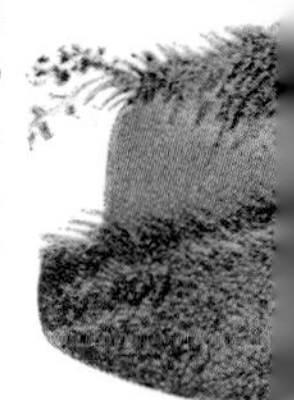

THE NORTHWEST TERRITORY

THREE YEARS before the American Revolution started, Moravian missionaries led a band of Christian Indians across the Alleghenies into the Ohio country and founded the towns of Schoenbrunn (Beautiful Spring) and Gnadenhutten (Tents of Grace). But their white neighbors, who lived in the shadow of tomahawk and scalping knife, considered the only good Indian a dead one.

Ten years after the gentle experiment began, militia, inflamed by frontier atrocities, fell on Gnadenhutten and, as the Indians prayed and sang hymns, brained them with rifle butts. The territory exploded in violence.

Yet tales of massacre could not check Ohio's destiny. The Northwest Ordinance of 1787 promised statehood when the region counted 60,000 settlers. They flooded in: veterans, squatters, New Englanders tired of farming rocks.

First came Rufus Putnam, a Massachusetts land speculator and cousin of Israel Putnam of Bunker Hill fame. He planted Ohio's earliest permanent white settlement at Marietta. His house, originally part of the stockade, and the Ohio Company Land Office are now sheltered in the Campus Martius Museum.

Other towns grew: Chillicothe, the first capital, where the Adena mansion is now restored; Gallipolis, with its tavern called Our House – Lafayette stayed there. "City of the French," Gallipolis was settled by artisans and artists from Paris and Lyons, "carvers and gilders to the king, coachmakers, frizeurs and perukemakers" who came expecting a paradise, and found only wilderness, hardship, and fever.

German Separatists found haven in Zoar village. Their leader's home, Number One House, remains. Franklinton (Columbus), Dayton, Cleaveland (they say a newspaper dropped an *a* to save space), and other land-company towns grew as fast as the 100-pound pumpkins and yard-long cucumbers that sprang from Ohio's rich soil.

The Indians, alarmed at the tide of settlement, fought for their homeland as furiously as Concord minutemen. They hacked to pieces the army of territorial governor

GEORGE ROGERS CLARK, SCULPTURED IN BRONZE BY HERMON A. MACNEIL, STANDS IN HIS MEMORIAL ROTUNDA AT VINCENNES

Arthur St. Clair in 1791. Drunk with victory, they scorned peace talks: "Restore to us our country, and we shall be enemies no longer."

Instead, President Washington ordered Gen. Anthony Wayne to regain control of the territory. For his heroics at Stony Point, New York, Wayne's Revolutionary War comrades had dubbed him "Mad Anthony." He hated defeat as he did the gout that plagued him. Now he drilled his troops to Spartan toughness and made them masters of the bayonet. In 1794 he built Fort Recovery on the site of St. Clair's defeat, shattered Indian assaults, then moved north to the Maumee River to build Fort Defiance. "I defy the English, Indians, and all the devils in hell to take it," Wayne proclaimed, and warned the redskins he would strike on August 17.

Knowing these tribes fasted before a battle, Wayne let them starve three days more, then swept down on their tree-strewn refuge—aftermath of a

NATIONAL GEOGRAPHIC MAP BY IRVIN E. ALLEMAN

Schoenbrunn's log cabins stand as a memorial to Ohio's first settlers. Here Moravians lived simply, died simply.

MERLE SEVERY, NATIONAL GEOGRAPHIC STAFF

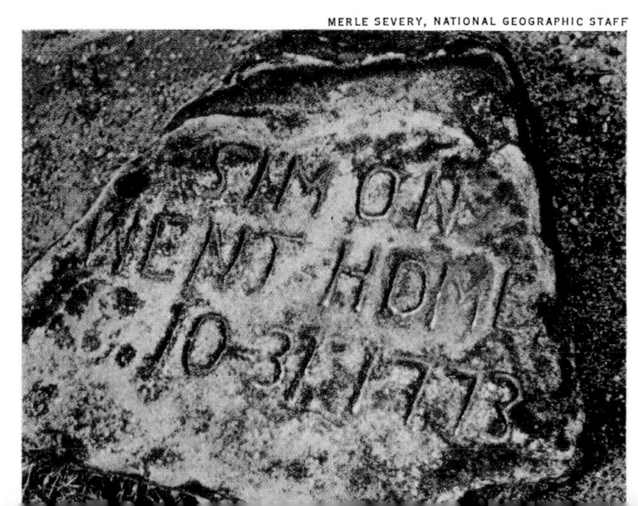

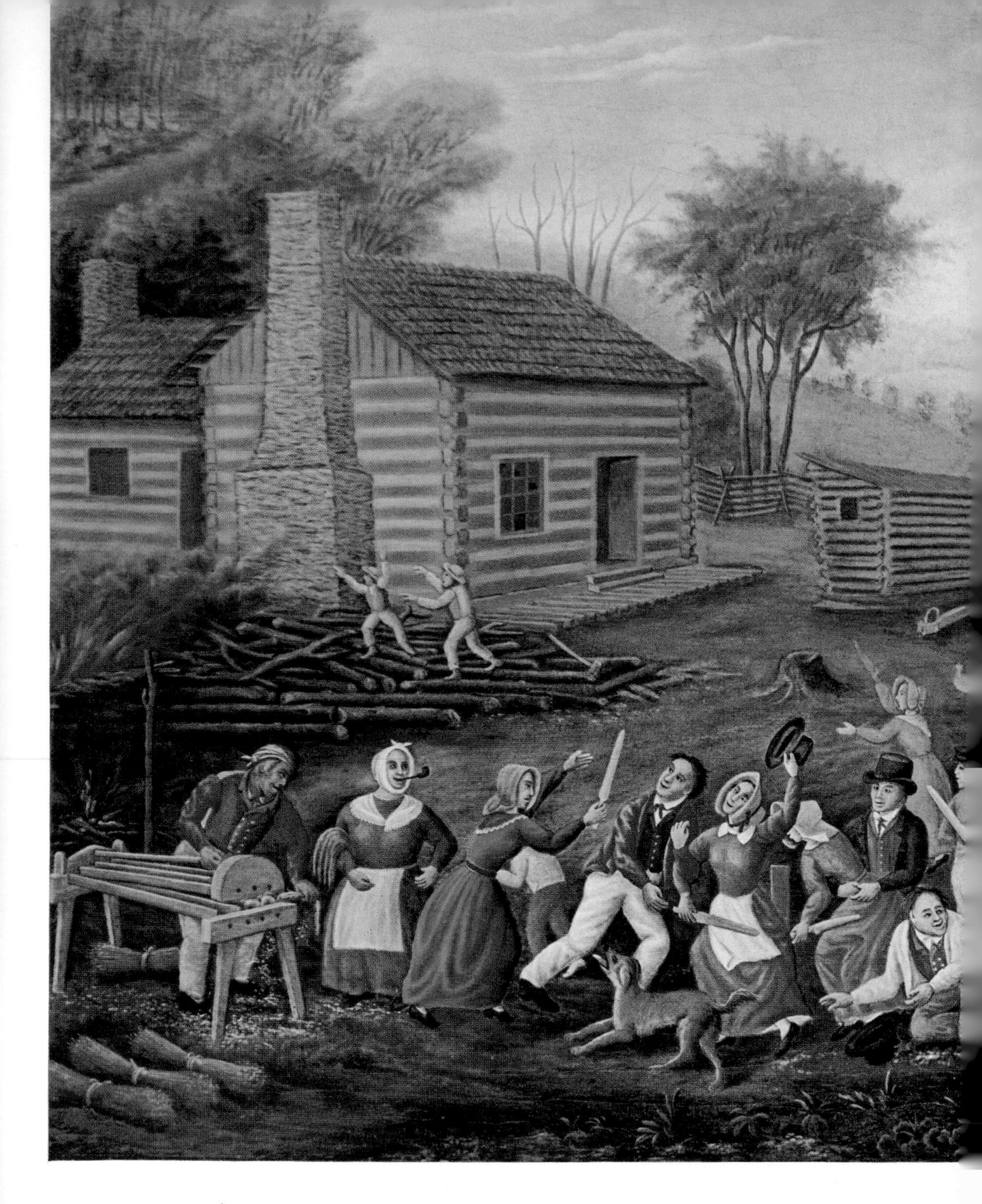

tornado—near present Toledo. Years later another soldier, Theodore Roosevelt, described how Wayne's Legion "dashed forward with bloodcurdling yells, pitchforked the enemy from behind entangled logs, shot them down as they fled."

The Battle of Fallen Timbers—it lasted less than one hour—crushed Ohio's Indians. In July, 1795, Wayne dictated terms at Fort Greene Ville and announced, "all the country, south of the great lakes, has been given up to America."

Peace came to Ohio, and in 1803 it became the first state carved out of the Old

NATIONAL GALLERY OF ART, GIFT OF EDGAR WILLIAM AND BERNICE CHRYSLER GARBISCH

Flax-scutching bee lightens frontier life

Neighbors help in the early American chore of preparing flax for weaving into linen. Scutching, or separating fibers from wood stalks, begins at left. The flax brake, or grinding machine, crushes the stalks. Paddles, called swingling knives, beat the fibers over boards until they break free. This assembly line, painted by Linton Park, son of a Pennsylvania pioneer, combines work with horseplay and courting. Chinks in cabin at right will be filled with moss and calked with clay.

Northwest. Settlers pushed into Indiana Territory where a man could buy a half section of land at $2 an acre, paying one-fourth down, and with a long rifle could shoot so many turkeys he'd keep his wife "two weeks behind with her pickin'." Thousands came, among them utopia-seeking Germans led by George Rapp who moved from Harmony, Pennsylvania, to New Harmony on the banks of the Wabash. Rapp worked his flock from dawn to dusk, urging them on with blasts from his trumpet. Finally he sold his utopia to another seeker, Robert Owen, and the Harmonists turned east to found Economy, near Pittsburgh.

Indiana's land rush inspired territorial governor William Henry Harrison to coin a phrase: "doing a land-office business." Lean and sharp-eyed, he governed from a small frame building in Vincennes that stands today near his mansion Grouseland. After parleys failed to keep the redskins off the warpath, Harrison and 1,000 soldiers marched on the Indian capital at Tippecanoe. That fight was a prelude to the War of 1812, and 29 years later furnished a slogan, "Tippecanoe and Tyler too," that boomed Harrison into the Presidency with running mate John Tyler.

In the Great Lakes wilderness to the north the fur trader still held sway. At Grand Portage, Minnesota, red-sashed French voyageurs smoked clay pipes, traded, drank heady wine. These burly woodsmen had canoed northern waters, dipping paddles in time to folk songs, for more than a century. Marquette founded St. Ignace, Michigan, in 1671; La Salle built a fort at Starved Rock on the Illinois River 11 years later; in 20 the French had settled Cahokia, oldest town in Illinois, and Green Bay, the oldest in Wisconsin.

CHICAGO HISTORICAL SOCIETY; JAMES L. STANFIELD

The tiny Fort Dearborn of 1803 grew into today's giant Chicago. Building to the right of uppermost bridge hides the site of the Chicago River fort. Television antennas soar from an apartment tower of futuristic Marina City.

When France lost her claims in 1763, and Sault Ste. Marie, Detroit, and other French posts hoisted the British flag, the voyageurs stayed on. When Chief Pontiac of the Ottawas fought two years to drive out the British, the French didn't lift a finger. Disgusted, he made peace, and Fort Chartres, center of French government in the Illinois country, lowered its *fleur-de-lis.*

Within 20 years the American flag rose above these old French settlements. The voyageurs simply shrugged and brought pelts to the trading posts at Mackinac Island and Prairie du Chien, centers of John Jacob Astor's fur empire.

The Stars and Stripes also waved over brand-new Fort Dearborn near the old Chicago portage used by Marquette and Jolliet. In 1830 only about 50 people lived in the village destined to become "Hog Butcher for the World, Tool Maker, Stacker of Wheat, Player with Railroads and the Nation's Freight Handler."

WAYNE BARRETT

EVERYDAY LIFE IN TOWN AND COUNTRY

MEN IN BUCKSKIN pierced the frontier, then settlers poured in, clearing, plowing between stumps, plotting cities. By 1800 Louisville, Cincinnati, Detroit, Cleveland, Pittsburgh had proclaimed manhood while still in swaddling clothes.

Here where so late the appalling sound
Of savage yells, the woods resound
Now smiling Ceres waves her sheaf
And cities rise in bold relief.

Cities? Rude settlements of log cabins walled in by forests, they were barren of literature, science, art. In them clustered land-hungry settlers, backward, boisterous, full of brag and optimism. Clad in homespun, brought up on Indian corn, salt pork, and hard liquor, they braved the Indian's tomahawk, endured dyspepsia, malaria, milk sickness, and homesickness. They fought drought, storm, mosquitoes, and each other. But they stuck it out and made good their boasts.

For the most part they came from New England. They left Puritanism behind

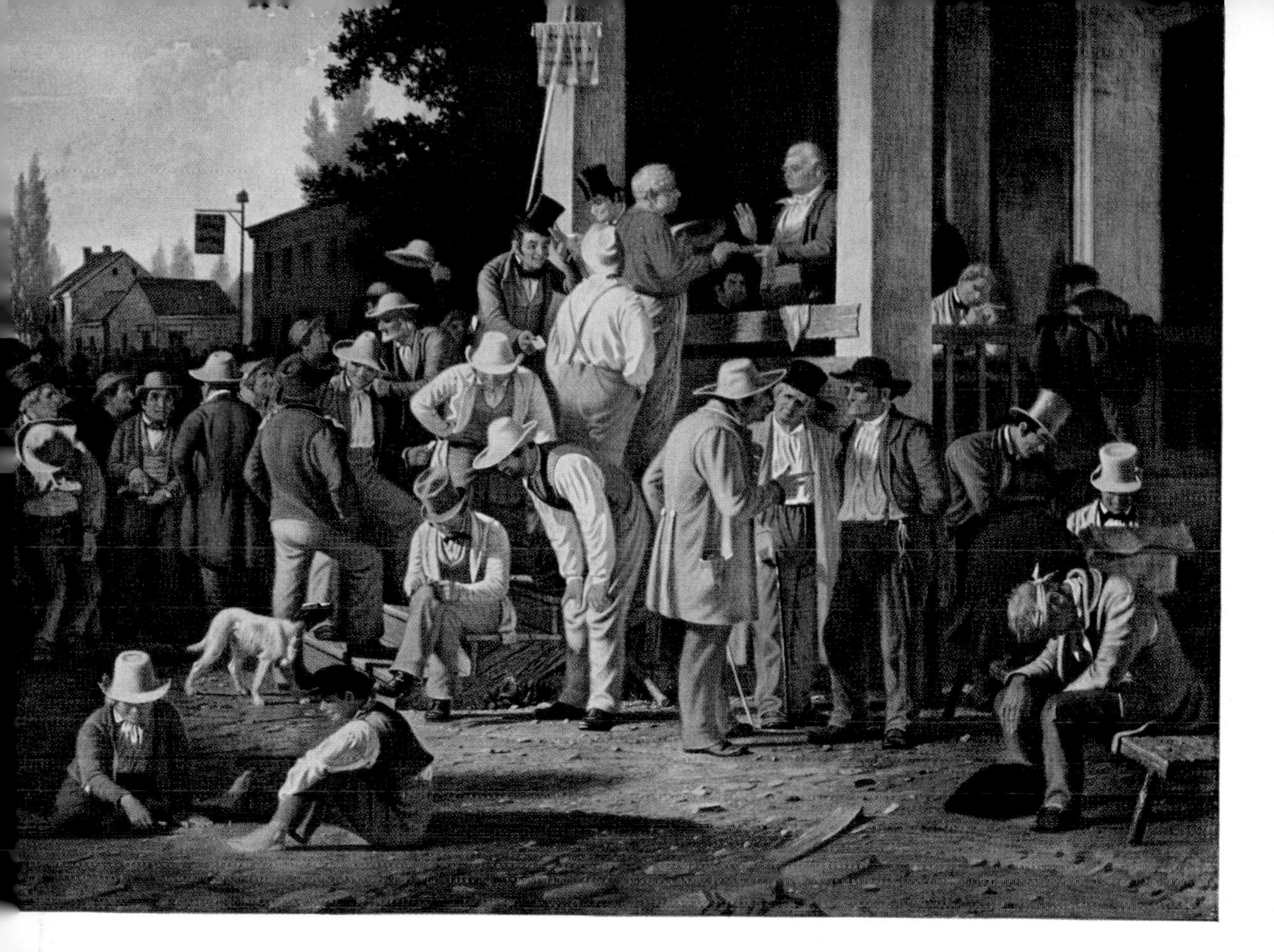

CLOCKWISE: "YANKEE PEDDLER" BY JOHN WHETTON EHNINGER, 1853, THE NEWARK MUSEUM
"COUNTY ELECTION (1851)" BY GEORGE CALEB BINGHAM, THE BOATMEN'S NATIONAL BANK OF ST. LOUIS
"THE SCHOOLROOM" BY AN UNKNOWN ARTIST, C. 1830, KENNEDY GALLERIES, INC., NEW YORK
"PAT LYON, BLACKSMITH" BY JOHN NEAGLE, 1826-7, BOSTON ATHENAEUM,
ON LOAN TO MUSEUM OF FINE ARTS, BOSTON

but kept the Sabbath—and "everything else they could lay their hands on." Frontier life echoed with the blacksmith's hammer, "'Lection Day" merriment, and young voices in the country school reciting from Noah Webster's *Blue-backed Speller.* And don't forget the glib Yankee peddler, dispenser of news and gossip as well as pins, pans, combs, cradles—and oak-leaf cigars. A rogue in fancy coat and high hat, he was our first traveling salesman, forerunner of the industrial age.

Industry marched to New England's measured pace. It started with the home loom and the village gristmill, stepped forward with the itinerant shoemaker and traveling tinker. Visionaries mulled over spinning jennies, cotton gins, and steam engines while "homebred" New Englanders, "wedded to their own way," sat back.

Old Sturbridge Village, on the Quinebaug River 60 miles southwest of Boston, recalls these halcyon days of 1800. Its 35 buildings house the tools, toys, textiles

Old Sturbridge Village, Massachusetts, gathered its buildings, such as "kissing bridge" (lower left), from far and near to portray life in the young republic. Tradition says courting couples stopped under its roof to make a wish.

Fresh-baked cookies disappear as if by magic, keeping the village bakery busy producing 57,000 dozen in an eight-month season. Mid-winter visitors jingle past the 1832 Meetinghouse (below) and quaff hot mulled cider at the Tavern on the Green.

B. ANTHONY STEWART, NATIONAL GEOGRAPHIC PHOTOGRAPHER, AND (ABOVE) LILLIAN H. STEWART

Cooperstown recalls when New York frontier folk met to barter and banter at the Village Crossroads. They made their own tools and fashioned fanciful weather vanes like the iron steed above.

our ancestors made and used. Visitors flock here all year; in midwinter they spend a "Yankee winter weekend" at the Publick House. They watch artisans mold pottery, dip candles, and make pewter. They dine on venison and bear pie, and sip sillabub before a crackling fire after a sleigh ride through the village.

Riding a "sledge," recorded Timothy Dwight, Yale president in the early 1800's, is a "favorite diversion in New England." He also listed "visiting, dancing, music, conversation, walking, riding, sailing, shooting at a

Folk sculpture was often the neon sign of yesteryear. The cigar-store Indian identified the tobacconist as the striped pole symbolizes the barber. This vain mermaid, apt for a beauty salon, instead was swayed by the slightest breeze atop a Massachusetts barn.

Weaving and other exhibits at Cooperstown and Old Sturbridge (above) show daily life on the farm frontier. Frugal villagers wore homespun until threadbare, then used it for patching. From leather they made leggings, aprons, even petticoats.

MERLE SEVERY, NATIONAL GEOGRAPHIC STAFF. RIGHT: WALTER H. MILLER
BELOW: EINARS MENGIS, SHELBURNE MUSEUM, VERMONT

A gimcrack of grandpa's day, this vending hen gives an egg and a cackle for a nickel. Items at Shelburne Museum, Vermont, range from wind-up toys and stagecoaches to a side-wheel steamer.

mark, draughts, chess, and unhappily, in some of the larger towns, cards and dramatic exhibitions." Puritan feelings forbade horse racing, but never got in the way of business. "John," the Yankee anecdote runs, "have you watered the rum?" "Yes, sir." "Have you sanded the sugar?" "Yes, sir." "Have you wet the codfish?" "Yes, sir." "Then come to prayers!"

Shakers, on the other hand, had a reputation for honest dealing that extended even to horse-trading. An offshoot of the Quakers, the Shakers trembled and shook during worship in their celibate communities. Fine farmers and craftsmen, they gained renown in the mid-19th century for their plain but sturdy furniture. Today at Hancock, Massachusetts, their past comes alive

DEAN CONGER, (UPPER LEFT) B. ANTHONY STEWART, AND (LOWER LEFT) ROBERT F. SISSON, ALL NATIONAL GEOGRAPHIC PHOTOGRAPHERS

Antiques and plaster mannequin in poke bonnet draw visitors to the Old Cranberry Barn at East Sandwich, Massachusetts. In the re-created village store at Stony Brook, Long Island (left), coffee grinder provides an aromatic treat. Only peppermint sticks are sold.

Handicrafts in home and shop pioneered mass production

Artisans of a bygone day poured hot tallow into pewter molds and turned out candles by the dozen—a great improvement over toilsome dipping and drying. Whale oil lamps represented another step forward. Many were made in Sandwich, renowned Massachusetts glass center. Such Cape Cod ware, sparkling like the rare pieces in the Sandwich Glass Museum (right), found their way into virtually every 19th century American home. True Sandwich glass has no identifying marks, inviting imitation.

DEAN CONGER AND (RIGHT) HOWELL WALKER, BOTH NATIONAL GEOGRAPHIC STAFF
CANDLEMAKING AT GREENFIELD VILLAGE, DEARBORN, MICHIGAN, BY NEIL P. DAVIS

in a scattering of buildings, a meetinghouse, and perhaps the world's first round barn.

Cooperstown on the Glimmerglass (Otsego Lake) preserves a slice of rural New York life and boasts a son who immortalized it. "The village was alive with business," wrote James Fenimore Cooper; "the artisans increasing in wealth with the prosperity of the country." Leatherstockinged yeomen walked behind plows in surrounding fields. Here Natty Bumppo came to life.

Cooperstown, with its Village Crossroads and Farmers' Museum, is a page out of the past illustrated with rustic crafts and folk art. Weather vanes and cigar-store Indians call to mind the whittling Yankee who, caught without a stick, might carve up the back of his chair.

Images of barn raisings, quilting parties, and husking bees haunt Shelburne Museum, nestled among Vermont's hills. Its old buildings were dismantled at original sites and re-erected timber by timber, brick by brick. A stone's throw from the Charlotte Meeting House and next door to Tuckaway's Barn sits the General Store. Summer visitors, ambling past the candy counter, catch a whiff of peppermint – or was it Wood's Pure Essence of Checkerberry? Shelves groan under teas, spices, remedies, and "just in case" items.

Early Americans read handset newspapers. At Worcester, "printer's devils" work a Revolutionary War press that printed the *Massachusetts Spy*.

In bygone days the country store rivaled the village inn as the social center. Crackerbarrel philosophers gathered round the potbellied stove and emphasized their points with jets of tobacco juice into the sawdust box.

Such forums of fiery opinion were all but snuffed out when the printing press came to town. The county newspaper gave a man his news. Its specialty shop advertisements wrote the obituary of the general store. With ready-made shirts and boughten woolens, the age of homespun now began to fade.

ELEUTHERIAN MILLS-HAGLEY FOUNDATION. RIGHT: B. ANTHONY STEWART, NATIONAL GEOGRAPHIC PHOTOGRAPHER

Hagley Museum traces industrial growth along Brandywine Creek in Delaware. Visitors inspect scale models such as this colonial water-powered flour mill, then ride out to see old Du Pont black powder mills, built open-backed to the river in case of accidental blasts.

RHODE ISLAND DEVELOPMENT COUNCIL AND (LEFT) CULVER SERVICE

Old Slater Mill, birthplace of America's textile industry at Pawtucket, Rhode Island, whirs and clanks for tourists today. Samuel Slater (left) built its complicated machinery from memory.

New England's cotton-spinning industry stands as a monument to Samuel Slater's memory. Royal decrees forbade the export of English machines and designs. So this master mechanic from Derbyshire memorized details of the Arkwright spinning process and smuggled them out in his head! With three partners he built a water-powered textile mill at Pawtucket, Rhode Island, in 1793.

In 1802 Eleuthère Irénée du Pont founded his powder mills near Wilmington, Delaware. They supplied the nation with explosives for more than a century. Here in the Hagley Museum today exhibits show the beginnings of American industry.

Hopewell furnace rekindles scenes of early ironmaking in Pennsylvania. Iron from oven at left was ladled into boxlike mold to make Franklin stoves. Water wheel drove pistons that blasted cold air into the furnace. The village, near Reading, is a national historic site.

JOHN J. PUTMAN

MERCHANTS AND SEA CAPTAINS

Rich cargoes build great homes

CIRCLING GULLS cried like lost souls, and the March wind whistled as it swept across the white-capped water of Salem harbor. To me the sounds seemed like voices out of the past. They spoke of days when merchant ships flying the American flag first sailed to the ends of the earth.

I turned up my collar, pushed my hands deep into my pea jacket, and strode past the Derby House and out old Derby Wharf. Here in 1787 Elias Hasket Derby's *Grand Turk* had dropped sail, the first New England vessel in the Far Eastern trade. Here merchants in cocked hats and scarlet coats had rubbed shoulders with swaggering captains, grizzled stevedores, and turbaned cabin boys from Calcutta.

I saw only snow-covered lobster traps. Yet the sea, murmuring and winking in the sun, beckoned me just as it did Salem boys 150 or more years ago. The old Custom House,

CROWNINSHIELD'S WHARF, SALEM, BY GEORGE ROPES, 1806, PEABODY MUSEUM OF SALEM
SAILOR WEATHER VANE, THE NEW YORK STATE HISTORICAL ASSOCIATION, COOPERSTOWN

Globe-circling Salem captains docked at Derby Wharf, then reported to the Custom House (background), both preserved by the Park Service. Handsome Federal homes along Chestnut Street (right) rose from profits of the Indies trade. The Pingree, Pierce-Nichols, and other houses reflect the comfort of merchant life and the skill of architect Samuel McIntire.

KATHLEEN REVIS JUDGE

the Peabody Museum with its maritime and Oriental treasures, and the stately merchants' dwellings recalled days when Salem had as many as 182 sail at sea. These square, three-story houses along Chestnut Street and around Washington Square stand like tall ships drawn up to wharves. My favorite, the Pierce-Nichols House on Federal Street, mirrors Salem traditions. "When merchant Jerathmeel Pierce built it," my guide told me, "he selected Salem's own Samuel McIntire as architect. When his daughter Sally chose a husband, it was George Nichols, a 23-year-old shipmaster." The groom's wedding gift? A bolt of muslin from Bombay.

Four weeks later Nichols had to sail for Sumatra. But I was relieved to hear he retired from sea at the ripe old age of 26 "to enjoy house and family."

Boston merchants rode to prosperity on the back of the sea otter. Captain Cook's journal had told how much the mandarins of China prized the soft, sleek fur; and sea otters abounded on America's northwest coast. In 1790 the *Columbia,* captained by Robert Gray, sailed into Boston after a three-year voyage that first carried the United States flag around the world. Copper-bottomed brigs fol-

lowed her course: around Cape Horn to barter gimcracks for pelts from Chinook Indians, thence to Canton and home, holds bulging with porcelain, silk, and tea.

On Beacon Hill I saw the houses that shipping fortunes built. Land was dear; homes rose in blocks. But on Louisburg Square the bowed fronts, big oak doors, and many-paned windows gave the residences a graceful look. Appropriately the city's great architect, Charles Bulfinch, owned shares in the *Columbia's* epic voyage. The Sears House, which he built on the hill in 1800, embodies the dignity of the Federal style that enhances so many New England towns.

Not all down-Easters pined for China. Marbleheaders wanted a fisherman's share, not a seaman's wage, and "no gaff from the mate, thank'ee." How well their rock-ribbed harbor reflects their character! Waves dash against granite. Gray houses march in twisted rows down to the water, where moored yachts now bob.

Gloucester still fishes. I viewed her green-hulled fleet clustered in the harbor, orange masts tipped with white, decks a jumble of rope and net. Boat names hint at the personalities of their skippers: *Rose and Lucy, Prosperity, Immaculate Conception, Cigar Joe.* But of all who went down to the sea in ships, the men of Nantucket fascinated me most. Living on "a mere hillock, and elbow of sand," as Herman Melville wrote in *Moby Dick,* they pursued the whale to the "remotest secret drawers and lockers of the world."

The Nantucket Whaling Museum shows the dangers they faced. Charles Sayle, a bearded mariner who makes ship models, piloted me. Charlie can't claim to be a genuine Nantucketer; he's lived there only 30 years.

He pointed to an 18-foot jawbone. "That came out of a bull sperm; 23 teeth on a side. It could smash a boat."

Nearby lay a double-ended, 28-foot whaleboat. It seemed ready to be lowered away at the first cry of "Thar she blows!" I hefted a harpoon and imagined standing in the bow as the boat closed in on a 60-foot "sparm."

"The harpooner would drive that iron barb deep, then it was 'Stern all, boys, stern all!' " Charlie explained. "When the line snapped taut, the boys were off for a Nantucket sleigh ride."

Nantucket lives by the summer trade, but its houses of weathered

Mystic Seaport re-creates the age of sail. *Australia,* oldest U. S. schooner afloat, is an exhibit at this Connecticut village.

ROBERT F. SISSON, NATIONAL GEOGRAPHIC PHOTOGRAPHER

B. ANTHONY STEWART AND (TOP RIGHT) ROBERT F. SISSON, NATIONAL GEOGRAPHIC PHOTOGRAPHERS

Sag Harbor shipbuilder Benjamin Huntting trod this stairway in days when his whalers carried Long Island boys to sea. Now a museum, the mansion typifies luxury built on blubber.

The "widow's walk" or "captain's walk" atop this house in Falmouth, Massachusetts, recalls lonely vigils of mariners' wives. From rooftops they scanned the sea for a ship gone two to four years, and hoped all was well. For when a harpoon struck, it was a "dead whale or a stove boat." In the Seamen's Bethel in New Bedford, marble tablets like that below commemorate men who never came home.

LIBRARY OF CONGRESS AND (BELOW) NORMAN FORTIER

shingle and clapboard are little changed from whaling days. On a blustery Sunday morning I walked down Main Street, where merchants dwelt. (Captains preferred Orange Street, mates lived on Union.) Cobblestones poked through snow; not a soul was in sight. I heard a rustle in an old house and half expected a whiskered shipowner to mount the "captain's walk" and con the sea for a whaler four years gone, his fortune in its hold.

At the foot of Main stands the Pacific Club, built by William Rotch as a counting house in 1774. "Used to be," Charlie told me, "you couldn't warm yourself by its iron stove unless you had captained a whaler in the Pacific."

New Englanders no longer hunt whale. In the 1860's kerosene replaced sperm oil in lamps. But New Bedford

In Memory of
CAPT. WM. SWAIN,
Associate
Master of the Christopher
Mitchell of Nantucket.
This worthy man,
after fastning to a whale,
was carried overboard by
the line, and drowned
May 19th 1844.
in the 49th Year of his age.

Be ye also ready; for in such an hour as ye think not, the Son of man cometh.

Andalusia's lavish drawing room shows Philadelphia shared in shipping profits. Built in 1795 by merchant John Craig, the Federal house (map, page 213) passed to financier Nicholas Biddle. A lover of things Greek, he added Doric columns. The mantel is Italian, the chandelier French.

Hampton (right), a national historic site near Baltimore, elegantly housed merchant Charles Ridgely. Chandeliers and Empire love seats evoke days when Eliza Ridgely entertained with a harp.

KATHLEEN REVIS JUDGE AND JOHN E. FLETCHER, NATIONAL GEOGRAPHIC PHOTOGRAPHER, AND (RIGHT) NATIONAL PARK SERVICE. "LADY WITH A HARP; ELIZA RIDGELY" BY THOMAS SULLY, 1818, NATIONAL GALLERY OF ART

cherishes its past with a splendid museum. Martha's Vineyard is proud of the captains' homes in elm-lined Edgartown and remembers that Gay Head Indians, like Tashtego in *Moby Dick,* won fame as harpooners.

To see how these men lived at sea, I went to Mystic Seaport in Connecticut, berth of *Charles W. Morgan,* last of the old-time whalers. Here the Marine Historical Association has re-created an early 19th century port. I passed sail and rigging lofts, shops of shipwright and figurehead carver, Spouter Tavern and Spicer Counting House.

Aboard the black-hulled *Morgan,* I gripped the wheel and peered 100 feet to the bluff bow. Three square-rigged masts towered over me; spars and lines crisscrossed the sky. I pictured myself driving her with the wind, hearing the sails ripple and snap as that bow rose and fell.

Forward squats the brick tryworks where slices of blubber, "Bible leaves," were boiled into oil. Melville told of nights when "the darkness was licked up by the fierce flames," and the smoke had "an unspeakable, wild, Hindoo odor about it . . . like the left wing of the day of judgment."

The work was hard, the food miserable, the forecastle like a dungeon. But a boy always had time to etch whale teeth or bone (scrimshaw), and someday might make captain, even own a ship—if he didn't succumb to storm and whale, "Feegee" cannibals, or impressment by the British navy. Little wonder that New Englanders looked on the sea as their own. Yet New York, Philadelphia, and other ports staked watery claims too. Baltimore's fame rode with her swift schooners and brigs, forerunners of the Baltimore clipper. During the Revolution they had served as privateers. As 1812 neared, there was talk of war. Baltimore's ships might fight again.

WAYNE BARRETT

THE WAR OF 1812

"Bombs bursting in air"

BIG GUNS THUNDER and shudder in the night. Their flashes etch stark tableaux of rain-spattered barbettes, cannon mouths, taut faces of American gunners. Above, a sodden furl of stripes and stars freezes in a rocket's glare. This is 1814, the night of September 13-14, and Fort McHenry, guarding the entrance to Baltimore Harbor, meets the onslaught of a British landing force.

Out of McHenry's range lie British men-of-war, pounding away with broadsides, arching mortar shells into the fort. A young Maryland lawyer, temporarily detained behind the fleet, has witnessed the bombardment all day. As it roars on through the long night, he paces the deck and strains his eyes for a glimpse of his nation's flag above the smoke-wreathed fort. Does it yet wave?

Then in dawn's early light he sees at last those broad stripes and bright stars. The flag still flies; Fort McHenry still holds; Baltimore is safe; the nation survives. In exultation at seeing "the discomfited host of its assailants driven back in ignominy to their ships," Key scribbles on the back of a letter a poem that comes from deep in his heart. Set to an old English tune, "The Star-Spangled Banner" will bring unborn millions to their feet.

Today McHenry faces not square-rigged men-of-war but an endless traffic of merchant ships headed in and out of Baltimore. The five buildings in the star-shaped fort are now museums. Inspecting the outer gun battery, the visitor can picture cannoneers ramming home powder and shot during the nightmarish ordeal, beating off the assault with crunching salvos while bomb fragments thwack into the earthen parapets.

The flag that Maj. George Armistead and his 1,000-man garrison kept flying hangs in the Smithsonian Institution in Washington, D.C. It was made by Mary Pickersgill at what is now the Flag House in Baltimore, a museum of the War of 1812. Those who see the fragile old banner today, and the fine houses of Baltimore that were shielded by Fort McHenry during the bombardment, may sense the emotion that gripped the sensitive soul of Francis Scott Key when he saw "that our flag was still there."

American triumphs in the War of 1812 were by no means everyday affairs. For this relatively little-known conflict had found the young United States woefully unprepared.

"THE STAR-SPANGLED BANNER" BY E. PERCY MORAN, PEALE MUSEUM, ON LOAN TO FLAG HOUSE MUSEUM, BALTIMORE
LEFT: VOLKMAR WENTZEL, NATIONAL GEOGRAPHIC PHOTOGRAPHER

Fort McHenry's flag flies 24 hours a day to honor the Star-Spangled Banner that Francis Scott Key saw still "gallantly streaming" after 25 hours of cannonading. The national monument and historic shrine juts into the Patapsco River in Baltimore.

Neutral America for years had fattened on trade with the Britain of George III and the France of Napoleon, locked in a life-and-death struggle. In 1806 the feast was over. The belligerents blockaded each other's ports and seized our ships. The Royal Navy, hard put to man Britain's first line of defense, stopped U. S. merchantmen at sea, searched them for deserters, and impressed crew members. England's frigates even patrolled off New York and Boston. When in June of 1807 the new U. S. frigate *Chesapeake,* guns still unmounted, put to sea from Norfolk, Virginia, she was immediately hailed by a British warship—four deserters might be aboard; kindly muster your crew. The Americans politely refused. Whereupon the British opened fire, boarded, and dragged off four men. Three claimed to be U. S. citizens who had previously been impressed into the Royal Navy.

THE CHESAPEAKE AFFAIR brought American tempers to a boil. The flag had been fired upon; American sailors shot down in cold blood. President Jefferson, endeavoring to avoid war, retaliated with the Embargo Act. But this curtailment of commerce stirred a hornets' nest in maritime New England, where fortunes were threatened; there was even talk of secession. A milder measure, the Non-Intercourse Act, restored limited trade. But impressment continued.

War was on the nation's lips in 1809 when that "withered little apple-John," James Madison, and his vivacious Dolley moved into the President's House. Negotiations to resume trade broke off; Britain showed only scorn for the "neutral rights" of her upstart offspring. John Bull rattled his saber and whispered intrigue to the Indians. War drums thumping at Tippecanoe echoed along the Great Lakes and into the north woods. Frontiersmen saw the hand behind the threat and declared the West could never be safe until the British were expelled from Canada.

Into troubled skies soared the War Hawks, fire-eating young congressmen from the South and across the Alleghenies who insisted that "war is the only means of redress." These men—Henry Clay of Kentucky, John C. Calhoun of South Carolina, Felix Grundy of Tennessee, and others—cast land-hungry eyes on Florida and Canada. "The militia of Kentucky are alone competent to place Montreal and Upper Canada at your feet," boasted Clay.

Eastern conservatives were shocked. Declare war on England? Not with our "paltry little navy rotting in the Potomac!" said Federalist leader Josiah Quincy of Massachusetts. "We have been embargoed and non-intercoursed almost into a consumption," shrilled John Randolph of Virginia; "this is not the time for battle."

Yet the War Hawks won their demand. On June 18, 1812, President Madison signed the declaration of war against Great Britain, the document of a bitterly divided Congress. The unready nation of less than eight million found itself in a war insisted on by the South and West in defense of the North and East, which didn't want to be defended. Several New England states went into mourning, with tolling bells and flags at half mast, and refused to raise militia and money for "Mr. Madison's War"—a war, intended to be waged on land, that was to bring glory on lake and sea, whose peace treaty would mention none of the issues ("Free Trade and Sailors' Rights") for which it was successfully fought, and whose greatest battle (New Orleans) would take place two weeks after the war was over!

Grand strategy in the summer of 1812 called for a four-prong attack on the British in Canada. One force was to strike from frontier Detroit; other columns were to sweep across the border from Fort Niagara at the western end of Lake Ontario, from Sackett's Harbor at the eastern end, and to move up the Lake Champlain corridor (see map in back of book). Command fell to two honored veterans of the Revolution, William Hull and Henry Dearborn, both long past their prime.

The plan failed miserably. From where the industrial city of Detroit now stands, Hull timorously led his undisciplined troops into Canada. Learning that British and Indians had taken Fort Mackinac to the north, he backtracked to Detroit and, besieged, ignominiously surrendered. That very day Fort Dearborn (Chicago), 250 miles west, was in flames, its garrison massacred.

On Champlain, militia balked at the border when Dearborn moved on Montreal.

A center prong got across the Niagara River not far from the thundering falls. Fighting seesawed; moments of bungling and skulking dulled the keen edge of valor.

Ghosts of blue-jacketed Americans in tall black leather shakos haunt the visitor to Fort Niagara in New York, which fell in 1813. Its mute cannon trigger scenes of nearby Queenston Heights, Chippewa, Lundy's Lane, and Fort Erie in Canada. When the smoke cleared, the British controlled the Niagara frontier; the Americans stood firm at Sackett's Harbor.

To the west, William Henry Harrison, taking command after Hull's debacle, built Fort Meigs, whose earthworks can still be seen on the Maumee River in Ohio. It withstood 1,000 redcoats, and 1,200 redskins under the brilliant Tecumseh. When the foe tested Fort Stephenson, southeast of Meigs, they found it too big a bite to swallow.

Now Harrison was ready to recapture Detroit—as soon as Lake Erie could be wrested from the British. Oliver Hazard Perry did that in September of 1813.

Ascending the shaft at Perry's Victory National Monument at Put-in-Bay, Ohio, visitors overlook the peaceful waters where

"We have determined to maintain this place, and, by heavens! we can."

GEORGE CROGHAN, a 21-year-old major, had orders from General Harrison to destroy Fort Stephenson and retreat. Why? Col. Henry Procter with 400 redcoats and Tecumseh with 2,000 braves were at the mouth of the Sandusky looking down Croghan's throat. One cannon and 160 men couldn't hold the fort. But Croghan got permission to try.

On August 1, 1813, Procter demanded the fort's surrender, "to spare the effusion of blood." Croghan replied that he would "blow them all to hell." That night British artillery roared. Next day the redcoats stormed the north wall and met rifle fire and an avalanche of spiked logs.

Now Croghan's cannon, "Old Betsy," peeked from her embrasure. WHAM! Grapeshot exploded in the enemy's face. The attack cost 150 men. Croghan lost one dead, seven wounded.

On the fort's site in Fremont, Ohio, Old Betsy guards the grave of heroic George Croghan.

RUTHERFORD B. HAYES LIBRARY AND (TOP) OHIO HISTORICAL SOCIETY

the tide of the northwestern frontier campaign finally turned for America, thanks to a daring young commodore who drove his ships through the British fleet as if leading a squadron of cavalry. Three weeks after Perry's victory Harrison's men entered Detroit. They poured on into Canada, caught up with the enemy, and won a resounding triumph at the Battle of the Thames, where valiant Tecumseh fell.

AT THE BATTLE OF LAKE ERIE Perry's flag bore the motto, DON'T GIVE UP THE SHIP. That flag hangs now in the U. S. Naval Academy at Annapolis, Maryland. Its words, which still stiffen midshipmen's spines, were spoken first by Capt. James Lawrence dying in battle. They symbolized the fighting heart of America's "cockboat navy." Iron men like Isaac Hull, David Porter, and William Bainbridge renewed the glory that John Paul Jones achieved in the Revolution and Edward Preble in 1804 won off the shores of Tripoli. The frigate *Constellation* fought in that Barbary War, and in the War of 1812. Later converted into a sloop of war and now preserved as a museum, she delights Baltimore tourists.

Queen of the Boston Navy Yard is the *Constitution,* veteran of Tripoli and 1812. Immortalized by poet Oliver Wendell Holmes, "Old Ironsides" was kept afloat in her old age by the pennies of school children, who now walk wide-eyed across her rebuilt deck, picturing the smoke and thunder of broadsides as she sailed undefeated through 26 actions. The oak-hulled frigate won her nickname off Halifax, Nova Scotia, where she pounded the British *Guerrière* into a hulk in August, 1812.

"PERRY ON LAKE ERIE" BY WILLIAM H. POWELL, U. S. CAPITOL

Commodore Perry transfers the colors from his disabled flagship *Lawrence* to the *Niagara,* fights on, and shatters the British fleet on Lake Erie, September 10, 1813. "We have met the enemy and they are ours." Sea Scouts re-enact "boarders away!" under the victory monument at Put-in-Bay, Ohio (top right). The 352-foot tower also commemorates peace along the United States-Canada border, one of the world's friendliest. The frigate *Constitution* (right) is berthed in the Boston Navy Yard. "Old Ironsides" is still on Navy rolls.

B. ANTHONY STEWART, NATIONAL GEOGRAPHIC PHOTOGRAPHER, AND (ABOVE) SINCLAIR OIL CORPORATION'S PUBLIC SERVICE ADVERTISING

Our navy found worthy brothers-in-arms in Yankee privateers—"militia of the sea." They took 1,300 prizes during the war, pursuing British merchantmen clear to the English Channel. Cocky Thomas Boyle in his trim Baltimore schooner even notified the British that he had "blockaded" all the ports of the United Kingdom!

Of course the fledgling republic was in no position to blockade anyone. It was fighting for its very life. Victorious over Napoleon in Europe, Britain now threw the weight of Wellington's Invincibles against America. In August, 1814, the British raided Chesapeake Bay, ransomed Alexandria, stampeded militia at Bladensburg, burst into Washington and left it in flames. Fleeing, Dolley Madison rescued the Stuart portrait of Washington that hangs in the East Room of the White House.

But Fort McHenry held, blunting the attack on Baltimore. And two days earlier, when 10,000 redcoats and an armed flotilla invading down Lake Champlain converged on Plattsburg, New York, Commodore Thomas Macdonough positioned his small naval force and exchanged broadsides. After two hours he reported:

"The Almighty has been pleased to grant us a signal victory." Events at Baltimore and Plattsburg persuaded the British to sign a peace treaty at Ghent in Flanders, Christmas Eve, 1814.

THE PEACE NEWS from Ghent could not reach New Orleans in time to stop Sir Edward Pakenham, brother-in-law of the great Wellington, from his attack on the city, key to the Mississippi Valley. Crag-faced Andrew Jackson, racked by dysentery, exhausted by campaigns against the Creek Indians, had

Battle of New Orleans, January 8, 1815: an eyewitness drawing. Redcoats carry ladders along the levee (foreground) to scale the rampart extending along Rodriguez Canal. Scarlet companies attack across the cane field, but the American wall of fire cuts them down. Jackson stands under U. S. flag. Chalmette Monument (right) overlooks the battlefield.

BY HYACINTHE LACLOTTE, ENGINEER IN THE LOUISIANA ARMY, 1815; COLLECTION OF EDGAR WILLIAM AND BERNICE CHRYSLER GARBISCH. ABOVE: NATIONAL PARK SERVICE

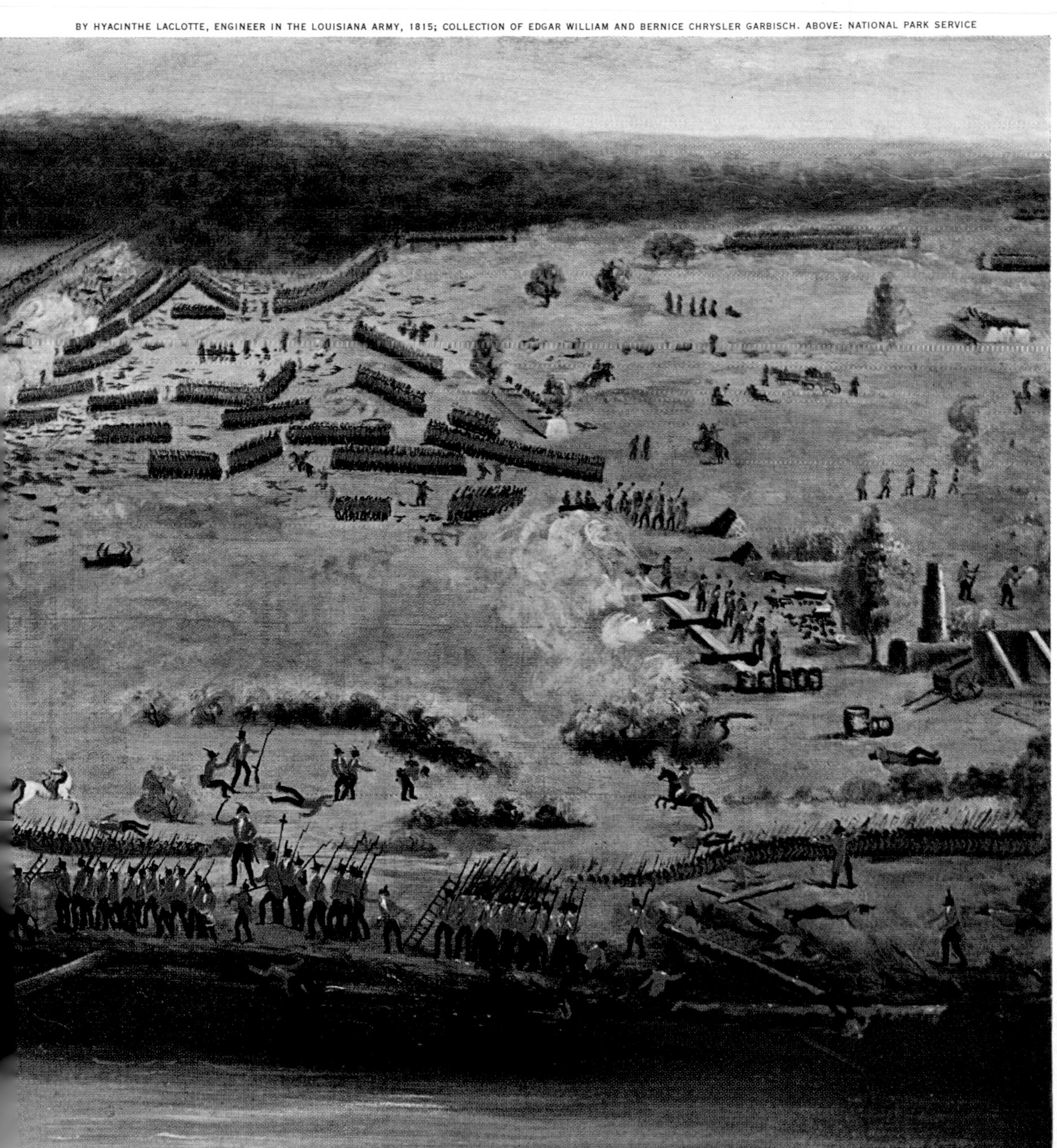

ALONZO CHAPPEL, CHICAGO HISTORICAL SOCIETY

Andrew Jackson, victor at New Orleans

I'M a prisoner of war, not a servant," snapped the 14-year-old Carolina boy, refusing to black the British officer's boots. Jackson's strong will—and the saber scar his Revolutionary War captor gave him—marked him while frontier lawyer, congressman, duelist, vanquisher of the Creeks at Horseshoe Bend, Alabama; first territorial governor of Florida; and President, 1829-37. "He's tough," admired a soldier. "Tough as hickory," replied another, and the nickname "Old Hickory" stuck.

His cotton profits built The Hermitage, near Nashville, Tennessee (below). Visitors today see original furnishings, and the garden laid out by his wife Rachel. When the "favorite of the people" moved into the White House, well-wishers and job hunters tracked mud on rugs, smashed china. "To the victors belong the spoils" was an apt slogan!

DAVID S. BOYER, NATIONAL GEOGRAPHIC STAFF

sprung from his sofa when he learned the redcoats were but nine miles off. "By the Eternal, they shall not sleep on our soil," he swore. Mustering 2,000 men, he struck the enemy camp that night, and after a savage melee fell back to the Rodriguez Canal, boundary of Chalmette Plantation.

Today's visitor to Chalmette National Historical Park, strolling among moss-draped cypresses, can see the abandoned millrace along which Jackson built a mud rampart from the Mississippi to an impassable swamp. It sheltered his motley army—Mississippi Dragoons, Louisiana Blues, Tennessee Mounted Infantry, U.S. Marines, Choctaw Indians, Santo Domingo Free Men of Color, and Jean Lafitte's "hellish banditti" from Barataria Bay, pirate nest 50 miles south of New Orleans.

The British celebrated New Year's with a barrage, but pirate gunners silenced some of the cannon. At night Tennesseans went "huntin' "; redcoat sentinels walked with fear. Jackson's army grew to 5,000, Pakenham's to more than 8,000.

January 8 dawned with a curtain of fog. It lifted to reveal two scarlet columns. Rockets signaled the British attack. Bayonets fixed, the redcoats marched... slowly... in step. Grapeshot tore their ranks. But on they came. Then the rampart exploded with the blast of 1,500 Kentucky rifles. Three deep, Jackson's men in rapid order fired and stepped back. The "constant rolling fire... resembled rattling peals of thunder." To a survivor it looked like "a row of fiery furnaces."

In less than two hours 2,000 British lay bleeding on that field of sugar cane stubble. Pakenham was dead. America's losses: seven dead, six wounded.

The British embarked, carrying the body of their general in a cask of rum.

In New Orleans citizens danced in the streets, sang hymns of thanksgiving. The battle was over. The second war of independence was over. The young nation had won respect in the eyes of the world.

PAINTING BY DE THULESTRUP, LOUISIANA HISTORICAL SOCIETY

December 20, 1803: The French tricolor descends, the Stars and Stripes rise over Place d'Armes. The young nation takes over the Louisiana Territory and nearly doubles in size.

New Orleans made history early. Spain claimed the lower Mississippi, but the French settled on the Gulf first in 1699, and 19 years later founded the city on low, quaky ground about 100 winding miles up the river: "If the river didn't get you from the front, Lake Pontchartrain watered you from the rear." Settlers fought flood, fever, and neglect, yet prospered. Kings granted riverside estates, and whispers told of court mistresses dispatched regretfully to *La Nouvelle Orléans* with small fortunes as consolation. Treaties in the 1760's tossed Louisiana from France to Spain. Then Spain passed the territory to Napoleon, who sold it to the United States. Visitors to the port today taste a rich gumbo of all three cultures.

W. D. VAUG

NEW ORLEANS

Visiting the city of three nations

THE MAN FROM IOWA took a breath of balmy night air, let his eye travel from the iron-laced gallery to the cup of ink-black coffee in his hand, and gave a slow sigh: "New Orleans—why, it makes living a pleasure!"

To this the Orleanian, of the French Quarter downtown, the Garden District uptown, the Mississippi River front, or crowded "backatown," politely agrees. His city, with its Latin heritage, has a special attitude best summed up by a local saying: "There are few things on earth worth a fit of indigestion."

When the Spaniards clanked into the town in the 1760's they soon succumbed to it, married French girls, and were absorbed. Then the youthful United States acquired this old city that not many Anglo-Saxons approved of. Years of clash followed. The Creole (a white descendant of French or Spanish settlers) sniffed at the American *arriviste*. To say that a fellow was American . . . *Monsieur*, that might lead to an insult, often settled with "pistols for two, breakfast for one."

Nowhere in America was it easier to be killed. Glance at a stranger, and you might be challenged for your "insulting attitude." Turn up your nose at New Orleans coffee, and next morning you might face cold steel. Best patronized meeting spot for these *affaires d'honneur* was under the moss-draped "Dueling Oaks" at Allard Plantation. Here fought Emile La Sére, who sympathetically helped bandage his fallen foes, and Pakenham LeBlanc, who once sensed a discourtesy at a dance, put the names of the board of managers in a hat, and drew one, a tyro, to challenge. But the "victim" shot first, and LeBlanc dueled no more.

Americans, too, were absorbed. Today's Orleanian may talk Brooklynese, but he'll quaff *café* during a business deal, spend an evening on a balcony in the Vieux Carré sipping from a tall glass, and eat long, quiet meals in a superlative restaurant. Some outsiders may agree with Mrs. Andrew Jackson: "Oh, the wickedness, the idolatry of this place!" But in time she too might have been Creolized.

Life in New Orleans long centered in the Vieux Carré or French Quarter, once a walled town, bordered by these four streets: North Rampart, a thoroughfare along the walls toward the swamp; Levee or Decatur, near the waterfront; Canal, originally a moat beyond which the Americans would build their town; and Esplanade, the parade ground below. Here one can still find buildings that look much as they did more than 150 years ago. To one side of the worn gray St. Louis Cathedral, focal point of Roman Catholicism in the Mississippi Valley, stands the Cabildo, seat of Spanish rule and scene of the formal transfer of the Louisiana Territory. On the other stands the Presbytère, for years part of the church's property. Rich examples of Spanish design, both the Cabildo and its twin the Presbytère have monumental arches below and magnificent stairways inside. But the details of the second floor are mainly Gallic. And years later Orleanians tacked on

Triple-spired St. Louis Cathedral, standing in the heart of the old city at Place d'Armes, now Jackson Square, honored Jackson's victory with a solemn *Te Deum.* Today it greets sightseers in the famous French Quarter, the Vieux Carré.

JUSTIN LOCKE

the oddly contrasting French mansard roofs. The buildings have, as New Orleans says, Spanish feet, a French head, and a mixed middle.

Stuccoed brick homes along nearby streets center about the courtyard, with an outer wall that rises on a line with the *banquette* (sidewalk). Iron-bordered galleries facing the street give the crowning exterior touch. A cool flagstone carriageway leads to the sun-splashed greenery of the patio. Vines twist among the iron scrolls of the galleries; flowers spread in tropical profusion. In the privacy of this semi-outdoor living room, a family eats meals or plays cards, a bird swings in a cage, a dog sleeps on the shady floor.

From a high floor Orleanians can look down on roof-line panoramas reminiscent of Paris: walls rising against walls, each house a separate unit, blue, pink, or purple, yet all in harmony with scene and weather.

The Garden District, the "American answer to the French Quarter," starts at Jackson Avenue. These Anglo-Saxons wanted no lines of close-built houses, backs to the street. They built the biggest residences New Orleans had seen, in the Greek Revival mode, and placed them in the center of spacious grounds, facing the street.

Wide galleries and halls, rooms sometimes 16 or 18 feet high, marble mantels, paneled doors with fanlights and pilasters reflect a design for commodious living. Oaks trail branches toward the railings, vines climb the pillars, flowering shrubs line the iron fencing. Magnolias, pecans, and palms, crape myrtles holding clusters of pink blossoms; sweet olives and figs among the rosebushes give the district its garden flavor.

To many tourists, New Orleans means jazz. And in this city of Jelly Roll Morton, King Oliver, and Louis (Satchmo) Armstrong, the wail and pound of "le jazz hot" goes deep into the night.

To others, New Orleans means fine food. When a Creole enters heaven, they say, he asks St. Peter where he can find the jambalaya. If he gets none of this piquant combination of shrimp, oysters, tomatoes, rice, and other items, he sidles over and inquires about food customs in the other place. From the

Lacy ironwork, the hallmark of New Orleans, was wrought first in Spain, then by Louisiana smiths. Flowering patios are another French Quarter feature. One-time slave quarters of a Royal Street mansion (right) overlook a tropical courtyard partly enclosed by the wall of an old convent.

French the cuisine derived a basic delicacy of taste. To this the Spanish added fragrant spices; the Indians contributed roots and herbs; the Negro, skills in mixing mouthwarming ingredients from the marshes and swamps, the river and the Gulf.

Any listing of restaurants is a catalog of personal preferences. Antoine's, superlative for generations, is notable for oysters Rockefeller. Galatoire's is celebrated for a *filet de truite Marguery,* trout smothered in a bland covering with shrimp, mushrooms, and hollandaise sauce.

Brennan's offers baked oyster specialties, with snails or shrimp in the center. Arnaud's is memorable for breast of turkey *en papillote,* a rich yellow concoction imprisoned with steam and aroma inside a paper bag. But the roster can quickly grow as long as a Broussard menu.

To millions, New Orleans means the Mardi Gras, the giddiest, most absurd, most magnificent thing in the city. It comes from France, a Christianized celebration that goes back to the pagan rites of spring.

Christmas over, men's societies (krewes) hold processions and balls behind closed doors. To be a queen ... for debutantes it's a matter for prayer. Fathers stave off creditors saving for daughter's supreme hour.

As "Fat Tuesday" nears, thousands watch street processions with glittering floats. Flares flicker, bands play. At last, on Mardi Gras, the city takes over the festivities. It masks and parades, prances, shouts, sings, and dances. Then at midnight Lent begins and New Orleans remembers the meaning of *carnevale:* farewell to the flesh. It begins to rest up for the next Mardi Gras!

Dinner at Antoine's is a gourmet's rite. To visit New Orleans without performing it is as unthinkable as to leave Paris without a look at the Louvre. But even oysters Rockefeller take a back seat when Mardi Gras (Fat Tuesday) rolls in. With costumed revelry and torchlight parades, the city goes mad. Born in 1857, the Mistick Krewe of Comus is oldest of some 65 festive groups. Here King Comus's masked krewemen dance at the season's final ball.

UPPER: JUSTIN LOCKE. LOWER: ROBERT F. SISSON AND JOHN E. FLETCHER, NATIONAL GEOGRAPHIC PHOTOGRAPHERS

THE OLIVIER PLANTATION NEAR NEW IBERIA IN 1861, BY ADRIAN PERSAC, COURTESY LOUISIANA STATE MUSEUM

THIS GENTLE FIGURE AT ST. MARTINVILLE MARKS THE GRAVE OF EMMELINE LABICHE, IMMORTALIZED AS EVANGELINE BY HENRY WADSWORTH LONGFELLOW.

Cajun country and the kingdom of cane

KETTLES BUBBLE and give off a steamy sweet fragrance. The yellowish-brown mixture grows thicker and darker. Men and women watch as if their lives depend upon it. In a sense they do. At length M. Etienne de Boré thrusts a long spoon into a kettle, stirs, and cries: "It granulates!"

That scene, enacted in 1795, changed Louisiana history. De Boré had gambled his plantation on this sugar mill. From it rose Louisiana's empire of sugar.

From the bayous below New Orleans—home of zesty, dark-eyed Acadians, or Cajuns—to above the capital at Baton Rouge, pillared houses rose along the Mississippi in a double line of splendor. Flanking each stood offices, guest houses, and a *garçonnière* for young bachelors. Grouped about were the kitchen building, perhaps a summerhouse beside the levee, and pigeon cotes. At back "the street" led through the slave quarters.

In early days, sugar homes stood on brick piers 10 or 12 feet high to escape flood and catch the breeze. Americans added Greek Revival to the Creole plan. Houses grew with great columns and neoclassic pediments.

The lower Mississippi was a "gold coast" where planters held little duchies and more retainers than many an English lord. Valcour Aime, "Louis XIV of Louisiana," once entertained a guest with a transcendent meal, then won $10,000 by showing that everything, even the cigars, had come from his plantation.

Another Creole, Marius Pons Bringier, was noted for arranging matches for his daughters.

Evangeline's wistful spirit haunts the bayou region of Louisiana, where Acadians settled after their exile from Canada in 1755. Acadian House in St. Martinville shows how her people lived and preserves memories of her "Gabriel" in Longfellow's poem. Mansions of the sugar kings flank the lower Mississippi. Many welcome visitors today.

Oak Alley, built by a sugar planter in the 1830's as *Bon Séjour* (Good Rest), was renamed by steamboat passengers who glimpsed its double line of live oaks, their boughs forming

JUSTIN LOCKE

a vaulted corridor to the mansion. Doric columns, 28 in all, girdle this showplace along the Mississippi, open to the public. One of the mighty oaks measures 29½ feet in girth!

WILLARD R. CULVER AND (OPPOSITE) CHARLES HARBUTT, MAGNUM

Elegance marks Houmas House, built by a son-in-law of Wade Hampton, South Carolina hero of the Revolution. David Weeks built Shadows-on-the-Teche (opposite) in 1830 as a town house for his vast domain of sugar land. The National Trust for Historic Preservation, which helped restore the grandeur of this monument to a bygone era, opens house and gardens to visitors daily.

He invited each prospect for a visit, then put the question: Will you be my son-in-law? Since M. Bringier was worth millions, there is no record that any blushing young man ever refused.

One gallant, with no known livelihood, yet the brightest of social gifts, accepted a plantation, Bocage, for marrying Bringier's 14-year-old daughter. She ran it while he played his guitar, painted pictures, wrote poetry, and had servants row him about in a cushioned, gilded barge.

The d'Estréhans, whose house stands near New Orleans, had a paterfamilias who erected a museum for his children and filled it with Greek statuary. He exposed them often to the cultural influence, but before each visit he had a slave cover the undraped figures with Mother Hubbards.

Upriver is Houmas House, imposing to the point of haughtiness. In 1857 a redheaded Irishman, bachelor John Burnside, bought the house and became the great man of the river, adding plantations as some growers bought necklaces for their wives.

A British traveler described some of the pitfalls of Houmas hospitality. One was the morning bath—iced. Another was the prebreakfast mint julep borne into the bedroom by a servant.

Perhaps the flamboyance of life in the mansions of the sugar kings is best told in the story of a grande dame who dropped a diamond earring at supper. "Don't bother," she waved away the man beside her. "The servants will sweep it up in the morning."

MISSISSIPPI
CORPS OF ENGINEERS, U.S. ARMY
MEMPHIS, TENNESSEE

THE GREAT RIVER

Canoes, flatboats, and stern-wheelers turn the Mississippi into Main Street

"WHOO-OOP! I'm the old original iron-jawed, brass-mounted, copper-bellied corpse-maker from the wilds of Arkansaw. . . . Cast your eye on me, gentlemen! and lay low and hold your breath, for I'm 'bout to turn myself loose!"

Yowling their challenges, men of the flatboats and keelboats, men of the Mike Fink breed, "half-man, half-alligator, and chock full of fight," reflected the big, powerful, dangerous river they rode to New Orleans.

The Mississippi revealed its tortuous brown course to De Soto in 1541, to Marquette and Jolliet in 1673, and finally yielded its entire length to La Salle in 1682.

The river waited another century before commerce came with the rush of a spring flood. Slender keelboats and boxlike flatboats carried tons of furs and produce downstream. Keelboatmen rowed, poled, towed their craft back to St. Louis and up the Missouri. Flatboats from the Ohio were knocked apart and sold for lumber; crews from Kentucky or Tennessee braved robbers and redskins as they walked home up the Natchez Trace.

What tales they could tell of the plantations and good-time towns they had seen! To a backwoods boy like 19-year-old Abe Lincoln, New Orleans with its French and Spanish peoples, its Old World luxury, and its slave market seemed another world.

But rivermen gaped even more when a wood-eating, smoke-belching steamboat came kicking round the bend in 1811. It launched an era of floating palaces with crystal chandeliers, thick carpets, and suave gamblers ready for a

"MARQUETTE AND JOLLIET DISCOVER THE MISSISSIPPI RIVER" BY CAL N. PETERS, MUSEUM OF HISTORY, PRAIRIE DU CHIEN; "THE JOLLY FLATBOATMEN" BY GEORGE CALEB BINGHAM, 1846, CLAIBORNE PELL COLLECTION; STERN-WHEELER BY W. D. VAUGHN

St. Louis hummed with river traffic when steamboats lined the levee and pioneers streamed through toward the setting sun. Today towboats jockey barges past 630-foot-high Gateway Arch, part of Jefferson National Expansion Memorial. The muddy Missouri, emptying into the Mississippi 15 miles north (left), helped funnel the nation westward.

friendly little game with greenhorn Easterners. The stern- and side-wheelers were sometimes deathtraps. Snags tore hulls; sparks lit fires; boilers burst as tobacco-chawin' captains raced and the whole valley laid bets. One ballad immortalizes Jim Bludso, engineer of the *Prairie Belle,* who burned alive saving her passengers.

There was runnin' and cursin', but Jim yelled out
Over the infernal roar,
"I'll hold her nozzle agin the bank
Till the last galoot's ashore."

A Missouri youngster, Samuel Clemens, savored the romance of the great river and stored it up for the day, as Mark Twain, he would write it into world literature.

"VIEW OF FRONT STREET" BY JOHN CASPER WILD, 1840, MISSOURI HISTORICAL SOCIETY, ST. LOUIS. BELOW: ARTHUR L. WITMAN. OPPOSITE: BRUCE DALE, NATIONAL GEOGRAPHIC PHOTOGRAPHER

TOM SAWYER'S TOWN

WILLARD R. CULVER (ALSO BELOW)

Duping a pal into whitewashing, Tom swaps brush for apple, "with reluctance in his face, but alacrity in his heart."

MARK TWAIN remembered it as a "white town drowsing in the sunshine of a summer's morning." Cupped on the shore of the Mississippi, Hannibal, Missouri, lies off the beaten track. It has neither beaches nor night clubs, yet it draws more than 150,000 visitors a year. For here, little changed by time, are the haunts of Tom Sawyer. Here stands the white frame house where Judge Clemens's next-to-youngest son Sam—known to the world as Mark Twain—had adventures he wrote into *Tom Sawyer*.

Mark Twain's boyhood home is restored throughout. Here Judge Clemens fiddled with a perpetual motion machine while his wife created tantalizing suppertime smells in a kitchen enlivened by 19 stray cats. Outside stands a replica of the fence Tom Sawyer hoodwinked his friends into whitewashing. "Aunt Polly's awful particular about this fence," he explained. "I reckon there ain't one boy in a thousand, maybe two thousand, that can do it the way it's got to be done."

Next door, the Mark Twain Museum displays the scarred cherry desk on which *Tom Sawyer* was written, along with a pilot wheel from a Mississippi steamboat

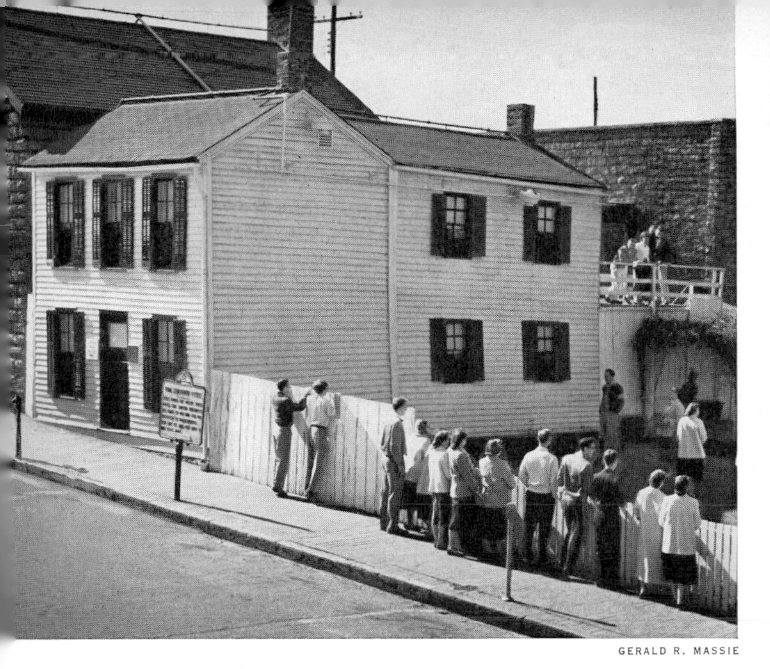

GERALD R. MASSIE

Hannibal's most famous home: A catcall in the night would bid Sam Clemens skin out a back window for a Tom Sawyer lark.

GEORGE PICKOW, THREE LIONS

Pilot wheel, young Clemens's symbol of glory, still awes youths at the museum.

and hundreds of other items. Across the street lived Laura Hawkins, Sam Clemens's pigtailed sweetheart who became the Becky Thatcher of *Tom Sawyer.* Being in love with her, and having an apple, Sam gave her the core.

"Steamboat a-comin'!" The cry once roused Hannibal as twin-stack packets churned round the bend to pick up cargoes of tobacco and slaves. A lone iron ring remains in the cobblestone wharf, the last of many to which steamboats were tied. Now cars park on the wharf, and the banks tremble as 3,000-horsepower towboats pound by pushing strings of barges. Sonic depth recorders replace the leadsman, whose call of "Mark twain!" indicated safe two-fathom water—and provided Sam Clemens with a pen name.

Almost any hot summer day finds Hannibal boys fishing and swimming naked from the banks of Jackson's Island. It is the same tangled jungle where Tom's friend Huckleberry Finn and the Negro Jim camped before starting their unforgettable raft trip down the Mississippi. Huck, in real life a friend of Clemens named Tom Blankenship, skinned a rabbit for bait and caught a catfish as big as a man. It was six-foot-two—"as big a fish as was ever catched in the Mississippi, I reckon." Today a fair-sized catfish is three-foot-four—as big as a boy.

Every American schoolboy knows the scene of Tom Sawyer and Becky Thatcher lost in the cave, huddling fearfully as their last candle burns to the end and leaves them in blinding dark. Sam Clemens and Laura Hawkins actually were lost there. Now wide-eyed children visit the cave and dodge aside when guides tell them, "Injun Joe died just where you're standing."

JERRY ALLEN

With the Mississippi as a back yard, Tom Sawyers and Huck Finns still pole rafts and play pirates and Indians.

DAVID LAVENDER

THERE NEVER WAS another American quite like the mountain man. You might see him—if you were an Indian in the 1820's or '30's—jogging along on his shaggy horse beneath snowy peaks, past crystal streams, across sagebrush plains. His big-bored rifle lies crosswise on his saddle; pistol, knife, and tomahawk are tucked in his belt. Beneath a wide felt hat his long hair falls to his shoulders. His stiff leather shirt and pantaloons are fringed with thongs, grease-smeared from numberless campfires.

His crinkled eyes have seen great bear and thundering herds of buffalo, have followed the trails of unnamed tribes. His elbows and knees may ache, for he spends much of his life in icy water hunting beaver. In the evening twilight of fall and spring he wades the mountain creeks searching out good sets for his traps. These he places under water in the animal's runway near the entrance to its lodge. At dawn he returns, reaching armpit deep to retrieve trap and drowned beaver.

His bones ache, and maybe his heart too. He's lived in the mountains for years; family, civilization are a dim memory. He shares a campfire with other mountain men, maybe takes a squaw. In early summer his lonely trail knits briefly with a hundred others at the rendezvous. Here in some isolated valley he meets the

BALTIMORE'S ALFRED JACOB MILLER SKETCHED MOUNTAIN MAN JOE WALKER IN THE ROCKIES IN 1837
WALTERS ART GALLERY, BALTIMORE, © 1951 UNIVERSITY OF OKLAHOMA PRESS

traders and their mule trains from St. Louis and swaps his pelts for raw alcohol, wool shirts, and year-old news. Then back into the mountains, where an Indian may lift his scalp if he doesn't take the Indian's first. And should he be killed his only epitaph will be the mountain man's lament: "Poor hoss. Out of luck."

A cruel life. Yet in that vast emptiness lying between the Missouri River and the tiny settlements of California, the mountain man is his own master. He savors the clean, bold lines of the untracked land, the free sweep of the wind in high valleys. The West is an itch under his skin. So had it been to others before him. Spaniards . . . Russians . . . Englishmen. All came in turn to stake their claim in the West. The first to know the land were the Spanish.

In 1528 a party of some 240 adventurers found themselves stranded on the coast of western Florida. Stitching together crude boats of horsehide, they sailed for Mexico. Miraculously they bobbed as far as Texas before a storm wrecked them. Half the men drowned. Then starvation, the lash of winter rains, and the horrors of Indian captivity carried off all but five. Toughest of these was Alvar Nuñez Cabeza de Vaca. Weary of the menial toil forced on him by his Indian captors, he persuaded them to let him serve as a trader, carrying into the interior "pieces of sea-snails, conches used for cutting, and a fruit like a bean." He brought back "skins, ochre, . . . hard canes of which to make arrows."

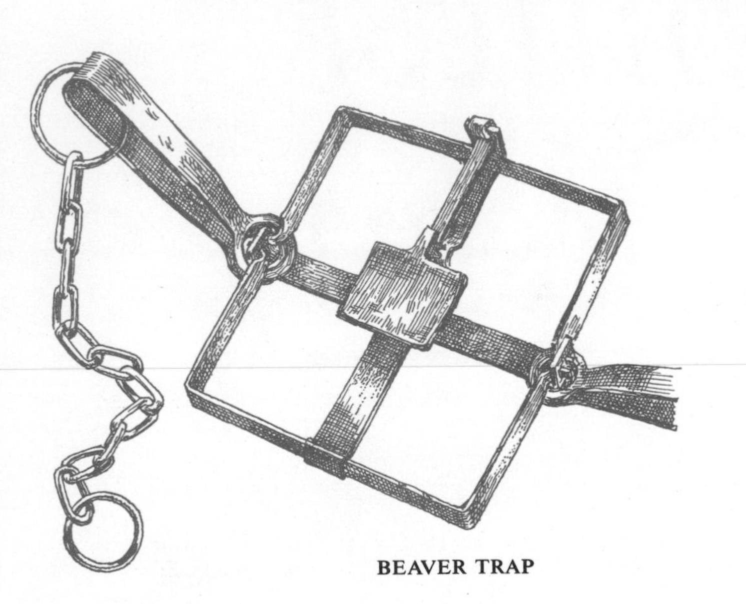

BEAVER TRAP

After six years of this life Cabeza de Vaca and three companions managed to escape and stumble west. They lived by fashioning combs, bows, and arrows to trade with Indians along the way, and by scraping and softening hides. They performed cures they had seen wrought by medicine men among their captors, and awed tribe after tribe. As many as 4,000 Indians clamored around them at a time. For nearly two years the men walked across southern Texas and northern Mexico to the Gulf of California. Then one day, sun-blackened and accompanied by several hundred worshipers, they met Spaniards from a Mexican settlement out hunting Indians for slaves. They "stared at me speechless, such was their surprise," Cabeza de Vaca wrote.

Taken to the City of Mexico, he unfolded an exciting story. He had fingered cloth woven of native cotton by the Indians; he had gaped at arrowheads made of "emerald" (probably malachite); he had gazed on "hump backed cows" (buffalo). What's more, he had heard of inland cities with dwellings four and five stories high. These were the pueblos of New Mexico. But in Spanish minds the "bighouse towns" became the fabled "Seven Cities of Cíbola."

The ancient civilizations of Peru and Mexico had yielded their treasures to conquistadores. Were there not more civilizations, more riches to the north?

To find out, Spanish officials sent a party headed by Fray Marcos de Niza. He took along Esteban, a Moorish Negro who had shared Cabeza de Vaca's adventure.

Esteban, with bells tinkling on his arms and ankles, was first to approach the Zuni pueblo of Hawikuh in western New Mexico. The Pueblo Indians killed him. Fray Marcos pressed close enough to glimpse the village, then returned to report it "larger than the City of Mexico."

That was enough for handsome Francisco Vásquez de Coronado. He donned his golden armor and in 1540 led an eager force north from Mexico (see map in back of book). They found Hawikuh, but to their disgust it was "a little crowded village, looking as if it had been crumpled all up together." The Indians resisted. Coronado was knocked unconscious by a stone.

But the defenders could not stand against Spanish armor and horses. Coronado seized food, then marched east to winter among the pueblos in the Rio Grande Valley.

There the bearded invaders watched young Indian men weave blankets to give to maidens as proposal presents; saw chattering groups grind corn to the tune of a fife; noted "cocks with great hanging chins" (turkeys); and learned something of the religious ceremonies in the underground kivas.

They found neither gold nor emeralds. Never mind. *Mas allá*—there is more beyond. Perhaps in golden Quivira.

Quivira was the invention of a shrewd Pawnee captive of the Pueblos who wanted to get home. The Spaniards called him *El Turco,* the Turk, because he wore a cloth headband. Following him, they trooped across parts of Texas and Oklahoma.

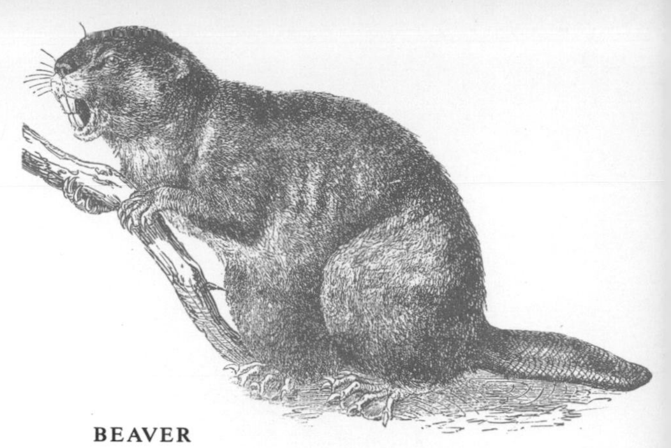

BEAVER

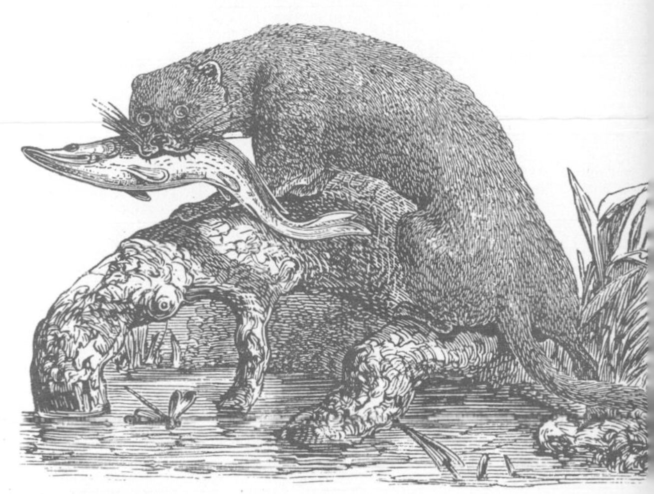

OTTER

FUR SEAL

The fur trade spurred the conquest of the continent. Beaver lured trappers west into the Rocky Mountains and on to the Pacific. The soft inner hair was made into costly felt hats, a status symbol in London and Paris. Seaborne hunters and traders flocked to the Pacific Northwest, harvested lustrous pelts worth fortunes, and nearly exterminated sea otter and fur seal.

BEAVER AND FUR SEAL, CULVER SERVICE. OTTER, BETTMANN ARCHIVE. TRAP BY PAUL R. HOFFMASTER

FROM A TREATISE ON THE NORTHWEST PASSAGE BY ENGLISH MATHEMATICIAN HENRY BRIGGS IN "PURCHAS HIS PILGRIMES," LIBRARY OF CONGRESS

"California . . . a goodly Ilande," reports this 1625 chart. The popular theory was disproved in the early 1700's by Father Kino, a Spanish missionary. But young George Washington in a school copybook dutifully listed "Calofornia" as one of North America's "Chief Islands."

Such featureless immensities! The springy grass left no sign of their passing. Gray wolves howled everywhere. Huge jack rabbits stared without fear at the strange horses. Incredible herds of buffalo darkened the plains. Following them came Indian nomads, their goods heaped on travois dragged by snarling dogs.

Some of Coronado's captains explored far afield. One found the Grand Canyon and tried for three days to reach its bottom. He failed. Another saw the village of Acoma, in New Mexico, perched on a white mesa so tall that "it was a very good musket that could throw a ball as high."

Coronado himself reached central Kansas. He found no golden Quivira, only the grass-thatched lodges of a few Wichita Indians. El Turco had lied. The Spanish put a rope around his neck, twisted it until he died, then began the bitter return. As they did so, another Spaniard was pushing north by sea.

Juan Rodríguez Cabrillo had heard that California was an island inhabited by lusty black Amazons. More tantalizing was his dream of finding a waterway leading from the Pacific through North America to the Atlantic. Geographers were sure there was such a passage and had even named it the Strait of Anian (later such an idea would be called the Northwest Passage). In 1542-3 Cabrillo's ships poked along the coast as far north as Oregon. They failed to find Anian.

Yet the myth persisted and 36 years later seemed proved when English swashbuckler Francis Drake swept up the west coast and vanished into the fog-shrouded north. Spaniards nodded in agreement: he had returned to the Atlantic by the Strait of Anian (actually, from Drake Bay on the coast of northern California he had sailed his *Golden Hind* west across the Pacific, then round Africa to England).

EAGER TO SEIZE THE STRAIT and lured by the promise of "great veins of silver," Spain began the colonization of New Mexico in 1598. Haughty Juan de Oñate spent a fortune outfitting his expedition in Old Mexico. Officers in glittering armor rode blooded horses and brought along gorgeous clothing, even solid silver dinner services. Behind them trudged several hundred soldier-colonists, their families and slaves, and missionaries. Livestock brayed and bleated; the broad wheels of baggage carts rasped in the sand.

Oñate stopped at a place he called San Juan, close to where Santa Fe would be founded 11 years later. His colonists dug irrigation ditches, introduced the cultivation of wheat, barley, and apricots, and built the first church in the Southwest. But their horses made the most telling imprint on the land. Spread by barter and theft, horses drastically changed the lives of the Plains and Rocky Mountain Indians. Mounted, the Indians could chase the buffalo far afield, could swoop down on enemies, could transport their tepee villages easier.

Oñate's dream, like that of Coronado, faded in the trackless land that yielded few riches. Missionaries strove to plant the seed of the Holy Faith, but tribesmen brooded over forced labor, whippings, hangings, the suppression of their ancient religion. Organized by a medicine man named Popé, the Indians revolted in 1680. They fell on settlements and farms, slaughtering 400 Spaniards. Survivors gathered at Santa Fe, broke through their besiegers, and fled south across the blinding sands of the *Jornada del Muerto* (Journey of Death).

Popé pushed Spain's New World border back to Old Mexico and worked feverishly to erase the alien culture that had been laid over his people. But 12 years later the dons returned to stay.

Redoubtable priests in quest of souls and knowledge helped Spain roll back the frontier. Eusebio Francisco Kino founded eight missions in Arizona and, alone or with only a few Indian guides, made more than 50 overland journeys of several hundred miles each. Father Kino dreamed of a land route from Arizona to the Pacific. And although such a discovery fell to others years later, he did traverse the fiery *Camino del Diablo* (Devil's Highway) between northwestern Mexico and the junction of the Gila and lower Colorado rivers in Arizona. He climbed the sun-blasted peaks, scanned the horizon with his telescope, and "discovered with all minute certainty and evidence that California is not an island."

Other padres and soldiers pushed into Texas, founding a mission (the Alamo) and a town (the beginnings of San Antonio) in 1718. Fifty years later the mission of San Diego de Alcalá and the town of Monterey rose along the California coast, soon followed by San Francisco and El Pueblo de Nuestra Señora, la Reina de los Angeles del Río de Porciúncula (Los Angeles). Braving sun-glazed deserts, gaunt mountains, and fierce Apaches, missionary-explorers sought a trail from New Mexico to the Pacific. Spurring the Spanish colonization of California was a threat that came from the north like a chilling wind—Russians!

PETER THE GREAT, the czar who westernized Russia, was fascinated by reports of a land bridge between Asia and America, and by the possibility that his nonseafaring nation might find the elusive Northwest Passage before the great maritime nations did. He sent Vitus Bering from St. Petersburg across the almost trackless wastes of Siberia to build a ship on the Pacific and explore toward America.

Twice Bering sailed from Kamchatka Peninsula, the finger of land that drops down from easternmost Russia. On his second voyage, in 1741, he detected through an opening in the clouds an incredible snow peak towering above a wonderland of islands, forests, inlets, and glistening icebergs. To this giant mountain on the underbelly of Alaska he gave the name it still bears, Saint Elias.

But weakened by his toils and depressed by the first stages of scurvy, Bering allowed his scientists only a few precious hours ashore before he weighed anchor. Fog shrouded his ship as it crept westward along the uncharted Aleutian Islands.

ALFRED JACOB MILLER SKETCHED "LARAMIE'S FORT" IN 1837. WALTERS ART GALLERY, BALTIMORE © 1951 UNIVERSITY OF OKLAHOMA PRESS

The sea seemed ghostlike; strange animal and bird voices wailed. Rain turned to sleet. A storm tossed the ship on an island that now bears the explorer's name. The men built huts of driftwood, sailcloth, and hides. Some survived the winter, but not Bering. The remainder built a clumsy boat, calked it with the tallow of sea cows, and sailed back to Kamchatka. With them they took the sea otter furs they had gathered to keep themselves from freezing.

Peter the Great had died, and his successors were indifferent to Bering's scientific discoveries. But the otter pelts triggered a stampede. Chinese merchants were willing to pay fortunes for the fur of *bobri morski,* as the Russians called the web-toed animal.

Promyshleniki (Siberian mountain men) rushed for Bering Island in flat-bottom river barges. Moving on to the Aleutians, they hopped from island to island, stripping each of fur. They offered trinkets and held Aleut women as hostages to get the Aleut men to chase the otter through tumults of white water onto barren reefs, and there club the animals to death.

Edging farther and farther south along the coast of Alaska, the Russians established their headquarters at Sitka on Baranof Island. Then in 1812 they built Fort Ross (*Rossiya,* or Russia) just 60 miles north of San Francisco.

But the Russians were not to enjoy the Pacific Northwest by themselves. In 1778 two British ships hove to in Nootka Sound on Vancouver Island. Aboard was the explorer, Capt. James Cook, come to find the Northwest Passage.

Cook watched as Indians clad in blankets woven from dog hair and cedar bark paddled out in high-prowed canoes, flinging out red dust and bursts of oratory. Their bodies were daubed with red clay and whale oil, their long black hair was streaked with fish oil and the white down of birds. The Nootkas had broad faces, small black eyes, and legs misshapen by lives spent crouching in their seatless canoes. Bits of metal dangled from their ears. But most exciting, many had draped over their shoulders, almost carelessly, priceless robes of sea otter and fox.

Cook's men traded briskly: "Whole suits of clothes were stripped of every button . . . copper kettles, tin canisters, candlesticks and the like, all went."

When the ships reached China the furs brought huge profits. Word spread and soon other ships were poking into the coves along America's northwest coast.

Yet England's strongest bid for the Pacific Northwest came overland—from the fur trading posts in central Canada. Two giant rivals, the Hudson's Bay Company and the North West Company, raced west. A doughty Scot, Alexander Mackenzie, struck out for the Pacific, took a wrong river, and ended up at the Arctic Ocean. Trying again, he breached the Rocky Mountains, floated down the Bella Coola River, and reached the coast of British Columbia. Others followed his path.

Fort Laramie, Wyoming outpost of the American Fur Company, raised the U.S. flag 800 miles west of St. Louis. It swarmed with Indians and mountain men, later supplied Oregon Trail travelers.

Last to enter the contest for the West was the infant United States. Her people had long known the pull of the West, the unfathomable urge to follow the setting sun over distant, blue-hazed mountains. George Washington had not yet been inaugurated as President when the author of a popular school geography wrote: "The period is not far distant, when the AMERICAN EMPIRE will comprehend millions of souls, west of the Mississippi."

Yankees first probed the Pacific Northwest when Boston merchants, hearing of Captain Cook's voyage, sent out two ships, one commanded by Robert Gray. In 1792 the young mariner discovered a mighty river flooding out of the forest.

For years there had been rumors of a great river flowing west. The "Oregon," one credulous Great Lakes traveler called it in his book, and another magic name entered our geography. Theorists speculated that the headwaters of the rumored Oregon, interlocking with those of the Missouri, would furnish the long-sought water route to the Pacific. Now Captain Gray proved the Great River of the West to be a fact. He named it the Columbia, after his ship, and the discovery gave the United States a claim on the Pacific shore.

THE TURN OF THE CENTURY brought fresh encouragement to the young nation. Spain yielded the vast territory of Louisiana to Napoleon. Pressed for money to finance his wars, he sold the 909,130 square miles to the United States for $15,000,000 (2½ cents an acre!). And suddenly the U. S. border leaped from the Mississippi to the Rocky Mountains.

But boundaries on maps didn't hold back fur traders. In 1810 Andrew Henry built in Idaho the first American post west of the Great Divide. That same year New York's John Jacob Astor sent his men around Cape Horn to establish Fort Astoria on the Columbia. Soon fur brigades roamed both sides of the Rockies.

The British forced Astor out. And to keep the Yankees out of the Oregon Territory, as the Northwest was coming to be called, the Hudson's Bay Company established Fort Vancouver on the Columbia, and sent trappers deep into Idaho and Montana to strip the country of beaver. But what the British government never gauged was man's hunger, not for gold or fur, but for *land* he could call his own.

This was the fulfillment the West offered Americans. Fired by its promise, sturdy homeseekers would move inexorably westward along trails blazed by trappers and traders. They would carry a conviction that it was their duty to fill the land with American culture and all its blessings. A New York editor would sum up the belief, writing that it was "our manifest destiny to overspread and to possess the whole of the continent which Providence has given us for the development of the great experiment of liberty and federated self-government."

Manifest Destiny! A new name for an old yearning. But it could never have been fulfilled if a continental awareness had not stirred the imagination of the people. This awareness in large measure grew from the expedition headed by Lewis and Clark that at last linked the shores of the continent by pushing up the Missouri farther than Frenchmen, Spaniards, or Englishmen had ever been able to go, crossing between the peaks of the Shining Mountains, and so reaching the headwaters of the giant river of the West, the Columbia.

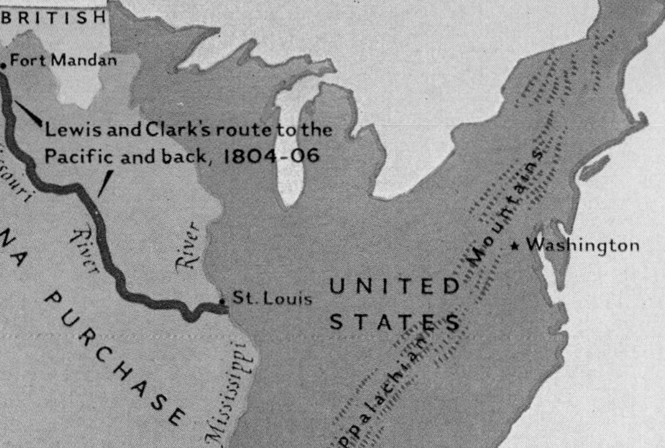

RALPH GRAY

WILLIAM CLARK

FOLLOWING THE TRAIL OF LEWIS AND CLARK

"EXPLORE the Missouri river, & such principal stream of it, as . . . may offer the most direct . . . communication across this continent." Penned by President Thomas Jefferson in 1803, those instructions launched the Lewis and Clark Expedition that opened American eyes to the marvels of a vast western domain.

Reading Jefferson's words, I grew eager to see for myself "the soil & face of the country." And what better way to show my three children—Judith, Mary Ellen, and Will—the wealth and splendor of their native land?

My hopes sprang to life one June day in Washington, D. C., when my wife and I, with about equal parts of help and hindrance from our youngsters, packed our station wagon with

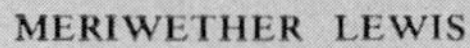
MERIWETHER LEWIS

PORTRAITS BY CHARLES WILLSON PEALE, INDEPENDENCE HALL COLLECTION camp gear, toys, cameras, and clothing. In a corner I installed a compact library featuring a set of the Lewis and Clark journals, our ready-made guidebooks. On top of the car we lashed our canoe *Trout.*

Jefferson, who bought the huge Louisiana Territory from Napoleon in 1803, chose his 28-year-old private secretary, Meriwether Lewis, to lead a small Army detachment up the Missouri to its unknown source, cross the Rockies, and descend the almost legendary Columbia to the Pacific. Captain Lewis asked William Clark, youngest brother of George Rogers Clark, to serve as co-captain in the trip's "fatiegues, it's dangers and it's honors." Clark jumped at the chance.

For five months the party outfitted at Wood River, 15 miles north of St. Louis, where the shifting Mississippi then received the Missouri. On the afternoon of May 14, 1804, the "robust helthy hardy young men" of the Corps of Discovery set out in a keelboat and two pirogues "and proceeded on under a jentle brease up the Missourie." They would not return until September, 1806. Lewis and Clark's initial appropriation by Congress for the three-year expedition was $2,500. Traveling frugally, our "expedition"—my wife, our children, and I—spent slightly more than that in three months following the party's trail.

The swirling milk-chocolate waters of "Big Muddy" led us west and north through Missouri, Mother of the West; wheat-growing Kansas; corn-belt Iowa and Nebraska; and the Dakotas, where farms gave way to range. We realized that a summer was none too long for following Lewis and Clark. We were always in a hurry. "When it comes to eating, you don't think of Duncan Hines," my wife reproached me. "You think of dunkin' doughnuts."

At Sioux City, Iowa, we paid homage at the grave of the first American soldier to die west of the Mississippi. Sgt. Charles Floyd was "taken verry bad all at once with a Biliose Chorlick" (bilious colic) and "Died with a great deal of Composure." He was the only fatality of the expedition.

The explorers sighted buffalo, prairie dogs, and pronghorns. Called goats by the captains, pronghorns were unknown to science. The plains teemed with game. The land was as

A 55-foot keelboat with a square sail carried the explorers halfway up the Missouri. If wind failed, they poled it like a Nile barge, rowed it like a Greek galley, or towed it from the bank like a Yangtze junk. They averaged ten miles a day against the strong current.

KEELBOAT FROM THE MOVIE "THE BIG SKY"; TOM KIISKILA

friendly as the river was hostile. Lewis and Clark quickly learned, as do those who live along the Missouri today, that it is a "devil-river" at war with humanity. Its current bore down upon them with unremitting force. Its mud banks sloughed off, nearly swamping their canoes. Its eddies devoured sand-bar islands as the men camped on them. In their 15-month uphill push against this river, the explorers covered 3,096 miles, by their count. The "Orange Crate" (Judith's nickname for our station wagon) drove the same distance in a few weeks.

In the Dakotas the children quickly learned to spot the dimples that indicate earth lodge sites of the Arikara, Minnetaree, and Mandan Indians. In Fort Abraham Lincoln State Park near Bismarck we saw five restored lodges rising like earthen bubbles under the green sod. One of them was completely furnished, with bunks around the edge, fire pit in the center, cache pits in the floor, and grinding basins for corn. A buffalo skull on a stick made a family altar.

It looked so homelike that Will asked, "Are you sure no one lives here?"

His mother reassured him. "But," she said, "it was in a house just like this that Sacagawea lived when she first saw Lewis and Clark."

"Oh, Sacagawea," Mary Ellen said. She stumbled over the difficult name. "We read about her in school."

"Yes, she was a Shoshoni living in the Rocky Mountains. Minnetaree raiders

Three forks converge in Montana to form the Missouri. Lewis and Clark named them the Jefferson (lower left), Madison (right center), and Gallatin (top) after the President and two cabinet members.

At the town of Three Forks, an annual pageant relives episodes of the explorers' journey, right. Sites of Mandan earth lodges, left, still dimple the North Dakota plains.

"MANDAN VILLAGE" BY GEORGE CATLIN, 1832, SMITHSONIAN INSTITUTION. RIGHT: RALPH GRAY, NATIONAL GEOGRAPHIC STAFF.
ABOVE: MELVILLE BELL GROSVENOR AND SUMNER GERARD, PILOT

captured her when she was about 12 and carried her away to the plains. There she remained a slave until a French fur trader bought and married her."

Lewis and Clark hired this man, Toussaint Charbonneau, as an interpreter and included in the deal his squaw Sacagawea and two-month-old boy. The explorers knew that at the source of the Missouri they would have to abandon their boats. The Shoshonis, Sacagawea's tribe, were the only people in that area from whom they might buy horses for the trip across the "Shining Mountains." Providence had sent them an ambassadress.

Building Fort Mandan, near Bismarck, Lewis and Clark wintered there, then pushed on in April of 1805. The keelboat had been sent down the Missouri to St. Louis with letters, dispatches, and specimens from the plains for the scrutiny of President Jefferson. Thirty-one men and Sacagawea set out to wrestle six canoes and the two pirogues—a little fleet "not quite so rispectable as those of Columbus or Capt. Cook"—up the dwindling river.

I could not miss the excitement in the journals as the party approached the Rockies. They were the first whites to encounter and describe in detail the fearsome grizzly: ". . . these bear being so hard to die reather intimedates us all; I must confess that I do not like the gentlemen and had reather fight two Indians than one bear."

Nearing the Rockies, we launched our canoe in the swift-flowing Missouri. North of Helena, Montana, a motorboat took us through the "Gates of the Rocky Mountains," where the journals describe gloomy cliffs rising nearly 1,200 feet. In the canyon, Lewis found nowhere to "rest the soal of his foot."

Winding south past the site of Helena, the explorers heard cheering news from Sacagawea: the three forks were not far away. Clark, walking ahead, discovered this point where three rivers unite to form the Missouri, 2,466 miles above its mouth. In the one-street town of Three Forks, Montana, we took rooms in the Sacajawea Inn. A restaurant cashier gave me four silver dollars in change and, as I hefted the unaccustomed weight, remarked, "Another Easterner!"

Moving west, Lewis and Clark were frantic to meet the Shoshonis. Nearly half their second summer was gone and they had no horses for crossing the mountains. The Indians were keeping out of sight, suspicious of this strange invasion. Lewis went ahead with three men, hoping to show his friendly intentions. Walking up Horse Prairie Creek to Lemhi Pass, he and his patrol became the first white Americans to stand on the Continental Divide: August 12, 1805. From here to the Pacific they would be outside United States territory.

Pushing down the opposite slope, Lewis enjoyed his first taste of Pacific-bound water. In a valley beyond, he found his Shoshonis—Chief Cameahwait and 60 warriors advancing toward him. The white man fearlessly put down his rifle and walked ahead, holding the American flag. Cameahwait "very affectionately" threw his arm over Lewis's shoulder and pressed his cheek against the stranger's. Other Indians followed suit; the whites "wer all carresed and besmeared with their grease and paint till . . . heartily tired of the national hug."

Sacagawea danced with joy, for Cameahwait proved to be her brother. Yet she chose to keep on with Lewis and Clark. The latter, especially, became fond of

"LEWIS AND CLARK MEETING THE FLATHEADS" BY CHARLES M. RUSSELL, HISTORICAL SOCIETY OF MONTANA. TOP RIGHT: RALPH GRAY, NATIONAL GEOGRAPHIC STAFF

the "little squar." He called her "Janey" and referred to her papoose, whom he called Pomp, as "my little dancing boy."

Bartering for horses, the explorers joyfully started across the mountains. But by the time they had struggled across the Bitterroot Range they were weary men. Entering the Lolo wilderness, they were told by Indians that a faint trail led to the navigable Clearwater, but that others had "suffered excessively with hunger." This was the hardest section of the whole trail. September snow threatened moccasined feet. Food gave out. The men killed a colt and ate it, as well as crayfish, bear's oil, and candles.

We found this wild Idaho upland little changed since the sick and starving explorers threaded it. Finally they reached the Clearwater and began to build dugout canoes in what is now Nez Percé National Historical Park. As their strength returned, they formed squares and danced to a fiddle.

Baby strapped to her back, steadfast Sacagawea shared the trials of the 31 men in Lewis and Clark's expedition. The mere presence of the young Shoshoni prevented attacks by Indians, for "a woman with a party of men is a token of peace," Clark noted. Her statue, by Leonard Crunelle, stands at Bismarck, North Dakota, 40 miles from where the explorers met her.

A large encampment of Flathead Indians (left) "received us friendly," Clark reported. White and red men met in Montana's Bitterroot Valley west of the Continental Divide. The Flatheads won their name because they left their heads flat as Nature made them, and did not elongate them in infancy with bindings or headboards as did neighboring tribes to the west.

On the entire venture, the party had only one fatal encounter with Indians. Attacked, Lewis and another man killed two Blackfeet.

RAY ATKESON. BELOW: MURAL BY FRANK SWARTZ IN ROTUNDA OF OREGON STATE CAPITOL, SALEM. RIGHT: LIBRARY OF CONGRESS

The Columbia River carried the weary explorers toward Mount Hood along what is now the boundary between Oregon and Washington. They portaged their heavy dugouts around Celilo Falls (below). Lewis and Clark direct the job; Sacagawea stands with her Canadian husband. Water backed up by The Dalles Dam today floods the site.

Northwestern Indians proved "assumeing and disagreeable." They even stole a peace

pipe passed among them! They wouldn't part with their fish, so "we purchased 8 Small fat dogs for the party to eate," wrote Clark. He sketched a white salmon trout "2 feet 8 inches Long," a scientific first, in his diary (right).

Curious Nez Percé Indians watched the caller "boss other mans how to do funny dance and sing songs, and all laugh"—still a pretty good description of a square dance.

By October 7, 1805, the dugouts were ready. Lewis and Clark pushed off on the last lap to the Pacific. I, too, canoed the Clearwater with a riverman in *Trout*'s stern. We shot many rapids, but stopped short of the one where the explorers struck a rock and lost a dugout.

Westward-running waters of the Clearwater, Snake, and Columbia sped Lewis and Clark toward their goal. Then on a wretched November day fog cleared and the Columbia widened into a bay. William Clark expressed the elation of the entire group:

"Ocian in view! O! the joy."

For us, reaching the Pacific, the sun burst out and bathed the Oregon coast in golden light. "From sea to shining sea" we had traced the steps of the men who made the phrase possible.

PAINTING BY WALDO LOVE, STATE HISTORICAL SOCIETY OF COLORADO

Jim Baker

Other trail blazers of the West

DAGUERREOTYPE BY MATHEW B. BRADY, C. 1850
CULVER SERVICE

John C. Frémont

EVEN as Lewis and Clark returned, mountain men were pushing west. They went to trap beaver but got trapped themselves by that extravagance of soaring, snow-topped peaks, endless plains, boiling springs, and spouting geysers where "Nature appears to lie some herself."

Gentle Jedediah Smith was first to cross the Great Basin and the Sierras; Jim Bridger

PHOTOGRAPH, 1866, HISTORICAL SOCIETY OF MONTAN

Jim Bridger. Right: Jedediah Smith

PHOTOGRAPH, C. 1865
STATE HISTORICAL SOCIETY OF COLORADO

Kit Carson

PAINTING BY CHARLES WILLSON PEALE, 1808
INDEPENDENCE HALL COLLECTION

Zebulon Pike

PAINTING BY WALDO LOVE
STATE HISTORICAL SOCIETY OF COLORADO

William Bent

found Great Salt Lake. Jim Baker, all beard and buckskin, took six squaws to wife during his long life; in his teens Kit Carson shot his first brave. Each year men rendezvoused along the Green River in Wyoming, the Bear River in Utah, or in Pierre's Hole, Idaho, selling pelts between gaming and spinning yarns. At outposts like Bent's Fort on the Arkansas River they outfitted for next season.

Trappers roved; soldiers explored (see map in back of book). Lt. Zebulon Pike probed Colorado. Lt. John C. Frémont scouted Oregon and California and publicized the West. Trail blazers were tough. Said Bridger as Dr. Marcus Whitman dug a three-year-old arrowhead from his back, "In the mountains, meat don't spoil."

"JEDEDIAH SMITH'S PARTY CROSSING THE MOJAVE DESERT IN 1826" BY FREDERIC REMINGTON, COLLIER'S, 1906, COURTESY AMERICAN HERITAGE

DAVID LAVENDER

WAGONS WEST

DEFYING snags and sand bars, paddle-wheel steamers thrashed upstream against the yellow spring flood of the Missouri River, then sidled toward the dock that served the frontier town of Independence, Missouri, five miles away.

Mountain men and Santa Fe traders watched them unload, casual interest turning to contempt as canvas-covered wagons rumbled ashore, followed by cows, chicken coops, washtubs, plows, and finally greenhorn farmers with harassed wives and flocks of awestruck children.

Their goal was 2,000 miles away: Oregon and California (magic words in the 1840's!). There, they had heard, days were sunny and land was almost for the asking.

They camped where they could, organized themselves into trains of 40 wagons or more, hired mountain men as guides, and argued over the best date for starting west. You couldn't move before the prairie grass was high enough to feed the stock; yet if you delayed too long, others would strip the forage.

They spent the waiting days buying supplies and animals. Independence, and later the river towns of Westport and St. Joseph, thrived on the business. At last the long whips cracked, men shouted, dogs yapped, oxen lunged forward, and broad wheels bit into fresh sod. They were on their way on the Oregon Trail.

At first drivers were busy persuading half-broken mules and oxen not to bolt, sulk in harness, or tangle themselves in picket ropes at night. Men eyed each other as potential captains. The leader of the train, said Marcy's handbook, *The Prairie Traveler,* should exhibit "good judgment,

"EMIGRANTS CROSSING THE PLAINS" BY F. O. C. DARLEY, LIBRARY OF CONGRESS

Fort Laramie: shelter on the trail

Fort Vancouver: haven at journey's end

Santa Fe: Mexican oxcarts met prairie schooners

Sutter's Fort: goal of weary emigrants

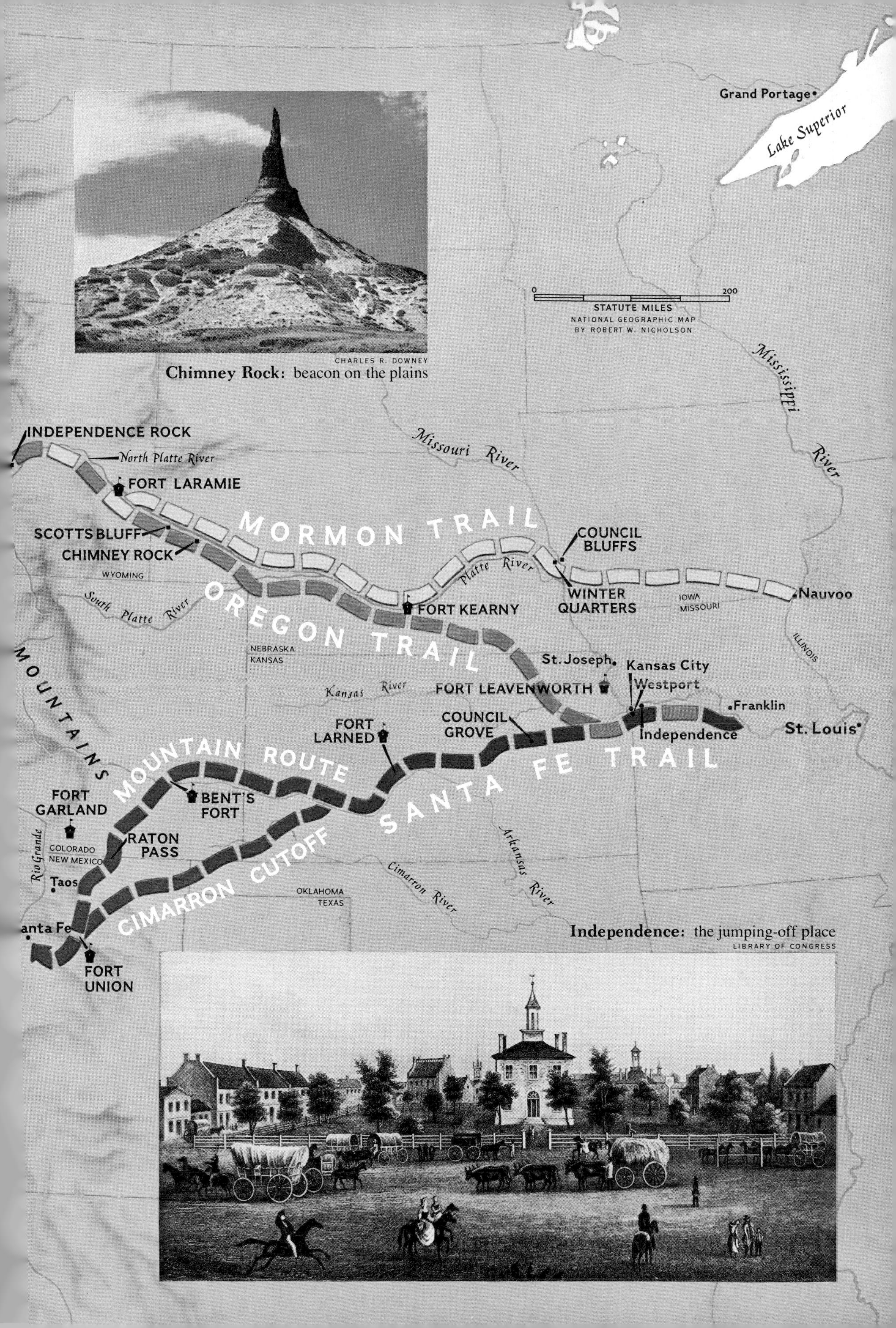

CHARLES R. DOWNEY

Chimney Rock: beacon on the plains

Independence: the jumping-off place

LIBRARY OF CONGRESS

SINCLAIR OIL CORPORATION'S PUBLIC SERVICE ADVERTISING

Scotts Bluff, landmark on the Platte, beckoned Oregon Trail travelers. Wagon trains drew up at its spring; campfires glimmered beside its face. Hoofs and wheels scarred Mitchell Pass in today's national monument.

integrity of purpose, and practical experience. These are indispensable to the harmony and consolidation of the association. His duty should be to direct the order of march, the time of starting and halting, to select the camps, detail and give orders to guards. . . ."

But the wayfarers were restless, opinionated individualists. Elijah White, leader of the 1842 caravan, was deposed when he ordered all dogs killed lest their barking attract Indians. Another captain was overruled when he tried to punish a youth who slept on night guard duty. The pioneers decided that since the lad couldn't stay awake, he need not stand guard at all!

The wagons moved across rolling hills spangled with verbena, wild indigo, tulips, and larkspur. Most of the emigrants found this first stretch exhilarating. But Edwin Bryant felt "the silence and desolation reigning over it excite irrepressible emotions of sadness and melancholy." And historian Francis Parkman wrote that the traveler's bed "will be a soft one, consisting often of black mud. . . . As for food, he must content himself with biscuit and salt provisions." Sudden, savage thunderstorms flooded camps, scattered stock, and drove rain through tents "as though they had been paper." Mountain man Jim Clyman declared one young wife "worthy of the bravest undaunted pioneer of the West." She "held an umbrella over the fire and her skillet with the greatest composure for near 2 hours and baked bread enough to give us a verry plentifull supper."

They sometimes crossed swollen streams at ferries, more often on makeshift rafts—hollowing a couple of cottonwoods into dugouts and linking them by crossbars. Lacking trees, men calked wagons and floated across.

Wagons often traveled several abreast so they could quickly be wheeled into a hollow square if Indians attacked. The husband walked beside heavy-shouldered oxen, "geeing" and "hawing," popping his whip when needed. Older boys prodded along the cow column. The wife sat on a wagon seat, eternally knitting. Younger children, hair bleaching in the sun, peered out the front or rear opening. Near the Platte River the soil grew sandier. You could wade the mile-wide river, "too thick to drink, too thin to plow." With no firewood, you cooked over buffalo

Narcissa Whitman's honeymoon was a perilous trek to the Northwest with her missionary husband and another couple in 1836. The wives were the first American women to make the journey overland.

WHITMAN MISSION NATIONAL HISTORIC SITE, MARVIN M. HENDRICKSON

Dr. Marcus Whitman set up his mission near Walla Walla, Washington. He and Narcissa taught Indians to pray and farm, and welcomed haggard emigrants. But when an epidemic of measles hit the Indians in 1847, they turned on the Whitmans, slew them and 12 companions. The Oregon Historical Society preserves the tomahawk (upper) that killed Marcus. A shaft overlooks the mission site.

MARCUS WHITMAN SCULPTURED BY AVARD FAIRBANKS, U. S. CAPITOL
NARCISSA WHITMAN, FROM OLIVER W. NIXON'S "HOW MARCUS WHITMAN SAVED OREGON"

OREGON STATE HIGHWAY DEPARTMENT AND (LEFT) OREGON HISTORICAL SOCIETY

Dr. John McLoughlin, "White-headed Eagle," sternly ruled Fort Vancouver for the Hudson's Bay Company, 1824-46, but aided weary American settlers. His home stands in Oregon City.

chips. Food tasted of dust and cow hairs, alkali stung your eyes. Fantastic landmarks rose from the plains, like Chimney Rock and massive Scotts Bluff.

Rest came at Fort Laramie, a trading post where Indians and trappers squatted in the shade and stared at the weathered wagons. Women eagerly washed clothes. Drivers refitted iron tires on wheels shrunken by dry air, and shod oxen, throwing them on their backs so their hoofs waved helplessly.

Off again. As oxen grew gaunt on the long climb toward the Rockies tearful women jettisoned prized furniture—claw-footed tables and heavy bureaus. Past Independence Rock, scarred with the autographs of earlier emigrants, the wagons groaned up Sweetwater River, as pleasant as its name. Pungent sagebrush flashed silver when wind turned up the gray leaves. Higher and higher they climbed until a sage-gray depression called South Pass pierced the backbone of the continent. They crossed it with cheers and gunfire. The Pacific ahead!

And then they recoiled with shock. For westward stretched "an immeasurable and sterile surface." Some swung south to trade at Jim Bridger's ramshackle fort; others plunged ahead over waterless Sublette Cutoff. Beyond Fort Hall those bound for California veered southwest. Oregon folks crossed the turbulent Snake River twice, then dragged themselves up among the cold evergreens of the Blue Mountains. At last, with winter so close, they sighted the curving sweep of the Columbia River breaking a gateway through the Cascade Range.

Below The Dalles, where dark canyon walls pressed the river into a "swelling, boiling & whorling" current, the emigrants pushed wagons onto rafts or abandoned them for canoes and bateaux. Downstream at Fort Vancouver, bastion of the British Hudson's Bay Company, the exhausted travelers were given succor.

A final laboring up the Willamette River brought them to Oregon City. Then they fanned out through green valley lands. Trail's end. Now a man could turn to his wife and say, "There—there's where we'll put the new house. There's home."

The Pig War

IN MOST WAYS Charles Griffin's pig was no different from any other. But it had the distinction in 1859 of leading Great Britain and the United States to the brink of war.

Griffin operated a farm for the Hudson's Bay Company on San Juan, one of a group of islands off the coast of present Washington State. At that time no one knew who owned the islands.

The two nations had long locked horns over the Pacific Northwest. After the withdrawal of Spanish and Russian claims, they had agreed to a joint occupancy. But as Americans spilled into the Oregon Territory, a crisis flamed. The United States claimed a boundary near the southern tip of Alaska; Britain called the Columbia River the dividing line.

The strident cry of "Fifty-four forty or fight" swept James K. Polk into the White House, and both nations sent warships to the Columbia. War was averted when in 1846 the conflicting claims were compromised at the 49th parallel, where the border stands today. But an ambiguity in the treaty left the San Juans a two-man's land.

The question came to a head when Griffin's pig wandered into Lyman Cutler's potato patch and began rooting. Cutler, an American, shot it dead. Griffin appealed to British authorities on Vancouver Island, who tried to talk Cutler into paying damages.

Feelings were running high on July 9, 1859, when U. S. Gen. William Harney visited San Juan. Americans urged him to dispatch troops. Harney sent 60 men under Capt. George Pickett, later to win Civil War fame. The British sent a fleet with 2,000 men. Pickett warned that whether they "landed fifty or five thousand men . . . he would open his fire."

But cooler heads prevailed, and the two forces settled in camps on opposite ends of the island. For 12 years, while awaiting a settlement, their only contest was to see which could serve the other the finest banquets.

In 1872 Emperor William I of Germany, as arbiter, awarded the San Juans to the United States. Today a blockhouse (below) remains at the English Camp; earthworks mark the American Camp. And in the Washington State Historical Society Museum at Tacoma rests the gun Lyman Cutler used to kill Charles Griffin's pig.

MERLE SEVERY, NATIONAL GEOGRAPHIC STAFF

Blizzards trap the Donner party in the Sierras

GEORGE DONNER was 62 years old when he decided to go to California with his brother Jacob and some neighbors from around Springfield, Illinois. He sold his prosperous 240-acre farm, took his tiny wife Tamsen and their five youngest to Independence, and joined a caravan. In the spring of 1846 they rolled west. Just short of South Pass a horseman showed them a letter from a California promoter, Lansford Hastings, urging emigrants to use a new short cut south of Great Salt Lake. The Donner party tried to overtake Hastings but missed him. They decided to tackle the Wasatch Range without a guide.

They moved boulders, dug wagonways along hillsides, chopped through mats of willows. It took 21 days to go 36 miles; six more days to cross the desert. Oxen stampeded; Indians stole horses and mules. Tempers snapped. One man was slain in a quarrel, one secretly murdered, a third left behind when he could not keep up. Charles Stanton, sent ahead to Sutter's Fort, returned with two Indian guides and seven muleloads of food. Not enough: the party was too far behind schedule.

Delayed by a broken axle, the Donner family was last to enter the Sierra Nevada. As the advance party neared the crest, a snowstorm struck. They retreated to an abandoned cabin below a little lake. As new storms roared in, they built crude huts. The Donners, a few miles below, made lean-tos. Snow fell inexorably. "Difficult to get wood," a diarist wrote. Then food gave out. The desperate pioneers ate hides, bark, bones. One man went mad.

Near Christmas five women, ten white men, and Sutter's two Indians set out on snowshoes made of oxbows and hides. Impossible travel! When several died, the survivors ate their flesh. When the Indians collapsed, they were shot and eaten. After 28 days two men and the five women staggered into an Indian camp.

Rescue parties found more traces of cannibalism at the lake, and packed out the pitiful survivors. Nearly half the party of 87 had perished, including George and Tamsen Donner, victims of bad advice, bad judgment, bad luck.

Donner Pass still deals treachery. Snow traps a streamliner for three days in 1952 (right), smothers U. S. Highway 40 (trench in trees). A century earlier 22-foot drifts gripped the Donner party; a monument overlooks their camp site.

U. S. NAVY AND (ABOVE) CULVER SERVICE

Brigham Young leads the Mormons to their Promised Land

As THE FIRST GROUP of Latter-day Saints, or Mormons, broke through the Wasatch Range and looked down on their new home in the West, they saw "a broad and barren plain hemmed in by mountains . . . the paradise of the lizard, the cricket and the rattlesnake."

Modern visitors who travel along Utah Highway 65 outside Salt Lake City catch the same view. True, the plain is now checkered with the green of irrigated farms and crowned by the great city. But it is clear that the Mormons, unlike most emigrants of the 1800's, did not choose their new Zion for richness of soil.

They sought refuge from a religious persecution unmatched in the story of America. Joseph Smith, the Saints' prophet, first stirred enmity when he told neighbors in New York State that he had been visited by God and His Son. As he published the *Book of Mormon,* founded his church, and attracted followers, he was hounded from New York to Ohio to Missouri to Illinois.

Settling in the Mississippi River town of Commerce, he renamed it Nauvoo and gathered the faithful about him. The city became the biggest in Illinois, with 15,000 inhabitants. But Gentiles, or non-Mormons, resented the Saints' political power and bridled at whispers of polygamy. When Smith ordered a critical newspaper destroyed, he was jailed and lynched. Raiders burned Mormon farms.

Leadership fell on Brigham Young, 43, a compact, heavily muscled man of

DAVID S. BOYER, NATIONAL GEOGRAPHIC STAFF, AND (RIGHT) WILLIAM BEAL

Utah Lake feeds the Jordan River, which Mormons tapped to irrigate thousands of acres of parched plain. Here Saratoga Springs, a resort, looks southeast toward the Wasatch Range. Mount Nebo (right) takes its name from the peak where Moses viewed the Promised Land.

uncommon ability. He determined to lead the Saints away from Gentile civilization. Reading the accounts of Frémont and other Western explorers, he chose the region of Great Salt Lake.

Mormons sold homes and furniture, bought oxen, and built wagons. In early 1846 the refugees fled across the ice of the Mississippi.

Young divided his moving throng into "hundreds" and "tens"; he sent advance units to establish ferries and plant crops; he assigned hunters, herders, and artisans to each party. Brass bands lifted spirits. "The angels of God will go with you, even as they went with the children of Israel when Moses led them from the land of Egypt," he promised.

The Saints spent the cold months of 1846-7 at Winter Quarters, near present Omaha, Nebraska, and in camps stretching across Iowa. In April, Young led an advance party to the chosen land. They dammed a creek to water the sun-baked earth, and planted potatoes. By fall 2,000 Mormons were in the valley.

Beset by frosts, crickets, and drought, Young put a bold plan into operation. The Saints, placing themselves fully under church control, began to build a

C. 1877, AMERICAN MUSEUM OF PHOTOGRAPHY

Brigham Young, bold and resolute, tamed a desert, built a religious empire, guided the Mormons with a firm hand, 1844-77. Yet he loved to see his people dance, sing, enjoy plays.

Seagull Monument in Salt Lake City commemorates birds that came "until the heavens were darkened," ate cricket invaders, saved pioneers' crops.

great city designed by the leader and the church's Twelve Apostles. Land and water were apportioned to all as needed. From the East and from Europe came thousands of converts. Some pulled handcarts, Young's answer to the high cost of wagons. He sent settlers throughout the Great Basin to found towns like Ogden and Provo, and proclaimed the huge State of Deseret (Honeybee).

But the creation of the U. S. Territory of Utah rekindled passions. Federal and church officials clashed; Gentiles accused Mormons of abetting Indian massacres; rumors of rebellion flamed. President Buchanan sent an army under Gen. Albert Sidney Johnston, and some 30,000 Mormons fled their homes. Peacemakers stepped in. But not until 1890, when polygamy was abandoned, did friction end.

Today's visitor glimpses the Mormon past in tiny settlements like Toquerville,

Mormon Temple in Salt Lake City fulfills a dream of Brigham Young. Begun in 1853 and finished 40 years later, it dominates Temple Square, focal point of world Mormonism. Behind the Temple, the domed Tabernacle houses a 10,000-pipe organ and the famed Mormon Choir.

Mormon fort at Pipe Spring in northern Arizona (left) guarded a ranch from Indians. The spring was named when a scout, camping here, shot the bottom out of a friend's pipe without hitting the sides of the bowl.

Mansion House of prophet Joseph Smith welcomes visitors to Nauvoo, Illinois, where the trek began (below). Nearby stand the Smith Homestead and the Brigham Young Home.

JAMES P. BLAIR, NATIONAL GEOGRAPHIC PHOTOGRAPHER. OPPOSITE: WILLIS PETERSON AND (LOWER) NATIONAL PARK SERVICE

Utah, or in mighty Salt Lake City. Along with the Temple, Tabernacle, and Capitol, the city displays the gabled Lion House, where some of Young's wives lived, and his Beehive House, restored to 1877 elegance and open to the public. The Pioneer Memorial Museum and a church museum re-create early days. East of the city the Pioneer Monument marks where the Saints first viewed their Zion.

Bullwhackers rejoice as they roll into Santa Fe, New Mexico. Lurching along at one mile an hour, they opened the Southwest to American trade and turned the Santa Fe Trail into a highway to fortune. In 1824 one wagon train set out from Missouri with $30,000 worth of goods and returned with silver and furs valued at $190,000. A fiesta reigns before the Palace of the Governors (below), oldest governmental building in the United States. The gala recalls resettlement of New Mexico by the Spanish in 1692 after Pueblo Indians, forebears of the Acoma woman (left), had driven them out 12 years before.

PAUL A. WAGNER

SANTA FE AND THE SOUTHWEST HERITAGE

THE 80-WAGON train creaked to a halt just east of Santa Fe. Oxen blew their fatigue, mules brayed their annoyance. But the bullwhackers and mule skinners paid no heed. They peered into mirrors, combed reluctant hairs, gingerly scraped off 60-day beards. Their clean shirts made them look more like Philadelphia drummers than Indian fighters who had cursed and cajoled their freighters over 775 miles of dusty plain, quicksand creek, and scorching desert.

But why not? Here was trail's end. Nine weeks without a sign of civilization—save for a few isolated forts and villages—could be forgotten amid the music of fandangos and the flashing eyes of señoritas in rebozos (shawls) and dainty mantillas.

The lead wagon turned into streets packed with shouting Mexicans. The drivers cut fancy didos with their whips and exaggerated their "Hoo-haw-w-w-s" as they circled the plaza

MUSEUM OF NEW MEXICO. ABOVE: "ARRIVAL OF THE CARAVAN AT SANTA FE" FROM JOSIAH GREGG'S "COMMERCE OF THE PRAIRIES," 1844, LIBRARY OF CONGRESS, AND (LEFT) WILLIAM BELKNAP, JR.

MERLE SEVERY, NATIONAL GEOGRAPHIC STAFF. BELOW: MUSEUM OF NEW MEXICO BY JUSTIN LOCKE

Taos Pueblo eyed conquistadores in 1540, greets tourists today. Beehive ovens bake bread.

St. Francis of Assisi Church at Ranchos de Taos, New Mexico, has gleamed in the sun some 250 years. Adobe walls and bell towers blend Indian and Spanish styles.

and rolled up to the warehouses. After a week of haggling over customs and bribes, the wagoners would barter the plows and farm tools, cotton goods and linens for silver and gold, mules and furs.

For years Spain had forbidden American merchants to enter New Mexico. But when Mexico won her independence in 1821, the Yankees were welcomed. William Becknell brought in a pack train the next year. By the 1830's traders in Westport and Independence were sending heavily laden caravans annually, at profits of up to 45 per cent.

As soon as the goods were placed in customs, the drivers turned to the delights of the town. Nowhere in Missouri could one see such sights! Girls with painted cheeks smoking tiny cigars; sombreroed vaqueros; brown-robed padres; Indians in serapes; dark-skinned altar boys in white surplices. Even the food was exotic: Spanish dishes, but with a Mexican hand on the pepper shaker. To quench the fire, liquid fire: "Taos lightning" or cactus juice or brandy from El Paso del Norte. For sport: shell games, cockfights, bullbaiting.

The Americanos had left the conventions of their own English puritanical society and entered a world where Spanish and Indian cultures mingled curiously.

Religious processions in the Royal City of Holy Faith carried carved images of saints reminding one of Indian gods. Tribal dances were interlaced with sword dances in which the Moors were symbolically driven from Spain. While La Conquistadora, a statue of the Virgin brought by the first settlers, was paraded to commemorate Spain's reconquest of New Mexico, Indians rattled noisemakers with enthusiasm.

Place names also reflected the mingling. To Yankee ears accustomed to trail markers like Rabbit Ear Mounds and Wagon Bed Springs,

Santos like these in a Santa Fe museum met the need of isolated settlers for religious statues. Wandering *santeros* (saint makers) lost touch with Spanish art and carved primitive, powerful images.

Acoma, believed the nation's oldest continuously inhabited town, dates from A.D. 1200. Spaniards

villages of Las Vegas and San Miguel del Vado were Spanish whispers. Indian pueblos of Taos and Acoma sounded as laconic as their inhabitants. And No Agua (No Water) and Ojo de Vaca (Cow Spring) were as plain and simple as the settlers.

To home building the Spanish colonists had brought a love of massive walls and shaded patios. But the walls were of Indian adobe, and corner fireplaces were patterned after the practical beehive ovens of the pueblos. Even a mule skinner could tell this intertwining of cultures was no recent thing. Before hitching up his rig for the trip home, he might learn that Santa Fe was a colonial capital in 1610—ten years before the Pilgrims landed at Plymouth. He was sure to mosey over to the Palace of the Governors, just as old, and past San Miguel Church, where prayers had been murmured for two centuries.

The founding of churches had marked Spain's expansion in the New World. Padres and soldiers had combined to explore the wastelands and mountain ranges, and then to subdue, baptize, and train the Indians. They grouped the docile tribes in missions, self-contained communities guided by religious zeal. The missions were not only a way of life; they were a Spanish formula for ruling an empire

"**Passed by here** the governor Don Juan de Oñate . . . 1605," reads the message carved on El Morro, a national monument in New Mexico. Indians, padres, troopers, teamsters added names to the mesa that shaded a pool.

MERLE SEVERY, NATIONAL GEOGRAPHIC STAFF, AND (BELOW) WILLARD R. CULVER

scaled 357-foot New Mexico cliffs to sack the Sky City. Tourists today ascend in peace by carved steps or road.

stretching thousands of miles over two continents. By 1630 a score of missions dotted the Southwest. Ruins at Gran Quivira National Monument in central New Mexico date from this period. Examples of later missions are San José, a national historic site in San Antonio, Texas, and San José de Tumacacori, a national monument in southern Arizona.

California's first mission was planted in 1769; 50 years later 21 stretched from San Diego to north of San Francisco Bay. Spaced about a day's journey apart, they formed links in *El Camino Real,* The King's Highway. Madrid hoped they and their *asistencias* (outlying stations) could fend off the Russians pushing down from Alaska. Certainly the *presidios* (military posts) were too few to do the job.

The 1,000 or so Indian neophytes of each California mission lived communally. Chanting hymns and greeting each other with *Amar a Dios* (Love God), they worked 40 hours a week as farmers, soapmakers, weavers, masons, or herders; and celebrated some 130 holy days a year.

Food was distributed daily, clothing and medical care when needed. Under the padres, fields were irrigated and golden grain shimmered. Paintings, religious objects were collected; libraries grew. Padres taught music with colored notes and learned dozens of dialects to spread their message. But they made enemies. Soldiers envied their power. Indians resented being chased down and whipped

San Xavier del Bac Mission rises from the desert like a ghostly mirage. Founded in 1688 by Father Eusebio Francisco Kino, it was rebuilt in 1797 after destruction by Apaches. It still ministers to the Papago Indians on their reservation south of Tucson, Arizona.

PIETRO BALESTRERO, WESTERN WAYS, AND (OPPOSITE) JAMES P. BLAIR, NATIONAL GEOGRAPHIC PHOTOGRAPHER

The altar screen, glittering in all the glory of Spain's Churrigueresque style, is adorned with images of patron saint Francis Xavier, the Virgin, and cherubs. Indian artisans loved vivid colors, smudged vegetable hues on walls and ceiling.

B. ANTHONY STEWART, NATIONAL GEOGRAPHIC PHOTOGRAPHER

Carmel Mission in California sounds its big bell for worship, smaller ones for festivals. Moorish dome, star window, simple façade and archway (right) reveal early Spanish heritage.

LEFT: THE ONLY AUTHENTIC PORTRAIT OF JUNIPERO SERRA; PAINTED FRO

California's Mission Trail reflects the vision of Father Junípero Serra

The Franciscan padre overcame "naked hills and stony deserts" and an ulcerous leg to found a chain of missions from San Diego to San Francisco. He tackled the project with elation: "What a joy! . . . I was about to see men who were ignorant of Christ, and who from this time on should be my friends." With a handful of padres and thousands of Indians he turned wilderness into farm lan strengthened Spain's claims, and filled desola spots with the Angelus' ring, "that this bell might be heard around the world." Father Serra died in 1784 and rests where he labored so long, at Carmel.

LIFE IN 1773, IT HANGS IN THE CHURCH OF SAN FERNANDO IN MEXICO CITY

for running away. Ranchers eyed the missions hungrily. One might have 20,000 sheep, 10,000 cattle, and 1,200 horses—all grazing on 50,000 acres.

In the 1830's a revolutionary Mexican government broke up the missions and opened the land to settlers. Intoxicated with freedom, the Indians looted and slaughtered livestock, then fled into the hills. Years of patient effort vanished.

But mission churches still stand. The tolling bells of restored San Diego de Alcalá recall the days of Father Junípero Serra, who founded California's first mission there. Santa Barbara, the only mission never to close its doors, has a museum tracing its 180-year past. The three naves of San Juan Bautista echo the same quiet litanies that fell on neophyte ears. At Mission Dolores in downtown San Francisco, thongs tied by Indian workers cling to the arched roof beams. San Luís Rey again bustles with brown-robed padres; this time as a Franciscan seminary. And yes, the swallows come back each March to the ruins of Capistrano.

San Francisco Solano, 1823, Sonoma
San Rafael Arcángel, 1817
San Francisco
San Francisco de Asís (Mission Dolores), 1776
San José de Guadalupe, 1797, Fremont
Santa Clara de Asís, 1777
Santa Cruz, 1791
San Juan Bautista, 1797
Monterey
San Carlos Borromeo del Carmelo, 1770, Carmel
Nuestra Señora de la Soledad, 1791
San Antonio de Padua, 1771, Jolon
San Miguel Arcángel, 1797
San Luís Obispo de Tolosa, 1772
EL CAMINO REAL
La Purísima Concepción, 1787, Lompoc
Santa Inés, 1804, Solvang
Santa Barbara, 1786
Pacific Ocean
San Buenaventura, 1782, Ventura
San Fernando Rey de España, 1797
San Gabriel Arcángel, 1771
Los Angeles
San Juan Capistrano, 1776
San Luís Rey de Francia, 1798
San Diego
San Diego de Alcalá, 1769
Point Loma
CALIFORNIA
BAJA CALIFORNIA
NEVADA
CALIFORNIA

CALIFORNIA DIVISION OF BEACHES AND PARKS

San Juan Bautista

Most of California's 21 missions shared their names with the settlements that grew in their shadow along *El Camino Real*, The Royal Highway, now closely followed by U.S. Route 101. Town names that differ are included after the mission founding date. Several of the *asistencias*, which served outlying districts, also stand today.

THOMAS NEBBIA

Santa Barbara

Juan Rodríguez Cabrillo, the "Columbus of California," landed here at Point Loma on San Diego Bay in 1542. In Mexican-built caravels resembling this model at Cabrillo National Monument, he explored north to where San Francisco now stands, but he missed the Golden Gate.

SAN DIEGO CONVENTION AND TOURIST BUREAU (ALSO LEFT)

San Diego de Alcalá

0 — 100
STATUTE MILES
NATIONAL GEOGRAPHIC MAP
BY ROBERT W. NICHOLSON

REDWOOD EMPIRE ASSOCIATION

Mission Dolores

J. BAYLOR ROBERTS, NATIONAL GEOGRAPHIC STAFF

San Luís Rey de Francia

KARL OBERT

San Juan Capistrano

Monterey each June salutes the days when it ruled California. Fiestas were frequent; rancheros and merchants entertained at the drop of a sombrero; horse races, bull-and-bear fights quickened the capital's languorous pulse.

Adobe houses with broad verandas and walled gardens recall its colorful youth under Spanish and Mexican flags. The Old Custom House, a museum, still stands at harborside.

B. ANTHONY STEWART, NATIONAL GEOGRAPHIC PHOTOGRAPHER

THE ALAMO

Texans fight for independence

DAWN, MARCH 6, 1836. The men huddled inside the old mission hear a bugle sound in the darkness . . . then the tramp of thousands of feet and shouts of "Viva Santa Anna!"

For the 187 Texans and Americans, rubbing sleep from their eyes and reaching for rifles and bowie knives, the moment of truth is at hand.

Twelve days ago these men of the Alamo watched the Mexican army march into San Antonio with all the pageantry of a bullfight: short scarlet jackets, bright blue pants, plumed shakos held erect by shining chin straps. And in the dust—bare feet.

The defenders saw the blood-red banner meaning "no quarter" hoisted on a church in the town, and answered with the blast of a cannon. They heard the Mexicans cheer the arrival of reinforcements, swelling Santa Anna's army to some 4,000.

And yet the tiny garrison stays. Some are still confident. They remember Anahuac, where the Mexican commander politely surrendered without a fight. And San Antonio, where three months ago they fought from rooftops, battered holes in walls, captured the big Mexican garrison.

But the fact is, 187 men can't hold the mission; with its walls and buildings, it sprawls over three acres. Col. William Barret Travis knows this. Looking at the men about him—Davy Crockett, the Texans, the volunteers from the United States—he writes a

Outnumbered 20 to one, Texans blaze away from the barricade, fire cannon atop the church and in the plaza to repel the army of Mexican dictator Santa Anna. On the 8th day 32 men and

A SCENE FROM JOHN WAYNE'S MOVIE "THE ALAMO"; THOMAS NEBBIA, NATIONAL GEOGRAPHIC PHOTOGRAPHER

boys from Gonzales, 70 miles away, reinforce the defenders in the sprawling mission near the San Antonio River. On the 13th day a tidal wave of troops breaches the walls. Dying in a nightmare of clubbing gun butts, slashing knives, and impaling bayonets, the 187 Texans exact a fearful toll—some 1,500—and give independence fighters a rallying cry: "Remember the Alamo!"

final dispatch: ". . . the victory will cost the enemy so dear, that it will be worse for him than defeat." Why do these men choose to stand and die? For much the same reason that minutemen stood at the bridge at Concord 60 years earlier.

Mexico allowed Stephen F. Austin and other American *empresarios* to found colonies in Texas in the 1820's. They would help fill the sparsely populated, Indian-infested area. The newcomers got land free and in turn became Mexican citizens. But friction arose. Former Americans resented trials without jury and

B. ANTHONY STEWART, NATIONAL GEOGRAPHIC PHOTOGRAPHER

CULVER SERVICE AND (LEFT) NEW YORK HISTORICAL SOCIETY

Davy Crockett of Tennessee (above) spun wild yarns but shot straight, claiming 105 bears one year. He scouted for Andrew Jackson in the Creek War, served in Congress, then headed west to give the Texans a hand. Georgia-born Jim Bowie, quiet but deadly in a duel, was famed for the bowie knife. Land speculator and prospector in Texas, he died with Crockett defending the Alamo, which stands restored as a museum in downtown San Antonio (left).

not having a say in government. They were outraged by new laws that would free their slaves and bar further immigrants from the States. They protested the garrisoning of troops among them and the highhandedness of officials. When Gen. Antonio López de Santa Anna overthrew the constitutional government, made himself dictator, and marched north to bring the Texans to heel, they fought back.

Now the cannon of the Alamo boom; rifles spit fire and death from the ramparts. Twice waves of Mexicans crash against the walls; they crumple from grapeshot, topple from scaling ladders, are trampled underfoot by retreating comrades. On the third assault they breach the north wall and pour into the compound like sheep. No time to reload. Texans swing their rifles like clubs, slash with big knives. They retreat into the stone "long barracks" and fight until their bodies are riddled with "grape, musket shot and the bayonet." In the old church Jim Bowie, bedridden, racked by fever, fires from his cot until killed.

That afternoon the Mexicans heap the Texans' bodies on layers of wood and cremate them. But Santa Anna has kindled a fire in Texas hearts he can't put out.

He marches northeast. Sam Houston and the Texas army fall back until they come to the San Jacinto River. There, on the afternoon of April 21, they shatter the Mexican siesta with the roar of cannon, the rattle of rifles, and the chilling cry of "Remember the Alamo!" In 20 minutes, while their improvised band toots a popular ballad, "Will You Come to the Bower I Have Shaded for You," the Texans kill 630 Mexicans and capture 730—including Santa Anna.

With independence won, the Lone Star Republic now struggles against bank-

S. SEYMOUR THOMAS, SAN JACINTO MUSEUM OF HISTORY

Sam Houston came to Texas "a man of broken fortune," won independence for the republic at the Battle of San Jacinto, then preserved it as president. He died in 1863 still protesting Texas' secession from the Union.

B. ANTHONY STEWART, NATIONAL GEOGRAPHIC PHOTOGRAPHER

Deep in the hearts of Texans abide the San Jacinto Battlefield Monument, marking the site of their most glorious victory, and the battleship *Texas,* veteran of two world wars. The 570-foot concrete-and-limestone shaft houses a museum in its base and looks out over a state park. Here in 1836 a force of 910 Texans attacked some 1,600 Mexicans under Santa Anna and killed or captured all but a few with a loss of only nine men.

ruptcy, Mexican hostility, and American indifference. Then U. S. opinion shifts; the fever of Manifest Destiny grips the land. The United States annexes Texas in 1845 and seeks to buy the neglected provinces of New Mexico and California. Mexico isn't selling.

Tension grows as both nations press claims along the Texas border. Mexico calls the Nueces the boundary. The United States draws the line at the Rio Grande and President Polk sends troops. Mexican cavalry cross over; war begins.

U. S. strategy is three-pronged. Gen. Stephen W. Kearny marches west, occupies New Mexico and California. Gen. Zachary Taylor knifes south, driving a wedge as far as Saltillo. Then Gen. Winfield Scott sails to Veracruz, battles his way over the mountains, and captures Mexico City. On February 2, 1848, Mexico accepts $15,000,000 for land which will become the states of California,

RICHARD CATON WOODVILLE, 1848, NATIONAL ACADEMY OF DESIGN

War news from Mexico via the newborn telegraph electrified the nation. The "wonder-wire" hastened troop movements, revolutionized news reporting, sped commerce. By July, 1848, it tied New York with New Orleans.

Nevada, Utah, and parts of New Mexico, Arizona, Colorado, and Wyoming.

Time has not been kind to the buildings that witnessed those stirring events. But today the Alamo still stands, and near Goliad the partly ruined presidio and the restored Mission Espiritu Santo recall the massacre there of 350 Texan prisoners by Santa Anna. In San Antonio is La Villita, a restored village with adobe houses that gives an idea of the old Texas towns. And at Huntsville stand the plain clapboard house where Sam Houston lived and the steamboat-shaped dwelling where he died.

The visitor to the Mexican War battlefields of Palo Alto and Resaca de la Palma near Brownsville may sense a tragedy beyond the American triumphs. For fellow officers in that war like Grant, Lee, Sherman, Jackson, McClellan, and Jefferson Davis were destined to meet again in a far bloodier struggle—as enemies.

CALIFORNIA DEPARTMENT OF NATURAL RESOURCES

Rebel Californians raise the Bear Flag

GEN. MARIANO VALLEJO sleeps peacefully as the dawn of June 14, 1846, breaks over Sonoma. There's a banging at the door; 30 men stand outside. "Surrender!" they shout.

He invites the leaders in, takes out bottles of wine. What's this about, he asks.

He can guess. Rawboned American traders and settlers have been trickling in for years. They seem to distrust and dislike Mexican rule. And the U. S. government hasn't helped. It keeps trying to buy California. Tension has been such that four years ago Commodore Thomas ap Catesby Jones seized Monterey on a rumor of war. Jones apologized, but then Captain Frémont and his armed explorers began to flit about the territory. And four days ago some Americans stole 200 army horses.

Vallejo refills the glasses, signs the surrender document, rides off a captive. The Americans proclaim a republic, elect William B. Ide president, and hoist a crude flag bearing a star, a grizzly bear, and the words CALIFORNIA REPUBLIC. But war between Mexico and the United States intervenes. In four years California will become the 31st state, its 92,000 people swelling the U. S. population to 30 million.

And General Vallejo? He will return to his Sonoma, become a leading citizen, and leave two handsome homes you can see there today.

"CLAY ADDRESSING THE SENATE ON THE COMPROMISE OF 1850," AFTER A PAINTING BY PETER F. ROTHERMEL, NEW YORK HISTORICAL SOCIETY

JOHN E. THIERMAN

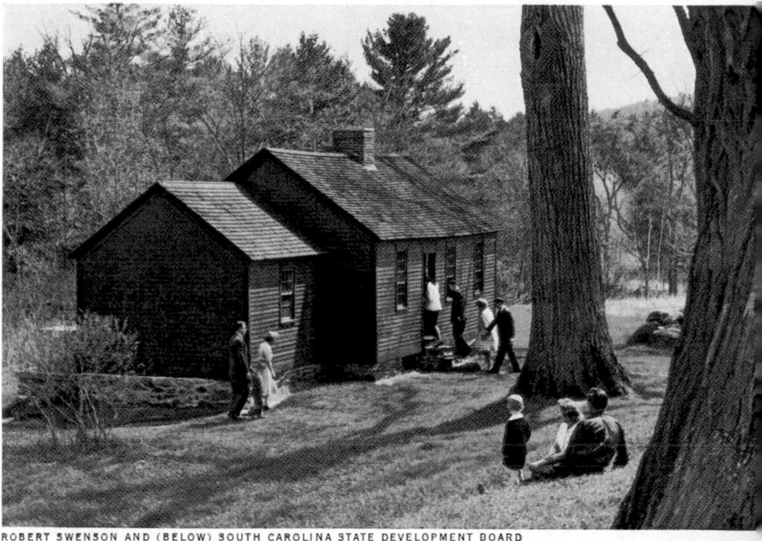

ROBERT SWENSON AND (BELOW) SOUTH CAROLINA STATE DEVELOPMENT BOARD

"The Great Compromiser," Henry Clay, offers resolutions that pacify free and slave factions in 1850 and save the Union. Thrice beaten for the Presidency, the senator yearned for Ashland, his home in Lexington, Kentucky, but died in Washington far from his four-poster (above).

Daniel Webster, head in hand at left, supported Clay, not "as a Northern man, but as an American." His birthplace, once the ell of his father's house, stands rebuilt (top right) near Franklin, New Hampshire. John C. Calhoun, standing third from right in the painting, fought the compromise though death stalked him. The champion of states' rights lived at Fort Hill (right), today on the campus of Clemson College in South Carolina.

WASHINGTON was cold and miserable during those wintry weeks in 1850 when the country almost fell apart over what to do about California and the lands acquired from Mexico. No decision could be reached without a bitter debate on the nation's ever ominous problem: slavery.

The Senate rang with the speeches of its three old giants. At 73 Henry Clay had left his sickbed to point out a middle road both North and South could travel. He would admit California as a free state—but he would make concessions to the South, among them a new, firm fugitive slave law. John C. Calhoun, his tubercular body wheezing beneath flannel wrappings, argued as eloquently (a friend read his address) that slavery was a positive good, that every Southerner had a right to bring slaves into the new territories and states. Last to speak was "Black Dan" Webster, voice of Northern industrialism. He would compromise; he would accept the prospect of runaway slaves being hunted in the North, for he hated disunion even more than the South's "peculiar institution." The Compromise of 1850 passed. The deepening rift between North and South was patched—but not healed.

JAMES H. CAFFERTY AND CHARLES G. ROSENBERG, MUSEUM OF THE CITY OF NEW YORK

Big cities burgeoned as the North expanded in population, industry, financial power. But New York's Wall Street quaked in the panic of 1857 (above). Towering buildings today dwarf Trinity Church and make a canyon out of "the Street."

THE NORTH

In bustling cities and on placid farms an ardent call is heard

THE STRENGTH of the North lay in its varied opportunities—factories as well as farms, cities as well as seaports, an eagerness to grow intellectually as well as materially. The face of the land pointed out the ways it was developing. Every waterfall offered cheap power. Every harbor along that rocky coast could nourish a town, perhaps a metropolis.

Small wonder, then, that by the mid-19th century young men of the northeastern states were drifting away from their serene, hill-cupped inland villages. They sought the marts of Boston, New York, or Philadelphia. They resettled beside red brick mills and helped make shoes, clocks, tools, toys, or textiles.

They went west, for among the Free-soilers of the frontier they found the same lusty confidence that marked their own infant industries. An obscure Midwestern politician put that attitude into words: "Men, with their families—wives, sons and daughters—work for themselves, on their farms, in their houses and in their shops, taking the whole product to themselves, and asking no favors of capital on the one hand, nor of hirelings or slaves on the other." So spoke Abraham Lincoln in 1859.

The rustic charm of farm villages hid much of the surge toward factories on the eve of war. Towns like East Corinth, Vermont, appear little changed today.

B. ANTHONY STEWART, NATIONAL GEOGRAPHIC PHOTOGRAPHER

Housing boomed when factory-made nails made possible the "balloon frame," a simple skeleton of two-by-four studs replacing the heavy pegged beams of yore. Quickly spiked together, it's still used.

European immigrants seeking freedom turned to the North and the West where work awaited men of many talents and backgrounds. Few went south. "Slave states are places for poor white people to remove *from,* not remove *to.*" Mr. Lincoln again.

Advances in transportation expressed the Northerner's restless spirit in a rich and self-reliant land. In the 1840's shipyards in New England and New York began turning out clipper ships, the swiftest vessels afloat. In bitter competition they sped passengers to California and raced for cargoes—among other things the Southern cotton that was now growing so profitably, thanks to the Yankee ingenuity of Eli Whitney, inventor of the cotton gin.

Railroads lined the map of the North and pushed westward. Forged iron for locomotives and rails came generally from Northern foundries. Engines ran on Pennsylvania coal. If soot was dusting the pastoral landscape, it was just too bad. Industry's profits could not be denied.

Yet the Southerner's image of the North as a land of

Northern mills and foundries throbbed with the youthful vigor of the industrial revolution. The Nashua Iron Company in New Hampshire banged out forged iron with a mighty trip hammer.

GLEASON'S PICTORIAL, 1851, LIBRARY OF CONGRESS. LEFT: ENGRAVING, 1855, METROPOLITAN MUSEUM OF ART

Graceful clippers slid down the ways to race for commerce and profits. *Flying Cloud,* launched from Donald McKay's shipyard at East Boston, once logged 433½ miles in a day.

LITHOGRAPH, 1859, THE OLD PRINT SHOP

Little red schoolhouses hummed with children learning the three R's. To this one, moved from Sterling to South Sudbury, Massachusetts, by Henry Ford, came Mary's little lamb.

flinty Yankees squeezing the last nickel out of a horse trade was a poor caricature. The North may have presented a coldly commercial face, but deep down it was warmed by traditions as sturdy as its hillside farms. It had given the country its first college, Harvard, and inspired the land-grant colleges that would soon dot the Midwest. It had provided the first tax-supported public library, at Peterborough, New Hampshire; the first public school, Boston Latin, in 1635; and the first effective school system, started by Horace Mann, a Massachusetts educator.

And ever since the days when Puritans first ranted against "the Devil, Quakers and Indians" and hanged witches, the North had thrived on moral causes.

Northern books, like the people, were self-illuminating and zealous. While Southerners remained enthralled over Sir Walter Scott's romances of chivalry, Northerners worried through the inward-searching works of Herman Melville, Nathaniel Hawthorne, Walt Whitman, Ralph Waldo Emerson, and Henry David Thoreau. The Common Man, coming of age, faced a barrage of ideas.

One idea was the abolition of slavery. William Lloyd Garrison grimly hammered it home with his paper, the *Liberator*. "I am in earnest," wrote Garrison, and the words are carved on his Boston statue: "I will not equivocate—I will not excuse—I will not retreat a single inch—AND I WILL BE HEARD." Heard he was, finally. Harriet Beecher Stowe made sure of that.

Her *Uncle Tom's Cabin* burst upon the world in the 1850's. Parisians wept over *La Case de l'Oncle Tom*. There was even an edition in Javanese. Mrs. Stowe insisted that God had stood at her elbow as she wrote. Never had the New England conscience been so well served.

Antislavery sentiment caused more than hearts to bleed. In 1854 a runaway slave was arrested in Boston and shipped to Virginia in strict compliance with the Fugitive Slave Law. The old city erupted with anger unknown since Revolutionary days. Faneuil Hall rang again with fiery speeches; a mob stormed the Court House and a deputy marshal was killed; black crepe festooned State and Court streets.

Recapturing that one Negro cost the United States $100,000. And Boston's reaction proved to all who cared to notice that some very hot blood could pulse through Yankee veins when a moral issue was at stake. EDWARDS PARK

Library of the famed Adams family adjoins their Old House in Quincy, Massachusetts. Painting is of President John Adams, who died on the 50th Independence Day murmuring "Jefferson still survives." At Monticello, Jefferson died the very same day.

ADAMS NATIONAL HISTORIC SITE BY KATHLEEN REVIS JUDGE. ABOVE: B. ANTHONY STEWART AND JOHN E. FLETCHER, NATIONAL GEOGRAPHIC PHOTOGRAPHERS

Wayside Inn, historic shrine to Henry Wadsworth Longfellow, still welcomes travelers

As Ancient is this Hostelry
As any in the Land may be,...
wrote Longfellow of the house in South Sudbury, Massachusetts, that inspired his *Tales of a Wayside Inn.* Washington and Lafayette stayed at the 17th century inn, oldest operating tavern in the country.

Longfellow, who in 1842 had written *Poems on Slavery,* condemned the surrender of fugitive slaves as "dirty work." Poets Whittier, Lowell, and Holmes also fought slavery with verse. Thoreau preached man's simple dignity, and found haven at Concord's Walden Pond (opposite, left). Emerson bought his Concord home (far right) in 1835. Literary neighbors were Hawthorne, Alcott.

Harriet Beecher Stowe's novel, trumpeting the horrors of slavery, roused the North to an old cause. "So this is the little woman who made the big war," said Lincoln on meeting Uncle Tom's creator. Her book sold 10,000 copies in its first week and persuaded millions that slavery must end.

Yet shortly before this literary bomb exploded, New England's Daniel Webster had lashed out at abolitionists: "I think their operations for the last twenty years have produced nothing good or valuable." Many in the North agreed. Bostonians threatened William Lloyd Garrison, the incendiary of abolition who considered the Constitution "a Covenant with Death" and publicly burned it. And an Illinois mob murdered Elijah Lovejoy as he tried to save his antislavery press.

Uncle Tom appeared in 1851 with brutal Simon Legree, and Eliza fleeing across the ice as bloodhounds bayed. And all the North seethed.

135,000 SETS, 270,000 VOLUMES SOLD.
UNCLE TOM'S CABIN
FOR SALE HERE.
AN EDITION FOR THE MILLION, COMPLETE IN 1 Vol., PRICE 37 1-2 CENTS.
" " IN GERMAN, IN 1 Vol., PRICE 50 CENTS.
" " IN 2 Vols., CLOTH, 6 PLATES, PRICE $1.50.
SUPERB ILLUSTRATED EDITION, IN 1 Vol., WITH 153 ENGRAVINGS,
PRICES FROM $2.50 TO $5.00.
The Greatest Book of the Age.

B. ANTHONY STEWART, NATIONAL GEOGRAPHIC PHOTOGRAPHER. OPPOSITE: NEW YORK HISTORICAL SOCIETY. BELOW: KEITH MARTIN

NATCHEZ

THE SOUTH

Where cotton reigns supreme

PROUD, INFLEXIBLE, the South scorned Mrs. Stowe as one who "hunts up crimes as beagles hunt their prey." The land had changed since 1794 when its most honored son, George Washington, noted: "Were it not then, that I am principled against selling negros, as you would do cattle . . . I would not, in twelve months . . . be possessed of one, as a slave." Even then Eli Whitney had invented his machine.

The cotton gin combed seeds from the short-staple cotton that grew in the deep South like a weed. Suddenly mills in the North and in England clamored for cotton. Planters put it in Georgia's clay and built white-pillared mansions on its profits, then seeking fresh soil moved to Alabama's prairie loam and Mississippi's flatlands. They produced fewer than 150,000 bales in 1815, nearly five million in 1860.

Slavery, waning in 1790, became essential for this cotton kingdom. Though few whites owned slaves, most excused the institution: "In the three million bags of cotton the slave-labor annually throws on the world . . . we are doing more to advance civilization . . . than all the canting philanthropists of New and Old England will do in centuries." Preachers found texts that sanctified and dignified slavery. Why, even children were taught to be considerate of slaves, but who cared for the "wage slave" of the North?

So some 3,500,000 slaves (generally treated much better than Uncle Tom) hummed spirituals after working the rich white fields. And wharves at New Orleans groaned under the South's baled treasure. And the planter turned angrily away from the abolitionist. Not worth a thought, Sir!

HOWELL WALKER, NATIONAL GEOGRAPHIC STAFF
FAR LEFT: EUGENE FISHER. ABOVE: "THE LEVEE—NEW ORLEANS," LITHOGRAPH BY CURRIER & IVES, LIBRARY OF CONGRESS

Natchez—symbol of ante bellum elegance

PERCHED ON A BLUFF overlooking the Mississippi River, Natchez sweeps the modern visitor back to days when cotton was king and a planter guarded his honor and his credit with equal attention.

You notice the land first. Loamy, buff-colored soil; slender pines and massive oaks bearded with moss; crimson splashes of azalea and camellia; and the broad river glimmering like a belt of bronze as the sun sets beyond the darkly wooded lowlands to the west.

In this lush Mississippi setting old mansions stand like sentinels of the past, each revealing something of life in the Old South. Massive D'Evereux, square and columned like a Greek temple, reflects the classical taste of the planter. Dunleith is circled by galleries, symbols of hospitality that seem to say, "Come sit a spell." Stanton Hall with its imported marble mantels, gold-leaf mirrors, and bronze chandeliers exudes the elegance of the cotton aristocracy.

You are welcomed to these and more than a score of other homes during spring Pilgrimage Month in Natchez. Hostesses, their voices as soft as a breeze from the river, don silk and brocade dresses of the mid-1800's for the occasion. It is not difficult to envision them in the roles of their great-great-grandmothers: welcoming guests who clatter up to the "big house" in fine carriages with liveried outriders, ushering laughing groups down the candle-lit great hall, presiding over a long table heaped with turkey, ham, strawberries, and bottles of champagne.

PLANTATION LIFE seemed specially made for young women. Visiting the bedrooms of these old houses, with their canopied beds and lacy curtains, one can imagine pretty Rebecca Mandeville sitting down to chronicle in her diary the spring days of 1848. "*March 2:* After dinner, trained my Brazilla vine up to the gallery . . . will now read a chapter in the Bible and then repose. *March 13:* I took Sissy and went on the bluff—put 2 or 3 ginger nuts in my bag first and eat them up there —dreadfully plebian! *April 12:* I don't think I ever passed a pleasanter evening— the party was composed of eight of us young girls and about as many gentlemen all in good spirits and ready for enjoyment—had two tableaux, scenes from Ivanhoe. *May 1:* Sewed this morning and began to read Hyperion. . . ."

But Rebecca may have found a wife's duties less serene. A planter often expected his spouse to rise with the sun, supervise the cooking, washing, and weaving, and teach, counsel, and nurse the slaves.

The master of the house relished his comforts but never forgot the cotton that made it possible. He'd fret at a dry spell or a dip in the London market, hum cheerily when he could boast of his fields: "No crop at all to compare with it, from half leg to waist high bolled & formed as well as can be." His pride and his pleasure were fast horses, politics, and a post in the Natchez Fencibles or Guards. Question him on these and you might be invited across the river for a duel. Refuse and the morning paper might read: "To the Public. I hereby denounce N. E. Turner a base poltroon and an arrant Coward . . . when yesterday a friend

Columned Melrose preserves the dignity and charm of the Old South. Reared in the 1840's of brick made by slaves, it is one of 30 homes on display each March in Natchez, Mississippi. Costumed hostesses are often descendants of first owners.

ROBERT F. SISSON, NATIONAL GEOGRAPHIC PHOTOGRAPHER

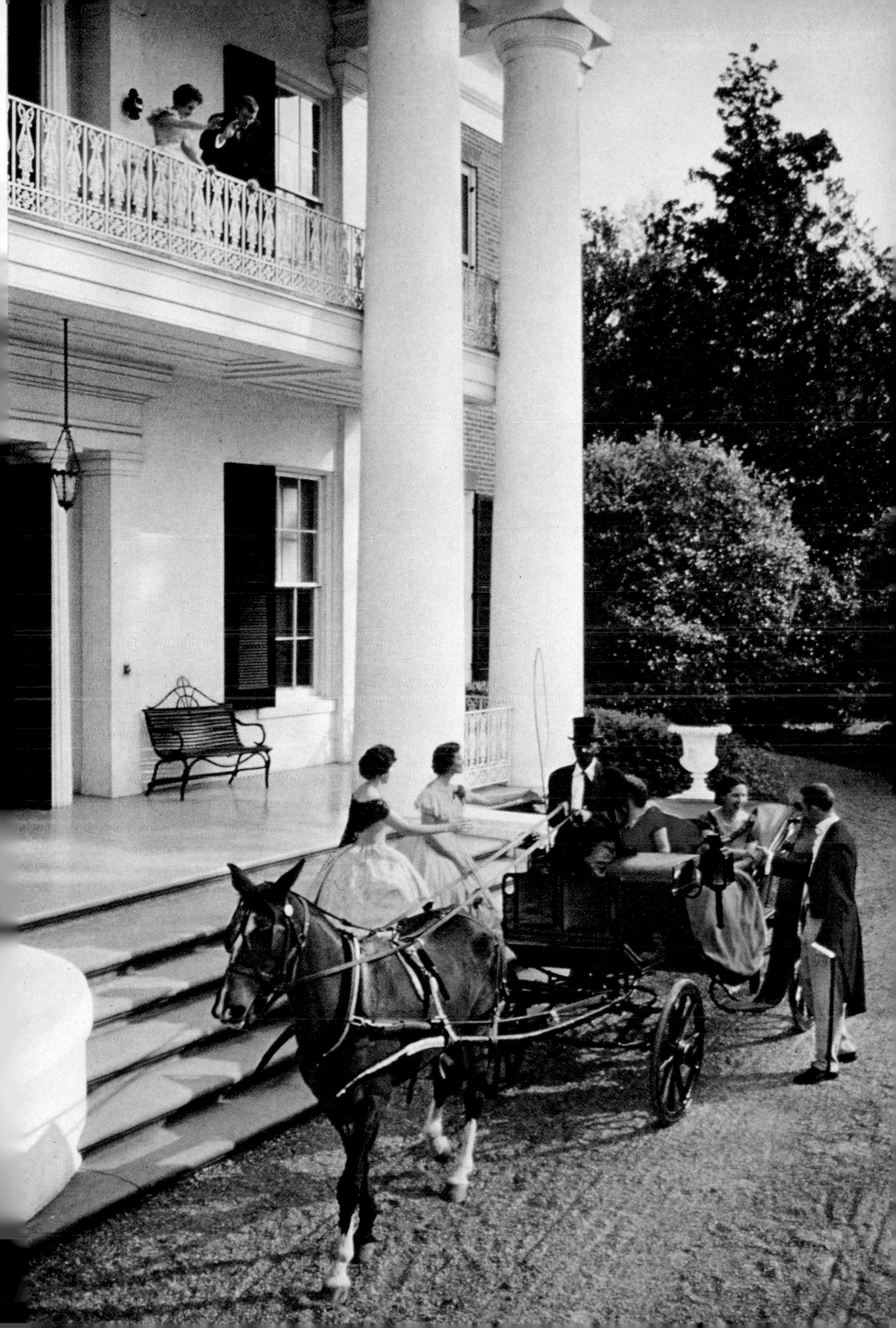

French brocatels, carved rosewood furniture, and lavish gilt adorn a Melrose drawing room, elegant reminders of the days when cotton built bale-sized fortunes in Natchez.

of mine Called on Him to Cross the river he basely Sculped from responsibility."

But with ladies the planter was more understanding, as one Natchez house testifies. Peter Little, master of Rosalie, was distressed by his wife's habit of entertaining the many itinerant ministers who passed by. He restored his privacy by simply building another mansion, The Parsonage, for the visitors.

Other dwellings help trace Natchez' colorful past. In 1716 French settlers under the Sieur de Bienville built a stockade on the bluffs. Forty-seven years later, at the end of the French and Indian War, Natchez passed to England with France's other New World possessions. Then while redcoats battled American revolutionaries, Spain slipped in to occupy the town. Hope Farm, Airlie, and Linden all knew the tread of booted Spanish dons.

Connelly's Tavern on Ellicott's Hill saw the U. S. flag hoisted for the first time on the lower Mississippi. Andrew Ellicott, a Pennsylvania Quaker sent to survey

ROBERT F. SISSON, NATIONAL GEOGRAPHIC PHOTOGRAPHER, AND (LEFT) WILLARD R. CULVER

Civil war dashed a dream of Byzantine grandeur at Longwood. Northern artisans dropped hammers and brushes and marched off to battle. Tools, pails remain where they left them.

the young nation's boundary in 1797, raised the flag despite protests by the Spanish garrison. A year later Spain ceded the area.

Connelly's vied with King's Tavern, oldest building in Natchez, to host the rude backwoodsmen, flatboatmen, peddlers, outlaws, adventurers, and settlers who traveled the Natchez Trace. Rowdies might brawl and wager in wicked Natchez-under-the-Hill, the old river town, but at Connelly's they followed the rules: "No more than five to sleep in one Bed.... No boots to be worn in Bed.... Organ grinders to sleep in the Wash House." The tavern might have added another rule—no conspiracy—for tradition says Aaron Burr, the statesman who killed Alexander Hamilton in a duel, met here to plot the creation of a Southwest nation.

Other Natchez visitors included Andrew Jackson, who wed his beloved Rachel at nearby Springfield; John James Audubon, who painted birds on the china now preserved at Green Leaves; Jefferson Davis, who wooed and won the pretty

WILLARD R. CULVER

Monteigne's formal garden beckoned ante bellum belles for a stroll with a favorite suitor—or suitors. More than 150 varieties of camellia japonica blossom on the old Spanish land grant. Come bath time, the pantaletted young mistress of Edgewood would find tin tub, hot-water kettle, and towels brought right into her own bedroom.

Varina Howell at The Briers; and Henry Clay, a frequent guest at D'Evereux.

Myrtle Grove holds fond memories too—of steamboat days. Its owner, Thomas P. Leathers, skippered the *Natchez* in its race with the *Robert E. Lee*.

Natchez reflects the life of the cotton aristocracy but not the whole South. After the United States bought Louisiana from France and Florida from Spain, the Southern states stretched from the bayous and sandy plains along the coast through rich deltas and prairies to pine hills and wooded mountains toward the north. Like the land, the nine million people in these states differed.

Most were small farmers who lived in "dog-trot" houses (two one-room cabins joined by a porch), tilled a modest number of acres, and enjoyed nothing more than hunting squirrel and rabbit with a good dog and a passable gun. Their wives socialized at quilting bees or with "dinner on the ground" after church services. Their daughters, unlike Rebecca Mandeville, knew what it was like to bend over a hot washpot or to chop cotton.

Yet something tied the planter and the small farmer together as Southerners.

Some say it was the cotton economy; some say it was the presence among them of three and a half million slaves; others claim they shared an almost mystical feeling for the land and a fear that man somehow loses something when he quits it for the factory or the counting house.

They had their grievances against the North. Everything they bought, from plowshares to coffin nails, seemed to fill Northern pockets. Even the cotton trade seemed in the grip of Yankee bankers and shippers. Abolitionists cried for a move that would strip the planters of much of their investment and create fearful new social problems. Finally, with California's entry into the Union, the South lost its powerful clutch in Congress. Wrote George Fitzhugh of Virginia: "In the Union there is no hope for us. Let us gather courage from despair and quit the Union."

Leadership lay with the planters. Men who managed their own farm communities seemed singularly equipped to govern. But plantation life did not teach conciliation. When pressed, Southern gentlemen like those of Natchez were more likely to reach for cane or pistol. JOHN J. PUTMAN

HARPERS FERRY

Festering conflicts focused here on wild-bearded John Brown

The Potomac River (foreground) swallows the tumbling Shenandoah at Harpers Ferry. Two rail-

THE GAUNT old man with the burning eyes had many logical reasons to strike at Harpers Ferry. Here, where North and South met, where an armory and rifle factory offered weapons—here was the place to start a general insurrection of slaves. Yet some say John Brown had another motive for his choice: that his heart leaped at the sheer setting of the Virginia town.

Still apt is the description of Harpers Ferry that Thomas Jefferson wrote

road bridges leap from Maryland to West Virginia; John Brown's bridge spanned islandlike piers.

VOLKMAR WENTZEL, NATIONAL GEOGRAPHIC PHOTOGRAPHER

VOLKMAR WENTZEL, NATIONAL GEOGRAPHIC PHOTOGRAPHER

Serene Shenandoah Street, the town's main thoroughfare, echoed to sporadic shots during the day and night that John Brown's party held the militia at bay. Later, Civil War fighting raged through Harpers Ferry. But floods account for the demise of the business section.

almost two centuries ago: "On your right comes up the Shenandoah, having ranged along the foot of the mountain an hundred miles to seek a vent. On your left approaches the Patowmac, in quest of a passage also. In the moment of their junction they rush together against the mountain, rend it asunder. . . . This scene is worth a voyage across the Atlantic."

Visitors still find it so at Harpers Ferry National Historical Park. The lower streets are those of a ghost town. Gray stone walls gape with empty window openings. Time and floods have been cruel to this onetime boom town, but history clings to it like mist on the rivers.

In 1747 Robert Harper began ferrying travelers across "The Hole," where Shenandoah and Potomac meet. A flood served notice that whatever settlement was planted here would be at the mercy of the two rivers. Yet Harpers Ferry prospered.

George Washington, mapping the mountain gap, noted its waterpower, timber, and signs of iron ore, and urged construc-

More sightseers invade Harpers Ferry, thanks to the national park, than did Rebels and Yankees, whose assaults on the strategic town are marked on the war map.

tion of an armory. The Chesapeake and Ohio Canal arrived and also the Baltimore and Ohio Railroad. A bridge spanned the Potomac. By the 1850's the busy little town had nearly 1,800 inhabitants, many working in the United States Rifle Factory.

Probably few of those townsfolk had ever heard of Osawatomie Brown, though he was known and feared in the Kansas-Missouri border country and carried a $250 price on his head for freeing slaves. Certainly no one had cause to suspect a "land and cattle buyer" who came unobtrusively to the Ferry in the summer of 1859.

He called himself Isaac Smith, and he rented the Kennedy Farm across the river in Maryland. Other strangers joined him there, hiding in the attic during daylight. Neighbors remarked on the number of shirts hanging from the clothesline—so many for one family. But no one paid heed, though the thing that John Brown and his followers were to do at Harpers Ferry would flicker over the nation like heat lightning before a distant storm.

On the night of October 16, 1859, Brown led 18 men across the covered wooden railroad and wagon bridge into the village. They carried guns, pikes, a sledge hammer, and a crowbar. They captured the bridge, broke into the federal armory, entered the rifle works, and sent a party toward Charles Town, now in West Virginia, to seize hostages and recruit slaves. This detachment came back with Col. Lewis Washington, George Washington's great-grandnephew, as prisoner. The first person fatally wounded by the raiders was the baggage master at the station, a free Negro who never heard the order to halt. An ironic casualty.

Brown's plans fell apart. The slaves had no heart for rebellion. Word of the raid spread, bringing militia and organized civilians into action. The outnumbered raiders retreated with some hostages into a little brick fire-engine house in the armory compound, knocked rifle ports through the walls, and waited.

Through that day and into the night shots echoed from the mountainsides. The militiamen avoided volunteering for any frontal charge. The mayor was shot dead

for venturing close. Near midnight, a detachment of U. S. Marines arrived by train from Washington. In charge was Col. Robert E. Lee. At dawn his aide, Lt. J. E. B. Stuart, approached the firehouse under a flag of truce to seek its surrender.

The door opened a crack and "Isaac Smith" poked his head out to parley. With a shock Stuart recognized old Osawatomie Brown, bearded now, but still the same fierce-eyed fighter Stuart had run across while on cavalry duty in Kansas. Brown would not agree to Lee's terms. The door closed. Stuart stepped aside and waved his cap. Marines battered at the door with sledges, then rammed it with a heavy ladder. It splintered and they poured through the gap as shots flashed and acrid

Marines smash down the firehouse door to capture five raiders. Ten were killed, as well as four townspeople and a marine. Thus did old Osawatomie Brown make good his prediction: "We've had enough talk about 'bleeding Kansas.' I will make a bloody spot at another point to be talked about." Awaiting execution, Brown welcomed martyrdom. "I cannot now better serve the cause I love . . . than to die for it." He also requested no attendants save "ragged, bareheaded & barefooted Slave boys & Girls." So grew the legend that he bent to kiss an infant slave while on his way to the gallows.

ABOVE: "SKETCH MADE ON THE SPOT BY OUR SPECIAL ARTIST," FRANK LESLIE'S ILLUSTRATED NEWSPAPER, OCTOBER 29, 1859, LIBRARY OF CONGRESS
RIGHT: "THE LAST MOMENTS OF JOHN BROWN" BY THOMAS HOVENDEN, METROPOLITAN MUSEUM OF ART

smoke seeped from the bullet-pocked building. John Brown was captured as he fought beside the bodies of two sons, one dying, one dead. He was led out, jailed, tried, and in December, 1859, hanged at Charles Town. One of the militiamen who witnessed the execution was John Wilkes Booth, destined to assassinate Lincoln.

Abolitionists made Brown a martyr. His raid crystallized the issues that were tumbling the nation toward war. He was buried near Lake Placid, New York, with a black rock to mark the spot, and soon the North's recruits were swinging off to camp roaring new words to an old hymn tune: *"John Brown's body lies a-mould-'ring in the grave, His soul is marching on!"* VOLKMAR WENTZEL

FLAG PRESERVED AT FORT SUMTER NATIONAL MONUMENT; DICK BURBADGE

FORT SUMTER

Southern guns blast the old flag

LIVE OAKS ARCH above the asphalt lane that leads to Fort Johnson, a point jutting into Charleston Harbor, South Carolina. From it you can see Fort Sumter rising on its sand bar a mile away, flat and round like a button on the vest of the bay.

Here stood Capt. George S. James, watch in hand, in the early morning of April 12, 1861. At exactly 4:30 he glanced at the taut faces around him, then pulled the lanyard of a ten-inch mortar.

Inside Fort Sumter, Sgt. James Chester, Co. E, 1st Artillery, heard a dull roar roll in awesome echo across the water and spotted the burning fuse of the mortar shell arching among the stars. Spiraling downward, building speed, the shell burst right over the fort—"a capital shot," noted Chester. Then on all sides guns opened fire. Telegraph keys clicked out the dreadful tidings:

"Charleston, April 12—the ball has been opened at last and the war is inaugurated."

In a sense, the first shot of the Civil War took decades to fire. Yet the last months of the 33-state Union, pinned together by compromise, saw events whirling fast, picking up momentum. And their vortex was South Carolina.

Pretending not to hear the growing talk of secession in 1860, the federal government was placating the South yet strengthening coastal forts. On November 20 Maj. Robert Anderson, a Southerner but loyal to the old flag, took command of Charleston's forts: Moultrie, Sumter, and Castle Pinckney. He set up headquarters at Moultrie;

First shot of the Civil War roused sleeping Charleston and sent a thrill through the nation. "The Rubicon was passed," wrote a Rebel officer. One lady, hearing the cannonade, "sprang out of bed and on my knees, prostrate, I prayed as I never prayed before." Her neighbors jammed the housetops. Sumter's riddled flag with its 33 pre-secession stars was hoisted at war's end by the same officer who had struck it four years before.

HARPER'S WEEKLY, MAY 4, 1861, LIBRARY OF CONGRESS
ABOVE: DIORAMA AT FORT SUMTER NATIONAL MONUMENT

VOLKMAR WENTZEL, NATIONAL GEOGRAPHIC PHOTOGRAPHER. OPPOSITE: NEW YORK PUBLIC LIBRARY

Lower casemate guns hit back at Charleston's Rebels during the 34-hour bombardment. Sumter entered the war with two tiers of cannon, but starting in 1863 savage Union gunfire pulverized upper levels and reduced the fort to rubble. Yet the South held it until 1865.

Sumter was unfinished. Exactly one month later South Carolina took the step that had become inevitable upon Lincoln's election. It seceded from the Union, and Charleston's church bells, ringing in jubilation, sounded a nation's alarm as well.

Fort Moultrie was vulnerable to land attack, so Anderson spiked its guns and took his command to Sumter—77 fighting men for a fort designed to hold 650; 15 guns ready to fire though the fort was planned for 135.

President Buchanan, who had tried to avoid trouble until his term ended, stiffened his spine and sent the *Star of the West,* an unarmed merchantman, to reinforce and supply Sumter. On January 9, 1861, cadets from Charleston's military school, the Citadel, fired on the ship and drove her off.

Georgia, Florida, Alabama, Mississippi, Louisiana, and Texas seceded. The Confederacy was established in Montgomery, Alabama, with Jefferson Davis, former senator from Mississippi and secretary of war, as president. Gen. Pierre Gustave Toutant Beauregard, "Napoleon of the Bayous," took command at Charleston the day before Lincoln's inauguration. Lincoln appealed to the South: "You have no oath registered in Heaven to destroy the Government, while I . . . have the most solemn one to 'preserve, protect, and defend' it."

But the silent siege of Sumter continued, and Lincoln decided to send another relief expedition. Confederates flocked to the Charleston batteries facing Sumter.

"God and Battle must decide the issue between the hostile hirelings of Abolition hate and Northern tyranny, and the people of South Carolina defending their freedom and their homes," bugled the Charleston *Mercury*.

On April 11 Beauregard demanded Sumter's evacuation or reduction. Anderson refused the ultimatum of his onetime West Point artillery pupil. The Confederate government sent a telegram from Montgomery, Alabama, asking when Anderson would evacuate. He hedged his reply with so many conditions that the Confederate emissaries rejected it, warning chivalrously ("We have the honor to notify you . . .") that Beauregard would open fire in one hour.

And so at 3:30 A.M., April 12, 1861, the envoys rowed the dark mile back to Fort Johnson and ordered Captain James to fire a signal shot at 4:30. A fire-eating Virginian, Roger Pryor, was offered the honor of pulling the lanyard. He shrank from the moment of truth: "I could not fire the first gun of the war." James fired the gun, fully aware of the historic moment—a thing to be told and retold to children and grandchildren. Seventeen months later he lay dead on a battlefield.

Shot and shell screamed over Sumter "as if an army of devils were swooping around it." At 7 A.M. Sumter's guns replied, aimed by the only ardent abolitionist in the fort, Capt. Abner Doubleday, famed for laying out the pioneer baseball diamond back in Cooperstown, New York. The Rebel gunners were happy to be answered. It absolved them from winning a cheap victory. As the guns dueled into the second day, the Southerners cheered every shot that came from the crippled fort.

Sumter's barracks caught fire. Smoke nearly suffocated the soldiers, workmen, and musicians. Flames raged near the powder magazine, threatening to blow the garrison to kingdom come. They used socks for cartridge bags, and had no food but salt pork. The flag was shot away, then rehung.

Beauregard sensed that the fort had taken about all it could. He sent aides "to offer assistance." Anderson finally agreed to surrender with full honors, including a salute to Old Glory.

So ended the first battle of the Great American War. Four men on each side were scratched. A horse of Rebel sympathies was slain. Two Yankees died when a gun misfired during Anderson's salute.

Walk through the entrance of Fort Sumter National Monument and you can almost smell the reek of black powder. The crumbled walls have been restored to their appearance after the 1861 bombardment, and dud Rebel shells lodge in them ("They refused to secede," says a visitor). A 42-pounder on a wooden carriage looks menacingly toward Fort Johnson. Surely a wisp of smoke curls from it. And seeing these things, you hear, it seems, a distant bugle. RALPH GRAY

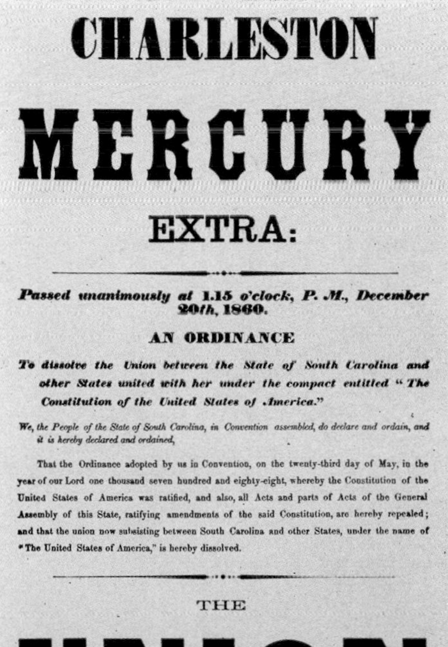

CHARLESTON

MERCURY

EXTRA:

Passed unanimously at 1.15 o'clock, P. M., December 20th, 1860.

AN ORDINANCE

To dissolve the Union between the State of South Carolina and other States united with her under the compact entitled "The Constitution of the United States of America."

We, the People of the State of South Carolina, in Convention assembled, do declare and ordain, and it is hereby declared and ordained,

That the Ordinance adopted by us in Convention, on the twenty-third day of May, in the year of our Lord one thousand seven hundred and eighty-eight, whereby the Constitution of the United States of America was ratified, and also, all Acts and parts of Acts of the General Assembly of this State, ratifying amendments of the said Constitution, are hereby repealed; and that the union now subsisting between South Carolina and other States, under the name of "The United States of America," is hereby dissolved.

THE

UNION

IS

DISSOLVED!

Ordinance of Secession answered Lincoln's election and made South Carolina a nation.

Landmarks of the Confederacy

DEEP SOUTH SPECIALTIES. TOP: MATHEW B. BRADY, C. 1860, NATIONAL ARCHIVES (LEFT), AND TOMMY GILES. RIGHT: ARLINGTON, NOW CUSTIS-LEE MANSION, THE ROBERT E. LEE MEMORIAL: DAVID S. BOYER, NATIONAL GEOGRAPHIC STAFF

Robert E. Lee and Jefferson Davis led the Confederate States of America during its four tragic years. Davis took oath as president February 18, 1861, at the State House in Montgomery, Alabama, in the ceremony re-enacted at left. When Virginia joined the C.S.A. after Sumter's fall, Richmond became the capital. Imprisoned at war's end, Davis finally settled at Beauvoir (far left) near Biloxi, Mississippi, where he wrote his memoirs.

Lee was born at massive Stratford (above) near the Virginia birthplace of his idol Washington. He married Martha Washington's great-granddaughter, acquiring Arlington (lower left), her home farther up the Potomac. Here he made his fateful decision: Virginia came first.

Richmond's White House of the Confederacy is now a museum rich with Rebel memories. After the city fell Lincoln visited Davis's office.

DAVID S. BOYER, NATIONAL GEOGRAPHIC STAFF
LEFT: J. DANNERSON, 1864, COOK COLLECTION, VALENTINE MUSEUM, RICHMOND

Flocking to the colors

EXULTANTLY the South cheered Sumter's surrender, while a growl of rage echoed through the North. No one received the news more calmly than Abraham Lincoln. On April 14, "Battle Sunday," he called for 75,000 state militia to serve the nation three months. The Confederacy, already training militia, called for more. North and South, farm boys and city lads jammed the recruiting stations while girls waved and local companies drilled on the town green. Many a proud Yankee posed in his dapper uniform—often of militia gray. Many a group of fire-eating "Southrons" showed off their fine bright clothes—many regiments wore blue—and bragged of what they would do with their pistols and long knives if only the war didn't end before they got into it. New Orleans applauded its Creole Guard that marched smartly to orders in French. New York mustered its firemen to form a regiment of Zouaves, a vastly popular designation for well-drilled men who wore baggy red pants and red fezzes. Bands blared—"Dixie" was popular in the North as well as South—and flags snapped and a New England youth bragged that he had kissed every girl in town after enlisting. Men marched off to camp and small boys strutted behind. This was the life! These were the brave, wonderful days of youth.

MATHEW B. BRADY, 1861,
LIBRARY OF CONGRESS
RIGHT: "PITCHING QUOITS"
BY WINSLOW HOMER, 1862,
FOGG MUSEUM OF ART
ABOVE: 1861, COOK COLLECTION,
VALENTINE MUSEUM, RICHMOND

EARL SCHENCK MIERS

IN THE STEAMING MID-JULY of 1861 the Northern army marched eagerly off to fight. Three months had passed since the bombardment of Fort Sumter, and the great majority of Northerners believed that one great pitched battle would end the rebellion and restore the Union. The quicker it was fought the better. Not a day went by without Horace Greeley's New York *Tribune* screaming the battle cry of the North's embittered millions from the head of its editorial columns: "Forward to Richmond! Forward to Richmond! The Rebel Congress must not be allowed to meet there on the 20th of July! BY THAT DATE THE PLACE MUST BE HELD BY THE NATIONAL ARMY!"

General in chief Winfield Scott, whose career stretched back to Lundy's Lane in the War of 1812, had opposed any headlong action. He knew that young armies are like young lovers: more prone to court trouble than avoid it. And this army, knocked together from state militiamen who had answered Lincoln's call for troops, was very young and gay and carefree. Moreover, Scott thought the Mississippi Valley, not Virginia, should be the arena for crushing the South. So he argued for delay to prepare and mass his forces.

Pacing the floor of the White House in a pair of old carpet slippers, Abraham

PICKETT'S MEN CHARGE TO THEIR HIGH-WATER MARK; UNION SUPPORTS STEM THE GRAY TIDE IN THIS SCENE FROM THE 353-FOOT CYCLORAMA, PAINTED BY FRENCH ARTIST PAUL PHILIPPOTEAUX, 1881-4, AT GETTYSBURG NATIONAL MILITARY PARK

"THE ARMY OF THE POTOMAC—A SHARP-SHOOTER ON PICKET DUTY" BY WINSLOW HOMER, 1862, LIBRARY OF CONGRESS

Lincoln had to face facts. Either the North struck a blow soon or he forfeited popular confidence. So in late June the cabinet met, overruled Scott, and decided on a campaign against Confederate forces concentrating at Manassas Junction in Virginia, 25 miles west of Washington. Scott must have known that the politicians would carry the day; he was all ready with a plan that had been worked out by one of his generals, Irvin McDowell.

Aged 42, McDowell had spent his adult life in the Regular Army. Shrewd, conscientious, and experienced, he had drawn up a sound scheme. He pointed out, correctly, that the key to any successful Federal movement on Manassas must rest in bottling up a second Confederate force that held Harpers Ferry, at the foot of Virginia's vital Shenandoah Valley. Scott and the cabinet agreed with McDowell. So Gen. Robert Patterson, a gallant 69-year-old veteran of the Mexican War, was sent to take command of some Union troops in Pennsylvania, attack Harpers Ferry, drive the Rebels up the Shenandoah Valley, and keep them too busy to help their friends over at Manassas.

Patterson started well. But he was old and soon lost steam. On July 15 he was 12 miles north of Winchester, Virginia, where the Confederates waited for him under the command of an able and experienced officer, Gen. Joseph E. Johnston.

Next day McDowell ordered his army out of Washington. So many Southern spies riddled the capital that Confederate General Beauregard, the cocky little Creole who had emerged as "Hero of Sumter," knew as much about Union troop movements as did McDowell himself. One lady who lived within a stone's throw of the White House already had written in cipher, "Order issued for McDowell to march upon Manassas tonight," and sent the message southward by courier even as the streets echoed to the tramp of Federal troops.

This bit of treason really was only of academic interest. All Washington erupted in holiday spirit, boisterously proclaiming that within a few days, perhaps hours, would come the smashing triumph that would end the war. Not wishing to miss the grand spectacle, politicos and civilians packed luncheon hampers, streamed out of the capital in hired carriages, chatted gaily as they picnicked along the way, and helped to clog the roads over which McDowell attempted to march his army.

FEW CONFLICTS have been bloodier than the Great American War. None, certainly, had a more ridiculous beginning. With rare exception the Federal troops leaving Washington that dusty July 16 were so inexperienced in warfare that before Sumter they had never seen a real soldier in uniform. In many ways their long column resembled a circus parade. Zouaves trudged along in their bright red bloomerlike trousers. One regiment sported the plumed hats of Italian *bersaglieri*. Many men had drilled with nothing more lethal than broomsticks until rifles could be issued. Most thought of battle in terms of a barroom brawl – too often they substituted braggadocio for the harsh discipline of genuine soldiers.

A relatively obscure, redheaded colonel named William Tecumseh Sherman despaired at his inability to keep his men from "straggling for water, blackberries, or anything on the way they fancied." Lt. George W. Bicknell of the 5th Maine was more sympathetic. He watched his comrades falling by the roadside, some "sunstruck," some "wind-broken," some crying with thirst. And when a brook flowed across the road he remembered later "the avidity with which our boys would drink of that water, in hundreds of cases using their shoes as dippers, horses and men side by side, the water thickened and yellow with dirt."

Scouts brought Beauregard intelligence of how the Federal march left the roads "strewed with blankets, haversacks, coats, thrown aside by the almost exhausted soldiers." But Beauregard took scant comfort from such reports. His own troops, spread out along a stream called Bull Run, were just as raw. "Old Bory" was plagued by dozens of worries. Most important: could Johnston's force from the Valley make it to Manassas in time to save him from catastrophe?

General Johnston himself barely reached Manassas ahead of McDowell's army. Back in the Shenandoah old Patterson's advance had come to a halt – nothing for the South to fear there. But here? Johnston found Beauregard devising a whole series of plans for crushing the Union force before it could strike. He would attack on Sunday morning, July 21. He would smite McDowell left and rear. He would crumple the invader and send him reeling from Virginia's sacred soil.

But on Sunday morning, two hours before Beauregard's assault was scheduled to begin, the Federal army hit hard across Bull Run. And that wasn't all. McDowell was inconsiderate enough to make this opening play a mere feint. His main blow was a thunderous full-scale attack on the Confederate left flank. It was the defender, not the invader, who started to crumple, Southern boys spinning away from the front on the verge of rout.

Colonel Sherman, a Mexican War veteran who never before had been in battle, was aghast at the sounds and sights around him: cannon balls crashing through trees and maiming human beings; the "terrible scare" of a Negro caught between the lines; "the fear lest we should be fired on by our own men." Lieutenant Bicknell was exhilarated by the shouts from the wounded as his 5th Maine hurried forward: "Go in, boys, the Johnnies are running."

Beauregard was in a fix and knew it. His troops were tumbling away from the driving Federals, scattering across the Warrenton Turnpike (today's U. S. Route 29-211), passing the Stone Bridge, and ducking through a shallow ravine beside the slope of Henry House Hill. But along that height stood a brigade commanded by Gen. Thomas J. Jackson, up to now physics teacher at Virginia Military Institute. He was trying to stem the rout while thunderous confusion filled the smoky air—more than 2,000 men "shouting each some suggestion to his neighbor, their voices mingling with the noise of the shells hurtling through the trees overhead, and all word of command drowned in the . . . uproar."

At this moment Confederate General Bee achieved immortality by crying, "Look at Jackson's brigade! It stands there like a stone wall! Rally behind the Virginians!" Beauregard ordered the colors advanced 40 yards, the men rallied, and the panic ebbed.

Still, as the afternoon wore on, the Union rolled ahead, its soldiers fighting without much style but with a savagery surprising in green recruits. McDowell believed he had won the battle. And Jefferson Davis, rattling up from Richmond in a special train to witness the action, was equally convinced that the South had lost it. Dejected Rebels crowding around the President's car offered no solace.

THEN, AT MIDAFTERNOON on that blazing day, Johnston's Confederates fresh from the Valley tumbled off the railroad cars and came howling like a tornado from a wood on the Federal right flank. Beauregard exulted. The charge was made "with such keeping and dash" that the Yankees were swept away in disorder. Sudden vignettes of disaster etched themselves on the mind of one New Yorker as the Union army fell apart: "Here a man, grasping his musket firmly in his hand, stone dead; several with distorted features, and all of them horribly dirty. Many were terribly wounded, some with legs shot off; others with arms gone, all of them, in fact, so badly wounded that they could not drag themselves away; many of the wretches were slowly bleeding to death, with no one to do anything for them."

Only moments before, McDowell, handsome and high-spirited in full uniform and white gloves, had jauntily waved his boys up a hillside. Now in dismay he watched a retreat that "soon degenerated into disorder, for which there was no remedy." Toward midnight the first shocked witnesses to the Union disaster stumbled into Washington. Lincoln, reclining on a couch in the Cabinet Room in the

White House, heard the grim stories and wondered if the Rebels were pursuing his disorganized army. By noon of the next day it became clear that they weren't, and Lincoln cheered up.

With eloquent simplicity Bavarian-born Col. Louis Blenker of the 8th New York, testifying before the Committee on the Conduct of the War, explained why he did not think it was "a blame for anybody to lose that battle." Said Blenker: "It was a panic, all at once," adding, with an apology for his poor English, "That is strange music—the bullet—and a strange feeling to be killed." Strange music too for both North and South were the casualty figures for First Bull Run or First Manassas: more than 4,500 young Americans dead, missing, or horribly wounded.

EVERYWHERE IN THE NORTH were portents that defeat had strengthened the people's will to fight secession. Gone was the holiday mood, replaced by determination to raise a trained, efficient army capable of winning battles. President Lincoln welcomed the change, for he felt that this "People's contest" must be won in the nation's mind and heart as well as on the battlefield. Within a few months of Bull Run a "hidden war" was smoldering. In New York City on February 21, 1862, a slave runner from Maine, Nathaniel Gordon, became the first and only American to hang for this crime. That same month Edward Lillie Pierce, a treasury agent sent to save 2,500,000 pounds of cotton captured in South Carolina, made a social experiment to see if Negroes could be "fitted for useful citizenship." Pierce wanted doctors, nurses, teachers, and social service workers, and got them, financed by private subscriptions. He was exhilarated by the speed with which Negro children learned; he admitted the grave problems that existed among offspring who had been raised to think they belonged more to the plantation than to their families. In this age, Pierce's enthusiasm sounded a fresh note, drew a concept of freedom in a new dimension.

Gordon dangling from the gallows, Pierce sending in rapturous reports on his experiment, and in Lincoln's mind words taking shape that would organize the hidden war that America was fighting—here was a mobilization of national purpose that the Confederacy could not match. Mr. Lincoln's Emancipation Proclamation, issued in 1863, achieved miracles as a tool of psychological warfare, at home and abroad.

The visible war, too, changed vastly after Bull Run. Gen. George B. McClellan had won a small victory in the mountains of western Virginia, a region that seceded from the Confederacy and became a state of the Union in 1863. After Bull Run he took over Union troops in Washington: "rather a mob than an army." McClellan saw to it that this Army of the Potomac was supplied, organized, and trained. Under this general, green troops were taught military discipline, whisky

UNION CAVALRYMAN IN ACTION,
SKETCHED BY WINSLOW HOMER, 1863, COOPER UNION MUSEUM

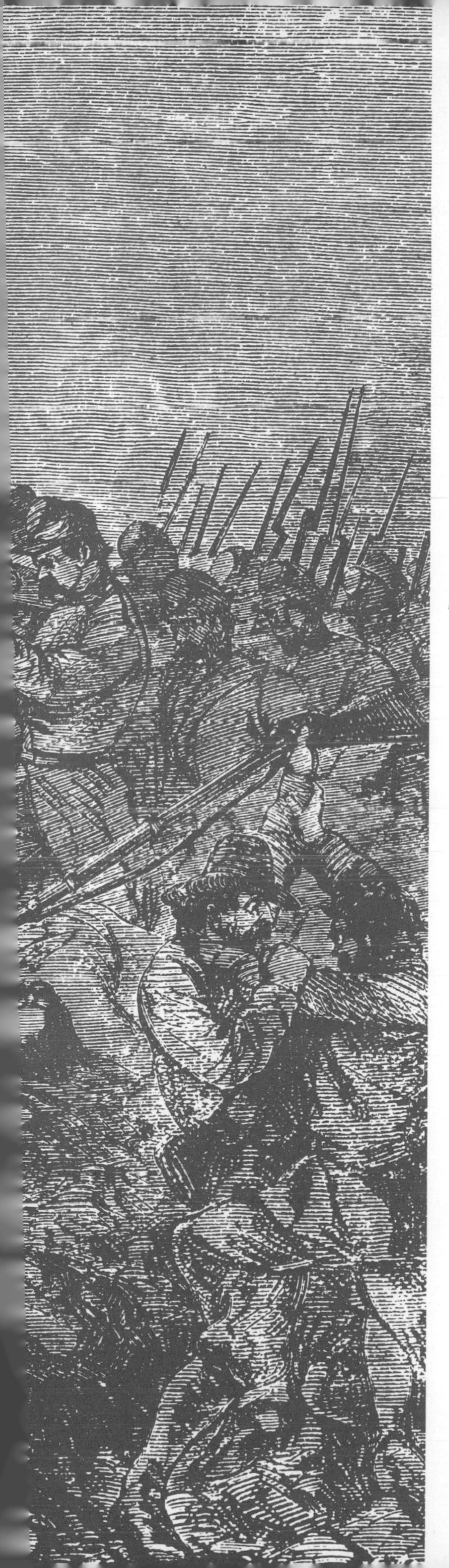

was prohibited in camp, and a provost marshal's department was created to end the rampant desertions and straggling. What in late July had been "a mere collection of regiments cowering on the banks of the Potomac," by autumn had been forged into a fighting force that began to acquire dignity, confidence, and military know-how.

Whatever critics say of "Little Mac"—that he never quite dared use this superb machine of his—he was one Northern general who understood that complex modern war could only be won by tending strictly to business, not by romantic skylarking.

THE GREAT AMERICAN WAR was unlike any the world had ever seen. As the months of tragic conflict ground on, farm boys and city clerks, fur trappers and waterfront bums, steamboat deck hands and sharecroppers learned to live with incredible realities.

They marched off to Manassas Junction filled with romantic notions of glory. Many thought a battle would be some sort of knightly tournament between brothers. That idea breathed its last when Pickett charged at Gettysburg, July 3, 1863.

It took time to grasp that the Great American War was thoroughly and irresistibly *American.* It was as proud as the Southern planter, as inventive as the Yankee trader, as earth-bound as the Western frontiersman, as contemptuous of life at times as a Comanche on a raid. Generals grew accustomed to balloons spying out positions, to reporters snooping, to photographers lugging wagonloads of equipment over cluttered roads, to civilian entertainers roaming the camps, and to hometown politicians bargaining for future votes with barrels of whisky. They heard doctors and nurses protesting about

Vicious infighting was caught by British correspondent Frank Vizetelly. Clumsy photography could not yet replace action sketches.

ASSAULT BY FEDERAL TROOPS ON BATTERY WAGNER, NEAR CHARLESTON; ILLUSTRATED LONDON NEWS, 1863, LIBRARY OF CONGRESS

slovenly camp kitchens and "death in the frying pan." They watched sutlers and cotton speculators vying with opportunistic fellow officers for quick profits and they saw the sawdust-filled soles of their soldiers' boots melt away as the men sloshed over muddy roads.

Soldiers grew accustomed to new weapons—rifled field guns, accurate at three miles; the repeating rifle, introduced late in the war, that shot as fast as a man could work the lever. They knew warfare was changing when they found themselves instinctively digging in whenever an advance slowed, when they lived for weeks in the gluey mud of trenches. Sailors knew it in that single battle between the ironclad *Monitor* and *Merrimac* when they hammered at each other with heavy turret guns and thus blew the world's wooden navies into oblivion.

Modern war rose like a phoenix from the ashes of Vicksburg. Its gospel: not just soldiers, but people in factories, on farms, people anywhere doing anything that sustained a hostile army—these are the enemy. And William Tecumseh Sherman, the colonel so shocked by bloodshed on the day of Bull Run, became the minister of this new, godless religion, to "make old and young, rich and poor, feel the hard hand of war." The terrible violence of those distant years stirred a prophecy from Henry Adams: "Some day science may have the existence of mankind in its power, and the human race commit suicide by blowing up the world."

THE NORTH began to change its attitude after Bull Run. The South was defeated by its success. Edward A. Pollard, editor of the Richmond *Examiner,* saw in the Southern victory "the greatest misfortune that could have befallen the Confederacy." Shocked, Pollard watched politicians "plotting for the Presidential succession" and states bickering over the site of the Confederate capital, "which they could not understand was yet imperiled by war."

Robert E. Lee, who had turned down command of the Union army and accepted that of Virginia's forces, believed the war could last ten years. He felt that Southerners must be taught to be "less boastful, less selfish, and more devoted to right and justice to all the world." It had galled Lee to sit in Richmond, a headquarters general, while fighting raged at Manassas. Later he led a force in western Virginia and failed miserably—but the moment was coming when he would step into history and legend, a remarkable figure in both.

The more representative men of the modern warfare came out of the West, and in one of them the North finally found its great general, Ulysses S. Grant. He was no borrowed martial image, no "Napoleon in Blue" like McClellan; Grant was a product of time and place—"the uncommon common man."

The war that Lee and Grant fought would be remembered by many names, but none would strike closer to the truth than the occasional reference to it as "Mr. Lincoln's War." It had touched the world, revitalized human aspiration, and won—what? For the nation, for the world there could be only one answer, spoken by Mr. Lincoln upon a gentle hillside at Gettysburg: . . . *that government of the people, by the people, for the people, shall not perish from the earth.*

Stonewall Jackson, guns on his right, still grimly awaits a Yankee attack on vital Henry House Hill back of Bull Run. Clover carpets meadows once torn and bloody at Manassas National Battlefield Park in Virginia.

THOMAS NEBBIA

WAR IN THE EAST

Lee seizes the initiative

MARSHY STREAMS, gloomy forests, gentle hills—this is the Peninsula, that strip of Virginia between the York and James rivers. It has changed little since the spring of 1862 when it offered a natural route for the Federals, landing from transports, to attack Richmond. Inching up it came a powerful, polished, steel-tipped machine, the Army of the Potomac under Gen. George B. McClellan. Defending were ill-organized Confederate troops. Robert E. Lee was still shackled to headquarters. But while the Union troops bent their line across the flooded Chickahominy and looked down on Richmond's spires from observation balloons, Lee seethed with a plan. It involved a second front—the distant Shenandoah Val-

EDWARDS PARK, NATIONAL GEOGRAPHIC STAFF

ley beyond the Blue Ridge. It depended on Stonewall Jackson, hero of Manassas. As the Peninsula aimed at Richmond, so did the Valley point at Washington. Turn Jackson loose to threaten there, reasoned Lee, and the pressure might ease here (see Civil War map in back of book).

It was done. Jackson turned into a bolt of lightning, smacking one Yankee outfit west of Staunton, then doubling back to whip another at Front Royal. Federals tried to stand at Winchester, were slugged again and sent reeling to the Potomac. Washington panicked and support for McClellan was shunted away to the Valley.

Isolated on the Peninsula, Little Mac's troops fought off a Rebel attack, wounding the Southern field commander, Joseph E. Johnston. The battle proved disastrous to the North, for to take Johnston's place came courteous Robert Lee, ever devoted to the idea of winning battles. Again he sent a message to Jackson.

Jackson—that Joshua in a mangy cadet cap, that mystic who drove his infantry like cavalry but hated to fight on the Sabbath—Jackson had been hitting his scattered foes in the Valley with both wings of his army at once. Now he vanished

Crashing field guns, thundering hoofs, a keening yell as infantry charged—thus did the Rebels fight

Stonewall Jackson's dashing Valley campaign, here reenacted, took pressure off beleaguered Richmond in 1862, allowed Lee to launch his Seven Days' Battles on the Peninsula, and kept Washington on the verge of nervous collapse. Jackson's lean, wolflike troops often marched 30 or more miles a day carrying little save rolled blankets and ammunition. Filthy, unshorn, their drab, catch-as-catch-can uniforms rotting, they still kept their rifles clean.

Jackson, a stern Presbyterian, would delay a battle to attend prayer meeting. Painfully shy, he spoke little, sucked a lemon for refreshment, and adored Lee, who sometimes teased him. In tactics the two read each other's minds. Their grim, hungry men would march anywhere for them, barefoot, and take on any odds.

like a gray wraith, only to turn up "red with the dust of three Virginia counties" at Lee's headquarters on the Peninsula. Plans were laid. It was June 25, high time for Lee's newly named Army of Northern Virginia to break McClellan's grip on Richmond. In the soft upland of the Valley, bewildered Federals wondered where Jackson would strike next. In the hot, dank woods of the Peninsula, Lee massed his men, Jackson felt for the Yankee flank, and the South began to move.

Just seven days later McClellan's big blue machine was being herded back into its James River base camp, supplies burning behind it. The General hated to see it get dented, and Lee had struck some heavy blows—Mechanicsville, Gaines' Mill, Savage's Station, Glendale. The Northern boys had fought with all the courage, precision, and flair that their toughest Old Army sergeants could wish. Time and again they had ripped the gray ranks that charged through the thickets yelling their eerie fox-hunting cry. And time and again as night fell the Yankees heard the inevitable order to retreat. The South lost men; the North lost the Peninsula.

Richmond National Battlefield Park, southeast of the city, explains and illustrates the details of the Peninsula Campaign. A 57-mile drive links the sites—a placid little house here, a shaded stream there, and finally the pleasant slope of Malvern Hill where Lee made his last attempt to crush McClellan. Gray regiments were blown apart as they stormed up toward massed Federal guns. The misty night that ended the battle echoed with the screams of wounded men. "It was not war," said a Rebel general. "It was murder." Yet next day McClellan was gone.

So Richmond was saved, at dreadful cost. Lee refitted, then turned his attention to the rest of Virginia. He sent Jackson to spar with Union General Pope near Culpeper. John Pope, fresh from the western theater of war, sneered at Easterners and bragged that his headquarters would be in the saddle. Veterans on both sides chuckled: that was where most people kept their hindquarters.

Jackson's rugged men marched rings around Pope, cut his rail line to Washington, robbed his base at Manassas, and jabbed him into position for an uppercut. Lee delivered it with a crash—the Second Battle of Bull Run—and Pope's disgusted soldiers trudged back to Washington, whipped again. That was all for Pope.

NOW LEE carried the war north. Early in September, 1862, the Army of Northern Virginia rolled through Leesburg, where its general was feted; then it forded the Potomac. "They were the dirtiest men I ever saw, a most ragged, lean, and hungry set of wolves," reported a Marylander. "Yet there was a dash about them that the Northern men lacked. They rode like circus riders. Many of them were from the far South and spoke a dialect I could scarcely understand. They were profane beyond belief and talked incessantly."

"Up from the meadows rich with corn," they tramped through quiet Frederick where lived an old lady named Barbara Fritchie—a friend of Francis Scott Key—who often displayed an American flag. Despite Whittier's poem, no Rebel paid her the slightest heed, nor did she to them so far as is known. But at Hagerstown a female patriot sang "The Star-Spangled Banner" right at General Lee. He gravely raised his hat and trotted on. He was worried by the dispersion of his force—Jackson off capturing Harpers Ferry. Now rumors were rife that the Army of the

Antietam Creek murmurs peacefully beneath Burnside Bridge, named for the Union general whose fallen troops stained the water red. His men fought their way across to hit Lee's flank in the 1862 Maryland battle.

W. D. VAUGHN

Potomac was high-tailing it after him. George McClellan was back in command.

The rumors were true. McClellan moved fast for once, stormed Lee's rear at South Mountain, and boasted he would bag the Virginian. After all, he'd picked up Lee's campaign orders wrapped around some cigars and he knew every plan in the Confederate's head. The trouble was, McClellan hated a showdown fight.

He got it at Sharpsburg, along Antietam Creek, in "the bloodiest day of the war." Lee whirled to face him there, and Jackson dashed up to help. McClellan committed about half his army, grudgingly, bit by bit, and the Yankees fought like savages as the Rebel lines writhed and shifted to meet attack after attack. The battle howled across a cornfield, and the corn looked "as if it had been struck down by a storm of bloody hail." Beside this field at Antietam National Battlefield Site is a sunken road, notorious "Bloody Lane." New Englanders blackened their faces and war-whooped before charging it. Sometimes the sun sets red again over Antietam as it did that hot September evening when the foes faced each other, bled white and glutted with war. Lee had to withdraw across the Potomac. McClellan couldn't follow. He'd had all he could take.

President Lincoln called on General McClellan (center) after Antietam and chided him for not destroying Lee's army. Leaving the camp, Lincoln gazed at the Army of the Potomac and sighed, "McClellan's bodyguard."

MATHEW B. BRADY, LIBRARY OF CONGRESS

"THE MERRIMAC AND THE MONITOR IN HAMPTON ROADS" BY C. RIESS, C. 1862, NORFOLK MUSEUM OF ARTS AND SCIENCES

Union blockade strangles the South

WITH DERISIVE laughter the South greeted President Lincoln's blockade of its coast. Swift ships ran the gantlet with little trouble at first, slipping in and out of Southern ports with precious supplies. To clear the James River of Yankee warships, Confederates fitted the captured Union frigate *Merrimac* with a superstructure of railroad iron, christened her *Virginia,* and set her to ramming wooden vessels off Norfolk. Federal officials wrung their hands, for this unwieldy but immune ironclad could bog down McClellan's Peninsula Campaign if it gained control of the lower Chesapeake Bay.

Then the U.S.S. *Monitor,* launched in the nick of time, puffed into Hampton Roads after a grueling voyage from New York. On March 9, 1862, she intercepted the slope-sided *Merrimac* steaming out to finish off the wooden *Minnesota,* which had been run aground the day before. The point-blank, slam-bang brawl between the two monsters (above) was a horror to their crews. The clanging, smoke-choked traps fought to a draw, but after the Rebels evacuated Norfolk the *Merrimac* was abandoned and burned. The *Monitor* eventually sank in a storm, but not before Northerners were smoking "El Monitor" cigars and dancing "Ericsson's Galop" in honor of John Ericsson, designer of the "cheesebox on a raft."

Federal ships and sailors, helped by young powder monkeys (right), gradually tightened the blockade. The South felt the pinch, and soon haughty plantation ladies were growing food; were spinning, weaving, and dyeing.

LIBRARY OF CONGRESS

The Gray holds fast at Fredericksburg

IN LATE OCTOBER, 1862, the President sent a telegram to McClellan: "I have just read your despatch about sore tongued and fatiegued horses. Will you pardon me for asking what the horses of your army have done since the battle of Antietam that fatigue anything?" McClellan had been sitting north of the Potomac, afflicted with what Lincoln called "the slows." Lee, refitting his army in Virginia, welcomed the respite.

In November, McClellan was replaced by Gen. Ambrose E. Burnside, famed for his side whiskers, a brave and honest man who believed he was not competent to lead such an army. He was right. The proof came when he took his troops into action at Fredericksburg on the banks of the Rappahannock.

Fredericksburg—a Virginia town rich in history, where Washington's mother once lived, where Monroe had a law office, where John Paul Jones kept house. Its colonial buildings still rise from the waterfront, and behind them can still be seen the high ground Lee's men lined with cannon and rifles that December day.

They had waited three weeks for the Federals to cross the river and attack and in that time had perfected their defenses—trenches south of town and a fine position in a sunken road at the foot of Marye's Heights just back of town. The gentle slope dropping toward the town from the sunken road is built up with new houses today. In 1862 it was a field. "A chicken cannot live on that field when we open on it," said one Rebel. Lee could scarcely believe that his new opponent, Burn-

side, would actually test such defenses. But as fog rolled away on the morning of December 13, here came massed blue regiments, stepping proudly with flags flying.

They struck at the trenches where Jackson commanded, and some nearly broke the tough Rebel line. Then the gray heaved the blue back.

Watching, Lee turned to Gen. James Longstreet, one of his trusted lieutenants: "It is well that war is so terrible —we should grow too fond of it!"

Incredibly, Burnside sent wave after wave of troops straight at Marye's Heights. The brown winter grass below it turned blue with bodies as the sunken road flashed and roared its answer. Yet on they came again and again, only to be shredded by massed artillery and a sheet of flame from tight-packed riflemen. Those on the firing line passed empty rifles back and got loaded ones in return, and their shots blended into a continuous snarl.

One gallant Yankee officer got 30 yards from the road before bullets riddled him. Old Union outfits that had earned the Rebels' respect at Manassas and Antietam seemed to vie with each other to see which made it nearest the road before being cut down.

Wounded lay 30 hours on freezing mud after that useless butchery. Poor, shaken Burnside finally left, and Lee wondered if he could have destroyed the whole Army of the Potomac.

Fredericksburg in winter's grip seemed peaceful as Federals awaited pontoons to cross the Rappahannock. Death lurked beyond the town. Prof. Thaddeus Lowe's balloons spotted Rebel works. Fired on often by rifled cannon, not one was shot down.

WIRT A. CHRISTIAN, JR., VIRGINIA STATE LIBRARY
ABOVE: LIBRARY OF CONGRESS

"GENERAL DOUBLEDAY CROSSING THE POTOMAC (JUNE, 1863)" BY DAVID G. BLYTHE, NATIONAL BASEBALL HALL OF FAME AND MUSEUM, COOPERSTOWN

Two roads to Gettysburg

LEE, PERCHED ABOVE FREDERICKSBURG, wondered what "those people" would do next. In January, 1863, Burnside's Army of the Potomac tried to move along its side of the Rappahannock and bogged down in winter mud while Rebel pickets hooted. That was all for Burnside. Handsome, flamboyant "Fighting Joe" Hooker replaced him. In April he crossed the river with more than 100,000 men.

Lee and Jackson daringly split forces. Lee held fast while Jackson led 28,000 troops around to hit the enemy flank. The Park Service preserves Jackson's route, a twisting, somehow ominous road through sunless woods around Chancellorsville. Motorists following it sense that they are slipping past the front of a great army, turning finally to strike it unawares. Cars humming east on Virginia Highway 3 recall to life the Rebel attack, for right here sat tired Yankees cooking supper on May 2 when Jackson struck with a howl and a crash of guns, rolling the Union flank up in a tangle while Lee smashed the front.

Brilliantly, Hooker got his men back across the river, but that was all for "Fighting Joe." Lincoln paced the White House moaning, "My God! My God! What *will* the country say?" Lee moaned too in the midst of triumph, for Jackson had been accidentally wounded by his own men. "Tell him to make haste and get well," said Lee. "He has lost his left arm; but I have lost my right arm." But Jackson died a few days later at Chandler's cottage, now restored.

To throw Union strategy off balance again and so relieve pressure against Confederate forces in the West, Lee marched north to Pennsylvania. Jubilantly his

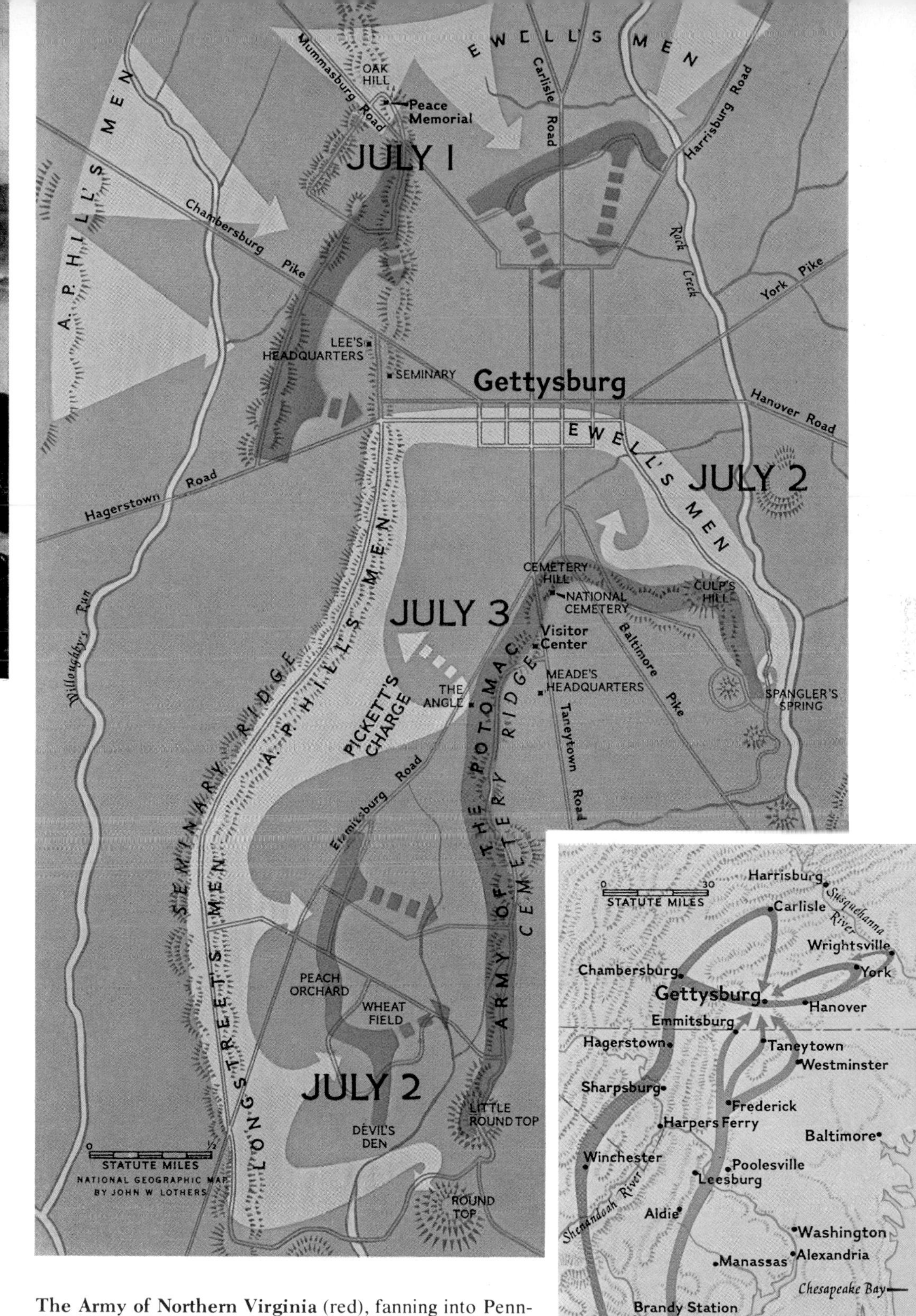

The Army of Northern Virginia (red), fanning into Pennsylvania, raced for Gettysburg when two of Lee's corps swamped Meade's advance units July 1. The Yankees held north of town, broke, then reformed on Cemetery Hill as the Army of the Potomac moved up. Lee hit the flanks July 2, smashed a salient in the Peach Orchard. Next day Pickett charged to the "high-water mark of the Confederacy."

NORTH-SOUTH SKIRMISHERS WATCH TARGETS AT A GETTYSBURG MEETING. PHOTOGRAPHS BY THOMAS NEBBIA.

veterans swung through country rich "like a land full of blubber to a Greenlander." But Lee lost touch with Jeb Stuart's cavalry, so was blind to actions of the Army of the Potomac, now led by scholarly George G. Meade.

Dispersed Rebel columns headed generally for Harrisburg. On June 30 a brigade marched toward the sleepy village of Gettysburg to find shoes. Instead they found Union cavalry. Next day a strong Southern force investigated. By now the Yankee troopers were backed up by some very straight-shooting, unafraid infantry. Rebel skirmishers cursed, so the story goes, "See those damn black hats? That ain't no militia—that's the Army of the Potomac." They had collided with the crack Iron Brigade, Midwesterners in black felt hats. Confederate troops came up faster than Federal. Even the Iron

ORNATE CONFEDERATE CAVALRY UNIFORM, PAUL JENSEN

UNION "TROOPS" MAN A FENCE NEAR SPANGLER'S SPRING
RIGHT: WELL-DRESSED YANKEE TROOPER AND (ABOVE) A REBEL DRUMMER BOY
PPOSITE: POWDER SMOKE FROM MUZZLE-LOADERS WREATHES THE FIRING LINE

Authentic weapons,
old uniforms, and the
gentle meadows of
Gettysburg.
Thus another generation
relives in its own way
the testing time
for all that was brave,
and firm, and true,
in all Americans.

Brigade couldn't hold them, nor the other Yankee veterans hurrying to the sound of guns. The men of two of Lee's great corps, A. P. Hill's and Richard Ewell's, tore into the fray. And as the sun lowered over those fenced fields north and west of town the Yankees drew back through the streets to Cemetery Hill, where a sign warned that use of firearms was prohibited.

Lee, sniffing another victory, urged Ewell to attack the hill and smash "those people" once more, but bald, wooden-legged Dick Ewell felt his troops could not take it. During the night, Lee spread his army from the streets of the town along a low, wooded rise extending south—Seminary Ridge, where today's Park Service road passes battery after battery of cannon.

Meade meanwhile was bringing up his army as fast as he could and placing it along a parallel rise, Cemetery Ridge.

Hit the flanks, Lee orders. On July 2 Ewell's guns open up and Longstreet moves out.

To parry the threat to the Union left, Gen. Daniel Sickles moves his men forward a mile to occupy higher ground in a peach orchard and wheat field. He anchors this salient on Devil's Den, that jumble of rocks where children like to play soldier.

The Rebs are not playing in 1863. Longstreet hammers at Sickles's salient, meanwhile reaching toward that stony hill, Little Round Top, at the end of the Union line. Undefended! Texans and Alabamians spring for it, but the Federals see the danger and rush men to hold it. A Maine regiment fights off overwhelming numbers among the rocks; support comes; the Yankee flank is saved. At Culp's Hill on the other flank, Ewell's infantry attacks at dusk. Fighting roars into the night

Devil's Den, haven for the sniper, fell to Confederates July 2. This Rebel fashioned a citadel of rocks. Then a shellburst took his life.

Little Round Top, bitterly contested on the second day, looks out over the now-serene wheat field and, beyond, the meadows of Pickett's charge. The first of Hill's Rebels approached Gettysburg at top right of picture on July 1. Spotters in the Seminary cupola warned Federal Gen. John F. Reynolds. Soon a bullet cut him down.

ALEXANDER GARDNER, LIBRARY OF CONGRESS. ABOVE: MERLE SEVERY, NATIONAL GEOGRAPHIC STAFF

as Rebels gain the crest, only to be heaved off next morning. Exhausted, smoke-blackened men fill canteens at Spangler's Spring.

At noon on July 3, portentous calm. Flies buzz and the scent of hay drifts through the weary battle lines. Then at one P.M. two cannon bellow, and in answer to the signal 138 Southern guns open, their shrieking shells plastering the Union line. Yankee guns reply and the earth shakes. Men huddle numb and deaf from the explosions. And then silence. Out from the wooded Confederate line step Pickett's Virginians and other crack troops. They align. Red flags brighten the butternut ranks. Gen. George Pickett, curly-haired and debonair, gestures them forward. And along the Yankee line Meade's brave men half rise to admire this last great massed charge, then nestle behind stone walls and cock their rifles.

Stand today beside the statue of Lee on Seminary Ridge and look across the field. It's not quite a mile to that other ridge. But it seems so far . . . so very far.

When they walked it that July day, cannon plowing them, rifles biting at them, it seemed to take so long. Yes, they reached that clump of trees. They broke through, crumpled. A few came back. "All this has been my fault," said Lee.

WAR IN THE WEST

"Unconditional Surrender" Grant sweeps the rivers

A DIFFERENT WAR thundered beyond the Appalachians, fought by a different breed of men—big and boisterous. They marched along thickly wooded river valleys, hip-deep in mud. They fought across steep ridges and through dense thickets. The confused western campaign pivoted around a soldier neither big nor boisterous, but stubbornly confident: Ulysses S. Grant. A West Pointer and Mexican War veteran, he cropped up in 1861 as an obscure colonel who soon tamed an unruly Illinois regiment. He became a brigadier, based at Cairo, Illinois, the jumping-off place for any river campaign.

Grant wangled permission to strike along the rivers. He joined forces with a gunboat fleet under Flag Officer Andrew Foote, and the expedition went puffing and thrashing south, up the Tennessee River to Fort Henry, a Southern stronghold. Between high water from the flooded river and hell from Foote's naval guns, Fort Henry collapsed like a soggy sand castle.

Over on the Cumberland River stood Fort Donelson—a tougher proposition. But Grant pressed his attack and forced down Rebel throats his demand for "unconditional and immediate surrender." This, the North's first major victory, brought fame to "Unconditional Surrender" Grant, and with it hundreds of gift cigars. A pipe smoker, he switched lest they be wasted.

As spring of 1862 approached, Grant moved farther up the Tennessee to cut Rebel communications. Grant planned to attack, but on the peaceful Sunday morning of

Ulysses S. Grant, shy and amiable, had resigned from the army and failed in various businesses when the Civil War called forth greatness. At Shiloh his men fought savagely to hold the Hornets' Nest salient (right).

MATHEW B. BRADY, 1864, LIBRARY OF CONGRESS

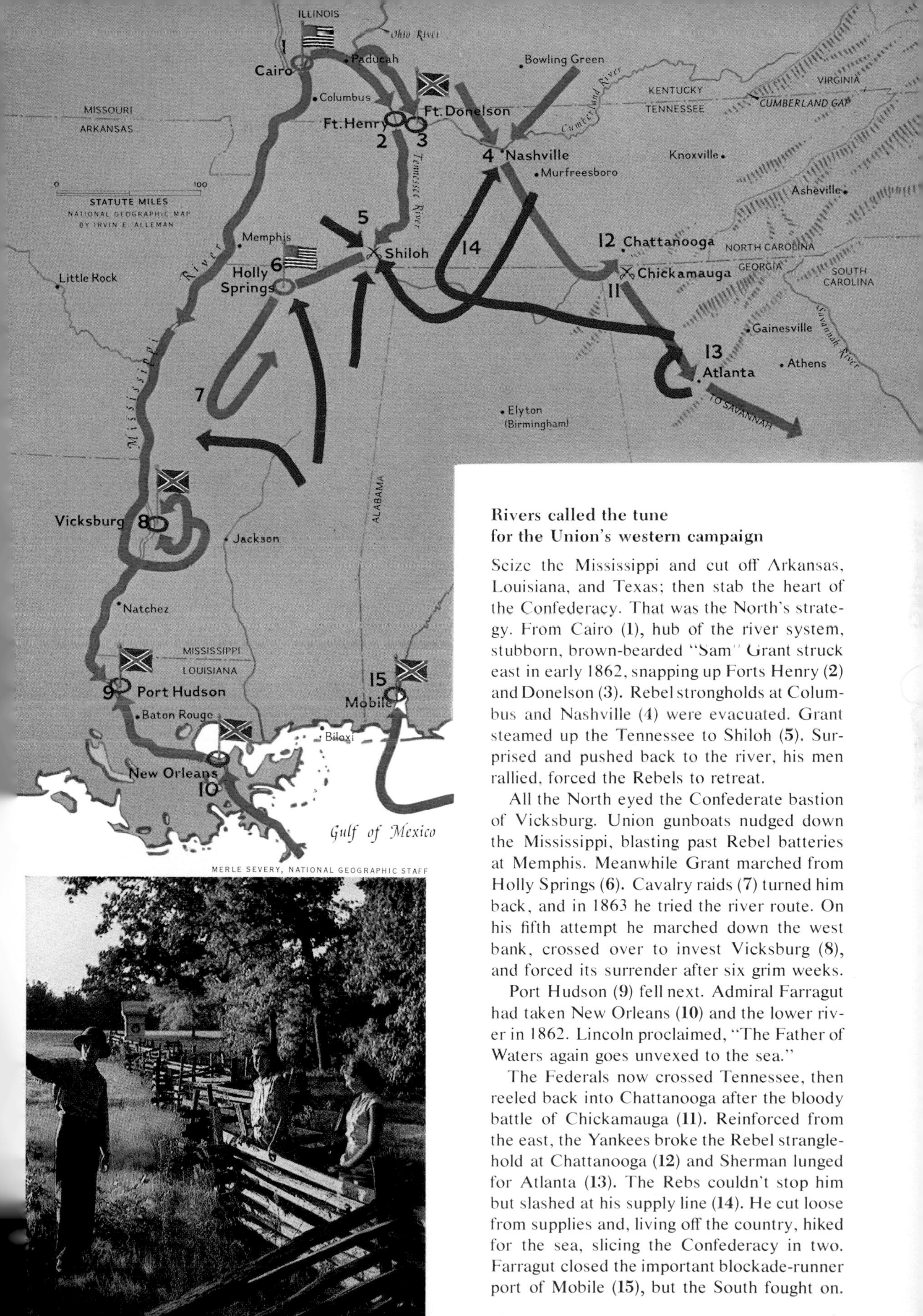

MERLE SEVERY, NATIONAL GEOGRAPHIC STAFF

Rivers called the tune for the Union's western campaign

Seize the Mississippi and cut off Arkansas, Louisiana, and Texas; then stab the heart of the Confederacy. That was the North's strategy. From Cairo (1), hub of the river system, stubborn, brown-bearded "Sam" Grant struck east in early 1862, snapping up Forts Henry (2) and Donelson (3). Rebel strongholds at Columbus and Nashville (4) were evacuated. Grant steamed up the Tennessee to Shiloh (5). Surprised and pushed back to the river, his men rallied, forced the Rebels to retreat.

All the North eyed the Confederate bastion of Vicksburg. Union gunboats nudged down the Mississippi, blasting past Rebel batteries at Memphis. Meanwhile Grant marched from Holly Springs (6). Cavalry raids (7) turned him back, and in 1863 he tried the river route. On his fifth attempt he marched down the west bank, crossed over to invest Vicksburg (8), and forced its surrender after six grim weeks.

Port Hudson (9) fell next. Admiral Farragut had taken New Orleans (10) and the lower river in 1862. Lincoln proclaimed, "The Father of Waters again goes unvexed to the sea."

The Federals now crossed Tennessee, then reeled back into Chattanooga after the bloody battle of Chickamauga (11). Reinforced from the east, the Yankees broke the Rebel stranglehold at Chattanooga (12) and Sherman lunged for Atlanta (13). The Rebs couldn't stop him but slashed at his supply line (14). He cut loose from supplies and, living off the country, hiked for the sea, slicing the Confederacy in two. Farragut closed the important blockade-runner port of Mobile (15), but the South fought on.

April 6 the Rebels struck first in thunderous onslaught—a gray sea that curled from the woods southwest of Pittsburg Landing and broke like surf on surprised Federals near a little Methodist church named Shiloh. Union troops stumbled back, past the landmarks still visible at Shiloh National Military Park. The wooded land looks the same, but a new church replaces the log structure where Yankees under Sherman were shoved back. Sherman was dripping blood from a minor wound. Grant rode up and found him gory, dusty, with tie askew, but cheerful.

In the Peach Orchard bullets cut so many blossoms that they drifted down like snow to rest gently on the dead. A small wood lot behind a sunken road sheltered stubborn Federals who formed a blistering salient in the sagging line. Rebels called it the Hornets' Nest and finally captured it. But the Yankees held on the riverside bluffs while reinforcements arrived. Sherman repaid Grant's call that night: "We've had the devil's own day, haven't we?"

"Yes," said Grant. "Lick 'em tomorrow, though."

And tomorrow they did, storming back to regain all the lost ground. By nightfall the armies were back where they started—as if there never had been a battle of Shiloh, with more than 23,000 casualties.

But the draw meant defeat for the South. Grant couldn't be stopped except by his superiors, and even they allowed him to go after Vicksburg while another Union force, the Army of the Cumberland, started southeast from Nashville. But Rebels sprouted from the ground. The Cumberlands were badly mauled at Murfreesboro beside wintry Stones River; Grant's march was forced back by cavalry

HUGO H. HARPER. BELOW: CURRIER & IVES, MARINERS MUSEUM

From Cairo, Illinois, strategic rail and river junction, Grant steamed up the Ohio (right) to the mouth of the Tennessee on his way to attack Fort Henry. Then gunboats churned down the Mississippi to take Memphis. Later, shielding its coal barges behind squat ironclads, the fleet fought past Vicksburg's batteries (below).

"FIRST AT VICKSBURG," U.S. ARMY. RIGHT: THOMAS NEBBIA

raids; Sherman took a drubbing at Chickasaw Bluffs, just to the north of Vicksburg.

Vicksburg overlooked a horseshoe bend in the river—it has changed course since then—and was guarded by bluffs and swamps laced with bayous. Grant tried building a canal, tried widening streams so gunboats could wedge through, finally moved down the west bank while gunboats under Rear Admiral David D. Porter lashed supply transports alongside and dashed by the roaring Rebel guns.

Crossing back to the eastern bank south of Vicksburg, Grant cut loose from supplies, beat a Confederate force at Jackson, then rammed the Vicksburg garrison that had come out to meet him. The Rebels scampered back to town and Grant drew his lines tight.

Vicksburg was bagged but didn't know it. People lived in caves to duck shells and ate fried rats. Soldiers got so tired of trenches that they sometimes emerged in informal truces to talk and swap things. The siege lasted six weeks. On July 4,

1863, the same day that Lee sadly led his torn troops away from Gettysburg, Vicksburg surrendered. After so many nights of gunfire, soldiers on both sides found it hard to sleep in the stillness.

Now the Mississippi was a Union river. Confederates west of it could no longer play a big part in the war. But the South was far from licked, and Grant's next task was to split it again.

Off marched the Army of the Cumberland, fit once more after its blood bath at Murfreesboro, aiming for Chattanooga and sidling past Rebel defenders so that they had to give way. The city fell without a fight, and the Yankees pushed through and fanned out to net fleeing Rebels. But these Confederates weren't a bit panicked. With reinforcements flocking in, they

In bitter attacks Federals tried to crack Vicksburg's defenses and end the siege. Yankees dug trenches close to Rebel works and enemy soldiers met and chatted between skirmishes. A Confederate guard once turned out to salute Grant as he inspected nearby Union lines. Grant returned the salute.

At peace in Vicksburg National Military Park, warriors share disputed ground.

were turning into a very muscular army, for once outnumbering the Northerners. And when they saw the Federals split into scattered forces, they made their move.

South of Chattanooga, beyond the ridges that wall the city, Chickamauga Creek flows through gently undulating fields and forest. Today's national military park is well tended, many of its trees standing high and clean above cropped grass. In September, 1863, it was a lonely, remote region clogged with scrub growth and thickets. The dispersed Union elements sensed they were losing touch; a foreboding made them grope back toward each other. Then the thickets flamed with rifle fire and a great Rebel horde poured death into them.

The Confederates waited just too long to smash the Union forces piecemeal. For a day the Army of the Cumberland held its own. But as the battle flashed and smoked into the second day a Union division was moved out of line by error. Rebels poured through, where the Brotherton House now stands, and routed much of the Yankee army. The rest held on Snodgrass Hill where a log cabin remains. Here Union Gen. George H. Thomas became "The Rock of Chickamauga."

Even the Rock gave up after dark. The beaten Federals crept away and holed up in the safety of Chattanooga. The Confederates laid siege to the town and from

 Serene Chickamauga Creek witnessed 1863's savagery. At Lee and Gordon's Mills Rebels tested

FRANK VIZETELLY FOR ILLUSTRATED LONDON NEWS, 1863, LIBRARY OF CONGRESS. BELOW: THOMAS NEBBIA

the Yankee flank. Confederate Gen. John B. Hood was wounded (above) as battle blazed through a fog of smoke.

Lookout Mountain gave Rebels a bird's-eye view of the Chattanooga rail center where the Union army lay. The position fell when Grant moved to break the siege. Chewing a cigar, he later inspected the objective (right).

In Union Station stands the *General,* the engine that starred in the great locomotive chase a year before the battle. A party of daring Yanks in civilian dress traveled deep into Georgia, stole the *General,* and raced north to destroy railroad bridges and so isolate Chattanooga. Rebels gave chase in a handcar and three engines. Only 18 miles short of the city Andrews' Raiders ran out of fuel. They split up and fled but were caught. Eight were hanged.

NATIONAL ARCHIVES. ABOVE: THOMAS NEBBIA

Lookout Mountain and Missionary Ridge watched the Yankees starve. Then Grant arrived and with the aid of a jerry-built river steamer opened a "cracker line" that fed the Yanks. In November he set about lifting the siege.

THE HEIGHTS above Chattanooga offer one of the world's finest views of a city. And the story of the fight for them is one of the great legends of warfare. Sherman had arrived with his Army of the Tennessee; Hooker had pulled in with two corps of the Army of the Potomac. Grant told Sherman to take the northern end of Missionary Ridge, Hooker to strike at Lookout Mountain on the other Rebel flank.

Hooker drove the outnumbered Rebs off Lookout Mountain without much fuss. Newsmen rhapsodized over "The Battle above the Clouds."

Sherman ran into a great deal of fuss and bogged down. Meantime the Army of the Cumberland, now commanded by Thomas, ached for a chance to get into action, break loose from the town, and wipe out the stain of Chickamauga.

Grant finally unleashed these men to storm rifle pits at the foot of steep Missionary Ridge. They poured over the pits like a wild blue wave, paused, then suddenly *sprang for the summit of the ridge*—without orders, without organization, with nothing in mind except to get up there and win.

It's a murderous climb, yet those men *raced* each other up while Rebels poured rifle fire into them, rolled cannon balls, cannon, and rocks down on them. Then all at once the Confederate troops turned tail and ran as though the sight of that vengeful blue tide were too much.

Chattanooga was wide open. The bitterness of Chickamauga was forgotten in the sweetness of Missionary Ridge.

MATHEW B. BRADY, LIBRARY OF CONGRESS

Sherman smashes Atlanta and

YOU COULD LOOK into the face of William Tecumseh Sherman and tell that by now he knew all about war. "Like the thunderbolt," he said, war "follows its laws and turns not aside even if the beautiful, the virtuous and the charitable stand in its path."

In March, 1864, he was allowed to wage his kind of campaign. Grant, called to Washington, handed him the victorious Union armies at Chattanooga and ordered him to crush Atlanta.

Sherman moved south along much the same path that U. S. Highway 41 follows today. When Rebel Gen. Joseph E. Johnston dug in at the mountain passes, Sherman simply swung around him. But at Kennesaw Mountain near

Rebels overrun a battery and a brick house just east of Atlanta, then fire from behind cotton bales as blue-clad Yanks counterattack. Federals kill horses (center) to prevent guns being

drives to the sea

Marietta, Georgia, he attacked frontally. Old cannon now brood along the crest that saw 2,500 Yanks die in the assault. Yet on September 2 Sherman could wire Lincoln, "Atlanta is ours, and fairly won!" Battered Rebs had slipped out of the city and begun a northwest march that would lead to a disastrous Southern defeat at Nashville, Tennessee. Sherman didn't follow. He proposed instead a march to the sea that would "make all Georgia howl."

On November 10 he ordered Atlanta's factories and depots burned, but his men got out of hand and the whole city went up in flames. Then 60,000 bluecoats swung off in four columns spread 60 miles wide. No army opposed them. "Bummers," or foragers, stripped every plantation of animals and food, then aided other soldiers in burning bridges, mills, barns, and houses. In late December Lincoln received a telegram from Sherman: "I beg to present you as a Christmas gift the city of Savannah. . . ." The General set up headquarters in the Green-Meldrim House and in February, 1865, set off again with his army, this time driving north through the Carolinas toward beleaguered Richmond.

hauled away. Twin-humped Kennesaw Mountain rises to the north. General Hood, who lost a leg at Chickamauga, defended the city but failed in desperate thrusts at Sherman's columns.

SCENE FROM THE 400-FOOT CYCLORAMA OF "THE BATTLE OF ATLANTA," PAINTED BY GERMAN ARTISTS IN THE 1880'S, COURTESY CITY OF ATLANTA

Gun muzzle to gun muzzle, the Union *Hartford* and the Confederate ironclad *Tennessee* swap fire in Mobile Bay. Admiral Farragut, clinging to the rigging for a better view,

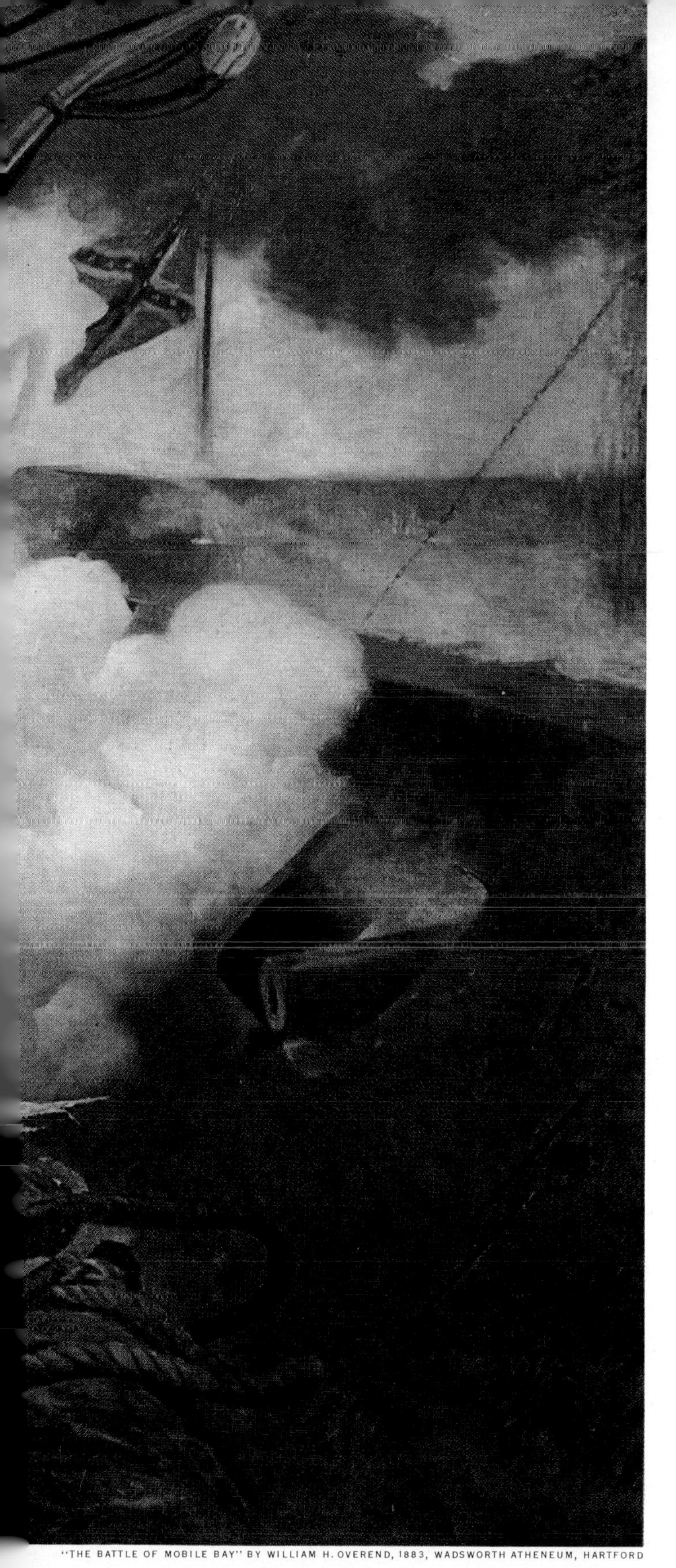

"THE BATTLE OF MOBILE BAY" BY WILLIAM H. OVEREND, 1883, WADSWORTH ATHENEUM, HARTFORD

watched shot bounce off the Rebel's six-inch armor, then ordered his wooden ships to ram her. Finally a monitor with 11-inch guns pounded her into helplessness and surrender.

Farragut at Mobile Bay

ON A SPIT of sand that almost severs Mobile Bay from the Gulf of Mexico stands an old sun-blistered fort called Morgan. Today children play around its cannon while parents admire the view from its ramparts.

On August 5, 1864, the cannon spewed death while a proud old warrior named David Glasgow Farragut, a salt since the age of nine, drove another nail in the coffin of Confederate hopes.

He sought to seal off Mobile, last important Rebel port on the Gulf. To do so meant running under Morgan's big guns. Shallows and torpedoes (as mines were called then) closed the rest of the entrance to the bay.

In the gray glimmer of dawn he sent his ships in. The fort's batteries opened fire, "mowing down the men, deluging the decks with blood." Amid the carnage, Farragut's lead ship faltered and blocked the channel. Almost simultaneously a monitor struck a torpedo and sank, her screw churning the air.

The admiral made a quick decision: "Damn the torpedoes! ... full speed!" His *Hartford* swung around the blocking ship, through the mine field, and into Mobile Bay. His fleet followed.

At eight o'clock, true to a promise, he had all hands piped to breakfast. Two hours later he battered a Rebel ram helpless. Fort Morgan fell and Mobile Bay found itself a Yankee "lake."

GRANT'S JUG HANDLE CAMPAIGN

"I propose to fight it out on this line . . ."

On a raw day in March, 1864, Ulysses S. Grant showed up in Washington to meet Mr. Lincoln, receive promotion to lieutenant general, and take command of Union troops in all theaters of war—more than half a million soldiers spread over half a continent. Grant and the nation both knew that his real task was to knock Robert E. Lee and the Army of Northern Virginia out of the war. No one was surprised when Grant called the tune for the Army of the Potomac, though General Meade, victor at Gettysburg, remained its commander.

Grant and Lee, the two champions, came to grips in early May when the Federals crossed the Rapidan River in Virginia and moved toward Richmond, passing into the same haunted forest where Stonewall Jackson had marched in the Battle of Chancellorsville exactly a year before. This time the Battle of the Wilderness stopped the Union advance. In gloomy woods and underbrush death came unseen. Officers led charges with one eye on their compasses. Friends fired into friends. Wounded men burned to death as artillery wadding set dry brush afire.

When Grant pulled out, soldiers on both sides expected a Union retreat north of the Rapidan to refit and plan new strategy. But this general was no McClellan or Pope or Burnside or Hooker. He sent the Army of the Potomac sidling to its left and then turned it south—toward Richmond. And Yankee veterans who had already faced death countless times knew they must face it again; yet they cheered because *this* was no retreat.

Lee saw what his new adversary was up to and raced to stop him. Five times the same maneuvers were etched on the map of Virginia—the South scrambling to meet the swinging blows of the North, Grant hitting hard, then circling around and hitting hard again farther south, so that his route looked like a series of jug handles (see map).

It was butchery, this new, relentless campaign: charred bodies in the Wilderness, the heaped-up dead and wounded around the Bloody Angle at Spotsylvania, where men stood on the bodies of their comrades to get at each other with bullets, bayonets, rifle butts, fists, and fingernails. Decades have passed since entrenched Rebels cut down Grant's

Park rangers still harvest Minié balls from duff in the Wilderness, at Spotsylvania, and at Cold Harbor (right), where these conical rifle bullets reaped thousands of young lives. In one field of fire trees more than 20 inches thick crashed down as slugs gnawed away the wood.

PAUL JENSEN AND (RIGHT) EDWARDS PARK, NATIONAL GEOGRAPHIC STAFF

Washington
Manassas
Fredericksburg
Richmond
Rapidan River
Rappahannock River
North Anna River
James River
Appomattox River
Potomac River
York River
Chesapeake Bay

0 25
STATUTE MILES
NATIONAL GEOGRAPHIC MAP
BY IRVIN E. ALLEMAN

1 Culpeper

The Army of the Potomac lies in camp near Culpeper in the spring of 1864, when Grant receives over-all command of the Union forces. He comes to supervise the activities of General Meade and stays with the army.

2 Wilderness

Fording the Rapidan, the Federals head south and are met by Lee in the Wilderness, May 5-6. In a vicious and confused fight, the woods catch fire, burning thousands of wounded. There is no clear decision, but Grant pulls his men out. Instead of retreating north to lick his wounds as other Federal commanders have done, Grant stays south of the Rapidan and moves on toward Richmond.

3 Spotsylvania

Lee faces Grant again at Spotsylvania, May 8-19. Stopped, Grant retreats again, but still southward. He proposes to "fight it out on this line if it takes all summer." It takes all summer, and all winter too, but Grant has replacements and Lee hasn't.

4 North Anna

Grant's next flanking movement is met by Lee at the North Anna River. The Federals take one look at the Rebel trenches, May 23, and pull out without offering battle.

5 Cold Harbor

Rolling toward Richmond, Grant gets within sight of its steeples, then finds Lee entrenched again at Cold Harbor. In a futile, badly prepared assault, Union troops pin paper "dog tags" on their tunics and go over the top, only to be cut down in droves in about 20 minutes of butchery, June 3.

6 Petersburg

Badly whipped, the Union army swings south of Richmond, crosses the James, and drives on Petersburg, for once catching Lee short. Richmond is close to crumpling June 9, but remembering Cold Harbor, overcautious Federals probe the feeble Rebel lines, then settle down to nearly 10 months of trench warfare.

7 Five Forks

Spearheaded by Phil Sheridan, Grant's force smashes Lee's flank at Five Forks, April 1, 1865. Grant orders an attack all along the Petersburg front. The weary Confederates cave in. Richmond falls April 3. Lee's men withdraw west toward the mountains.

8 Appomattox Court House

Union troops race the decimated Rebels west. Sheridan's cavalry gets to Appomattox Court House first, blocking the way. When the Confederates coil to drive through, the troopers trot aside, revealing long, grim lines of blue-clad infantry. The game is up. Lee calls for terms and finally meets Grant face to face at the McLean House, April 9. "Don't cheer," Grant orders his troops. "The Rebels are our countrymen again."

charging regiments at Cold Harbor. But the place chills the visitor with its trenches, rounded by the years, still waiting in the forest. Here fell 7,000 Federals within less than half an hour—more casualties in minutes than all those recorded for the entire War of 1812! "I have always regretted," wrote Grant years later, "the last assault on Cold Harbor."

Grant's plan to bludgeon straight down to Richmond had failed. He had misjudged Lee and the enormous staying power of the Army of Northern Virginia. But Grant could be deft as well as stubborn and he proved it by spiriting 100,000 Union troops from under Lee's nose, stealing across the James River, and moving on Petersburg, vital rail center south of Richmond. Only a handful of hastily assembled Confederates managed to bluff the Federal van out of walking right into town and perhaps ending the war. But the Union field commanders hesitated, Lee rushed into position, and both armies dug in for prolonged trench warfare, June 1864 to April 1865.

IT WAS GRIM AND FILTHY. Men lived in dust or mud, their blue or butternut uniforms taking on a universal moldy yellow tinge. Sharpshooters picked off anyone who showed himself; mortars thumped down on the trenches with nice precision. Yet sometimes soldiers would arrange informal cease fires and converse across no man's land.

As summer progressed, Rebels in one sector kept hearing faint sounds of metal striking earth under their feet. Coal miners from a Pennsylvania regiment tunneled 511 feet from their own trench and set a charge of gunpowder. Early on July 30 the mine was exploded, blowing men, horses, and cannon sky-high and digging a huge crater.

Yankees poured into the breach and again it seemed that the war might end. But though the Army of the Potomac was generally a first-rate fighting force, it still had weaknesses in organization and they showed up now. The attack fizzled. Men milled around in the bottom of the crater without leadership. The shaken Rebels reformed and began slaughtering Yankees at close range. So the big pit that remains today at Petersburg National Battlefield proved nothing. "The saddest affair I have witnessed in the war," General Grant said.

To divert Grant, Lee sent bearded Jubal Early out to the Shenandoah Valley to stir up trouble. General Early whipped the Yankees, crossed into Maryland, and swept down on the capital like a grizzled Genghis Khan. Washington was used to crises and accepted this one coolly though its forts were ill-prepared and its troops mostly invalids and headquarters men. Early got inside the District of Columbia, within sight of the Capitol dome, before some of Grant's veterans swung into Fort Stevens and scared him off. Lincoln came out to glimpse war and insisted on walking the parapet in his tall hat while Rebels sniped at him. His officers told him to "get down, you damn fool!" And grinning a little, he did.

Weary Union veterans squat in the mud of Petersburg's trenches during a 10-month siege. Grant finally broke Lee's lines on April 1, 1865, forcing the Rebels to abandon Richmond. But not before the Confederates put to the torch supplies and stores of tobacco. Southern troops and citizens fled across Mayo's Bridge from an inferno of flaming warehouses and exploding ammunition.

CURRIER & IVES, LIBRARY OF CONGRESS. BELOW: MATHEW B. BRADY, 1865, NATIONAL ARCHIVES

Rude, pugnacious Gen. Philip H. Sheridan chased Early through the Shenandoah Valley. The story goes that Sheridan's chaplain kept asking him to pause for Sunday service, and "Fighting Phil" finally consented one peaceful Sabbath, "if you let me announce the hymn." The chaplain agreed, the men assembled, and Sheridan announced: "Hymn 42: 'Early my God I will seek thy face'!"

Sheridan cleaned out the Valley. Back on the Petersburg lines Lee's gaunt army made a last gallant attack, seizing Fort Stedman but losing it again. The end was coming along with spring in 1865, and everyone knew it.

On April 1 Sheridan smashed Lee's flank at Five Forks. Grant hit the Rebel line early on the 2d. Gunfire from Lee's trenches dimmed and winked out like candles of hope. Petersburg fell. President Davis was in St. Paul's Church, Richmond, when a messenger whispered and he rose and left. Richmond fell.

Gamely Lee raced his hungry, beaten soldiers westward, but Grant moved faster. At last the Confederate van met a line of Yankee cavalry blocking their way, and when guns were rolled up, the troopers moved aside and disclosed a front bristling with Federal infantry. The end had come.

On Palm Sunday, April 9, 1865, Lee and Grant, the two great antagonists, met face to face in the small brick McLean home at Appomattox Court House. They spoke quietly of arranging terms imposing the least hardship on men in the ranks, of feeding the starving Confederates. When Lee left, Grant raised his hat in salute. Lee answered the gesture and rode toward his men, ragged, decimated, crowding around him now to touch his stirrup and shout, "God bless you, Uncle Robert!"

Somewhere on the Federal line troops cheered. Grant ordered silence. "The Rebels are our countrymen again."

It would never be quite the same country. More than 600,000 had died, as many as in all our other wars combined. The bleeding nation faced the agony of reconstruction. But it was a nation. Once more these were the United States.

MATHEW B. BRADY OR ALEXANDER GARDNER, 1865, LIBRARY OF CONGRESS. BELOW: BURTON HISTORICAL COLLECTION, DETROIT PUBLIC LIBRARY
OPPOSITE: LEE SURRENDERS TO GRANT AT APPOMATTOX COURT HOUSE, PAINTED FOR NATIONAL GEOGRAPHIC BY TOM LOVELL

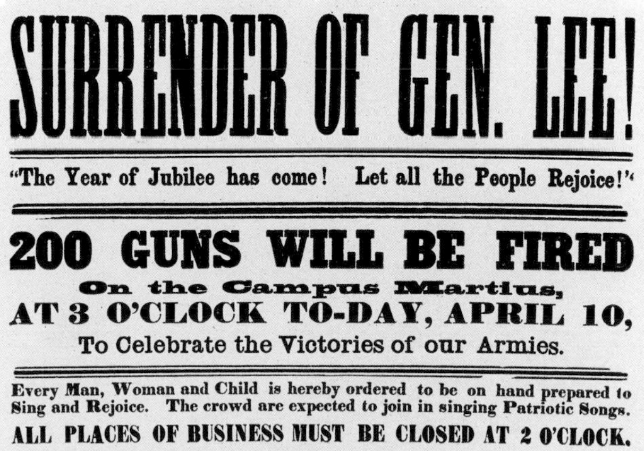

SURRENDER OF GEN. LEE!

"The Year of Jubilee has come! Let all the People Rejoice!"

200 GUNS WILL BE FIRED

On the Campus Martius,

AT 3 O'CLOCK TO-DAY, APRIL 10,

To Celebrate the Victories of our Armies.

Every Man, Woman and Child is hereby ordered to be on hand prepared to Sing and Rejoice. The crowd are expected to join in singing Patriotic Songs.

ALL PLACES OF BUSINESS MUST BE CLOSED AT 2 O'CLOCK.

Hurrah for Grant and his noble Army.

By Order of the People.

In jubilation, Union armies parade up Pennsylvania Avenue in Washington. Lee's surrender (in the McLean House, opposite) was followed by Joseph E. Johnston's to Sherman. Devastating in war, Sherman proved as generous as Grant in victory. Broadsides like the one (left) appearing in Detroit urged celebrations. But tragedy accompanied triumph. Lincoln, who longed for peace, barely lived to see it.

THE STORY OF ABRAHAM LINCOLN

IT WAS APRIL 8, 1865, the day before Appomattox. The President had visited Richmond, ravaged by pillagers, partly blackened by fire. From their homes the conquered had stared silently at the conqueror. War's terror still hung in the air. As the President boarded the *River Queen* for Washington a military band struck up. To the musicians' surprise, the President called for "Dixie." He wanted it to be a good-will song of the reunited states. That was Abraham Lincoln.

Carl Sandburg summed him up in these words: "Not often in the story of mankind does a man arrive on earth who is both steel and velvet, who is as hard as rock and soft as drifting fog, who holds in his heart and mind the paradox of terrible storm and peace unspeakable and perfect."

He was only 22 when he arrived as "a piece of floating driftwood" at New Salem, Illinois, a log-cabin village crowning a bluff above the Sangamon River. Lincoln was used to cabins. He had been born in one in the Kentucky Barrens, second child of Thomas and Nancy Hanks Lincoln. He had lived five years as a child in another on nearby Knob Creek, and to him this first remembered home forever represented "stinted living."

The family had moved on to Indiana and Abe worked the land and "went to A.B.C. schools by the littles." At 19 he helped drift a flatboat of produce down the Ohio and Mississippi rivers to New Orleans. Now in New Salem he worked in the store and mill of Denton Offutt who, as he recalled in his third-person autobiography, "conceved a liking for A., believing he could turn him to account."

New Salem offered opportunities surprising in a pioneer community never larger than 25 homes and stores. Lincoln debated, "studied English grammar, imperfectly, of course," and mathematics. He ran for the state legislature telling the voters that if he lost, "I have been too familiar with disappointments to be very much chagrined." He lost. But in 1834 he tried again and won. He began law studies "in good earnest."

W. D. VAUGHN

Reconstructed New Salem, Illinois (left), recalls Abe Lincoln the Rail Splitter. He came at 22, 13 years after burying his mother near Rockport, Indiana. A "friend of her Martyred Son" erected the stone (right).

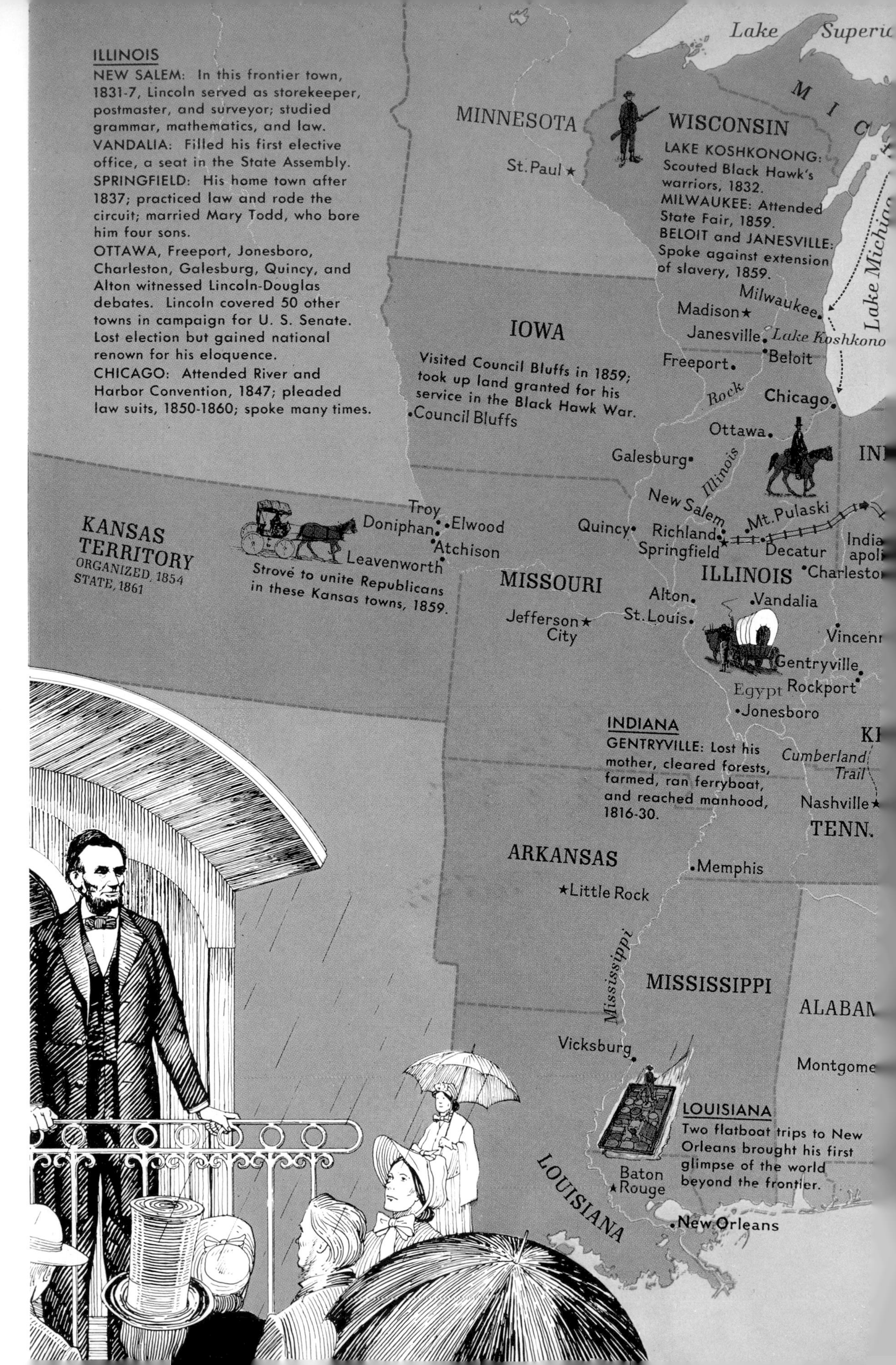
ILLINOIS
NEW SALEM: In this frontier town, 1831-7, Lincoln served as storekeeper, postmaster, and surveyor; studied grammar, mathematics, and law.
VANDALIA: Filled his first elective office, a seat in the State Assembly.
SPRINGFIELD: His home town after 1837; practiced law and rode the circuit; married Mary Todd, who bore him four sons.
OTTAWA, Freeport, Jonesboro, Charleston, Galesburg, Quincy, and Alton witnessed Lincoln-Douglas debates. Lincoln covered 50 other towns in campaign for U. S. Senate. Lost election but gained national renown for his eloquence.
CHICAGO: Attended River and Harbor Convention, 1847; pleaded law suits, 1850-1860; spoke many times.
MINNESOTA
St. Paul
WISCONSIN
LAKE KOSHKONONG: Scouted Black Hawk's warriors, 1832.
MILWAUKEE: Attended State Fair, 1859.
BELOIT and JANESVILLE: Spoke against extension of slavery, 1859.
Lake Superior
Lake Michigan
Milwaukee
Madison
Janesville
Lake Koshkonong
Beloit
Freeport
Rock
Chicago
IOWA
Visited Council Bluffs in 1859; took up land granted for his service in the Black Hawk War.
Council Bluffs
Ottawa
Galesburg
Illinois
New Salem
Mt. Pulaski
Quincy
Richland
Springfield
Decatur
ILLINOIS
Charleston
KANSAS TERRITORY
ORGANIZED, 1854
STATE, 1861
Troy
Elwood
Doniphan
Atchison
Leavenworth
Strove to unite Republicans in these Kansas towns, 1859.
MISSOURI
Jefferson City
Alton
St. Louis
Vandalia
Vincennes
Gentryville
Rockport
Egypt
Jonesboro
INDIANA
GENTRYVILLE: Lost his mother, cleared forests, farmed, ran ferryboat, and reached manhood, 1816-30.
Cumberland Trail
Nashville
TENN.
ARKANSAS
Little Rock
Memphis
Mississippi
MISSISSIPPI
ALABAMA
Vicksburg
Montgomery
LOUISIANA
Two flatboat trips to New Orleans brought his first glimpse of the world beyond the frontier.
LOUISIANA
Baton Rouge
New Orleans

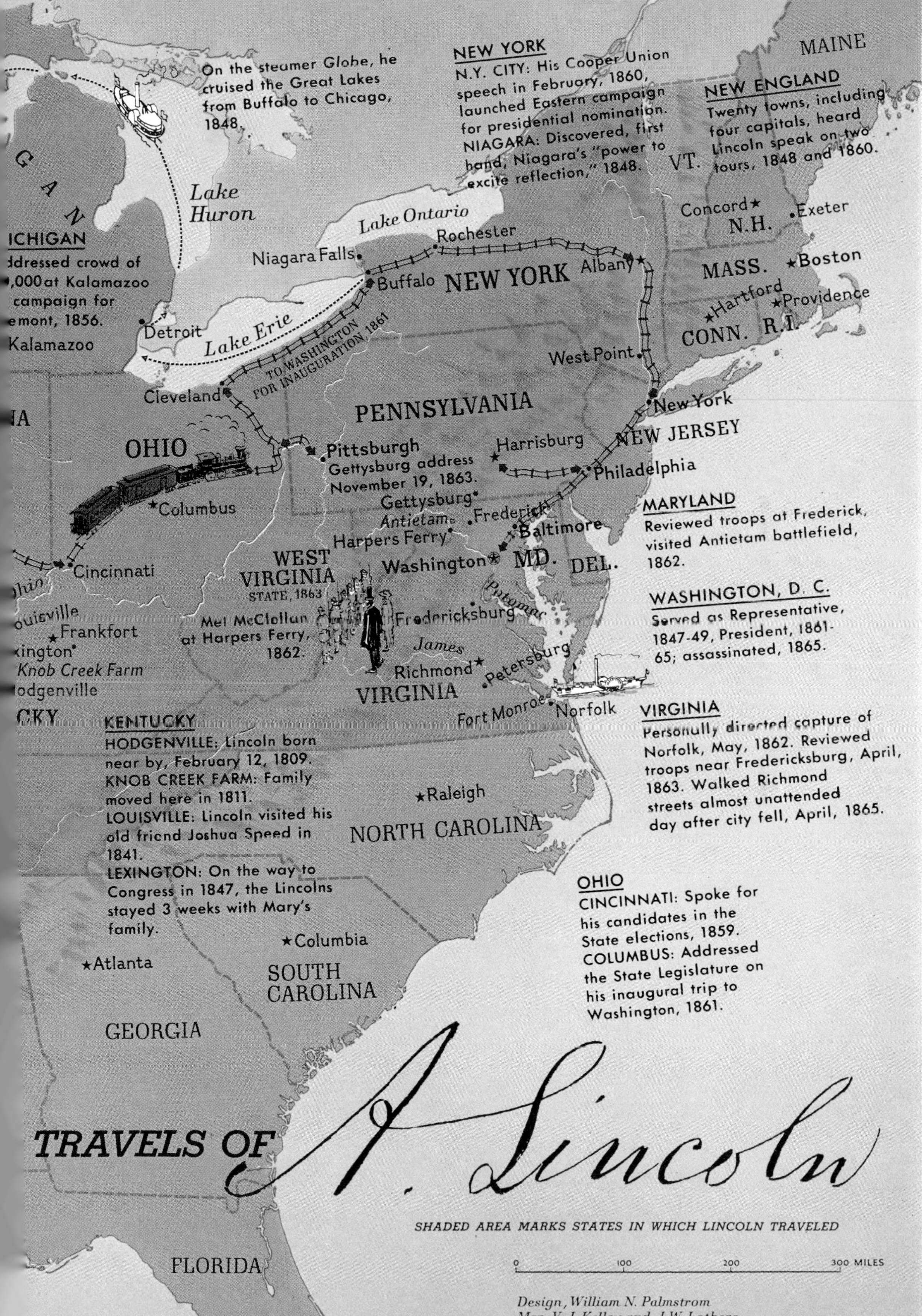

CANADA
On the steamer Globe, he cruised the Great Lakes from Buffalo to Chicago, 1848.
NEW YORK
N.Y. CITY: His Cooper Union speech in February, 1860, launched Eastern campaign for presidential nomination.
NIAGARA: Discovered, first hand, Niagara's "power to excite reflection," 1848.
MAINE
NEW ENGLAND
Twenty towns, including four capitals, heard Lincoln speak on two tours, 1848 and 1860.
VT.
Lake Huron
Lake Ontario
Concord
Exeter
N.H.
ICHIGAN
ddressed crowd of ,000 at Kalamazoo campaign for emont, 1856.
Kalamazoo
Rochester
Niagara Falls
Buffalo
NEW YORK
Albany
MASS.
Boston
Hartford
Providence
Detroit
Lake Erie
TO WASHINGTON FOR INAUGURATION, 1861
CONN.
R.I.
West Point
Cleveland
PENNSYLVANIA
New York
NEW JERSEY
OHIO
Pittsburgh
Gettysburg address November 19, 1863.
Harrisburg
Philadelphia
Columbus
Gettysburg
Antietam
Frederick
Baltimore
MARYLAND
Reviewed troops at Frederick, visited Antietam battlefield, 1862.
Harpers Ferry
Cincinnati
WEST VIRGINIA
STATE, 1863
Washington
MD.
DEL.
WASHINGTON, D. C.
Served as Representative, 1847-49, President, 1861-65; assassinated, 1865.
Met McClellan at Harpers Ferry, 1862.
Fredericksburg
Potomac
ouisville
Frankfort
xington
Knob Creek Farm
odgenville
James
Richmond
Petersburg
VIRGINIA
Fort Monroe
Norfolk
VIRGINIA
Personally directed capture of Norfolk, May, 1862. Reviewed troops near Fredericksburg, April, 1863. Walked Richmond streets almost unattended day after city fell, April, 1865.
KENTUCKY
HODGENVILLE: Lincoln born near by, February 12, 1809.
KNOB CREEK FARM: Family moved here in 1811.
LOUISVILLE: Lincoln visited his old friend Joshua Speed in 1841.
LEXINGTON: On the way to Congress in 1847, the Lincolns stayed 3 weeks with Mary's family.
Raleigh
NORTH CAROLINA
OHIO
CINCINNATI: Spoke for his candidates in the State elections, 1859.
COLUMBUS: Addressed the State Legislature on his inaugural trip to Washington, 1861.
Columbia
Atlanta
SOUTH CAROLINA
GEORGIA
TRAVELS OF A. Lincoln
SHADED AREA MARKS STATES IN WHICH LINCOLN TRAVELED
0 100 200 300 MILES
FLORIDA
Design, William N. Palmstrom
Map, V. J. Kelley and J. W. Lothers
Sketches, I. E. Alleman
©N.G.S.

Knox College at Galesburg, Illinois, heard Lincoln and Douglas debate in 1858. Bronzes of the two flank door of Old Main. Outwardly the building has changed little.

C. 1859, COLLECTION OF FREDERICK HILL MESERVE

Stephen A. Douglas

1860, LIBRARY OF CONGRESS

Abraham Lincoln

"Of all the damned Whig rascals about Springfield, Abe Lincoln is the ablest and most honest." So Stephen A. Douglas, Democratic veteran of the U. S. Senate, sized up the man he debated in his 1858 bid for re-election.

The 24 years between Lincoln's election to the state legislature and the Republican nomination for the Senate had prepared him for the coming race. He had honed his wit against that of other attorneys and made campaign speeches across Illinois. In 1846 the voters had chosen him for the House of Representatives. After one term he had stood aside to let another run. Accepting the nomination to run for the Senate against Douglas, he had stirred the nation with the words: " 'A house divided against itself cannot stand.'

To Springfield, Illinois, came Lincoln at 28, a self-taught lawyer lacking enough cash to buy bed linen. When he said farewell from the only home he ever owned (right), it was as President-elect. He had bought the house for $1,500 after his marriage in 1842. It remains a state memorial to him.

W. D. VAUGHN (ALSO TOP)

I believe this government cannot endure, permanently half *slave* and half *free.*"

Douglas, known as the Little Giant, traveled to the debates in style aboard a private railway coach. A cannon on a flatcar boomed out his arrivals. Ottawa, Freeport, Jonesboro, and Charleston welcomed the candidates with carnivals and brass bands. At Knox College in Galesburg the largest turnout of the debates braved a cold wind. Twenty thousand heard Lincoln say of his opponent: "He is blowing out the moral lights around us, when he contends that whoever wants slaves has a right to hold them." The debaters dueled at Quincy and at Alton, where an observer saw Lincoln stand "like some solitary pine on a lonely summit."

When Douglas won the Senate seat, Lincoln compared himself to the boy who stubbed his toe: "It hurt too bad to laugh and he was too big to cry." But he was elected President in 1860 and left Springfield for Washington on his inaugural journey. Feelings were running so high that Lincoln's train was secretly rerouted at Harrisburg, Pennsylvania, because of a rumored attempt to assassinate him in Baltimore. Less than two months later the storm broke.

The North's claim of victory at the Battle of Antietam in 1862 gave Lincoln the military success he needed to announce the Emancipation Proclamation freeing the slaves. Then Union victory at Gettysburg doomed the Confederacy, though few realized it. Lincoln traveled to Gettysburg on November 18, 1863, to dedicate the military cemetery.

On the battlefield next morning Lincoln listened to Edward Everett's two-hour oration, then spoke only two minutes. The address "fell on the audience like a wet blanket," he said later. He could not know then that the world would acclaim it.

Four score and seven years ago our fathers
brought forth, upon this continent, a new nation, conceived in Liberty, and dedicated to the proposition
that all men are created equal.

Now we are engaged in a great civil war, testing whether that nation, or any nation, so conceived,
and so dedicated, can long endure. We are met
here on a great battle-field of that war. We ~~are~~ have
~~met~~ come to dedicate a portion of it as ~~the~~ a final resting place ~~of~~ for those who here gave their lives that
that nation might live. It is altogether fitting

In a bedroom of the David Wills home in Gettysburg, Lincoln revised his famed address. He held the second draft (above) in his hand as he spoke the next morning.

On Good Friday, 1865, the President was talking to a friend: "Everything is bright this morning. The war is over. . . . We are going to have good times now, and a united country."

Behind was the Second Inaugural Address and its moving benediction: "With malice toward none; with charity for all. . . ." Behind, too, was a disturbing dream in which he heard the mourners sob and a soldier explain, "The President . . . was killed by an assassin!"

That evening the President and his wife went to Ford's Theater in Washington where crazed John Wilkes Booth fired a derringer point-blank at Lincoln's head. Mortally wounded, the President was carried across 10th Street and into the Petersen House. At about seven the next morning Abraham Lincoln was dead.

ROCKER PRESERVED AT GREENFIELD VILLAGE, DEARBORN, MICHIGAN; WILLARD R. CULVER

Booth Stable

Supposed Course of Booth on horseback

Public Alley

Public Alley

Passage

Stage

Booth's course after he jumped

The Box over these is where the assasination occured.

Lower P. Box

ORCHESTRA

Auditorium

Lobby

Office

10th Street

This Plan is drawn from memory

Jno T. Ford

LIBRARY OF CONGRESS

Bloodstained rocker stirs memories of assassination; John T. Ford's plan of his theater shows how the killer escaped. Booth crept into the Presidential box, shot Lincoln from behind, then leaped to the stage. He caught a spur on a draped flag and broke his leg, an injury that led to his capture.

JOHN E. FLETCHER, NATIONAL GEOGRAPHIC PHOTOGRAPHER, AND W. D. VAUGHN

Ford's Theater started as a Baptist church, was remodeled, then burned in 1862. Ford rebuilt in time for the Lincoln tragedy. Afterward public feeling forced its sale. It housed offices in 1893 when the floors collapsed, killing 22. Now the Park Service maintains it as the Lincoln Museum.

"Now he belongs to the ages." Each year nearly six million people make a pilgrimage to Lincoln Memorial in the nation's capital. Slowly they pass between the columns (there are 36, one for each of the reunited states at the time Lincoln was assassinated). They stand silently,

W. D. VAUGHN

sometimes for a long time, before the thoughtful figure of the Great Emancipator sculptured by Daniel Chester French in Georgia marble. They read the Gettysburg Address inscribed on one wall and the Second Inaugural Address across the chamber. And they leave, quietly.

S. LINDER
THE HOFFM

WILLIAM C. EVERHART

SHORTLY AFTER MIDNIGHT on January 1, 1863, Daniel Freeman filed the first land claim in Brownville, Nebraska Territory, under the Homestead Act. He had dragged the land-office agent from a New Year's party to register 160 acres near the town of Beatrice. Thousands took up claims in the months that followed, for even during the Civil War the West demanded its share of the nation's energies. In 1864, as Grant launched his drive on Richmond, white-topped wagons of 75,000 settlers rolled west over the Oregon Trail. "It was one of the great pulses of American life that went on beating amid the din of war."

An army veteran, bragging about the recent war back east, might have lied in a small sort of way. But once he crossed the Missouri he began to take lessons from the prairies. In the clear air he seemed able to touch mountain ranges a hundred miles away. Streams appeared to run uphill. Buffalo and horses raced upside down in shimmering mirages. "You can't tell the truth about the Great West without lying," said an observer. He hit it about right.

Almost as unbelievable were the West's wild towns. Tombstone, Arizona, was a brawling honky-tonk place where three frontiers collided—the miner's, cattleman's, and Indian's. Tombstone drew more than its share of gunslingers and

"IN WITHOUT KNOCKING," 1909, NOW IN THE AMON CARTER MUSEUM OF WESTERN ART AT FORT WORTH, TEXAS, PULSES WITH THE VIGOR AND REALISM OF MONTANA COWBOY ARTIST CHARLES M. RUSSELL. © BROWN & BIGELOW

peace officers, although few could tell them apart. On a memorable day near the O.K. Corral mustachioed Marshal Wyatt Earp and Doc Holliday, "lean, consumptive, sardonic, and deadly," reduced the cowboy population of Arizona Territory by gunning down badmen Billy Clanton and Frank and Tom McLowery.

In the cowtowns homicidal exhibitionists of the Jesse James and Billy the Kid stripe occasioned a high turnover in peace officers, who frequently played leading roles in funerals. Wild Bill Hickok, suave and natty, was marshal at Abilene, Kansas. But he spent most of his time at the card table in the Alamo Saloon, leaving the game occasionally to exercise his ivory-handled pistols.

The last, and some say the wildest, of the frontier boom towns was Deadwood, in Dakota Territory. There Wild Bill, "Prince of Pistoleers," played his last hand as he sat with his back to an open door. Mike Russell, a sawed-off Irishman with a long beard, kept bar. Everyone was welcome with two exceptions—women and children. Calamity Jane could get a drink, Mike said, because she was an exception that proved the rule. Those fortunate to have seen hard-riding, straight-shooting Calamity in action agreed. Yet all the West was exceptional, totally different from anything the Eastern pioneer had known. The men who founded Rough and Ready, Hangtown, Poker Flat, and Murderer's Bar were bound to be different from those who named their towns Plymouth, Jamestown, and Boston.

THE ACCIDENTAL DISCOVERY OF GOLD at Sutter's Mill in January of 1848 turned eyes westward to behold the glittering vision of a new El Dorado. When President Polk announced that the amount of gold "would scarcely command belief," the world exploded, and the fragments landed in California. "Greenhorns" from the East, "Sydney Ducks" from Australia, "Paddies" from Ireland, "Coolies" from China, "Cousin Jacks" from Cornwall, "Keskydees" *(Qu'est-ce qu'il dit?)* from France flooded the mining camps.

Returning home early in 1849 after a few months' absence, a New Yorker would hardly have recognized his city. Men in broad-brimmed hats and high boots kept honest folk from their labors with tales of wealth in the wilderness. Boxes, barrels, and bales hid store fronts. Hundreds of drays pushed through the crowded streets, headed for the wharves. There wild-eyed Argonauts fought to get aboard every hulk the shipping companies could send far enough out to sea not to attract attention when it sank. Everywhere was heard a new word—California!

Tens of thousands went overland. They swarmed into the Missouri River embarkation towns—Westport, Independence, St. Joseph—covering the surrounding fields with wagons and tents. When spring came the great wagon trains rolled out on the prairie, beginning a 2,000-mile journey which the survivors would never forget. Asiatic cholera scattered 5,000 graves along the trail to the Rockies. But nearly 80,000 forty-niners got to California, transforming it from wilderness to statehood in a single year.

No hamlet in all the 30 United States was left untouched. One historian has estimated that the number of homes broken by the Gold Rush was "but little less than inflicted by the Civil War ten years later."

There was gold aplenty, just as all the guide books had claimed. Every miner who arrived at the diggings panned dust. He did, that is, if he was willing to stand for hours in icy streams, wield pick and shovel from dawn to dusk, then collapse in his tent after downing a supper of greasy pork, beans, and coffee. The trouble was, not many miners found very much gold. Probably nine out of ten made less money in California than they would have at home.

Although the California surface mines petered out in the early 1850's, gold fever hopelessly infected the miners. In 1858 more than 20,000 streamed north to the Fraser River gold fields in British Columbia. Like quicksilver they were off in all directions, exploring an unmapped wilderness, finding rich lodes along the rivers of Oregon, Washington, and Idaho, in the deserts of Arizona and Nevada, in the mountains of Colorado and Montana.

With all their hectic living, the miners developed effective if quick rules of justice and the framework of local government. "Congregate a hundred Americans anywhere," a foreign observer noted, "and they immediately lay out a city, frame a state constitution and apply for admission into the Union, while twenty-five of them become candidates for the United States Senate."

Miners invariably formed vigilance committees to round up the badmen. Juries appointed by the committee might listen to testimony but seldom had the patience for lengthy argument. Two men found with stolen horses in the California diggings

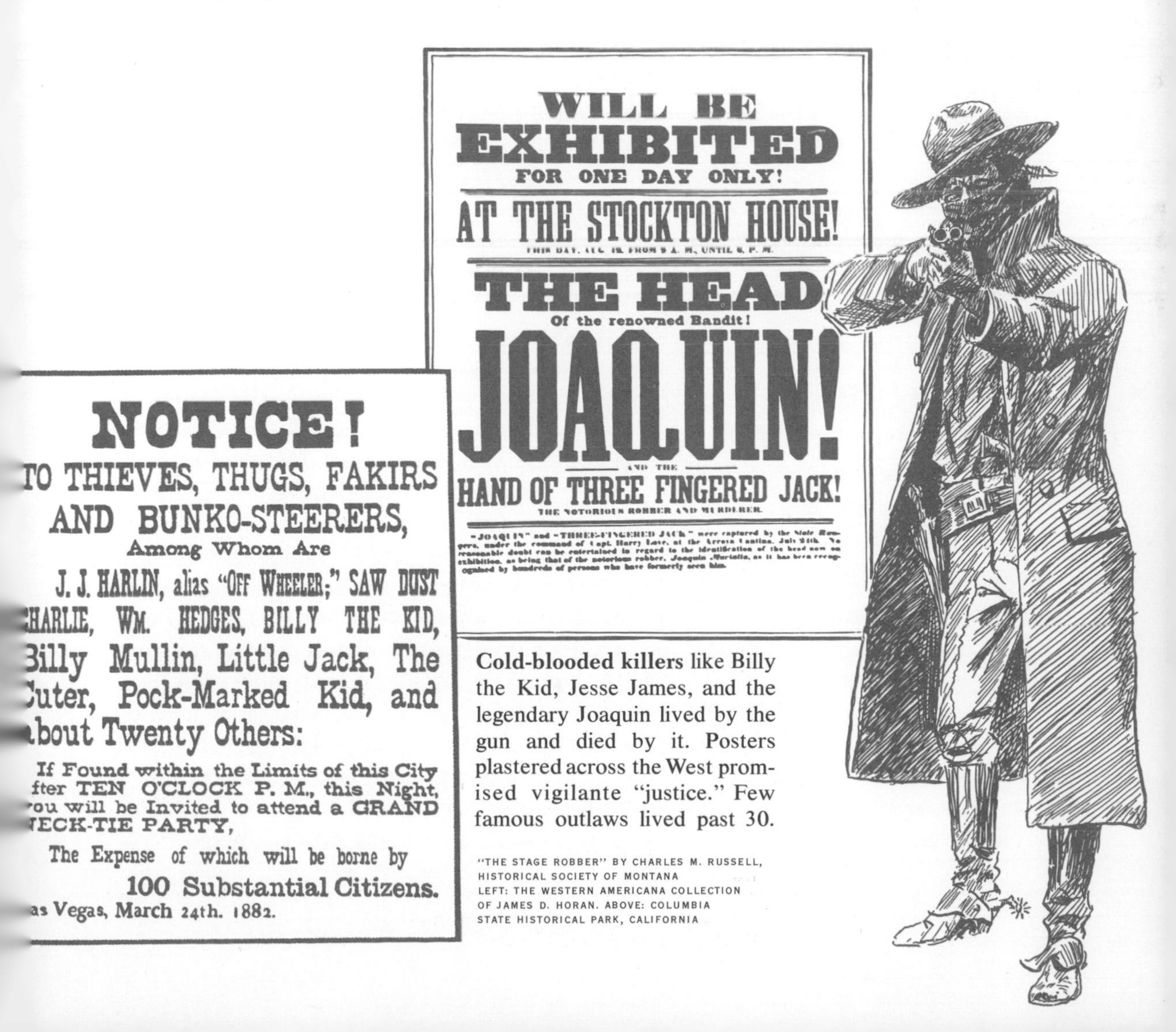

WILL BE
EXHIBITED
FOR ONE DAY ONLY!
AT THE STOCKTON HOUSE!
THE HEAD
Of the renowned Bandit!
JOAQUIN!
AND THE
HAND OF THREE FINGERED JACK!
THE NOTORIOUS ROBBER AND MURDERER.
NOTICE!
TO THIEVES, THUGS, FAKIRS
AND BUNKO-STEERERS,
Among Whom Are
J. J. HARLIN, alias "OFF WHEELER;" SAW DUST
CHARLIE, WM. HEDGES, BILLY THE KID,
Billy Mullin, Little Jack, The
Cuter, Pock-Marked Kid, and
about Twenty Others:
If Found within the Limits of this City
after TEN O'CLOCK P. M., this Night,
you will be Invited to attend a GRAND
NECK-TIE PARTY,
The Expense of which will be borne by
100 Substantial Citizens.
Las Vegas, March 24th. 1882.

Cold-blooded killers like Billy the Kid, Jesse James, and the legendary Joaquin lived by the gun and died by it. Posters plastered across the West promised vigilante "justice." Few famous outlaws lived past 30.

"THE STAGE ROBBER" BY CHARLES M. RUSSELL, HISTORICAL SOCIETY OF MONTANA
LEFT: THE WESTERN AMERICANA COLLECTION OF JAMES D. HORAN. ABOVE: COLUMBIA STATE HISTORICAL PARK, CALIFORNIA

were "condemned by acclamation" and hanged on the spot. Lacking jails, the vigilantes specialized in quick punishment: whipping, branding, or ear-cropping. Claim jumpers, stage robbers, thieves, and murderers, along with unlucky victims of mistaken identity, all received the benefits of frontier justice. Such remedies were brutal—and final. But as one who knew the situation asked, how else could the miners protect life and property in a country devoid of law?

Fastidious, well-mannered Henry Plummer provoked a spectacular case of vigilante action. His gang systematically pillaged the 90-mile road between Virginia City and Bannock, two rip-roaring Montana mining camps. Wisely taking the precaution of becoming sheriff, Plummer had no trouble learning the schedule of bullion shipments. The miners were more than patient, but after 100 of their colleagues had been robbed or murdered they formed a vigilance committee and set out to even the score. The ringleader and 23 henchmen stretched hemp—Plummer from gallows he had built when sheriff.

During the 1850's miners demanded that the government provide better communications between mining camps and with civilization. In 1858 the Butterfield Overland Mail inaugurated regular postal and passenger service. The 2,600-mile trip from Tipton, Missouri, via El Paso, Texas, to San Francisco—the tortuous "oxbow" route—consumed about four weeks. A fat man in a crowded coach meant agony for those next to him, for the busy Overland Mail operated on the theory that the coach was never full. "Three in a row we would solemnly rise from our seats, bump our heads against the low roof, and, returning, vigorously ram the again-rising seat we had incontinently left."

WANTED

YOUNG SKINNY WIRY FELLOWS not over eighteen. Must be expert riders willing to risk death daily. Orphans preferred. WAGES $25 per week. Apply, *Central Overland Express, Alta Bldg., Montgomery St.*

PONY EXPRESS MUSEUM, ST. JOSEPH, MISSOURI

While stagecoaches creaked across deserts and mountain ranges, a slim young rider in red shirt and high-topped boots impatiently waited through a ceremony at St. Joseph, Missouri. When the speeches ended on that April 3, 1860, he galloped the first leg of a historic cross-country run. Nine days and 23 hours later the first Pony Express rider reached Sacramento.

Men, or rather boys, who rode for the Pony Express displayed an almost fanatic devotion to duty. They swam flooded rivers, led their horses through howling blizzards in the mountain passes, and raced through bands of Indians waiting in ambush. Relay stations were raided, riders shot. In emergencies riders such as "Buffalo Bill" Cody stayed in the saddle nearly 24 hours and covered more than 300 miles without relief. Only one of the semiweekly mails never arrived. But even as young men flashed across the plains, laborers were

"THE OVERLAND PONY EXPRESS," HARPER'S WEEKLY, 1861, DRAMATIZES DARING RIDERS AND THE TELEGRAPH THAT REPLACED THEM. LIBRARY OF CONGRESS

planting the posts and stringing the "talking wire" of the transcontinental telegraph. It carried Great Medicine, they told the Indians, and gave them an occasional shock. The gang in the tepee got the message and caused little trouble.

The telegraph killed the Pony Express after only 19 months. Death came shamefully, considering the tedious telegram the builder sent his wife: "This being the first message over the new line since its completion, allow me to greet you."

AS CIVIL WAR GUNS COOLED, restless Americans discovered new wealth in the West—gold on the hoof. The long drive of Texas cattle to Kansas railheads and Wyoming ranges is an American saga told and retold in dime novels and on movie and television screens. In the face of marauding Indians, rustlers, and farmers with shotguns, despite fractious longhorns that might stampede at the flash of a match or a clap of thunder, cowboys "pointed north" millions of cattle.

Kansans who had seen buffalo darken their plains stared in disbelief at the wild-eyed longhorns pouring north, overflowing the prairie, and crowding the riverbanks. From a hilltop one cowboy saw seven herds to his rear and eight in front, with the dust of 13 more in sight. "All the cattle in the world seemed to be coming up from Texas," he marveled. "Bully chaps for glue," scoffed critics of the stringy longhorn. "We have seen some Buffaloes that were more civilized."

Herds of about 2,500 head were drifted in a long slender line along dusty trails that became as "well defined as the course of a river." For long stretches the half-wild longhorns were without water, and controlling them was almost beyond the power of men. Cattlemen's historian Ernest Osgood caught the vivid scene: "To all those who saw that long line of Texas cattle come up over a rise in the prairie, nostrils wide for the smell of water, dust-caked and gaunt, so ready to break from the nervous control of the riders strung out along the flanks of the herd, there came the feeling that in this spectacle there was something elemental, something resistless, something perfectly in keeping with the unconquered land about them."

Whether riding point or eating dust back with the "drags," cowboys spent all day and part of the night in the saddle. After a supper of beans, bacon, and coffee, they took turns guarding the herd. "To ride around the big steers at night, all lying down full as a tick, chewing their cuds and blowing, with the moon shining on their big horns, was a sight to make a man's eyes pop."

At the end of the long drive lay the cowtown. Cowboys came in like sailors hitting a liberty port. After months on the trail a man wanted to forget the dirt and the heat and the stampedes, and he figured he couldn't do it sitting around the general store. If he got so drunk he couldn't hit the ground with his hat in three throws, it was worth the money and something to remember on the way back to Texas.

Cowboy artist Charlie Russell told a tale that put it pretty well. "Ma," asked a wide-eyed girl, inspecting the manly cowpuncher sitting tall in the saddle, "do cowboys eat grass?" "No, dear," the old lady replied, "they're part human." Hugely human, his spirit as unfenced as the Great Plains he conquered, the cowboy left his brand on the West—and in every youngster's dreams.

The cowboy had nothing but contempt for the "sodbuster," except on Saturday nights when he slicked down his cowlick, swallowed his pride, and went courting the farmer's pretty daughter. Nevertheless the farmer, last in the long march of civilization westward, pressed gradually onto the cowboy's Great Plains. When he arrived with his cow, his plow, and his spotted sow, the solitude disappeared.

"Uncle Sam is rich enough to give us all a farm," ran a popular song of the 1850's. The Homestead Act fulfilled that sentiment. "If you strike off into the broad, free West," bubbled editor Horace Greeley, "and make yourself a farm from Uncle Sam's generous domain, you will crowd nobody, starve nobody, and neither you nor your children need ever beg for something to do."

Ironically, the cattleman paved the way for the sodbuster, for the success of the cattle industry on the plains discredited the myth of the Great American Desert. "Garden of the West," someone relabeled it, and millions believed it. Fired by the prospects of a better life, settlers swarmed onto the plains during

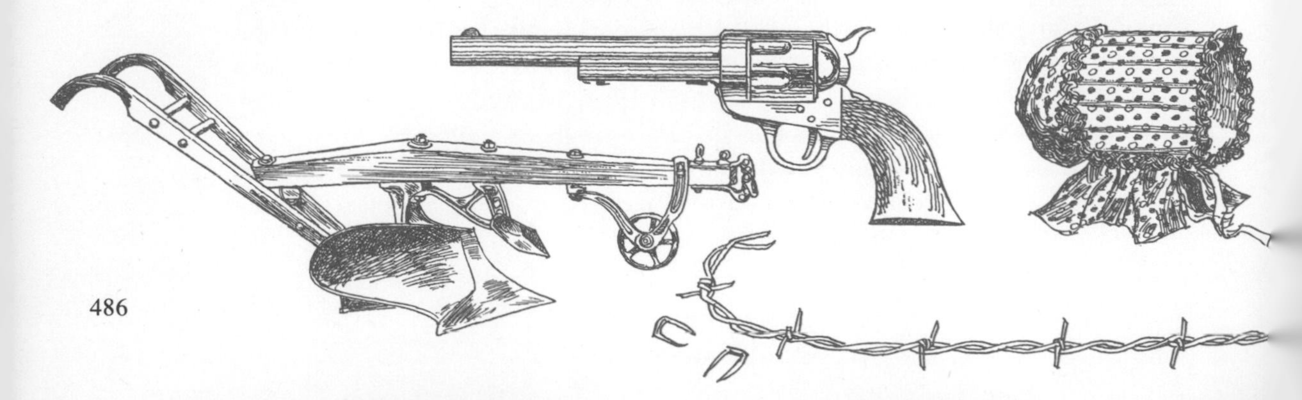

the last three decades of the 19th century—the greatest movement in United States history. They took up more land than in all the years since Jamestown.

The great migration stemmed partly from the advertising of transportation companies. Anxious for fares, steamship lines "marred the walls of half the Continent with their Posters." The railroads carried farmers to prairie railheads at reduced prices, sold them cheap land—then quickly upped freight rates.

Getting land was easier than protecting it. Free-roaming livestock trampled wheat and corn. The cattleman refused to build fences, the farmer could not afford to. Split rails shipped to his 160-acre homestead on the treeless plains might cost $1,000. "Good fences make good neighbors," the saying goes. Plains life in 1870 saw neither fences nor neighborliness. Farmers tried hedges. Thorny Osage orange—"pig tight, horse high, and bull strong"—took four years to grow. Schemes for "thorn wire" and "pricker" fences deluged the patent office but didn't catch on. Plains newspapers debated the problem more than they did politics or foreign affairs. Then, in 1873, a bewhiskered Illinois farmer twisted together two metal strands entwined with a spur. Joseph Glidden had perfected barbed wire. A promoter showed that it could turn back charging longhorns. Soon barbed-wire fences crisscrossed the prairie.

The farmer also demanded something that would break thick prairie sod. In 1868 James Oliver obliged with his chilled-iron plow. Soon after came the sulky plow that the farmer could ride instead of walk behind.

Watching it all, a cattleman was unconvinced when told the sodbusters constituted the "bone and sinew" of the country. "D___n such bone and sinew," he raged. "They are the ruin of the Country, and have everlastingly, eternally, now and forever, destroyed the best grazing land in the West."

But the "nester" had come to stay. Theodore Roosevelt, a plains rancher himself, saw where the future of the region lay. "The homesteaders, the permanent settlers, the men who took up each his own farm on which he lived and brought up his family, these represent from the National standpoint the most desirable of all possible users of, and dwellers on, the soil."

Westering pioneers stepped out of their industrial revolution to encounter primitive people who had not progressed beyond the flint arrowhead of the Stone Age. The white man was contemptuous, and he found Indian ways incomprehensible. The Indian was no less contemptuous, for his was the pride of a people who were at one with their land and who believed fiercely in their future. The Indian's Sun Dance was as meaningful as the white man's Christmas. An Arapaho ceremonialist in a rabbit skin commanded the dignity of a robed bishop.

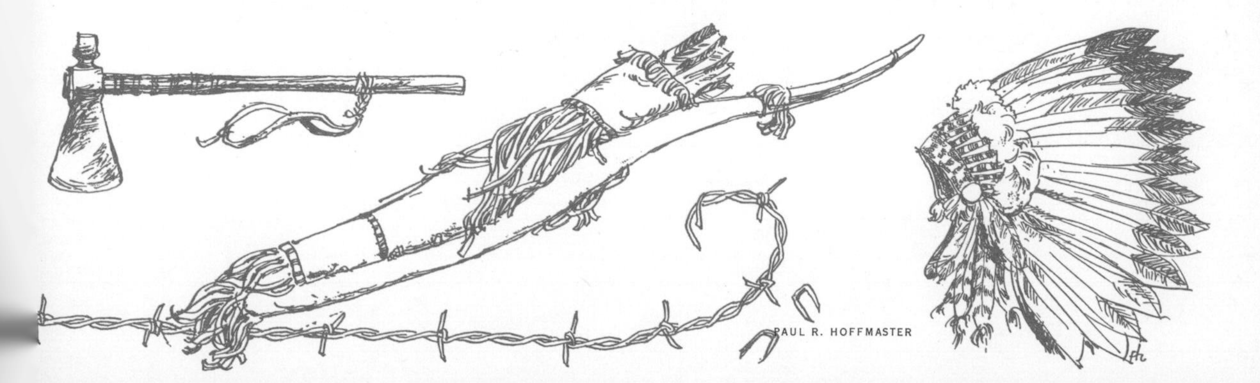

Despite the cleavage between cultures—one dynamic and acquisitive, the other inert with simple wants—Western Indians showed little hostility to white men before 1860. They seldom attacked parties during the early years on the Oregon Trail. On one caravan to Santa Fe so many companionable Kiowa tagged along that the party consumed 1,000 buffalo en route. Still, the white man preferred trading horses, the Kiowa stealing them.

Soon after the Spanish brought the horse to the Southwest, Indians were creeping into camps, howling like wolves, and stampeding the corrals. The horse passed northward from tribe to tribe—stolen, traded, or caught wild on the prairie. With this wonderful animal the Plains Indian became less agricultural, more nomadic. By 1800 his culture centered on the horse and the buffalo.

Buffalo had roamed for an eternity across the limitless grasslands of the plains. In vast dark herds they drifted over the West as the stars moved. It seemed that no power less than another Ice Age could destroy them.

Every hour of the day reminded the Plains Indian of his dependence on the shaggy beast. The food for his children, strings for his bow, the covering for his bed all came from the buffalo. The hunt, dangerous and marvelously colorful, was a test of courage and wove its way into the Indian's religion. The Plains Indian danced the return of the buffalo as other tribes danced for sun and rain. After a successful hunt he took his finest buffalo robe, intricately painted and quill-embroidered, to a high hill. There he left it, an offering to the Great Unknown and to all the buffalo that had died so their brother the Indian might live.

INDIAN AND WHITE MAN were destined to clash. The stakes? Land. Defiant Plains tribes slowed the white tide. North of the Platte River lurked the Sioux and the Blackfoot, independent and warlike. South waited the Arapaho and the Cheyenne, proud and intelligent. In the Southwest reigned the Apache and the Comanche, cruel and elusive. "Finest light cavalry in the world," said Gen. George Crook, who fought Geronimo's braves.

Intermittent but savage conflicts crippled the red man. Samuel Colt's revolver, "which multiplied every soldier by six," offset daring Indian horsemanship. More devastating was the slaughter of the buffalo. It began in the late sixties with the building of the Union Pacific Railroad. Hide hunters took as many as three million buffalo a year. An 1883 expedition found fewer than 200 in all the West.

Destitute without the buffalo, decimated by wars, the Indian finally submitted to life on the reservation. Old men put away the sacred relics and refused to teach young men the tribal lore. "I am tired of fighting," lamented Chief Joseph of the Nez Percé. "It is cold and we have no blankets. The little children are freezing to death. My people, some of them, have run away to the hills and have no blankets, no food. No one knows where they are—perhaps freezing to death. I want to have time to look for my children and see how many of them I can find. Maybe I shall find them among the dead. Hear me, my chiefs. I am tired. My heart is sick and sad. From where the sun now stands I will fight no more forever."

Indians, sodbusters, cattlemen, forty-niners—men with the West in their eyes! They created the legend of the Lusty West. Its spell persists.

"MINERS PROSPECTING FOR GOLD" BY FREDERIC REMINGTON, 1887, EDWARD EBERSTADT & SONS

GOLD IN THEM THAR HILLS

BOYS, I BELIEVE I'VE FOUND A GOLD MINE!" James Marshall rushed into Sutter's Mill on January 24, 1848, carrying flakes of gold in the crown of his hat. The millwright had stumbled onto washings from California's Mother Lode, a vein of gold-bearing quartz stretching 150 miles along the western foothills of the Sierra Nevada. Marshall and his boss, feudal baron John A. Sutter, tried to keep the strike a secret. But soon the cry rose: "Gold! Gold! Gold from the American River." It touched off the greatest mining orgy in history.

"Gone to the Diggings"—shopkeepers hung signs on their doors, and overnight

San Francisco became a ghost town. Then gold-crazed Argonauts streamed into the harbor, shipments of bullion rattled down from the hills, and the town exploded into the metropolis of the Golden West. Prices, measured by the pinch of gold dust, soared. Saloons bulged with unshaven miners, dapper gamblers, and painted women. Bunco men swindled the greenhorn; gunmen downed the miner for his poke. In the first eight years of the Gold Rush, more than 1,000 murders rocked "the gayest, lightest hearted, most pleasure loving city of the western continent."

It was just as hectic at the diggings. Where streams had tumbled unnoticed down the Sierras, forty-niners swarmed. Camps were thrown together: shacks of juniper posts, potato sacks, and old shirts; smoky hovels of mud and stone. Prospectors argued over ore samples. Bummers cadged drinks. Those who wanted

Sutter's Fort was the hub of California's golden past. Here John Sutter ran his 146,000 acres, his tannery and distillery, his traffic with Russian fur traders. In 1841 he bought their Fort Ross (right), north of San Francisco. His millwright discovered gold at Coloma (cairn below marks site), and towns like Columbia mushroomed. Its Wells Fargo office (upper right) weighed some $50,000,000. A flake of Sutter's gold (lower) balances beside an 82-ounce nugget at the Smithsonian Institution in Washington, D. C.

J. BAYLOR ROBERTS, NATIONAL GEOGRAPHIC STAFF, AND (ABOVE) REDWOOD EMPIRE ASSOCIATION

"I was everything," John Sutter recalled, "patriarch, priest, father, and judge." Persuading Mexico to give him a chunk of California, the Swiss-born "General" employed hundreds, lived and ruled like a king. "My best days," he lamented, "were just before the discovery of gold." It ruined him. Laborers deserted, squatters overran his land, his empire collapsed. He died poor, vainly seeking indemnity from Congress.

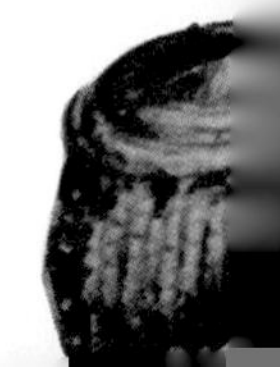

wholesome entertainment found "nothing to do but hang around the saloons, get drunk and fight, and lie out in the snow and die." Violence was rife. In one mining town 72 bodies reposed in the cemetery before the first citizen died of natural causes. Camps grew furiously, then dwindled or died with the gold supply. Sun-bleached buildings and rusted machinery are today's mementos of Gold Rush days.

More than a hundred camps flank the "Mother Lode Highway" (appropriately Cali-

CLOCKWISE: DEAN CONGER, MERLE SEVERY, VOLKMAR WENTZEL, ALL NATIONAL GEOGRAPHIC STAFF. JOHN A. SUTTER BY WILLIAM S. JEWETT, 1856, EDWARD EBERSTADT & SONS

San Francisco drowsed before the Gold Rush as a military post, mission, and village. *Californios* (right) called the settlement Yerba Buena for its good herb (mint). Frémont labeled the Golden Gate.

SAN FRANCISCO IN 1847 BY VICTOR PREVOST, CALIFORNIA HISTORICAL SOCIETY

RIGHT: FROM ROBERT K. HEIMANN'S "TOBACCO AND AMERICANS," McGRAW-HILL BOOK COMPANY

Ships rotted at 'Frisco in the early fifties when their crews followed the jaunty forty-niner (right) off to the gold diggings. Dragged ashore, the hulks served as warehouses, even lodgings.

From dance-hall bawd of Gold Rush days, from rubble heap after the 1906 earthquake and fire, San Francisco has flowered into a cultured beauty. Bay Bridge funnels traffic into Yerba Buena Island tunnel.

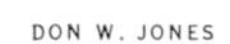

DON W. JONES

fornia Route 49) and draw sightseers as gold drew prospectors. At Coloma, the town that sprang to life around Sutter's Mill, Marshall in bronze points to the spot where he discovered gold. A little south sits storied Placerville. Once called "Hangtown" because of its "suspended sentences," it also helped a few businesses get off the ground. J. M. Studebaker built wheelbarrows for miners; Philip Armour ran a butcher shop, Mark Hopkins a grocery.

Off the highway lies Volcano, rich in ruins and memories. Its golden lava built the usual saloons, California's first public library, and the St. George Hotel, which still rolls out the welcome mat. Down 49 at Carson Hill tourists gape at the "glory hole," which produced the nation's largest nugget—a 195-pounder worth $73,710. A mining shaft nearby descends almost a mile.

Mark Twain, on the lode a century ago, heard a yarn at Angels Camp in Calaveras County, then wrote about the "Celebrated Jumping Frog." It catapulted him to fame and inspired the town's International Frog Olympics. Fellow writer

SMITHSONIAN INSTITUTION AND (RIGHT) STATE STREET BANK AND TRUST COMPANY, BOSTON

Hoofs thunder, a savage shrieks, and the "nigh leader" stumbles, pierced by arrows of Plains Indians. Downing the lead horse on the left hopelessly snarled a team. In the 1860's scenes like this bloodied Apache Pass in Arizona, farther south. Stage passengers wore side arms and a "wide-awake hat." Drivers rode for triple pay. Wheel ruts dug by the Butterfield line still scar the earth. At the east end of the pass crumbling Fort Bowie keeps lonely vigil. Amid mesquite and buckthorn lurk specters of Cochise and Geronimo.

Bret Harte immortalized Roaring Camp nearby, also Poker Flat and Fiddletown.

Best preserved of California's mining camps is Columbia, "Gem of the Southern Mines." Saloons, a firehouse and school, ruins of Chinese stores and old fandango halls survive near yawning pits which yielded some $87,000,000. There children can ride in an authentic, four-horse Wells Fargo stagecoach—and they don't have to worry about Black Bart. Bard of the bandits, he robbed 28 coaches single-handed and sometimes left a calling card signed "Black Bart, the PO 8" (poet):

Let come what will I'll try it on
My condition can't be worse
And if there's money in that box
'Tis munny in my purse.

Indians preyed on stage lines too. At a Utah station they killed a bald-headed agent. Because he had "a good growth of whiskers on his chin, they scalped that."

"DOWNING THE NIGH LEADER" BY FREDERIC REMINGTON, FROM HAROLD McCRACKEN'S "FREDERIC REMINGTON," COURTESY J. B. LIPPINCOTT COMPANY

Stage routes followed the miner, and he was always on the move. A greenhorn could work the surface or placer deposits. But when these played out, mining became big business. Labor gangs drove shafts deep into the mountains; hydraulic systems washed hillsides into long sluices; stamp mills pulverized gold-bearing quartz. The miner became a day laborer, turned farmer, or strapped his pick and pan on his burro and plodded off in search of a new El Dorado.

Fanning out from California, prospectors panned "color" from Idaho to Arizona. In 1859 they hit pay dirt on the Nevada slope of the Sierras. But it was difficult to mine, for troublesome "black stuff" encased it. That black stuff proved to be loaded with silver! Twenty thousand flocked to stake claims here on the Comstock Lode. Mark Twain found the area "fabulously rich in gold, silver . . . thieves, murderers, desperados, ladies, children, lawyers, Christians, Indians, Chinamen . . . poets, preachers, and jackass rabbits." Comstock wealth helped finance the North in the Civil War, even shook the world's monetary systems. But the best was

BATES LITTLEHALES, NATIONAL GEOGRAPHIC PHOTOGRAPHER, AND (RIGHT) RAY MANLEY, WESTERN WAYS

Tombstone, powder-burned and bloodstained but "too tough to die," lives on in the Bird Cage Theater (above). The 1880's also come alive in the Crystal Palace Saloon and Cochise County Courthouse. Each October "Helldorado" gunmen ape Wyatt Earp in the battle at the OK Corral.

Cap pistols shoot it out on Tombstone's Boot Hill (right). "Legally hanged" on marker doesn't include one lynched.

The toy stagecoach at left doesn't leave Frontier Museum in Custer State Park, but this youngster's Colt .45 would protect it if it did! In nearby Custer, South Dakota, stands a log cabin (now a museum) built in 1875 by troops who tried to keep miners out of the Black Hills of the Sioux.

Virginia City, Nevada, atop 600 miles of Comstock tunnels, boomed like no other Wild West town. A ground squirrel made the strike. In 1859 prospectors panned its diggings and the rush was on. Today the spire of St. Mary's-in-the-Mountains rises above weathered buildings filled with relics. Visitors tour an old mine (above).

to come. In 1873 miners struck the Big Bonanza—a 54-foot-wide section of the lode filled with some $200,000,000 in gold and silver. Virginia City reigned as Queen of the Comstock, housing 30,000 free spenders. Its nabobs showered gold double eagles on favorite actresses. One dropped $38,000 on the flip of a faro card.

Today sightseers find Virginia City's old saloons and houses of chance still operating, and the pretentious but unpainted mansions of bonanza kings clinging to Mount Davidson. They visit the *Territorial Enterprise,* "first newspaper in the howling wilderness of Nevada." In Piper's Opera House they walk the dance floor that was mounted on springs so stomping miners would not destroy it. They tour old mining works, and in nearby Carson City inspect a full-scale model of a mine at the Nevada State Museum, once a mint that coined Comstock metal.

Colorado prospectors found gold near Pikes Peak, and 100,000 "fifty-niners"

MERLE SEVERY, NATIONAL GEOGRAPHIC STAFF

rushed to one of mining's greatest fiascoes. But fortunes in silver waited at Leadville and at Aspen, today a skiing resort. Cripple Creek blossomed on a "$300,-000,000 cow pasture"; it boasted 46 brokerage houses, 14 newspapers, 70 saloons. Driving through its satellite camps the motorist is never out of sight of ore dumps, shafts, hoists, and crumbling buildings.

Accidental birth, furious growth, decay or death—that's the history of Colorado's Tin Cup, Crystal City, Gold Park, Jimtown, Sunshine, and Fairplay. In 1858 gold was "dug with a hatchet in Cherry Creek and washed out into a frying pan"—and Denver was born. Central City laid a path of silver bricks for President Grant. The bricks are gone, but a well-preserved mining town greets today's tourists. Narrow, saloon-lined streets guide them to the old opera house, which each summer resounds with an opera and play festival.

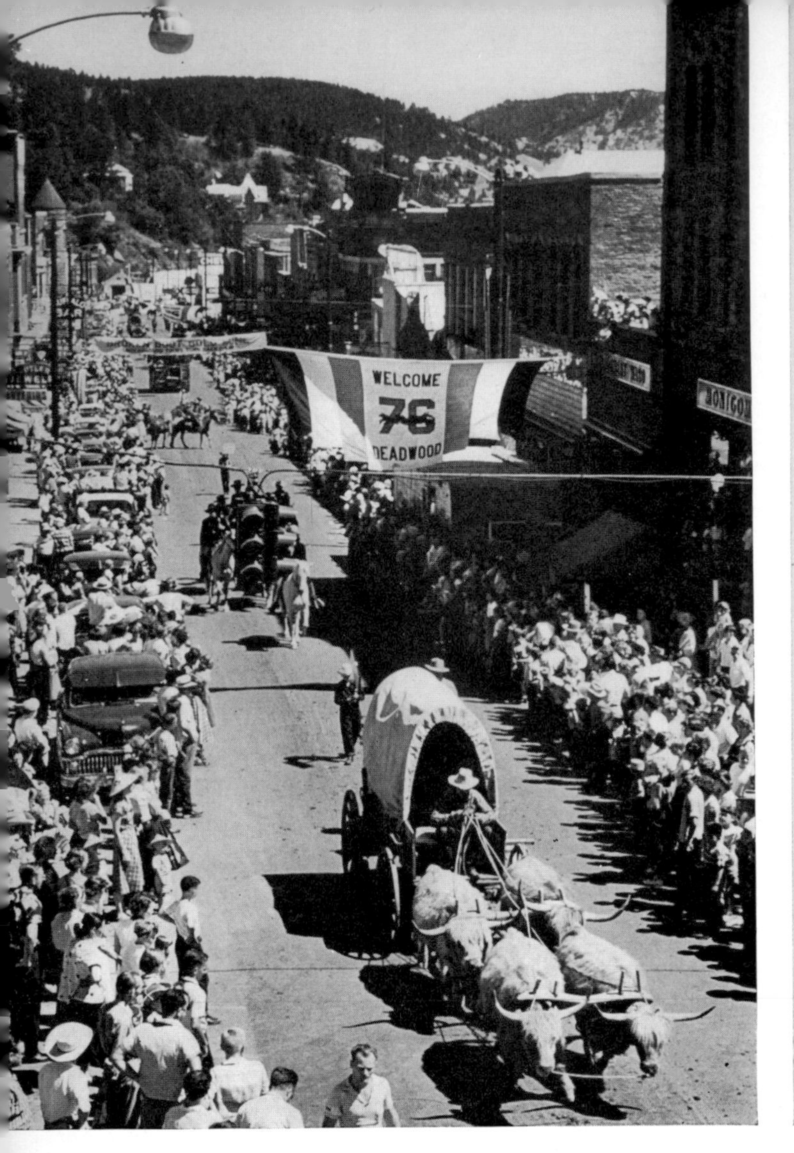

Calamity Jane ("Scorn Martha Jane Canary and you court calamity") dressed, drank, and fought like a gunman. Belle of the Black Hills, she haunts Deadwood, South Dakota. Each August it revives the gold rush spirit of 1876.

"Mellerdrammers" delight visitors to the opera house in Virginia City, Montana. Scene of many a "drygulching" which stocked its Boot Hill, the old mining town relives its past in the Bale of Hay Saloon and Wells Fargo Coffee House.

Until the 1870's the Black Hills of Dakota escaped the prospector's pick. Then an expedition under Gen. George Armstrong Custer confirmed the rumors of gold. Failing to stem the tide, the government threw open the area to those willing to risk attack by the Sioux. Some 15,000 miners streamed in, and the Sioux went on the warpath. The Indians were finally tamed; but the miners went wild—gold in Deadwood Gulch! Wide-open, ramshackle Deadwood shook with a great spasm of lawlessness: "There the faro games were wilder, the hurdy-gurdy dance halls noisier, the street brawls more common, than in any other western town."

Today sightseers stroll Deadwood's Main Street with the ghosts of Wild Bill Hickok, Calamity Jane, Poker Alice, Deadwood Dick, and Crooked Nose Jack McCall. Here youngsters in cowboy suits stalk phantoms of Sam Bass and Joel Collins, fugitives from another frontier—the dry and dusty world of the cattleman.

RAY MANLEY, WESTERN WAYS. LEFT: BATES LITTLEHALES, NATIONAL GEOGRAPHIC PHOTOGRAPHER, AND BETTMANN ARCHIVE

Virginia City, Montana, like its sister city in Nevada, enjoys a travel boom a century after miners struck gold, strung up outlaws, and paid $150 for a sack of flour. Rank's Drugstore (above), oldest active store in the state, displays merchandise of the 1860's.

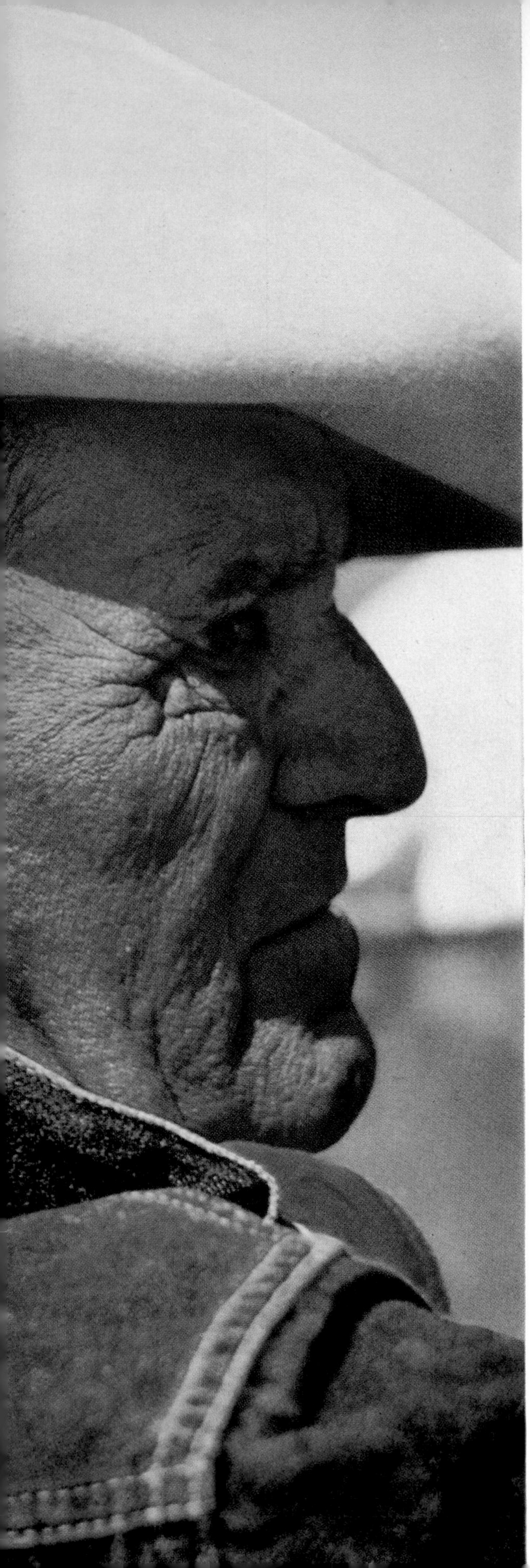

CATTLEMAN'S

IT ALL STARTED IN TEXAS. There roamed the cowboy, the cow pony, the longhorn steer. Put them together and you have the makings of the cattleman's empire.

Ancestors of the longhorn came to the New World with the Spaniards 450 years ago. Strays grazed along the Nueces and Rio Grande, multiplied, and mixed with scrub cattle brought in by American settlers. Horns lengthened, the body grew rangier, and by the Civil War there was your longhorn—tall, bony, coarse-haired and slab-sided, tail dragging the ground, short on looks but long on endurance.

The cow pony, too, was a Spanish stray *(mesteño)* living like a wild animal. Mustang, *yanquis* called him. Small and scrubby, sure-footed and fleet, he'd run all day and kick his rider's hat in the air at night.

The cowboy grew up in the land that Stephen Austin pioneered. From the *vaquero* (Mexican cowherd) he learned to cut out and rope; from the mounted Plains Indian, to fight at a gallop. Before long the tough men of the "Texas breed" were ready to ride into the nation's folklore.

At the end of the Civil War more than five million longhorns roamed the Texas chaparral, hardly worth roping and branding. Then Joseph G. McCoy, an audacious livestock shipper, found a way to connect the $4 steer in Texas with the $40 market in the booming North. In 1867 he built pens and loading chutes at Abilene and invited Texans to drive their herds here for shipment on the Kansas Pacific Railroad.

McCoy opened the floodgates. In two decades Texas drovers "pointed north" ten million longhorns, aiming for Kansas railheads or the open range.

First the North Star, then hoof-carved paths guided the long drives. "Cowboy, roll out!" A dozen weathered cowpunchers

THOMAS NEBBIA

EMPIRE

would rub the dust from their eyes, wash down beans with coffee, mount cayuses, and drift their 2,500 cattle toward the next water hole. With them went the temperamental cook in the chuck wagon and a youthful apprentice ("Little Joe, the wrangler") who tended the extra horses.

Fording the Red River into Indian Territory (Oklahoma), the drovers paid tolls to the tribes or saw them drive off part of the herd. At night, singing soothed cattle made jittery by distant heat lightning:

Oh, it's bacon and beans most every day,
I'd as soon be a-eatin' prairie hay.

On to the Kansas plains they plodded. Mirages danced in the sun, and farmers brandished guns and strung barbed wire.

Not all the long drives ended at a Kansas cattle car headed for Chicago. Some longhorns went to feed army garrisons and reservation Indians. Others stocked grasslands where the buffalo once roamed.

MEN RUSHED WEST to get rich on cattle. Easterners, Englishmen, even Australians bought dubious range rights, slapped their brand on a bunch of longhorns, and were on their way to becoming cattle kings. Speculation ran wild and profits were enormous—"riotous feastings on the rim of the crater of ruin."

Ruin came in the mid-eighties. Cattle overgrazed the grasslands, died in drought and blizzard, glutted the market. The stream of longhorns dwindled to a dribble and the cattleman's empire faded.

But not that "ordinary, bowlegged human," the cowboy. He mows hay on a tractor, "rides fences" in a jeep, and rounds up the herd from a helicopter. And he's still the wholesome hero of millions of Americans. On the dude ranch he puts the

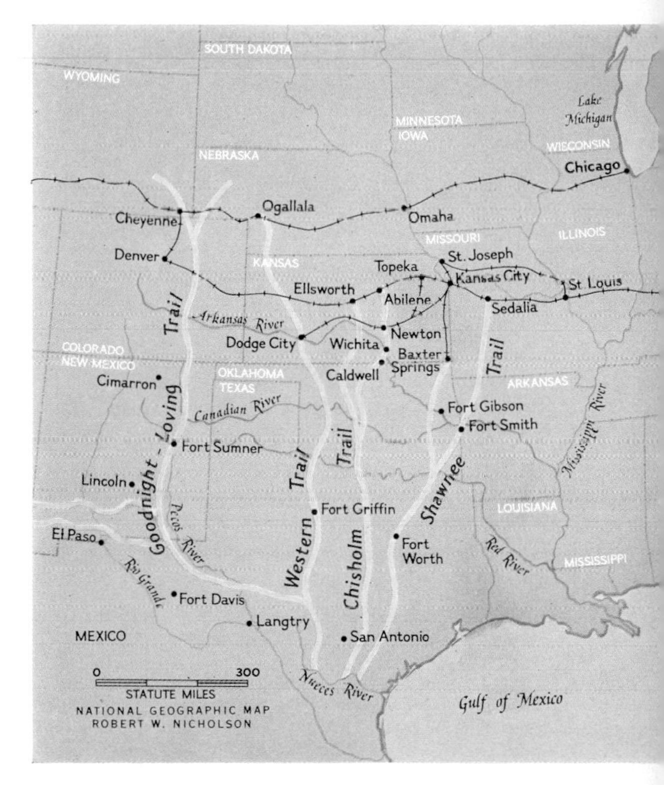

Trails from Texas were the cattleman's highways to northern buyers and open range in the 1860-80's. Bandit-infested Shawnee Trail, guarded by Fort Gibson and Fort Smith, led to Missouri and Kansas railheads. The Chisholm Trail met the railroad at Abilene. Today that beaten path can be seen by tourists "pointing north" on U. S. 81 in Oklahoma. The Western Trail funneled longhorns past Fort Griffin (now ruins) to Dodge City, where "Hands up" was as common as "Hands off." The Goodnight-Loving Trail led to summer grasslands.

unsteadiest rider on the steadiest "hoss." He visits some 500 towns a year with the rodeo. At extravaganzas such as Frontier Days at Cheyenne, Wyoming, and Oregon's Pendleton Roundup, visitors rise in their seats with the broncobuster, groan when he "smells corral dust," gasp while he bulldogs a steer to the ground.

Texas still leads the nation in beeves, but now its 9¼ million are Herefords, Shorthorns, and Anguses heavy with porterhouse and prime ribs. King Ranch, larger than Rhode Island, breeds the Santa Gertrudis, cross between the Shorthorn and India's sacred, fever-resisting Brahman. Missing is the tough old longhorn;

Roundup! Cowboys still lasso and throw 'em, as here on the huge Waggoner Ranch near Vernon, Texas. But the downed critter is a Hereford not a longhorn, and butane heats the branding

crossbreeding for tender steaks almost refined him into oblivion. In 1927 government agents combed south Texas to build herds visitors see at Wichita Mountains Wildlife Refuge in Oklahoma and Fort Niobrara Game Reserve in Nebraska.

Fire and progress have destroyed most of the cattle kingdom's shanties and false-front buildings. But at Langtry, Texas, Judge Roy Bean's "hall of justice"—the Jersey Lilly Saloon—still stands. He proclaimed himself the "Law West of the Pecos," fined culprits a round of drinks for the crowd, and pined for actress Lily Langtry. Lincoln, New Mexico, still echoes the Lincoln County War. In 1878

irons. In the 1870's, heyday of the open range, one roundup might cover 5,000 square miles. Each rancher cut out cows that bore his mark and burned his brand on their bleating calves.

B. ANTHONY STEWART, NATIONAL GEOGRAPHIC PHOTOGRAPHER

MERLE SEVERY, NATIONAL GEOGRAPHIC STAFF

rival cattle barons ended it with a three-day gunfight in the streets. The long drive, the roaring six-shooter, and the Indian ambush are captured for visitors in art collections at Oklahoma's Gilcrease Institute in Tulsa and Woolaroc Museum near Bartlesville; at the Amon G. Carter Memorial Museum in Fort Worth, Texas, "Where the West Begins"; at the Whitney Gallery in Cody, Wyoming; at Montana's State Museum in Helena and C. M. Russell Gallery in Great Falls.

Indestructible are the legends of rip-roaring Kansas cowtowns. "At this writing," warned the Topeka *Commonwealth* in 1868, "Hell is now in session in Abilene." Such sessions erupted at Ellsworth, Newton, Wichita, Caldwell, and Dodge City as those towns grew along the westward-nosing railroad tracks.

Looking for a year's fun in a week, Texas drovers warmed their stomachs with whisky and their feet with dancing, shot at the stars when happy and to kill when angry. Lawmen like the Earps and Mastersons kept what little peace there was. Often the last word in an argument was an epitaph: "T. Brown Died 1875 of Lead Poisoning." Killers often went free. But not when "Hanging Judge" Parker presided. At Fort Smith, Arkansas, he hanged 88 badmen. Visitors shudder at his gallows, which accommodated a dozen at once.

When the last bawling longhorns trailed to Dodge City, acres of wheat ringed the city, and hogs were rooting up prairie sod. By 1888 the cowtown was so prudish that it fined a woman $5 for "unlawfully, feloniously" wearing "male attire." The farmer—moral, marrying, and permanent—had taken over.

Dodge City, Queen of the Cowtowns, gloried as the "Beautiful Bibulous Babylon of the Frontier." It slaked the thirst of Indian fighters from nearby Fort Dodge and shipped hides during the Kansas buffalo slaughter. It boomed as the world's largest cattle market, 1875-84, when Texans trailed in more than a million head to its railyard. Cowboys stampeded to the Long Branch Saloon, and some stayed forever in Boot Hill. On a rebuilt section of Front Street (left) visitors see a replica of the beat patrolled by Wyatt Earp and Bat Masterson.

Below: Cowtown bullets find their mark, and gunmen die with their boots on. The commotion, caught on canvas by Charles M. Russell, who vividly chronicled the heyday of the Wild West, could have been over a girl, a poker hand, or a lingering Civil War grudge.

"WHEN GUNS SPEAK DEATH SETTLES DISPUTES" BY CHARLES M. RUSSELL, THOMAS GILCREASE INSTITUTE OF AMERICAN HISTORY AND ART, TULSA

REWARD

($5,000.00)

Reward for the capture, dead or alive, of one Wm. Wright, better known as

"BILLY THE KID"

Age, 18. Height, 5 feet, 3 inches. Weight, 125 lbs. Light hair, blue eyes and even features. He is the leader of the worst band of desperadoes the Territory has ever had to deal with. The above reward will be paid for his capture or positive proof of his death.

JIM DALTON, Sheriff.

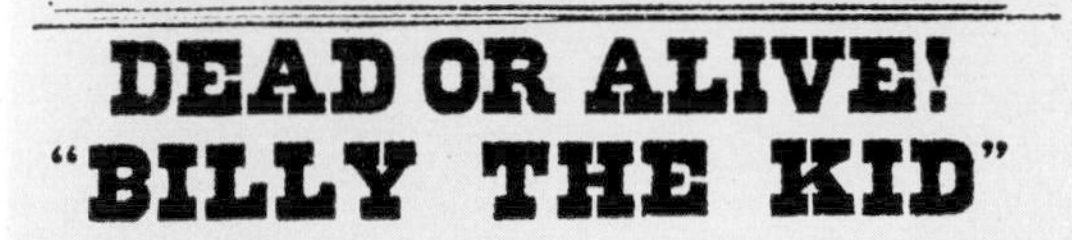

DEAD OR ALIVE!
"BILLY THE KID"

"Hello, Bob," said Billy the Kid. He gave the jailer both barrels and leisurely left the Courthouse at Lincoln (below). Each August the New Mexico cowtown re-enacts the 1881 escape. They say William Bonney (not "Wm. Wright" as on the poster) had a notch on his gun for every year of his life when Sheriff Pat Garrett ended it at 21.

LINCOLN COUNTY COURTHOUSE STATE MONUMENT, NEW MEXICO STATE TOURIST BUREAU

SODBUSTER'S EMPIRE

BEGINNING IN THE 1860's, men edged, then cascaded onto the Great Plains, fired with the hope of a new start in life. Government grants, sales by railroads, squatting—all helped satisfy land hunger. Inexorably (and illogically to the cattleman) the sodbuster plowed up grass that was right side up in the first place, strung barbed wire, and brought women to the Wild West.

He soon found reports of the good life exaggerated. Droughts withered crops; blizzards froze livestock; grasshoppers ate everything but the mortgage. Dust on the horizon could be a twister — or Indians. The drabness, the fear, the endless toil, the sod house dripping yesterday's rain exacted a toll from the farmer's wife.

Inventors supplied new plows and reapers, flour mills and windmills. The sodbuster learned to dry farm, to irrigate, to plant hardy wheat. He and his sturdy wife brought up children without doctors, taught them without schools. They meant to put down roots, and did, in the domain of the fierce, nomadic Plains Indian.

The Pioneer Woman (left) in Ponca City, Oklahoma, stands as a bronze memorial to the homesteader's partner. Cook, mother, midwife, she stood by him as he dented the wilderness with his corn patch. Acreage came easy. When Indian lands in Oklahoma were thrown open in 1889 (upper right), thousands staked claims in a day. But hard years followed in a "soddy" (lower). Today travelers near Beatrice, Nebraska, can see a frontier cabin and its furnishings at Homestead National Monument, site of one of the first claims under the 1862 act.

"OKLAHOMA RUN" BY ROBERT W. LINDNEUX, UNIVERSITY OF OKLAHOMA
LEFT: STATUE BY BRYANT BAKER; B. ANTHONY STEWART, NATIONAL GEOGRAPHIC PHOTOGRAPHER
BELOW. SOD HOUSE IN CUSTER COUNTY, C. 1887, NEBRASKA STATE HISTORICAL SOCIETY

"WESTWARD HO" BY WILLIAM R. LEIGH, WOOLAROC MUSEUM, BARTLESVILLE, OKLAHOMA. RIGHT: B. ANTHONY STEWART, NATIONAL GEOGRAPHIC PHOTOGRAPHER

THE INDIANS FIGHT BACK

MINERS, CATTLEMEN, HOMESTEADERS—to the Plains Indian they were only invaders overrunning lands promised the tribes "as long as the grass shall grow." Reservation life, the effort to turn nomadic warriors into farmers and users of soap, was the final degradation. Little wonder the Indians fought back.

When "white eyes" clashed in civil war, red men seized their chance. In 1862 the Sioux massacred more than 700 settlers in Minnesota. South to Texas the tribes terrorized the frontier. Enraged Colorado volunteers retaliated, killing several hundred sleeping Cheyenne and Arapaho. So it went for 30 years.

After the war Northerners and ex-Confederates ("galvanized Yankees") joined ranks against the menace. In the Southwest they hunted the Apaches, "tigers of the human species," whose reign of terror almost swept civilization before it. Cochise tied captives to anthills, burned them, chopped chunks of flesh from their

The battle was glory to the Plains Indian and had the ritual of a medieval joust. To touch the enemy—a coup—meant more than to scalp, though the Cheyenne settled for either when attacking a wagon train (left). Plains finery (above) symbolizes the Indian today.

feet until they died. Victorio fled army columns in grim chases that totaled 90,000 miles before he was shot down. Geronimo, raiding between drinking bouts, slaughtered scores before he led the last of the Apaches to the reservation in 1886.

Kiowa, Comanche, and Cheyenne rose against the reservation system in 1874 and launched the Red River War. They plundered Texas and Colorado, then fled to the searing Staked Plain. Pursuing soldiers became crazed with thirst; some opened their own veins in search of moisture. After 14 battles the repentant red men straggled back to Indian Territory. Relative calm came to the southern plains.

To the north the Sioux defended their land with a ferocity that checked the white tide. In 1866 Red Cloud led his warriors against soldiers in Wyoming, hunting ground of the Sioux. First he sniped, picking off woodcutters and sentries. When 81 men under Capt. William Fetterman sallied out to even the score, Red Cloud sprang an ambush that wiped them out. Then he hurled thousands of warriors against a handful of men commanded by Capt. James Powell. Wave after wave crumpled before the defenders. Red Cloud lost hundreds of braves learning of the

MERLE SEVERY, NATIONAL GEOGRAPHIC STAFF (ALSO TOP RIGHT)

army's new breech-loading rifles. But the United States was tired of warfare and called back the army from the land of the Sioux.

Soon more white men came, gold seekers rushing to the Black Hills in Dakota. This was sacred hunting land. In 1876 Sioux and Cheyenne massed by the thousands to defend it. Army units moved to round them up.

At the head of the 7th Cavalry rode George Armstrong Custer, searching out the hostiles in Montana. The Civil War general found them June 25 on the Little Big Horn and advanced on their camp. Indians boiled out like bees from a hive, circled on horseback, closed in on foot. Bullets and arrows rained. Custer confidently expected his carbines would rule. He dismounted his command—some 225 well-disciplined troopers—and took a stand along a barren ridge. Though outnumbered ten to one, his men "were fighting good," an Indian recalled. "The dust and smoke was black as evening." But the Indians stampeded Custer's horses, cutting off all escape. In two howling charges, it was all over. Custer and his troopers went down fighting to the last man.

Generals George Crook and Nelson Miles drove the hostiles to the reservation, but the Sioux drama had one more act. In 1890, seized by the "Ghost Dance" craze and spurred on by medicine man Sitting Bull, they chanted in a frenzied vision of deliverance from the white man's yoke. Settlers grew nervous, troops moved in. When Indians resisted being disarmed, violence flared at Wounded Knee in South Dakota. More than 200 Indians fell. The power of the red warrior was broken forever.

Fort Larned, Kansas, once known as Camp Alert, rose in 1859 to guard the Santa Fe Trail. A fine example of a frontier post, it recalls when hundreds of wagons would head westward in a single day.

Fort Union in New Mexico (left) heard the brazen call of the bugle as cavalry rode out after raiding Utes, Comanches, and Apaches. Biggest post in the Southwest, it was built on the Santa Fe Trail in 1851, abandoned 1891. The National Park Service preserves its ruins.

Stockades (below) were fair game for the Indian, striking with stealth and fire. But he preferred better odds: wagon trains, hunting parties, small troop units he could cut up with howling, hard-riding attacks.

"DEFENDING THE STOCKADE" BY CHARLES SCHREYVOGEL, FROM THE COLLECTION OF BRONSON TREVOR

Custer's luck runs out at the Little Bighorn

George Armstrong Custer, "Yellow Hair" to the red men, had a regiment, courage, and Civil War memories of dashing cavalry charges. Sitting Bull, braided Sioux medicine man, had ten times the men and a vision that they would win. Custer's heroic defense above the Little Bighorn River on June 25, 1876, made the nation yearn for details that no white man lived to tell.

Shrill war cries of Sioux and Cheyenne, the hoarse shouts of 7th Cavalry troopers seem to resound from this canvas by Edgar S. Paxson. After years of research on the scene, he painted the death struggle in 1899. Indians said Custer, depicted in buckskin, fell early.

Graveyard silence haunts Custer Battlefield National Monument in Montana; markers show where soldiers died in the last great victory by Plains Indians. Custer rests at West Point.

MELVILLE BELL GROSVENOR. UPPER: CUSTER BY MATHEW B. BRADY, AND SITTING BULL, BOTH NATIONAL ARCHIVES. LEFT: "CUSTER'S LAST STAND," WHITNEY GALLERY OF WESTERN ART, CODY, WYOMING

STEWART H. HOLBROOK

The Growing Giant

LONG BEFORE the West was won, prophets hailed a new era, even gave it a name: The Age of Enterprise. Filled with the thunder and lightning of business and industry, 19th century America smelled of smoke, coke, coal, oil, dust, sage, and pine. What had happened? A rich continent, free of political shackles, had been thrown open for development. It seemed as if every one-man shop with power from river or brook had suddenly grown into a factory. And many were installing steam engines, to operate come high water or low.

Along with pioneer industrialists came inventors. One and all had something to ease the labor of the man who earned his keep by the sweat of his brow. Who could have guessed that an obscure kettlemaker in Eddyville, Kentucky, was to become the first man in the world to turn dull iron ore into bright steel in a matter of minutes by blowing cold air into the molten mass? William "Crazy" Kelly's invention of the mid-1800's, known later as the Bessemer process, revolutionized an industry. And what prophet could have foretold that a resident physician of the New York City Alms House was to perfect the common one-piece pin, and to design a machine for sticking pins into paper folds? Dr. John I. Howe's invention was a marvel of the 19th century. What seers could have guessed that in a hundred rising cities, in a thousand hamlets and crossroad villages, unknown tinkerers

STEELMEN "SLAG THE LADLE" (REMOVE DROSS) BEFORE POURING MOLTEN STEEL INTO MOLDS AT A BESSEMER FURNACE IN SPARROWS POINT, MARYLAND. BETHLEHEM STEEL COMPANY

would devise plans or formulas for flying machines, digging machines, sewing machines, threshing machines; would figure out recipes to harden or soften materials, even to change the nature of a thing—as wood into paper. Many of these men were downright crackpots, fanatic about their visions. Yet an astonishing number of them had that divine spark of originality that made their creations work!

In 1790 the United States Patent Office opened for business. No fewer than a dozen inventors—"all from Connecticut," said one account—waited at the door. And as the years rolled by, urgent dreamers from every state, from every territory offered all manner of new things: posthole diggers, apple parers by the dozen, writing machines, a steam carriage, a combination churn-and-rocking chair. The man in the Patent Office might scratch his head in wonder, but he was polite. It seemed almost everybody got his patent.

U. S. Patent No. 1 went to Samuel Hopkins for an improved method of "making Pot ash and Pearl ash" from wood ashes. These were ingredients for glass making. Mr. Hopkins wasn't the first to profit from America's vast woodlands. Nor the last.

PRODUCTS OF THE FOREST had been among the first exports from the colonies. Not for nothing did the District of Maine put a pine tree emblem on its flag. At South Berwick in 1634 colonists built a dam and harnessed the Salmon Falls River so it swished an up-and-down saw—America's first sawmill. A son of Pilgrim John Alden ran a sawmill on Maine's Saco River. Another early timber baron, Sir William Pepperrell of Louisbourg fame, appeared at his log landings in a scarlet coat. I like to think that from this influence stemmed the loggers' liking for bright red sashes, shirts, Mackinaws, and stockings.

Colonists found the all-covering forest both friend and enemy. From it came wood for houses, ships, and fuel. Yet marauding Indians lurked in its sinister depths. Also it kept the soil dark and damp so grain couldn't grow. Thus for at least two centuries the man who erected a sawmill and cleared the ground was reckoned a public benefactor.

"Daylight in the swamp!"—classic morning cry of the logging boss—signaled the time to start chopping. And chop and saw they did, the generations of woodsmen, properly called loggers. In 300 years they hewed out what was called The Big Clearing from eastern Maine to western Oregon. Barring the plains, where trees were too sparse to count, they cut a swath 3,000 miles long.

Yet this mighty industry did not hit full stride until independence was won. England's monarchs forbade the cutting of pines and "okes" suitable for navy masts. Royal representatives branded these trees with a broad arrow. But the Revolution ended that practice. Ambitious men bought the former crown lands by the millions of acres. Ingenious men perfected—and patented—devices like circular saws, cant dogs, sleds, double-bitted axes, log turners, chain saws, and a thousand more items right down to the method of using gamma rays to determine the density of wood in a tree.

Perhaps the best known inventor in the lumber industry was Joe Peavey, a Maine blacksmith. He devised the improved cant dog, made a patent sketch of it, but got sidetracked in a Bangor saloon. When he revived, he found another blacksmith had signed and entered his patent application. Nevertheless, "peavey" has long been generic for the riverman's logrolling tool.

Names of outstanding lumbermen rise from the forest of timber merchants. William Bingham was one. In 1793 he bought some two million acres of northeastern white pine and spruce. For more than a century woodsmen hacked away at it, driving logs from the "Penobscot Million" downriver to Bangor, Maine, and from the "Kennebec Million" down to Augusta.

In their urgency for timber Penobscot and Kennebec loggers sometimes crossed axes. Usually they fought for the sheer fun of it. Gouging and ear chewing were highly thought of.

But you couldn't kill a lumberjack with a poleax. Rough, tough, lusty, he lived in a tree and hung by his tail, it was said. He was immune to disease and slept soundly when the thermometer was "two feet below zero." He was a catfooted man with steel calks in his boots who chased logs downstream. Throw a bar of soap into the water and he would ride the bubbles to shore.

He was an exaggeration but no myth, a pioneer fit to follow in the tracks of the explorer and trapper. When a forest had been cut, he would shoulder his ax and hit out over the next hump.

The timber line moved steadily west and sawdust cities flourished as the forests fell. Glens Falls, New York, and Williamsport, Pennsylvania, were logging capitals in the 1860's. But within a decade Saginaw, Michigan, was the lumber colossus with 74 sawmills. Cutting in Wisconsin and Minnesota closed out what some call the golden age of lumberjacks. By 1900 loggers were leaping the bare Dakotas to harvest the heavily timbered Northwest. From Idaho into

LOGGING'S ROARING ERA
LIVES ON IN LEGENDARY PAUL BUNYAN;
PAUL R. HOFFMASTER

the Sierras stretched a sea of pine. On the banks of the Columbia and around Puget Sound grew Douglas fir so thick a man could hardly swing an ax. Near Humboldt Bay in California towered monstrous redwoods. A logger wasn't likely to forget the first time he saw one fall. "Tim-berrr!" There is a dry tearing as though the clouds are being ripped apart, and the swishing undertone sounds like a hurricane being born. A long rumbling crash booms in your ears and shakes the ground.

You could tell a logging town by the mile upon mile of logs in lake or river waiting their turn at the murderous band saws. One of these glittering steel ribbons could and did make 500,000 feet of boards in a day. Summer or winter made little difference, for some thoughtful lumberman had pushed a pipe carrying live steam into a frozen log pond. Lo, the hot pond was born! Night or day it was pretty much the same, for refuse burners billowed fire and smoke for months on end, often for years. In the deepest woods, burners gleamed and winked like lost stars in the night, all because barns and houses had to be built and the northern plains fenced, and in a hurry too. All America was in a hurry.

In 1909 American sawmills made 44½ billion feet of lumber, an all-time peak. Then consumption started to fall. The cities that were first built of lumber had come to be built of almost everything else. Instead of public benefactor, the lumberman suddenly became a public enemy, accused of leaving nothing but stumps in his wake. It was a grossly unfair charge. Certainly the logger left stumps; he also left farms and ranches, towns and cities.

In logging's red-eyed heyday fortunes billowed and sometimes vanished within a decade: Poor boy today; tomorrow a plug hat, gold-headed cane, and a cellar of champagne. One lumber baron enclosed his estate near Waters, Michigan, with a

wall built of champagne empties. The house has gone but part of the wall still stands. Mark it well for it spells an era.

With the Growing Giant housed, lumbermen agreed they should not work the forest as a mine, then abandon it. The woodland was a farm which would yield crops again and again, so long as men protected it from decay, blowdown, and fire. Public indifference and carelessness had made fire prevention a gigantic task in the old days. Lumberjacks said the Peshtigo fire in Wisconsin, raging the same night that Chicago burned, bred a thousand moosebirds—dead loggers reincarnated as Canada jays. Happier landmarks of America's oldest industry are the millions of acres of registered tree farms on once-abandoned timber cuttings. Let the wide-ranging tourist go see for himself. New crops of timber supply an industry which technology has changed until lumber is merely one of a thousand items manufactured from cellulose and lignin, the components of wood.

NEARLY ALL INNOVATIONS, it seems, must be preceded by prophets. One of the greatest, and most disregarded, was cantankerous Oliver Evans, born in Delaware in 1755. When he was 17 he learned about the steam engine that James Watt had perfected in England. Devising ways to use it engrossed Evans's genius the rest of his life.

Right after the Revolution he petitioned Pennsylvania and Maryland for exclusive rights on his "improvements in flour mills and steam carriages." As a prophet of steam railroads Evans went to the top of his class.

He envisioned a railway between New York City and Philadelphia "for the transportation of heavy produce, merchandise, and passengers on carriages drawn by steam engines." He suggested paths for the wheels to run on, "with a rail between them, set on posts, to guide the tongue of the carriage so that they might travel by night as well as by day." Critics yawned and snickered. Evans talked on and on of parallel logs on the ground, flattened on top and with a three-inch plank pinned to them. A wooden railway, he said, would require less upkeep than a turnpike. People could safely travel 15 miles an hour, 300 miles a day.

Poor old Evans, blower of bubbles, rider of rainbows. The good old stagecoach, Mr. Evans, will never be supplanted. Besides, if the Lord had intended us to ride in steam carriages, Sir, he would have invented them.

Evans never wavered in his belief that steam engines would pull carriages over rails. "But," he reflected, "one step in a generation is all we can hope for. If the present generation shall adopt canals, the next may try the railway with horses, and the third generation use the steam carriage."

The steam carriage would not have to wait nearly so long. In 1815, four years before Evans died, New Jersey granted John Stevens of Hoboken permission to build a railroad across that state. Failing to pry capital out of complacent men, he designed and built in 1825—at the age of 76!—a steam locomotive, then ran it on a circular track in the yard of his home.

The snorting toy worked. The dam of apathy and ignorance burst. In 1827 the Baltimore and Ohio Railroad was chartered. A year later old Charles Carroll, sole surviving signer of the Declaration of Independence, leaned on a spade and turned

Steam mechanized 19th century farms as well as factories. This Rube Goldberg-like monster was the forerunner of today's gasoline tractor.

NEW YORK PUBLIC LIBRARY

a sod while a band played and cannon boomed. But the B & O fooled with sail cars and horsepower before it took the big step to steam.

Meanwhile the West Point Foundry in New York built the locomotive *Best Friend of Charleston* for the Charleston & Hamburg in South Carolina. Over its six miles of track in December, 1830, rolled the first train of cars ever moved by steam in the United States. This event truly fathered American railroading—not the much-heralded race several months earlier between Peter Cooper's *Tom Thumb* and a gray horse, the horse winning hands down.

Five years after the *Best Friend* made its epic run, there were 1,098 miles of steam railroad operating in the United States. It was the beginning of a nostalgic age. Locomotives had diamond stacks and conductors wore immense mustaches and fine cutaway coats. Horse-drawn omnibuses "met the train" at the depot, where brassy "news butchers" hawked tobacco, candy, and newspapers. Oliver Evans would have gloried in the spectacle.

WHAT "MARK TWAIN" SAYS ABOUT IT.
Hartford, March 19, 1875.

GENTLEMEN: Please do not use my name in any way. Please do not even divulge the fact that I own a machine. I have entirely stopped using the Type-Writer, for the reason that I never could write a letter with it to anybody without receiving a request by return mail that I would not only describe the machine, but state what progress I had made in the use of it, etc., etc. I don't like to write letters, and so I don't want people to know I own this curiosity-breeding little joker. Yours truly,

SAML. L. CLEMENS.

THE FIRST AUTHOR TO USE A TYPEWRITER WROTE THIS TESTIMONIAL FOR REMINGTON; LIBRARY OF CONGRESS

"Nothing is invented and perfected at the same time," an old saying has it. This applies not only to Evans but to "Doc" Samuel M. Kier, something of a Barnum in Pennsylvania. Knowing that seepage oil had been used for years as a panacea for human ills, he began to bottle it. Kier's Rock Oil sold so well that he put 50 red and gilt wagons on the road, their sides ornamented with paintings of the Good Samaritan ministering to the afflicted.

Now he attempted to make an illuminant from his Rock Oil. In Pittsburgh he rigged a still—actually the first oil refinery in the United States—and succeeded in producing a wine-colored liquid he named carbon oil. Then he invented a lamp burner that would consume it and give a fairly good light. But it stank most horribly. Ten years were to elapse before the odor was removed. Kier neglected to patent his refining process and it was appropriated by later experimenters.

On August 27, 1859, the first drilled oil well in the world began spouting at the rate of 25 barrels a day. Titusville, Pennsylvania, recalls the strike with the restored derrick and a museum in a state park. Driller Edwin L. Drake, who had been a conductor on the New York and New Haven Railroad, was to petroleum what James Marshall was to gold. But this event, in the long run, far surpassed the discovery of gold in California. Petroleum would change the lives of people the world over.

At first it simply changed western Pennsylvania from backwoods to an industrial jungle, reeking with the fumes from small refineries, spotted with derricks, laced with pipelines. On the banks of slimy creeks wild-eyed men built hideous

SCIENTIFIC AMERICAN, 1890, LIBRARY OF CONGRESS

Traffic jams plagued New York even in the Gay Nineties. Visionaries urged elevated sidewalks over streets to train stations and ferry slips.

towns and named them Oil City, Pithole, and Petrolia. The scene was duplicated over and over in Ohio and West Virginia, in Texas, Oklahoma, and California.

Long before oil became something more than a patent medicine, imaginative men had kindled the fires of industry. One-man shops burgeoned into factories. Sons of farmers, and daughters too, flocked to them. Individual enterprises banded together, sold stock to the public, and borrowed from bankers.

As the machine industries boomed ahead, the sons of farmers became corporation presidents. Clerks became full-fledged merchants. Mill hands became technicians. Immigrants from the Old World marveled at the ease with which Americans changed not only their job and place of residence but their position in society. The fluidity of vertical movement was a startling sight for Europeans.

Among the welter of new industrialists emerged the Giants, Titans, or Moguls. That the terms of robber, pirate, and rascal were also applied to them alters nothing; what counted most was that they never were called feeble. Consider Daniel Drew and Jim Fisk. Both were country lads, but there any similarity ends. All his long life Drew dressed and played the part of a yokel in the big city, a sort of rustic fallen among thieves. "I got to be a millionaire," he liked to say, "afore I knowed it, hardly." Often he spent his evenings in a cheap hotel quietly chewing plug tobacco and reading the Bible. His Christian pose, however, never interfered with his cattle dealings. He had drovers salt his steers and let them drink their fill before weighing. "Watered stock" became a Wall Street term.

Jim Fisk milked millions from the Erie Railroad. He refurbished the New York

City Grand Opera House and leased it to the Erie for $75,000 a month. Its carved oak doors, gilded balustrades, cut glass chandeliers, and ceilings with "Pompeian designs of intertwining vines and flowers hiding naked cupids and rosy nymphs" formed a fit setting for the Prince of the Erie. He ruled from a walnut desk on a dais and sat in a chair studded with gold-headed nails. "Nothing is lost save honor," he said of the conspiracy to corner the gold market in 1869 which resulted in the Black Friday Scandal, with a taint that spread even to Congress.

ALONG WITH GREAT WEALTH the moguls accumulated personal characteristics that became legendary. John Warne "Bet-a-million" Gates was a rollicking, Falstaffian soul who wore diamonds on his shirt and on each gallus buckle. In one evening he lost $400,000 at cards. Cornelius Vanderbilt was playing whist when one of his railroads came under fire for allegedly violating New York law. "Whist is a game," he told his eager interrogator, "that requires one's undivided attention." Right down to his last illness in 1876 the Commodore was always good for a quote. When a doctor suggested champagne to the patient, the old man figured the cost, then replied: "I guess sody water will do."

John D. Rockefeller, who neither smoked nor drank liquor, got sustenance chiefly from milk and graham crackers. Andrew Carnegie enjoyed oatmeal. Philip D. Armour was a glutton for work. "I like to turn bristles, blood, bones, and the insides and outsides of pigs and bullocks into revenue," he said.

J. Pierpont Morgan's ruby nose added to his fame. It was "part of the American business structure," he once remarked; another time he quipped that it "would be impossible for me to appear on the streets without it." He sometimes commanded his chauffeur to drive on the sidewalk when bogged down in traffic.

James Jerome Hill, who got his start in what had been the raw settlement of Pig's Eye (rechristened St. Paul), once fired an employee on discovering his name was Spittles. Again, when the mayor of a Minnesota town objected mildly to all-night switching, the irascible railroader swore its people should walk, then had the depot torn down and set up two miles away. On the other hand, when a section crew was trying to clear track for a train stalled in a Dakota blizzard, he sent workers into his private car for hot coffee while he shoveled snow.

Industrial America of Hill's time was a boisterous state where the effective way to remove weaklings was to set a pace which only the most rugged could survive. Horatio Alger said it again and again. You got to be railroad president by *working harder than the other fellow*.

Wherever railroads came, change was sure to follow. They created countless jobs and altered America's habits as nothing else. "They go and come," said Henry Thoreau of the trains that passed his pond, "with such regularity and precision, and their whistle can be heard so far, that the farmers set their clocks by them, and thus one well-conducted institution regulates a whole country. Have not men improved somewhat in punctuality since the railroad was invented? Do they not talk and think faster in the depot than they did in the stage-office?"

Yes, indeed they do.

"**The Pacific Railroad** is finished," the telegraph clacked. "San Francisco annexes the United States!" Californians boasted. Across the nation bells rang and cannon boomed with the wedding of rails at Promontory, Utah. The ceremonial golden spike and silver maul, mementos of that May day in 1869, repose at Stanford University.

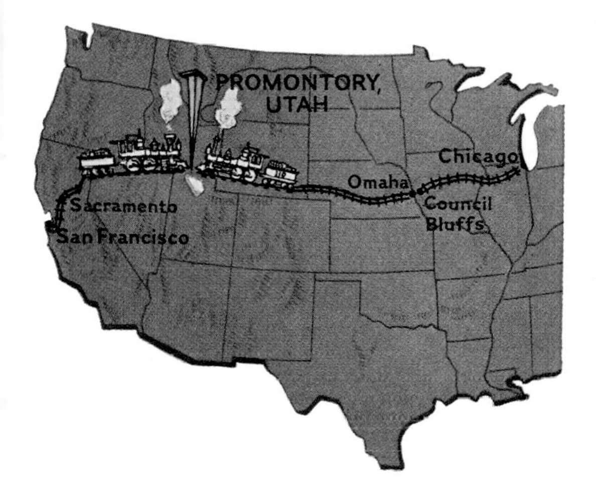

B. ANTHONY STEWART, NATIONAL GEOGRAPHIC PHOTOGRAPHER

A GOLDEN SPIKE JOINS THE NATION

IN SACRAMENTO STANDS a modest monument to an engineer and prophet—Theodore Dehone Judah, also known as Crazy Judah. A more fitting monument would be the long, long ribbons of steel that tie Pacific swells to rolling plains. Judah wasn't the first to dream of a transcontinental railroad. Men had talked of that almost from the birth of the iron horse. But when Judah spoke, enthusiasts heard their Moses. He made believers of editors and congressmen. He raised capital from California merchants—among them Leland Stanford, Charles Crocker, Mark Hopkins, and Collis P. Huntington. He created the Central Pacific.

On July 1, 1862, President Lincoln signed the act subsidizing that company and the Union Pacific to build a railroad from the Missouri River to the Pacific Ocean. "We have drawn the elephant," telegraphed the jubilant Judah. "Now let us see if we can harness him up." His partners, eager for government land and loans that accrued with each mile of track laid, wanted to build fast and cheap. Judah, in charge of construction, wanted nothing to do with a makeshift road. He sold out and sailed for New York. There, a week after landing, he died of fever.

But his idea lived, became a deed, finally became a legend. Eastward from Sacramento inched the Central Pacific. Bull-throated Charley Crocker, finding brawn scarce, hired Chinese to lay track. Averaging about 110 pounds soaking wet, the pig-tailed, basket-hatted coolies worked like devils, their picks beating a steady

tattoo on the Sierra granite. Through snow and avalanche they blasted and bored to the Nevada flats, leaving 15 tunnels in their wake.

Westward from Omaha thrust the Union Pacific. Its construction gangs of Civil War veterans, mountain men, mule skinners, and tough Paddies from Ireland toiled across Nebraska and Wyoming trailing a raft of gamblers and painted harpies. Often laborers had to help troops fight the Cheyenne, for as Gen. George Crook tartly remarked, it was difficult to surround three Indians with one soldier.

In Utah the subsidy-hungry companies built roadbeds feverishly—right on by each other! Rival crews traded pot shots and set off blasts to destroy opposing grades. Finally, after a nudge from Congress, the rails met at the shack and tent town of Promontory, about 40 miles northwest of Ogden. At noon on May 10, 1869, bearded officials hammered in the golden spike that joined East and West.

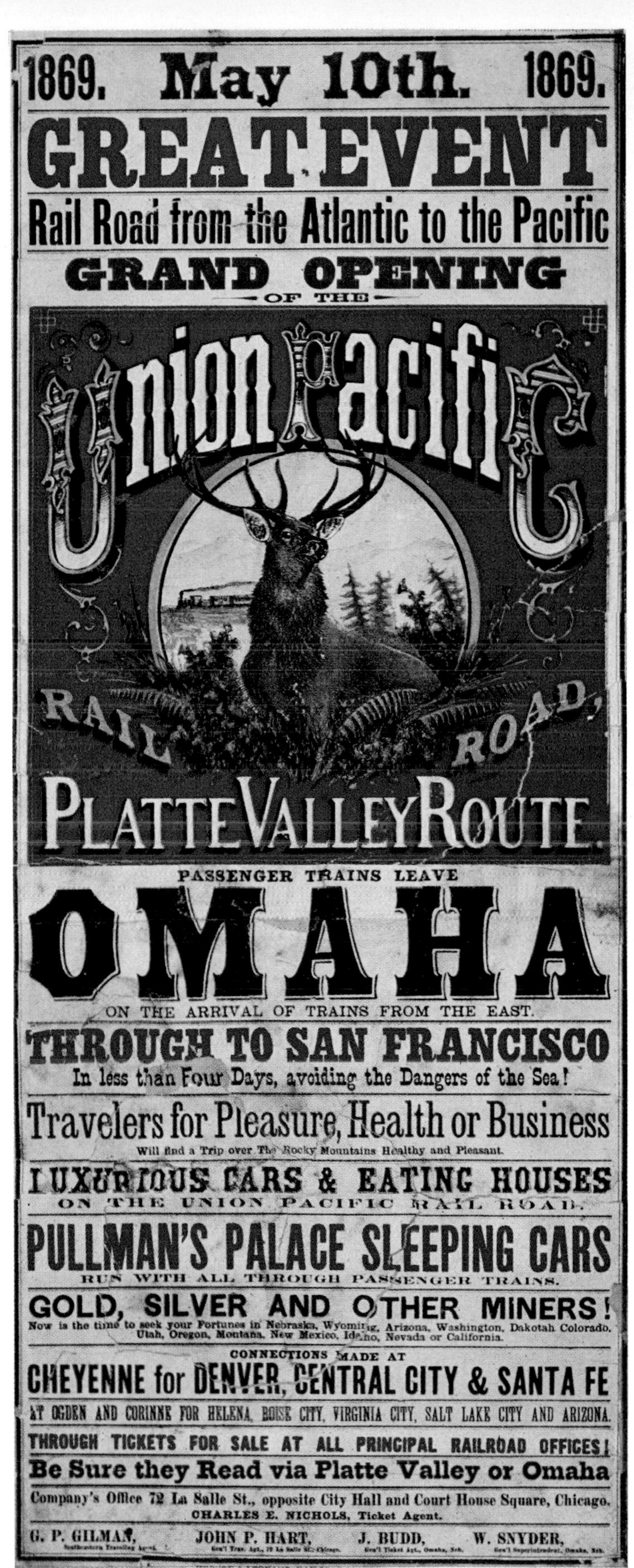

Promontory, Utah, blazed in glory, then faded when the transcontinental junction was moved to Ogden. Visitors to the Golden Spike National Historic Site hike through sand and sage to find traces of the original line. Some "Hell on Wheels" towns like Cheyenne, Wyoming, prospered.

Romance of the rails touched nearly every American hamlet and heart. Men still sing "Casey Jones" and gaze at old-time locomotives in parks or in Baltimore's B & O Transportation Museum.

UNION PACIFIC RAILROAD COLORPHOTO
ABOVE: SOUTHERN PACIFIC COMPANY

A trip to yesterday

A WHISTLE SCREAMS, steam hisses, couplings clank. We chug out of Durango, Colorado, and clickety-clack into the San Juan Mountains. Yellow coaches with open platforms, hand brakes, and potbellied stoves bulge with tourists. Many, en route to Mesa Verde National Park, have stopped on U. S. 160 to make this all-day, 90-mile round trip to Silverton ("We have silver by the ton").

Why? For the thrill of riding one of America's last narrow-gauge steam railroads through immense scenery to a false-front mining town straight out of the gilded 1880's.

Black smoke billows; the diamond-stack engine pants along three-foot tracks that hairpin and S-curve where standard gauge (4′8½″) could never go. Camera fans hang from windows as cracker-box cars squeal around a narrow shelf far above dizzying Animas Canyon. Threading the gorge, the little train climbs amid a jumble of 13,000-foot peaks. The conductor points. "See those switchbacks of the old stagecoach road? Only way to reach the mines before the rail route was blasted in 1881-82."

With bonanza days gone and the Million Dollar Highway, U. S. 550, sapping its business, the Silverton branch was dying when movies and tourists discovered it. Now the iron pony will go puffing on each summer day so long as enthusiasts keep it from the roundhouse of oblivion.

MERLE SEVERY

MERLE SEVERY, NATIONAL GEOGRAPHIC STAFF. OPPOSITE: ELIOT ELISOFON, COURTESY LIFE, © 1959 TIME INC.

Iron pony drinks deep after cliff-hanging in Animas Canyon. At 9,300 feet tourists pile out to enjoy Silverton, old Colorado boom town.

"UNVEILING THE STATUE OF LIBERTY" BY EDWARD MORAN, 1888, COURTESY OF MRS. SETON HENRY

LIBERTY AND OPPORTUNITY BECKON

THE STATUE OF LIBERTY National Monument rises 300 feet above New York Harbor to lift her lamp "beside the golden door." Within her copper form, hued green by time's alchemy, visitors climb a spiral stairway to peer from windows in her massive crown. Masterpiece of Alsatian sculptor Frédéric Auguste Bartholdi, gift from France, this "Mother of Exiles" inspired poet Emma Lazarus, whose words adorn the pedestal. *Give me your tired, your poor, your huddled masses yearning to breathe free. . . .*

Standing in the center of old Fort Wood on Liberty (Bedloe's) Island, the 225-ton statue tends freedom's greatest portal. She has been strengthened, her

"IN THE LAND OF PROMISE: CASTLE GARDEN" BY CHARLES F. ULRICH, 1884, CORCORAN GALLERY OF ART

torch brightened since her unveiling in 1886 at the flood tide of immigration.

In the 19th century, famine and strife sent torrents of aliens to the United States. Let them come, exulted Emerson: "The energy of Irish, Germans, Swedes, Poles, and Cossacks, and all the European tribes,—and of the Africans, and of the Polynesians,—will construct a new race, a new religion, a new state, a new literature."

From 1855 to 1890 more than seven million streamed through Castle Garden, New York. Boston, Seattle, San Francisco, Honolulu established other depots. But Ellis Island, New York, outstripped them all. By the time it closed in 1954 after 62 years, 20 million immigrants had poured in. Before quotas checked the flow, men claimed that for every steamship arriving, teeming with passengers, a new steel plant rose in Pennsylvania, a new textile plant sprang up in Massachusetts, and 1,000 more pick-and-shovel men pushed railroads west from Chicago.

B. ANTHONY STEWART AND (BELOW) BATES LITTLEHALES, NATIONAL GEOGRAPHIC PHOTOGRAPHERS

ANDREW H. BROWN, NATIONAL GEOGRAPHIC STAFF

Polyglot America! Not even Babel heard more tongues. Old World heritages, though largely fused with those of the New, can still be seen, heard, and tasted. Tulips and wooden shoes mark the May festival in Holland, Michigan; Scottish bagpipes skirl in Cleveland's Cultural Gardens, where nationality groups don native garb for "One World Day"; barbecued duck basted with honey tempts appetites any time in San Francisco's Chinatown restaurants.

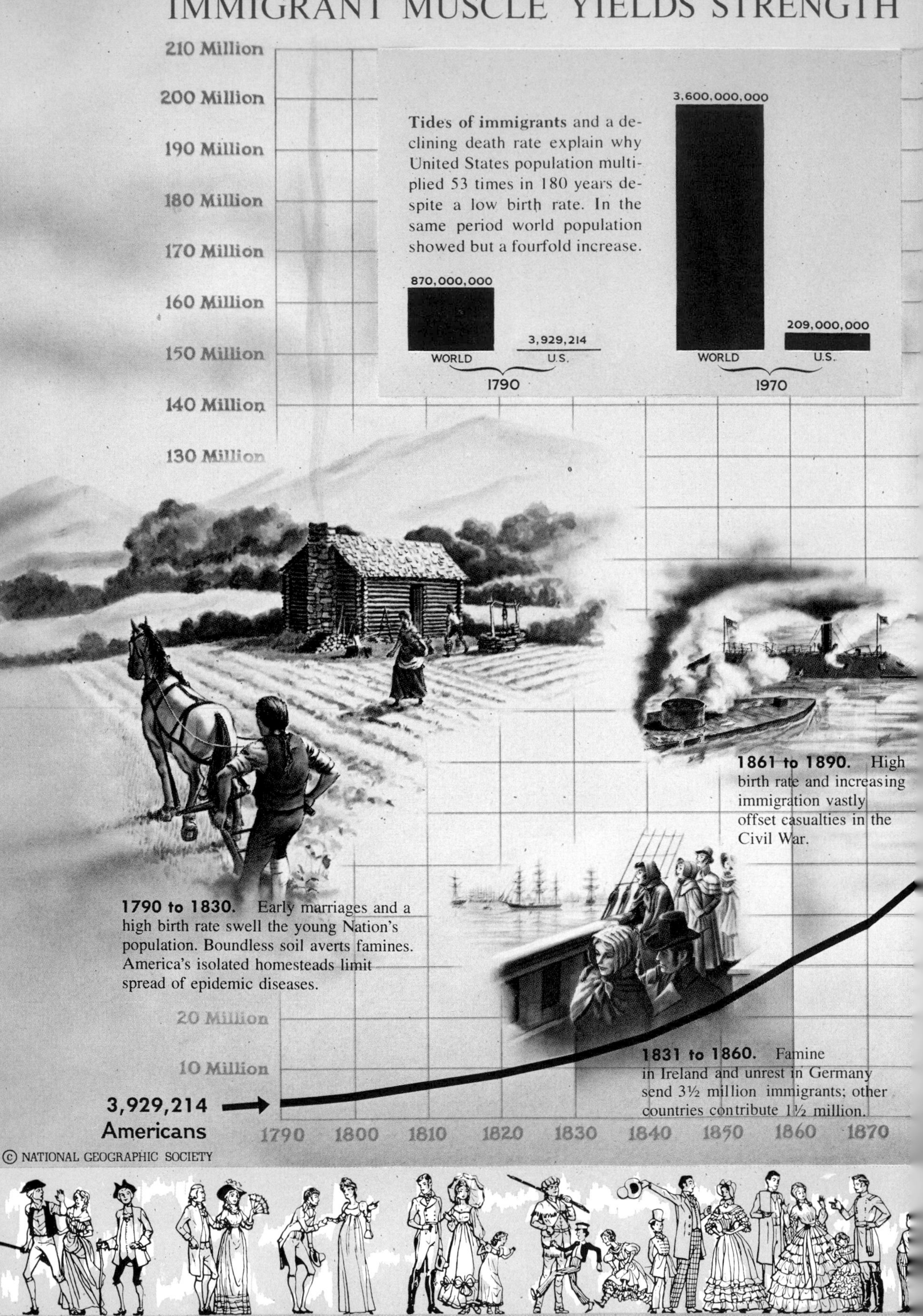
IMMIGRANT MUSCLE YIELDS STRENGTH
210 Million
200 Million
190 Million
180 Million
170 Million
160 Million
150 Million
140 Million
130 Million
Tides of immigrants and a declining death rate explain why United States population multiplied 53 times in 180 years despite a low birth rate. In the same period world population showed but a fourfold increase.
870,000,000
WORLD
3,929,214
U.S.
1790
3,600,000,000
WORLD
209,000,000
U.S.
1970
1861 to 1890. High birth rate and increasing immigration vastly offset casualties in the Civil War.
1790 to 1830. Early marriages and a high birth rate swell the young Nation's population. Boundless soil averts famines. America's isolated homesteads limit spread of epidemic diseases.
20 Million
10 Million
1831 to 1860. Famine in Ireland and unrest in Germany send 3½ million immigrants; other countries contribute 1½ million.
3,929,214
Americans
1790
1800
1810
1820
1830
1840
1850
1860
1870
© NATIONAL GEOGRAPHIC SOCIETY

FOR THE GROWING GIANT

209,000,000
Americans
1961 to 1970. Population passes 200 million in mid-1967 and heads for 209 million by the end of the decade. Birth rate decline and a leveling of the falling death rate hold the gain steady. Experts predict a sharp rise in the 1970's when girls of the post-World War II baby boom reach childbearing age.
1951 to 1960. Unprecedented prosperity, earlier marriages, larger families, and new life-saving drugs trigger a population boom. Newly admitted Alaska and Hawaii help to swell the decade's gain to 29 million.
1941 to 1950. Rising birth rate, falling civilian death rate, and controlled immigration offset World War II losses and net a gain of 19 million.
1931 to 1940. Depression, lowest birth rate in the country's history, and immigration barriers lessen population growth.
1921 to 1930. Postwar prosperity brings a new flood of immigrants leading to end of free entry. Boom ends in '29.
1911 to 1920. World War I slows immigration; birth rate declines; influenza kills half a million. Result: slower growth.
1891 to 1910. Expanding industry and cheap steamship fares attract 12 million immigrants, the majority from southern and eastern Europe.
1890
1900
1910
1920
1930
1940
1950
1960
1970
R.W. Nicholson

BLAST FURNACES IN BIRMINGHAM, ALABAMA, BY J. BAYLOR ROBERTS, AND (LEFT) WASHINGTON LUMBERJACK WALKING A SPAR TREE, BY B. ANTHONY STEWART, BOTH NATIONAL GEOGRAPHIC STAFF

Resources and industries build fabulous fortunes . . .

IN THE LATE 19th century America's smoldering industry burst into flame and spread like wildfire. Business became BIG business. "Poor boys," as Andrew Carnegie labeled them, "trained in that sternest but most efficient of all schools – poverty," became tycoons.

They built factories, railroads, skyscrapers; manufactured steel, explosives, gasoline. They sensationalized newspapers and capitalized on the nation's muscle. Tough-minded, encased in rhinoceros hides, these men in a hurry

HOMESTAKE MILLS AT LEAD, SOUTH DAKOTA, SIT ON AMERICA'S RICHEST GOLD LODE; BATES LITTLEHALES, NATIONAL GEOGRAPHIC PHOTOGRAPHER

set the national style. America rewarded them handsomely. With their legendary wealth they bought everything but eternal life. They fashioned the Gilded Age.

Many of its monuments and memories endure. Monuments such as 2,509 Carnegie libraries; Vanderbilt University; the Guggenheim, Du Pont, Rockefeller, and Ford Foundations; the National Gallery of Art in Washington, gift from banker Andrew Mellon. Memories such as $100,000 parties in Fifth Avenue

LUCAS GUSHER OPENED TEXAS OIL ERA; BEAUMONT CHAMBER OF COMMERCE. RIGHT: PORTRAITS BY WAYNE BARRETT, NATIONAL GEOGRAPHIC STAFF

Cornelius Vanderbilt, first American mogul, sired a dynasty synonymous with wealth (grandson Cornelius reigned in the 1890's). The crusty Commodore wrote the book on railroad monopoly.

John D. Rockefeller amassed a huge fortune fueling the world's kerosene lamps and gasoline engines. His philanthropies, fortunes in themselves, inspired his son and grandsons.

John Pierpont Morgan, financial wizard, architect of corporations, helped shape U. S. industry. "God made the world," steelworkers joked, "and it was reorganized in 1901 by J. P. Morgan."

James Jerome Hill laid rails and deposited immigrants from St. Paul to Puget Sound. The country bloomed; Hill reaped millions.

Andrew Carnegie, King of the Vulcans, giver of libraries, forged frail companies and dynamic men into an empire of steel.

. . . and a gilded age

mansions; round-the-world voyages in Commodore Vanderbilt's *North Star;* the private Pullmans of Jay Gould and Leland Stanford. But the most opulent symbols of the Gilded Age were its castles and "cottages."

Millionaires spent kings' ransoms on retreats at Bar Harbor, Maine; in the Berkshires in Massachusetts, and on Long Island.

At Newport, Rhode Island, storied playground of New York's "400" in the Gay Nineties, sightseers now stare in wonder at a score of palaces, particularly The Breakers, the 70-room, multimillion-dollar cottage of Cornelius Vanderbilt. Come summer, station wagons crammed with kids and grandmas parade down Ocean Drive where liveried coachmen drove phaetons and broughams behind silver-harnessed horses. On broad Newport lawns Whitneys and Vanderbilts raced newfangled horseless carriages; and one cottager, John Jacob Astor, could remark that "a man with a million dollars is as well off as if he were rich."

Tourists can see what untaxed millions bought in William Rockefeller's 20-room cottage on Jekyll Island, Georgia, and George W. Vanderbilt's Biltmore estate in North Carolina. Nor did price deter James Deering, farm machinery magnate, who built the Italian villa Vizcaya near Miami. Visitors gaze at its art—bought by the shipload.

"The Blue Boy" by Gainsborough and "Pinkie" by Lawrence crown the collection of railroad titan Henry E. Huntington at his San Marino estate near Los Angeles. At San Simeon, on California's Highway No. 1, William Randolph Hearst had his own zoo!

DRAWING BELOW BY CHARLES DANA GIBSON

Biltmore, George W. Vanderbilt's château near Asheville, North Carolina (above), covers four acres and is surrounded by 12,000 more. Touring the estate, visitors are wafted back to the Gilded Age of the coach-and-four and the 300-foot yacht. George's brother Frederick built the $660,000 Vanderbilt Mansion overlooking the Hudson at Hyde Park (opposite) as a country home. Gibson Girl (right) endures as a nostalgic symbol of high society of the 1890's.

B. ANTHONY STEWART, NATIONAL GEOGRAPHIC PHOTOGRAPHER, AND (BELOW) WAYNE MILLER, MAGNUM

San Simeon, a dream come true, dazzles with its art and architecture

Now a California state historical monument, the $30,000,000 estate of publisher William Randolph Hearst draws busloads of tourists the year round. Through grounds where zebras, mountain goats, and antelope roam, they ride up to La Casa Grande. This Spanish-Renaissance castle crowns The Enchanted Hill, high above the Pacific.

Flemish tapestry and Sienese banners deck the Refectory (left), with its carved ceiling from an Italian palace, its convent dining tables and monastery choir stalls. Here Hearst's dinner guests might find homely ketchup bottles and mustard jars beside gleaming silver candelabra. "We grew up in a museum," said William Randolph, Jr., "but a comfortable one."

A Roman temple (above), its façade built from ancient fragments, adorns the marble-tiled Neptune Pool. Three Graces at right commune near a guest villa.

B. ANTHONY STEWART, NATIONAL GEOGRAPHIC PHOTOGRAPHER

FRANK FREIDEL

ALASKA

LIKE TOILING ANTS, pack-laden men struggled up the passes between Alaska and Canada in the winter of 1897-8. The age-old lure of gold brought them to this northern frontier from the corners of the earth – but mostly from the United States, now settled from sea to sea. Thirsting for wealth and adventure, they boarded ships to Dyea or Skagway in the Alaska panhandle, then toted mountains of gear up the icy slopes and down into the Yukon country. Scrabbling for gold along the Klondike River, they fought, suffered, and starved. Many went home. Some went "clean mad for the muck called gold." A few got rich. A few moved on to new strikes in Fairbanks and Nome and so rediscovered Alaska.

A century and a half had passed since the prospect of furs lured Russians to Alaska. In 1799 the Czar chartered the Russian-American Company, which governed for 68 years and ran a fur monopoly from the capital at New Archangel, soon to be known by its Indian name, Sitka. Today Sitka National Monument, famed for its totem-pole exhibit, marks the site where company manager Alexander Baranof broke Indian resistance.

By 1867 Russia had lost interest. Secretary of State William H. Seward was able to buy Alaska for $7,200,000 – less than two cents an acre! Critics sneered at "Seward's Icebox" and "Walrussia," and Congress failed to establish any government. Only the fish canneries and fur companies profited.

SOURDOUGHS PACK THEIR SUPPLIES OVER CHILKOOT PASS, AN ALASKAN GATEWAY TO THE KLONDIKE. WEBSTER & STEVENS, 1898

Then in 1880 prospector Joe Juneau found color in the panhandle. The biggest gold mine in the world developed in the town that bears his name—now the capital. Today a ghostly quiet hangs over the Juneau mines that yielded $150,000,000 before the last and the biggest—the Alaska-Juneau—closed in 1944. There is little traffic in the tunnels, only the daily tourist trip in an old ore train. On the mine tailings, golfers have staked out fairways that contain flecks of gold. They call their links the "Million-dollar Golf Course."

In Skagway, residents put on a "Days of '98" show and re-enact "The Shooting of Dan McGrew," Robert W. Service's famous ballad. Visitors find the town much the way the miners left it, old saloons and boardwalks lining the main street.

As gold fever passed, sourdoughs discovered that Alaska offered other riches: fertile soil, timber, waterpower, oil. World War II and the cold war brought an influx of

Sitka shines like silver along the west coast of Baranof Island. Founded in 1804, the Alaskan settlement thrived as the capital of the Czar's fur empire and became an industrial center. Flour and lumber mills, iron and brass foundries shipped products as far away as Hawaii.

Russian influence lives on in the Orthodox religion. St. Michael's Cathedral, completed in 1850, hummed to the chant of robed priests until fire destroyed the building in 1966. Icons (right), rescued from the domed church, are still used by the congregation.

W. E. GARRETT AND (RIGHT) THOMAS J. ABERCROMBIE, BOTH NATIONAL GEOGRAPHIC STAFF

servicemen. Cities mushroomed. Anchorage, a mere railroad camp not long before, boomed into a gleaming metropolis, Alaska's largest. The mining town of Fairbanks burgeoned into second place.

In June, 1958, Congress passed a much-debated bill and Alaskans went wild with joy. Bonfires blazed, sirens wailed, bells pealed as Alaska became the 49th state.

Alaska has 300 million acres of public land free for homesteading, most of it accessible only by air or water. Recently the state beckoned to the "South 48" for more people by developing a ferry system along the Inside Passage. Fast, far-ranging boats in two years carried 187,000 passengers and opened seven towns and 1,500 miles of coastline to cars and trucks.

Southeastern Alaska hasn't seen so many strangers since gold rush days—and this is only the beginning.

HAWAII

On August 12, 1898, while sourdoughs panned gold in the bleak Klondike, Americans were cheering themselves hoarse in a flower-scented paradise 3,000 miles away. They had gathered at the Iolani Palace in the mid-Pacific city of Honolulu to watch President Sanford B. Dole of the Republic of Hawaii turn over to the United States what Mark Twain called "the loveliest fleet of islands that lies anchored in any ocean."

Their discoverer, Capt. James Cook, was killed in 1779 at Kealakekua Bay on the island of Hawaii. His paradise grew into a united kingdom under gigantic Kamehameha I and became a Pacific crossroads for ships of many nations. In 1816 Russians began building a redoubt in Honolulu where Fort Street now runs. France acquired rights in 1839, and four years later Britain was ceded the kingdom but turned it back. Americans took the most interest. Merchants

THOMAS NEBBIA, NATIONAL GEOGRAPHIC PHOTOGRAPHER

Surf riding, sport of Hawaiian kings, thrills Mainlanders scudding toward Waikiki Beach in outrigger canoes and on dancing surfboards. Visitors who explore beyond the view of Diamond Head (above) find Oahu and the six other inhabited islands rich in cane sugar, pineapples, and scenic grandeur. Orientals and Occidentals have mingled successfully here in the 50th (Aloha) state, a harmonious melting pot. Now they vote together (below).

bought Hawaiian sandalwood for the China trade, whalers put in for provisions, and in 1820 a brig arrived with 19 New England missionaries.

Through schools and New England-style churches, many still standing, the missionary families significantly changed the Polynesian way of life. They even counseled Hawaiian kings. Abraham Lincoln wrote of Hawaii: "Its people are free, and its laws, language, and religion are largely the fruit of our own teaching and example." Hale Hoikeike, a museum on Maui, preserves a missionary's home and female seminary. Its plaster was strengthened with human hair donated by Hawaiian ladies.

Trouble erupted in paradise when Queen Liliuokalani, author of *Aloha Oe*, tried to restore royal power. She was deposed, to live out her life at Washington Place, now the governor's residence in Honolulu. During the Spanish-American War the United States annexed strategically important Hawaii, and in 1900 made it a territory.

On the infamous date, December 7, 1941, Japanese planes snarled over Diamond Head to devastate Pearl Harbor. Postwar appeals brought statehood in 1959. Today's state governor sits in Iolani Palace, home of kings.

Kamehameha I, his statue garlanded with 40-foot leis, consolidated the islands by conquest. Monarchs ruled from Iolani Palace (top); royal trappings (above) rest in Bishop Museum. Sunken *Arizona* (right) honors Pearl Harbor dead. A simple slab (far left) marks where Captain Cook fell.

THOMAS NEBBIA AND (FAR LEFT) WALTER MEAYERS EDWARDS, NATIONAL GEOGRAPHIC STAFF
ABOVE: ROBERT MOSIER

AMERICA'S INVENTIVE GIANTS

IN THIS NATION of tinkerers, many found new frontiers right in their workshops. The 19th century inventor, according to romantic tales, knew little of science. Dreamy and impractical, he experimented hit or miss and with luck made his fortune.

A few worked this way. Charles Goodyear was one. He labored to improve rubber so that raincoats and overshoes wouldn't turn into a smelly, sticky mess in hot weather. Always in debt, he worked at his project inside jail and out and wore rubber clothes to demonstrate his early products. Someone said of Goodyear: "If you meet a man who has on an India rubber cap, stock, coat, vest and shoes, with an India rubber money purse without a cent of money in it, that is he." In 1839 he accidentally dropped a mixture of rubber and sulphur on a hot stove. It "vulcanized," and the rubber industry was born.

Most successful inventors built upon the scientific discoveries of others. Hundreds of mechanics had tried to build a workable reaper before Cyrus McCormick methodically combined seven vital principles and in 1831 brought his clattering machine out on a Virginia field, where it did the work of six strong men with scythes. McCormick set up a plant in Chicago, revolutionized American agriculture, and was a millionaire at 40.

Samuel Colt could design a new gun at the drop of a hat. At 16 he was whittling a mock-up out of wood. In 1836 he patented the first practical revolver and set about mass-producing it. He planned to use interchangeable parts and an assembly line—radical proposals in the early 1800's. Colt's partners vetoed them, and the company went bankrupt. Then the Mexican War brought a demand for revolvers. Colt got a contract, pushed through his scheme for mass production, and built the arms empire that helped win the West.

Great advances had been made in electrical knowledge when, in 1832, Samuel F. B. Morse wondered "why intelligence may not be transmitted instantaneously by electricity." Morse, a talented and characteristically impoverished painter,

These men pioneered the Age of Invention. From left: William Thomas Green Morton, demonstrated use of ether as anesthetic; James Bogardus, machinist, used cast iron in construction, making skyscrapers possible; Samuel Colt, invented the revolver; Cyrus Hall McCormick, the reaper; Joseph Saxton, the foun-

"MEN OF PROGRESS" BY CHRISTIAN SCHUSSELE, C. 1860, MELLON COLLECTION, NATIONAL GALLERY OF ART

tain pen; Charles Goodyear (seated, arm on table), first to vulcanize rubber; Peter Cooper (behind Goodyear), built *Tom Thumb*, first American-made railway locomotive, financial backer of transatlantic cable; Jordan Lawrence Mott, anthracite stove; Joseph Henry (standing, left of column), physicist, organized Smithsonian Institution; Eliphalet Nott, educator, heating; John Ericsson (standing, right of column), developed the screw propeller, designed the *Monitor;* Frederick Ellsworth Sickels, steam engines; Samuel F. B. Morse, telegraph; Henry Burden, machinery; Richard March Hoe, printing equipment; Erastus Brigham Bigelow, power loom for carpet manufacture; Isaiah Jennings, dentistry tools; Thomas Blanchard, machine tools for making tacks and turning gunstocks; Elias Howe, the sewing machine.

made use of the electromagnet—already invented—and developed a sender, a receiver, and a code. Congress voted money for a transmission line between Washington and Baltimore and in 1844 Morse tapped out the historic message: "What hath God wrought!" His electric telegraph swiftly linked all parts of the nation.

Morse did something else: he hired inventors to assist him. This forerunner of the industrial laboratory pointed the way for other giants of invention who were probing the frontiers of science and engineering. Their work drastically changed the American scene and raised the living standards of millions of their fellow men.

Thomas Edison switched on the world's lights

VITALLY INTERESTED in the world around him, Thomas Alva Edison felt an uncontrollable urge to improve it. As a newsboy on a train, he set up a chemical laboratory in the baggage car. It finally caught fire. Edison became a telegrapher—one of the best in the country—but would neglect his messages to use the lines for electrical experiments. While still in his 20's he sold the rights to an improved stock ticker for $40,000. He sank the money into producing the machines.

In 1876 he built a laboratory at Menlo Park, New Jersey, and with a trained staff began making "inventions to order." This team created the phonograph and, after trying 6,000 kinds of filaments, the first practical incandescent electric lamp.

In 1886 Edison set up an invention factory, equipped to "build anything from a ladys watch to a Locomotive," at nearby West Orange. There during his last 44 years he and his assistants tested devices that brought 520 patents. These wonders include the motion-picture camera, long-playing record, and the alkaline storage battery. The battery alone took 50,000 experiments.

Edison described genius as "one per cent inspiration and 99 per cent perspiration." Perhaps his greatest invention was the modern research laboratory.

VOLKMAR WENTZEL, NATIONAL GEOGRAPHIC PHOTOGRAPHER. BELOW: NATIONAL PARK SERVICE. OPPOSITE: NEAL P. DAVIS

Edison shouted "Mary had a little lamb" into a horn, made adjustments, and the horn squeaked the words back at him! That first 1877 phonograph used tin foil to pick up the squiggles of a stylus. A decade later, spurred by Alexander Graham Bell's development of a practical wax record, Edison plunged into work on his neglected phonograph. After a final 72-hour marathon he perfected a wax-cylinder model (below). Music from this marvelous talking machine delights young visitors to his West Orange laboratory (above), now a national historic site.

Edison's gift of abundant light came from his earlier laboratory at Menlo Park, New Jersey. Lab and lamp (left) have been moved to Greenfield Village, Henry Ford's Americana museum at Dearborn, Michigan.

George Eastman made "snapshot" an everyday word

IN THE FALL of 1877 a serious-minded, industrious young Rochester bank clerk, George Eastman, decided to take up photography as a hobby. He purchased $94.36 worth of equipment and made an unpleasant discovery.

"I learned that it took not only a strong but also a dauntless man to be an outdoor photographer. My layout, which included only the essentials, had in it a camera about the size of a soap box, a tripod, which was strong and heavy enough to support a bungalow, a big plate-holder, a dark-tent, a nitrate bath, and a container for water. The glass plates were not, as now, in the holder ready for use; they were what is known as 'wet plates'—that is, glass which had to be coated with collodion and then sensitized with nitrate of silver in the field just before exposure.... Since I took my views mostly outdoors ... the bulk of the paraphernalia worried me. It seemed that one ought to be able to carry less than a pack-horse load."

From Eastman's exasperation came a revolution in photography. He perfected and marketed glass plates that were already sensitized. Then in 1888 he put out the Kodak, using roll film. It was so easy to operate anyone could use it. "You press the button, we do the rest," said his slogan.

Eastman House, a museum presenting photography's past and its miracles today, trains Rochester Institute of Technology students and welcomes visiting "shutterbugs." Youngsters examine an 1839 Daguerre, first camera sold to the public. Four-lens camera in background made card-size pictures. Orange hood covers an 1869 portable darkroom.

B. ANTHONY STEWART, NATIONAL GEOGRAPHIC PHOTOGRAPHER. OPPOSITE: NEAL P. DAVIS AND (LOWER) EASTMAN HOUSE

Head in a vise, a victim poses rigidly for long seconds before the tintyper at Greenfield Village. "American Film," a gelatin-coated paper patented by Eastman in 1884, simplified photography and put it within reach of millions of people. He tested it on his portrait at 29 (below).

This box camera, loaded with a 100-exposure roll, cost $25. When the film was exposed, you sent the camera to Rochester, New York, where technicians developed the round pictures, made a print of each one, and sent back your reloaded camera, all for $10. As Eastman pointed out, this system enabled "the whole public to practice the art."

Eastman's nitrocellulose film, in Edison's motion-picture machine, gave birth to the movies. Photography came to serve science and industry many ways.

George Eastman, who had known poverty as a child, gave millions to education. His home is now a museum, a living memorial to "the man who brought photography to everyone."

GILBERT M. GROSVENOR, NATIONAL GEOGRAPHIC STAFF. SKETCHES OPPOSITE © BELL FAMILY

Bell Museum at Baddeck, Nova Scotia, preserves mementos of the wide-ranging inventor.

Alexander Graham Bell gave wings to man's voice

NO ONE could have been better prepared to invent the telephone than Alexander Graham Bell. He was the third generation in his family to be an expert on the human voice. In 1871 the Boston Board of Education invited the young Scottish-born scientist to lecture on his father's system of "visible speech" to teachers of the deaf. His success led him to open his own school of "vocal physiology," the anatomy of the vocal cords. His quest to develop a scientific device that would help teach the deaf to speak spurred him to investigate the anatomy of the human ear with its delicate vibrating membrane.

By setting an exhausting pace, Bell found time to work on this and other experiments. He was helped by an altruistic Boston lawyer, Gardiner Greene Hubbard, later first president of the National Geographic Society. Mr. Hubbard's daughter Mabel, deaf since childhood, became Bell's pupil and soon the couple fell in love. But marriage had to wait, for the scientist was still relatively poor.

Industry promised rich rewards for a device that would send several messages at once over the same telegraph wire. Bell, trained in acoustics, thought of sending the signals in different pitches. He experimented with reeds that acted like tuning forks, those at the receiver vibrating only when their own signals were transmitted.

While perfecting this multiple, or harmonic, telegraph with his assistant Thomas A. Watson, Bell found a way to make an electric current vary in intensity instead

Dr. Bell opened service between New York and Chicago in 1892, only 14 years after predicting long-distance voice communication. He sketched the telephone (upper) in 1875, the rocket plane in 1893. Hydrofoil boat (lower) appears in his 1917 notes.

of simply pulsing when the tuned reeds vibrated. Bell recognized the key to transmitting not just signals but sounds. Immediately he set to building an apparatus with membranes and electromagnets. When it was completed, he spoke over it the simple words, "Mr. Watson, come here; I want you." Watson came.

Bell patented his telephone in 1876 and it soon became part of American life. He devoted himself to research in Washington, D. C., where he used an award to establish the Volta Bureau "for the increase and diffusion of knowledge relating to the deaf." While serving as president of the National Geographic Society, 1898-1903, he engaged Gilbert Grosvenor as editor and backed him in transforming its small technical journal into a profusely illustrated one written in terms the layman could understand. Membership in a nonprofit, educational society, not merely subscription to a magazine, was Bell's idea.

At his summer home on Cape Breton Island his researches took him into such fields as aeronautics, marine engineering, medicine, and genetics. Everything was grist for his mental mill. He tested rocket- and jet-powered rotor blades for his conception of a helicopter more than 40 years before one was perfected. His tetrahedral kite carried a man aloft. His hydrofoil speedboat, developed with F. W. Baldwin, set a world record—70.86 miles an hour—in 1919. He experimented with solar stills to convert sea water to fresh. He even bred a flock of twin-bearing sheep.

Much of his remarkable legacy to science is displayed at the Bell Museum, a Canadian government memorial to a great American who, if asked to state his profession, invariably replied, "I am a teacher of the deaf."

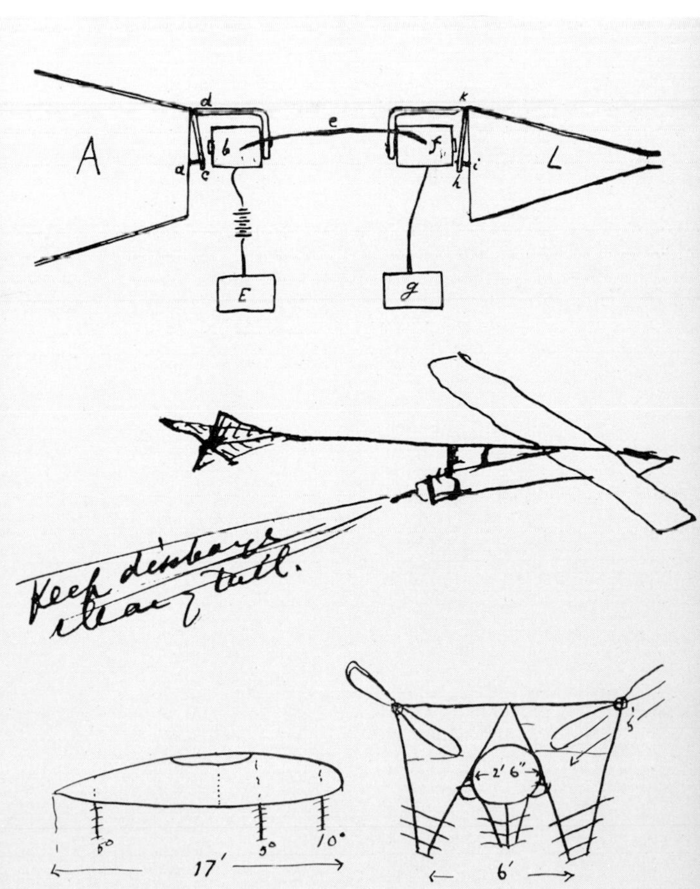

U. S. DEPARTMENT OF AGRICULTURE

George Washington Carver discovered secrets of nature's alchemy

SOME SCOFFED at the thin, bent old man. He was so frugal. He improvised most of his laboratory equipment from discarded junk. But George Washington Carver, applying his discoveries to the service of man, was making his life an inspiration to his fellow Negroes in the South.

Born of slave parents in Missouri, hungry for knowledge, he worked his way through school, finally abandoning art and music and turning to botany and agriculture. He wanted most to make things grow. On graduation from Iowa State College he was appointed to the faculty.

In 1896 Booker T. Washington, head of Tuskegee Institute in Alabama, asked him to join the staff, and the chance to serve his people sent Carver south to stay 47 years. He showed the impoverished farmers how to use what was around them: compost and cowpeas to enrich fields, garden vegetables to improve their diets, hillside clays to whitewash cabins. Grow less cotton, he taught, and more sweet potatoes and peanuts—and in his laboratory he derived more than 300 products from peanuts.

Tuskegee honors him with a museum. A national monument marks his birthplace.

SLAVE CABIN PICTURED AT GEORGE WASHINGTON CARVER NATIONAL MONUMENT, NEAR DIAMOND, MISSOURI; JACK E. BOUCHER, NATIONAL PARK SERVICE

THEY CALLED Luther Burbank the "plant wizard," but he had nothing more mysterious than Yankee keenness and industry combined with a flair for showmanship. He started a nursery in Santa Rosa, California, in 1877, a time when orchardists badly needed superior fruit to ship to Eastern markets. Burbank got plum trees from Japan, crossed them with others, and came up with the dramatically successful Santa Rosa plum.

He went on to develop apples, peaches, tomatoes—some 240 varieties of fruit. His Santa Rosa acres also yielded potatoes, squashes, walnuts, the Shasta daisy and other flowers, and after 16 years of experiment, a spineless cactus!

A Dutch botanist who visited Burbank reported he was "a very plain man, more a gardener than a savant, with clear blue sparkling eyes, full of life and fun." Yet he was so sensitive he would burst into tears at lavish praise or an unkind word.

Burbank pioneered by trial and error; today plant inventors redesign species for home and industry with Atomic Age tools.

Burbank's birthplace and garden office can be seen at Greenfield Village.

BROWN BROTHERS

Luther Burbank trained plants to work for man

PLANT VARIETIES IMPROVED BY BURBANK INCLUDE PLUM, CORN, RHUBARB, TOMATO, PEA, POTATO, CHERRY, BLACKBERRY, QUINCE, CANNA, DAHLIA, POPPY, GLADIOLA, DAISY, ROSE; SKETCH BY PAUL R. HOFFMASTER

Greenfield Village brings to life horseless carriage days

ON SOME 200 ACRES in Dearborn, Michigan, time takes a vacation. Here stand a 1634 Cape Cod windmill and an 1886 Detroit power plant. Among the 100-odd buildings visitors find a slave cabin based on George Washington Carver's memories of his birthplace, a courthouse where young Abraham Lincoln practiced law, and Thomas Edison's Menlo Park laboratory, transported board by board with seven carloads of New Jersey soil thrown in to give the old building a familiar foundation.

This is Greenfield Village, repository of Americana, conceived and built by Henry Ford, the millionaire automobile manufacturer who never forgot his humble background as a Michigan farm boy.

Born in 1863, Ford grew up with no taste for farming but a love for machinery. He repaired his father's plows and fixed neighbors' watches for the fun of it. From his 12th year, when he thrilled to the sight of a steam thresher lumbering down the road under its own power, he dreamed of making a machine that would run along a road.

Many others shared that dream. Inventors built vehicles powered by steam or gasoline engines; most were elaborate and expensive. Ford wanted something cheaper, "to lift farm drudgery off flesh and blood and lay it on steel and motors."

Laboring long hours after his day's work, he assembled his first automobile in a brick workshop behind his Detroit home. It weighed less than 500 pounds

Horseless carriages meet annually at the Village. This Stanley Steamer shows off before Martha-Mary Chapel on the green.

NEAL P. DAVIS

and ran on bicycle wheels powered by a two-cylinder engine. He finished it before dawn one rainy June morning in 1896 and had to hack away part of the wall with an ax to get it out. Then he cranked the engine and off he went.

Ford's was not the first car built in Detroit, and European manufacturers were turning out large models for wealthy customers. Competition was sharp, as Ford discovered when he formed a company in 1899. He had at least 57 rivals! By building racing cars the lanky mechanic got publicity. His racers set spectacular records: the first hit 72 miles per hour in road trials. Organizing a new company in 1903, Ford now tackled the problem of building a car so cheap the farmer could afford it.

His first Model A cost $800. Several models that followed were higher priced. Then in 1907, while manufacturing his Model S, he planned for mass production a durable machine capable of jouncing over the rocky, rutty, muddy roads. He tooled up to produce it and in October, 1908, unveiled the Model T. In 1910 he shifted production to his big new factory in Highland Park, Michigan.

To cut production costs Ford standardized the Model T, making no basic changes from year to year. But he constantly improved his methods of manufacture. He introduced continuously moving assembly lines in 1913 and slashed the time required to put together a Ford chassis from 12½ hours to 1½. He cut the car's base price from $950 in 1909 to $440 in 1914, then made an announcement, incredible for that time: he would pay no worker less than five dollars a day.

Ultimately Ford lowered the price of the Model T to $290. By 1927, when he discontinued production, he had sold more than 15,000,000 of them. The stubby, high-riding, wheezy Tin Lizzie, beloved butt of innumerable insults ("Danger! 100,000 jolts!"), had literally put the nation on wheels. And it had made Henry Ford one of the most famous and widely quoted men in the 20th century world.

"HISTORY IS BUNK," was one of Ford's often quoted remarks. By that he could have meant no more than that he disapproved of senseless clinging to outmoded methods. As he grew older and richer he collected and preserved countless mementos of the simpler past that mass production and the automobile age were leaving behind. At South Sudbury, Massachusetts, he restored the Wayside Inn that Henry Wadsworth Longfellow had made famous, and surrounded it with buildings illustrating the old handicrafts. Still that did not go far enough.

The idea grew on him of assembling an entire community in which to display his treasures, to give future generations a vivid picture of the life their ancestors led, especially the men of America's industrial revolution. Hence Greenfield Village.

Here history comes alive, as at Williamsburg. Mills and machine shops hum, children recite from McGuffey readers, the potter twirls his wheel, the glass blower bends before his torch like a votary before the sacred fire, the tintyper poses his subjects, and a stern-wheeler chunks down the man-made Suwannee River past Stephen Foster Memorial House while a minstrel sings the composer's songs. Covering 14 acres nearby is the Henry Ford Museum, its entrance modeled after Independence Hall. Here are gathered "every household article, every kind of vehicle, every sort of tool" people used in past generations. Students visit to learn mechanical theory, tourists just to savor. All leave knowing their country better.

Tin Lizzie's earliest ancestor sits in the doorway of the shed where Henry Ford built it in 1896 from old carriage parts and bits of pipe. Steered with a tiller, this first Ford could hit 20 miles an hour. The shed was moved to Greenfield Village from Detroit.

WILLARD R. CULVER

December 17, 1903: Bicycle makers from Dayton, Ohio, make history on the sands at Kitty Hawk,

DAWN OF A NEW AGE

THE FRAIL CONTRAPTION of wood, muslin, and wire trembled as a cold wind whipped Kill Devil Hill. One of the brothers held a wing, the other lay in a wooden cradle beside an idling engine whose carburetor had been made from a tomato can. "After running the motor a few minutes to heat it up," Orville Wright wrote, "I released the wire that held the machine to the track, and the machine started forward into the wind." Wilbur Wright walked, then ran alongside, steadying the wing. He let go, and the little truck made of bicycle wheel hubs that bore the weight of the *Flyer* lifted off the two-by-four rail.

For 12 marvelous seconds that December morning in 1903 the world's first powered heavier-than-air machine flew above the sands at Kitty Hawk. A dream as old as man's aspirations had come true—man flies.

Today the historic *Flyer* rests in the Smithsonian Institution in Washington,

LIBRARY OF CONGRESS

North Carolina. Wright Brothers National Memorial preserves this birthplace of powered flight.

D. C., for all to wonder at. Yet at first the Wright brothers' epochal flight went unheralded—a strange reaction in an age of exuberance and confidence. For this was the bright new 20th century, and this was the gay and lusty United States of America where dreams *could* come true and where new frontiers were much in demand.

Theodore Roosevelt, in the White House, personified these vigorous, buoyant times. He was bulling the Panama Canal across the Isthmus—and through Congress. He was waving his "big stick" at foreign powers and using it to break up big business monopolies at home. He delighted in books, children, the sheer joy of life at Sagamore, his home in Oyster Bay, Long Island. Visitors to this well-preserved mansion and to his brownstone birthplace in New York can capture the essence of T. R. and the brave world around him.

Roosevelt himself "discovered" flight in 1910, when he flew for 3½ minutes. By then the Wrights' accomplishment had triggered a surge into the frontier of the air. Soon Eddie Rickenbacker was dueling in the skies over France; Charles A. Lindbergh soloed across the Atlantic; Richard E. Byrd flew over the North and

B. ANTHONY STEWART, NATIONAL GEOGRAPHIC PHOTOGRAPHER

Wizardry at Oak Ridge, Tennessee, points the way to the future. Ultraviolet light bathes a scientist (above) studying the model of a sodium chloride crystal, or table salt. Red circles represent sodium atoms; yellow are chlorine.

Oak Ridge, a child of World War II, came of age in 1959, when the U. S. government turned the town over to its citizens. Here students visit the world's oldest existing atomic reactor, now a national historic landmark. Holes in the wall once held uranium fuel for this atomic pile, started up in 1943, a year after physicist Enrico Fermi built the first atomic pile in Chicago. Nearly two million persons have toured Oak Ridge's American Museum of Atomic Energy, which tells the story of the atom and its many services to mankind.

In today's age of scientific miracles men even walk in space (opposite).

South Poles. The speed of air progress can be gauged by the fact that within 60 years the wingspan of a large airliner was greater than the 120-foot distance of the Wrights' first flight, and experimental planes were bettering 4,000 miles per hour.

In the same breath-taking fashion the United States shot into the nuclear age in the summer of 1945. During World War II thousands of workers in huge plants at Oak Ridge, Tennessee, Hanford, Washington, and Los Alamos, New Mexico, labored on materials for a secret weapon. Man had learned how to unlock the power of the atom, and its mighty force helped end that war though not the threat of a holocaust that might destroy mankind.

Happily, nuclear fission also opened the door to endless benefits. Scientists set to work on peaceful uses for atomic energy: radioactive isotopes ("tracer atoms") that serve agriculture, industry, and medicine; nuclear power plants to generate electricity and to propel ships and aircraft. Atomic power may hold the key to interplanetary travel.

Less than six decades after the Wright brothers' first flights, astronauts rode flaming rockets to probe that farthest frontier of all—space. On January 31, 1958, three months after Russia's Sputnik I, the United States sent an instrumented satellite into orbit around the earth from a site that is already historic: Cape Kennedy, Florida, then called Cape Canaveral. Weather and communication spacecraft blasted off from there and other bases to reach toward the sun, moon, and planets. On May 5, 1961, the first American rocketed into space when Alan B. Shepard, Jr., zoomed 116 miles above the Atlantic in a 15-minute sub-orbital flight.

Other U. S. spacemen followed from the sandy cape. John H. Glenn, Jr., circled the globe three times in February, 1962. A year later L. Gordon Cooper, Jr., brought Project Mercury to a triumphant close with 22 orbits.

In June, 1965, Edward H. White II thrilled the world when he left Gemini twin James A. McDivitt at the controls and climbed out of his capsule to take a 17,500-mile-an-hour stroll across the United States (right). Tethered by a cord, White used the guidance gun in his right hand for maneuvering and thus became the first self-propelled spaceman. By year's end astronauts had rendezvoused two orbiting spacecraft.

On the ground, scientists worked feverishly on Project Apollo, final phase in Cape Kennedy's program to land Americans on the moon and then bring them back safely to earth.

Today at this landmark of the Space Age the future seems very near.

SPACE WALK FROM GEMINI 4 PHOTOGRAPHED BY JAMES A. MCDIVITT, NASA

INDEX *How to use the index to plan your vacation trip to America's Historylands*

Specific historic sites as well as towns, cities, people, and events have been included. Look up the places you would like to visit; the text will tell you what sites are important, and why. Consult one of the special maps (see p. 571) or the big historical pocket map of the United States for ideas on interesting side trips. Illustrations and illustrated text references are indicated in **boldface** type.

CAPE KENNEDY, FLORIDA: A MIGHTY, FOUR-STAGE ROCKET BLASTS OFF TO HURL A SATELLITE PAST THE MOON; LUIS MARDEN, NATIONAL GEOGRAPHIC STAFF

INDEX TO MAPS

FOR REFERENCE

Some 900 issues of the *National Geographic Magazine* contain a wealth of information on America's historic landmarks. Check the Index.

These colorful National Geographic books will add meaning to your vacation trips:

America's Wonderlands
Indians of the Americas
Wild Animals of North America
Song and Garden Birds of North America
Water, Prey, and Game Birds of North America
Wondrous World of Fishes

Publications catalog on request from National Geographic Society, Washington, D. C. 20036.

NATIONAL GEOGRAPHIC SOCIETY

WASHINGTON, D. C.

Organized "for the increase and diffusion of geographic knowledge"

GILBERT HOVEY GROSVENOR
President, 1920-1954; Editor, 1899-1954
Chairman of the Board, 1954-1966

The National Geographic Society is chartered in Washington, D. C., in accordance with the laws of the United States, as a nonprofit scientific and educational organization for increasing and diffusing geographic knowledge and promoting research and exploration.

Since 1890 the Society has supported 380 explorations and research projects, adding immeasurably to man's knowledge of earth, sea, and sky. It diffuses this knowledge through its monthly journal, NATIONAL GEOGRAPHIC; more than 26 million maps distributed each year; its books, globes, and atlases; 30 School Bulletins a year in color; information services to press, radio, and television; technical monographs; timely exhibits from around the world in Explorers Hall; and now a nationwide series of programs on television.